THE VIVEKACŪḌĀMAṆI OF ŚAṄKARĀCĀRYA BHAGAVATAPĀDA

for isa

there is an unending cacophony in
the forest of life until the lion
of vedanta roars its thunderous silence!
know that the child of a lion
is also a lion
this book is for you
and all sons and daughters
everywhere

The Vivekacūḍāmaṇi

of

Śaṅkarācārya Bhagavatpāda

An Introduction and Translation

Translated and Edited
by
JOHN GRIMES
Kodaikanal International School,
South India

MOTILAL BANARSIDASS PUBLISHERS
PRIVATE LIMITED • DELHI

First Indian Edition: Delhi, 2004

ISBN: 81-208-2038-x (Cloth)
ISBN: 81-208-2039-8 (Paper)

MOTILAL BANARSIDASS
41 U.A. Bungalow Road, Jawahar Nagar, Delhi 110 007
8 Mahalaxmi Chamber, 22 Bhulabhai Desai Road, Mumbai 400 026
236, 9th Main III Block, Jayanagar, Bangalore 560 011
120 Royapettah High Road, Mylapore, Chennai 600 004
Sanas Plaza, 1302 Baji Rao Road, Pune 411 002
8 Camac Street, Kolkata 700 017
Ashok Rajpath, Patna 800 004
Chowk, Varanasi 221 001

Printed in India
BY JAINENDRA PRAKASH JAIN AT SHRI JAINENDRA PRESS,
A-45 NARAINA, PHASE-I, NEW DELHI 110 028
AND PUBLISHED BY NARENDRA PRAKASH JAIN FOR
MOTILAL BANARSIDASS PUBLISHERS PRIVATE LIMITED,
BUNGALOW ROAD, DELHI 110 007

Contents

Preface

śruti smṛti purāṇānām ālayaṁ karuṇālayam
namāmi bhagavatpādaṁ śaṇkaraṁ loka śaṇkaraṁ

I salute the divine feet of the great Śaṅkara,
the repository of sacred scriptures,
an abode of immense compassion,
who ever accomplishes the good of the world

Śaṅkara (*c.* 650–700 CE, or Common Era) is considered to be a giant among giants, a living legend and probably the most venerated philosopher in India's long and hoary history. Advaita Vedānta hagiographies declare that a youthful Śaṅkara composed the *Vivekacūḍāmaṇi* (*Crown Jewel of Discrimination*) in the *āśrama* of his Guru, Govinda Bhagavatpādācārya, along the banks of the Narmadā river, when he was barely a teenager.[1]

The *Crown Jewel of Discrimination* is in the form of a dialog between a preceptor (*guru*) and a pupil (*śiṣya*) in which the pupil humbly approaches the preceptor and, having propitiated the teacher with selfless service (*seva*), implores to be rescued from worldly existence (*samsāra*). The *guru*, being pleased, and convinced of the student's qualifications and earnestness, promises to teach the way to liberation (*mokṣa*) which culminates in the ecstatic experience of one's own Self.

Advaita Vedānta tradition avers that not every individual will possess the necessary qualifications (i.e., knowledge of Sanskrit grammar, the requisite philosophical training, and so on) to study the three foundational sourcebooks (*prasthāna traya*).[2] Thus teachers, out of compassion, composed what are known as independent treatises (*prakaraṇa grantha*) which serve as introduction manuals. Such works contain four indispensable elements (*anubandha catuṣṭaya*): the determination of the fitness of a student for the study of the treatise (*adhikāri*); the subject matter (*viṣaya*); the mutual relationship between the treatise and the subject matter (*sambandha*); and the object to be attained by the study (*prayojana*).[3] The *Crown Jewel of Discrimination* is one such work whose clarity makes it extremely popular both among spiritual adepts and aspirants alike. Further, the *Crown Jewel of Discrimination* places paramount importance upon discrimination (*viveka*) in one's quest for liberation. Its main purport is to analyse the Self (*ātman*) and reveal that the individual self (*jīva*) is really the Supreme Self (*ātman*) or That (*Brahman*).

This book contains an annotated English translation[4] of the *Vivekacūḍāmaṇi* or '*The Crown Jewel of Discrimination*'. This translation is based upon the original Sanskrit text found in the Samata edition of the *Complete Works of Sri Sankaracharya*, volume III.[5] This book also contains a rather lengthy introductory essay and copious cross-referencing to relevant Upaniṣadic verses.

These cross-references are a unique feature of this translation and, besides mirroring a time-honored Indian philosophical practice, demonstrate the text's familiarity with, and relevance to, Upaniṣadic thought. I have also given definitions and notes to select words in the verses. The basis for choosing these terms was to further elucidate on the meanings of terms which will be of great interest and consequence per the import of the verse.

Any translation of an ancient text always poses many diverse problems of understanding and interpretation, both for its readers and for its translator. In regards to 'translating', Gerald Larson wrote,

> The verb 'translate' refers to the activity of conveying the content and style of a meaningful utterance from one linguistic medium to another, and the substantive or participial word 'translating' refers to the various components involved in accomplishing that activity, namely:
>
> a) the meaningful utterance (text) of a speaker (writer) in a first linguistic medium (or what is 'translatable');
> b) the 'translator' who understands the meaningful utterance in the first medium, but is also competent in a second medium;
> c) the recasting of the utterance by the translator from the phonology, morphology, syntax and semantics of the first linguistic medium into the second medium (or the 'translating');
> d) the 'translated' utterance or the 'translation' in the second medium;
> e) the meaningful utterance (text) in a second linguistic medium understood by a hearer (reader).[6]

With nine English translations already in existence, why another one? Circumstances and contexts change. Assessments and interpretations are legion. Every language contains innumerable ambiguities, nuances and subtleties. Strategic decisions vary and, as Larson has pointed out, there are at least four such strategic decisions: (1) stylistic; (2) pedagogical; (3) interpretive; (4) motivational.[7]

Translations present difficult questions. Some translators emphasize *content* while others emphasize *form*.[8] Some employ primarily the historical approach and others the structuralist approach.[9] Then there are the issues of gender and feminist perspectives involved.[10]

In my translation I have attempted to be aware of internal textual problems (a single term can have more than one meaning, depending upon its context) while balancing technical precision with philosophical clarity. However, my own particular bias is reflected most in an attempt at readability combined with religious sensibility. The final word (*siddhānta*) of Advaita, both implicitly and explicitly, is that every individual is the Absolute (*ayam ātman brahma; tat tvam asi; aham brahmāsmi*). Thus, to be faithful to this insight I have used inclusive language in my translation and made it reader-friendly for both sexes. I am aware of those scholars who invoke Advaita's (so-called infamous) male-oriented bias. In reply, I maintain that my particular prejudice can be answered in numerous ways. The truth of history is the truth of the historian.[11] Time, place, context, tradition, audience, and so on all have their parts to play. To the best of my ability, I have attempted to appropriate what I take to be the meaning of the text. I have reflected on what I believe the text meant *then* and what it means *now*. I am not an advocate of Sanskrit for Sanskrit's sake. Going beyond a mere professional interest, my desire was to present a text which speaks to those who read it today.

With great gratitude I offer my thanks to Dr Kevin Lee for his exquisite jacket painting of Śaṅkara and to Aditya and Tara Mcnon for compiling the index.

John Grimes
Gurupūrṇimā 2003
Kodaikanal International School
Kodaikanal, South India

Notes

1 Kulkarni, *Adi Sankara: The Saviour of Mankind*, p. 116.
2 *Upaniṣads, Bhagavadgītā, Brahmasūtras.*
3 Grimes, *A Concise Dictionary of Indian Philosophy*, p. 235.
4 English translations of the *Vivekacūḍāmaṇi* include: *Śaṅkara's Crown Jewel of Discrimination*, tr. by Swami Prabhavananda and Christopher Isherwood, Vedanta Press: Hollywood, 1947. *Vivekacūḍāmaṇi of Śrī Śaṅkarācārya*, tr. by Swami Turiyananda, Sri Ramakrishna Math: Madras. *Vivekacūḍāmaṇi*, tr. and commentary by the Śaṅkarācārya of Sṛṅgeri, Bombay: Bharatiya Vidya Bhavan, 1988. *Vivekacūḍāmaṇi of Śrī Śaṅkarācārya*, tr. by Swami Madhavananda, Advaita Ashrama: Calcutta, 1966. *The Crown Jewel of Wisdom*, tr. by Charles Johnston, New York, 1925. *Talks on Sankara's Vivekachoodamani* by Swami Chinmayananda, Bombay, 1970. *Vivekacūḍāmaṇi*, ed. and tr. by R. Balasubramanian, *The Voice of Samkara* 7, 1982–10, 1985. *Vivekacūḍāmaṇi or Crest-Jewel of Wisdom of Śrī Śaṁkarācārya*, tr. by Mohini Chatterji, Theosophical Society: Adyar, 1932. *Vivekacūḍāmaṇi*, tr. Chunilal C. Bohra, *Brahmavādin* 17, 1912: 394, 445, 480. Summarized by Karl Potter in *Encyclopedia of Indian Philosophy* 3, 1983. The *Vivekacūḍāmaṇi* was translated into German by M. Chatterjee as *Das Palladium der Weisheit*, Leipzig, 1895.
5 The Samata Books edition is in ten volumes and includes 118 works including small tracts and hymns. See Volume III, *Upadeshara-chanavali* pp. 3–111. I consulted nine other editions of the text and, whenever there was a divergence of the text, I always opted for the Samata version.
6 Larson, 'The Song Celestial: Two Centuries of the Bhagavad Gītā in English'. *Philosophy East and West* 31, no. 4 (October, 1981), pp. 518–519.
7 Ibid., p. 519. To mention but a few examples: Swami Prabhavananda's translation significantly departs from the original Sanskrit; technical terms and problems frequently disappear, and the resulting simplification often borders on the simplistic. Swamis Prabhavananda, Turiyananda and Madhavananda, all being Ramakrishna Vedanta monks, present a neo-Vedanta interpretation of the text. Their bias is clearly 'apologetic' and they are believers in their tradition. The

Śaṅkarācārya of Sṛṅgeri's Commentary was in Sanskrit and itself needed to be translated. Of all the works noted, it is clearly the most scholarly and faithful to the original style. Being a 'Śaṅkarācārya' himself, perhaps this is to be expected.

8 See Thomas Coburn, *Encountering the Goddess*, p. 5.

9 Structuralism's proponents include Piaget, Levi-Strauss, M. Biardeau, C. Malamoud, A. Hiltebeitel, S. Kramrisch, and Wendy Doniger O'Flaherty. For assessing the merits and defects of structuralism, see Jacob Neusner, *Method and Meaning in Ancient Judaism III*, Chico: Scholars Press, 1981, pp. 233–234.

10 An insightful book on this is *Feminist Perspectives on Biblical Scholarship*, ed. Adela Yarbro Collins, Chico, Scholars Press, 1985.

11 See Fiorenza's 'Remembering The Past in Creating the Future: Historical–Critical Scholarship and Feminist Biblical Interpretation', in *Feminist Perspectives on Biblical Scholarship*, for a wonderful presentation of the pitfalls of invoking (what one thinks is) history.

Scheme of Transliteration

अ	a	आ	ā	इ	i	ई	ī		
उ	u	ऊ	ū	ऋ	ṛ	ॠ	ṛ		
ऌ	ḷ	ए	e	ऐ	ai	ओ	o		
औ	au	अं	aṁ	अः	aḥ				
क्	k	ख्	kh	ग्	g	घ्	gh	ङ्	ṅ
च्	c	छ्	ch	ज्	j	झ्	jh	ञ्	ñ
ट्	ṭ	ठ्	ṭh	ड्	ḍ	ढ्	ḍh	ण्	ṇ
त्	t	थ्	th	द्	d	ध्	dh	न्	n
प्	p	फ्	ph	ब्	b	भ्	bh	म्	m
य्	y	र्	r	ल्	l	व	v		
श्	ś	ष्	ṣ	स्	s	ह	h		
ळ्	l	क्ष	kṣ	त्र्	tr	ज्ञ	jñ		

Text Abbreviations

AitUp	Aitareya Upaniṣad
AmrtUp	Amṛtanāda Upaniṣad
AV	Atharvaveda
BDh	Bandhāyana Dharmasūtra
BG	Bhagavadgītā
BGBh	Bhagavadgītābhāṣya
BṛhUp	Bṛhadāraṇyaka Upaniṣad
BṛhUpBh	Bṛhadāraṇyaka Upaniṣad Bhāṣya
BṛhUpBhV	Bṛhadāraṇyaka Upaniṣad Bhāṣya Vārttikā
BS	Brahmasūtra
BSBh	Brahmasūtrabhāṣya
ChānUp	Chāndogya Upaniṣad
ChānUpBh	Chāndogya Upaniṣad Bhāṣya
ĪśaUpBh	Īśa Upaniṣad Bhāṣya
KaUp	Kaṭha Upaniṣad
KaivUp	Kaivalya Upaniṣad
KauṣUp	Kauṣitaki Upaniṣad
MaitrīUp	Maitrī Upaniṣad
MāṇḍUp	Māṇḍūkya Upaniṣad
MuṇḍUp	Muṇḍaka Upaniṣad
US	Upadeśasāhasrī
RV	Rgveda
ŚvetUp	Śvetāśvatara Upaniṣad
TaittSaṁ	Taittirīya Samhitā

TaittUp	Taittirīya Upaniṣad
TaittUpBh	Taittirīya Upaniṣad Bhāṣya
V	Vivekacūḍāmaṇi
Yajna	Yājñavalkya Smṛti
YS	Yogasūtra

Legendary Episodes in the Life of Śaṅkara

650 CE	Birth
652	Could speak, read, and write Sanskrit
653	Tonsure (*cūḍākarman*) ceremony
655	Sacred thread ceremony (*upanāyana*)
655	Death of father
655	Goddess partook of his ritual offering and he composed the hymn, *Devībhujangastava*
656	Shower of golden *āmalaka* fruits and the composition of the *Kaṇakadhārāstotra*
657	Altered the course of the Cūrṇi River for his mother
657	Wrote his first book, the *Balabodha Samgraha*
658	Mastered all four *Vedas* and *Vedāngas*
658	Meeting with King Rajaśekhaṛa; vision of Vaṣudeva and rescue of the image of Kṛṣṇa
658	Episode with the crocodile; renunciation; leaves home
658	Meets his guru, Govinda Bhagavatpāda; composes 'Six Stanzas on Liberation' (*nirvāṇa ṣaṭakam*); takes formal *sannyāsa*
658–662	Resides in *āśrama* of Govinda; composes a number of hymns as well as the *Vivekacūḍāmani*; altered the course of the Narmadā River
662	Visits Gauḍapāda at Badarikāśrama along with Govinda
662	Resides in Kāśī; writes commentaries (*bhāṣya*) on *Brahmasūtras, Upaniṣads, Bhagavadgītā*; meets Vyāsa; meets Śiva as a *cāṇḍāla*; meets his first disciple Sanandana (Padmapāda)
666	Last rites for his mother; *mahāsamādhi* of Govinda
667	Meeting with Kumārila; debate with Maṇḍana
668	Digvijaya; establishment of *maṭhas*
682	Śaṅkara's *mahāsamādhi*

PART ONE
An Introduction to the Life and Thought of Śaṅkara

It is said unthinkable, unborn knowledge is not different from the known. The known is that which reveals the unknown.

Approaches to the Study of Śaṅkara

There exists both a plethora of source material on Śaṅkara as well as a problematical void. He is considered by many to be the most venerated sage of Indian philosophy. In addition, he has a secure place among the world's greatest philosophers. His reputation is immense and his writings command the highest respect and homage. Unbelievably multi-faceted, he was a teacher, a thinker, a reformer, a commentator, an organizer, a philosopher, a poet, a theologian, a missionary, a mystic, a scholar, a saint, a *siddha*, a *mukta*, a divine incarnation, a living legend.

However, this being acknowledged, very little may be said with any precision on the basis of firm historical evidence about his date of birth, life, or writings. What is available is comprised of bits and pieces, speculations, and legends, derived either from his own works, from hagiographies, or from references in other works. Virtually everything about him has been questioned. Though there do exist many professed biographies of Śaṅkara (known under the rubric of 'Śaṅkara Vijayas'), all the extant ones date from the fourteenth to the eighteenth centuries and thus are posterior to him by anywhere from six hundred to a thousand years.[1] Further, the hagiographies or literature about the life, legends, and writings of Śaṅkara contain a profusion of prophecies, signs, and wonders. They are filled with incredible, miraculous accounts. They also, upon analysis, most likely contain exaggerations, distortions, contradictions, and inconsistencies. These works give an enormous amount of information concerning the legend of Śaṅkara, but they are not historical biographies in the modern sense of the term.[2] Thus, to date no extant materials are known of from which to reconstruct the life of Śaṅkara with *certainty*.[3]

Scholarship is replete with the works of those who have attempted to plumb the mysteries of Śaṅkara. Indologists, philosophers, religionists, historians and artists, are but some more recent representatives of this endeavor. Virtually all are in agreement that it is almost impossible to come to any definitive conclusion. Classical scholarship was perhaps over-authoritatian and dogmatic while a lot of the contemporary scholarship was perhaps over-hostile. Thoughtful research may best be enhanced by becoming aware of the strengths and weaknesses of any given position. Traditions develop and there is usually a grain of truth latent in 'old wives' tales'.

The material which exists for a study of the life and times of Śaṅkara has been viewed from at least three paradigmatic perspectives,[4] each attempting to make coherent and meaningful sense of the material. These are the historical approach, the philosophical approach and the traditional approach. Each perspective possesses certain strengths and weaknesses. Each perspective makes certain presuppositions. Each perspective has a contribution to make.

First, there is the historical approach.[5] Being the most recent of the three approaches, it also proclaims the greatest objectivity. Be that as it may, the strength of this position lies in the fact that it is the accepted modern paradigm for determining what is 'factual' and therefore true; correct; authentic. Its concern is with empirical evidence. However, it has often been said that 'the truth of history is the truth of the historian'. Today's truth very often becomes tomorrow's myth. The historical approach is, in fact, only one of a number of approaches, employing a particular perspective, and to claim a monopoly on the truth is nothing more than a dogmatic and arbitrary fabrication. Taking note of this precaution, the historical method has made its contributions to what can and cannot be stated about Śaṅkara, especially in regards to determining his dates. Without a doubt it has added another dimension and perspective to the investigation – even if it cannot legitimately claim to be the definitive conclusion.

Next, there is the philosophical approach. This perspective consists of an investigation and an interpretation of Śaṅkara's works, primarily to determine which compositions traditionally ascribed to Śaṅkara can be regarded as genuine. This method allows for great variety, and issues raised include colophons, mention in other works, stylometric analysis, and considerations of language, style, content, and ideas.[6] This approach, however, has the tendency to reduce Śaṅkara to (merely, solely, primarily) a philosopher. There is little justification for such a reduction. If anything, tradition declares that Śaṅkara was, first and foremost, an expounder of liberation (*mokṣa*); both what it is and the means thereto and second, that he wrote his philosophical works at the request of his *guru*. Therefore, it would appear that his interest in philosophy was not primarily for philosophy's sake, but as an aid to liberation and as a clear and perpetuating declaration of what that entailed. This point has often been forgotten or, perhaps, conveniently ignored.

If it is granted that Śaṅkara was not only a philosopher, but also a teacher, then it does not necessarily follow that terms need always be used in an identical manner. Śaṅkara was located firmly within the Upaniṣadic tradition and certainly employed many of the techniques found therein and these techniques have a bearing on precision, context and competence:

> One such method is described by Śaṅkara in his commentary on the *Bhagavadgītā*. This method has been time-honored in the Advaita tradition as the traditional method for teaching the transphenomenal *Brahman*.[7] It employs the technique of prior superimposition and subsequent denial (*adhyāropa* and *apavāda*). First, qualities and relations like omniscience, omnipotence, omnipresence, causality, etc., are superimposed upon the Absolute so as to enable one to form some sort of understanding. Then, gradually these attributes are negated as a deeper and deeper analysis is performed. From the familiar, one is led to the unfamiliar. From the known, one is led to the unknown. As Śaṅkara put it: 'Their aim (religious knowledge) is to be the means of detachment from the objects towards which one is naturally attracted.'[8]

A teacher need not always employ a particular term or terms in an identical manner. As long as it may be demonstrated that Śaṅkara did not employ a term in a manner which is inimical to the fundamental doctrine of Advaita, then I believe a useful purpose may be served in its particular employment. To cite one example, sometimes it may serve one's purpose to distinguish between the waking and dreaming states and, at other times, it may be illustrative to equate them. To deny this is to deny the skill of a teacher. Further, it is well known that Śaṅkara's teachings employed many key terms which are polysemous and thus capable of more than one designate. This built-in ambiguity has been considered by some an asset and by others as a defect. It is up to the reader to decide. Precision is important but context usually decides a given meaning. Śaṅkara is famous for his internal and intertextual consistency. Thus, it behooves one to identify and be continually aware of Śaṅkara's own perspective.

As well, even by employing the philosophical approach to determine which writings are authentically Śaṅkara's, a tremendous amount of uncertainty still prevails. The issue is complex and complicated and one is sometimes tempted to remove the 'errors of antiquity' by substituting one's own. Whether one employs a careful analysis of Śaṅkara's use of certain technological terms,[9] or colophons,[10] or a stylometric approach comparing word frequencies,[11] the results remain deductive and confusing. Some of his works are beyond doubt.[12] But whether a person with Śaṅkara's genius could have employed different terminologies, analogies, styles, meters, and approaches cannot always definitively be determined from a philosophical analysis. The question as to whether Śaṅkara was a theist, a poet, a Śaivite, a Vaiṣṇavite, a tantric, a yogin, or exclusively an Advaitin cannot be definitively answered. Nor is it the case that such labels are mutually exclusive. To cite but one example, Jñāneśvar Maharaj is claimed alike by Śaivites, Vaiṣṇavites, tantrics, *yogis*, *jñānis*, and *bhaktas*, and each have advanced claims that his doctrine is theirs. It is a generally accepted rule that the greater an exposition, the simpler and more universal it is.

Finally, there is the traditional approach. In one sense, this approach deserves first mention for it is the oldest method and obviously the method that the author of this text intended for his audience. Prerequisites are stated (*sādhana catuṣṭaya*).[13] Not only must discrimination and detachment be cultivated, but 'an intense longing for liberation' (*mumukṣutva*) must also be present as well as the text's declaration,

> That person who desires to know the truth of the Self and who possesses the above mentioned qualifications should approach a Master, a knower of the Self, who confers freedom from bondage. (V. 33)

Religious seekers, devotees, and staunch believers do not question when Śaṅkara was born, all that he did or did not do, where he died, or what he wrote. To them there is a sense of absolute conviction and the only question is, 'How can we understand and follow his teachings and experience liberation?' Their predominant interest lies in boons, blessings, spiritual instructions, and Self-realization.

The question of determining the authenticity of the writings attributed to Śaṅkara is a complicated issue. The fact that he allegedly lived such a short life, coupled with the plethora of works of such diverse character attributed to him, makes the issue all the more difficult. Which ones are genuine? Tradition wants to accept them all. Modern critics tend to be at the other extreme and exhibit a reluctance to accept more than three or four of the more than four hundred possibilities.

Determining the Dates of Śaṅkara

To fix with any certainty the exact dates of Śaṅkara is one of the most perplexing and controversial problems in the history of Indian philosophy.[14] This is a common difficulty experienced in regard to many Indian historical personalities due to a paucity of records as well as conflicting traditions which appear in different parts of the country.

In attempting to determine the date of Śaṅkara, investigators have utilized (1) professed biographies of Śaṅkara known under the rubric of 'Śaṅkara Vijayas'; (2) internal evidence from Śaṅkara's undisputed works; (3) astrological data;[15] (4) records or succession lists (*maṭhāmnāya*) from the Śaṅkara *maṭhas*; (5) epigraphic corroboration; and (6) legends from the living tradition of Advaita Vedānta in India.

The most popular, oft-quoted, and commonly accepted date (according to modern historians and scholars and the Śṛṅgerī Maṭha) is 788–820 CE.[16] The traditional or orthodox view (as championed by most of the Śaṅkara monasteries or *maṭha*) is 508–476 BCE.[17] However, this later view appears to be readily dismissable as it makes Śaṅkara a contemporary of Buddha and we know with certainty that Śaṅkara was clearly posterior to such Buddhist scholars as Dignāga (end of fifth century CE) and Dharmakīrti (beginning of seventh century).[18] Taking note of all the analysis that has gone before him, G.C. Pande proposes that Śaṅkara should be placed somewhere near 650–700 CE, a date which agrees with that given in the *Darśana-prakāśa* and the Śṛṅgerī tradition.[19]

The Life of Śaṅkara

The lion of Vedānta appeared;
the universe of duality rejoiced

Though Śaṅkara's place within both Hinduism and the Advaita Vedānta philosophical tradition is tremendous and he commands the highest respect and reverence, studies about his life are scant[20] and controversial. They contain a profusion of legends and are filled with incredible miracles, seeming exaggerations and distortions, contradictions, and inconsistencies. Whether this is a strength of the various accounts, or a weakness, depends upon one's perspective and interpretive abilities. Before us is a record of experiences, stories, legends (however incomplete), exaggerated, and unresearched, for which there are no simple explanations. At least a thousand years have passed and still we have but partial understandings, misinterpretations, and naive interpretations.

It has been said that legends about the life of Śaṅkara were shaped by three factors.[21] First, there are the traditional accounts which declare that Śaṅkara was an incarnation of Śiva.[22] Second, there was the need for the orthodox tradition to provide a genealogy, authentification, and support for the new monastic tradition which Śaṅkara supposedly created along with its religious, spiritual and social declarations. Third, there was the growing polemic of the Advaita tradition with its desire to highlight Śaṅkara's wondrous, victorious life (*digvijaya*).

The upshot of these three factors was the presentation, acceptance, and adoption of an ever-growing faith in, and reverence for, both Śaṅkara and the monastic centers which he supposedly founded. What is important to note here is that believers and spiritual aspirants are primarily looking for a personal experience, for personal liberation, for that which inspires and uplifts them and not just for information about, no matter how wonderful or interesting or even divine. It is because these legendary accounts further their belief in, and reverence for, Śaṅkara and his teachings that they are accepted, adopted, and repeated, whether or not they are historically true.

On the other hand, there are scholars and intellectuals who presuppose that the life and works of Śaṅkara can be meaningfully discussed and understood independent of a belief in them. The consequence of this type of postulation is that information becomes not only relevant, but all-important. This is the domain of 'those who want to know' in contrast to the previously above-mentioned 'those who want to be' (or believe). Pious devotees or staunch believers generally do not ask such questions, not seriously at any rate, for they focus on their own personal experience(s) or else on how to achieve such experiences. Their predominant interest lies in boons, blessings, and/or Self-realization.

Tradition declares that Lord Śiva was Śaṅkara's family deity and, flowing from this, the Śaṅkara literature has long been seen as a genre by means of which Śaṅkara was ultimately deified into an incarnation of Lord Śiva.[23] Traditional accounts of Śaṅkara's life begin with Lord Śiva – Lord Śiva as the primordial teacher (*ādiguru*); Lord Śiva as the boon-giver to Śaṅkara's parents; Lord Śiva as incarnating as Śaṅkara:

> How strange! Under the banyan tree are old men. Their teacher is only a boy. His explanation consists in silence. Yet the disciples have been made free from doubts.[24]

> The Great God Śiva, the Self-created, the Merciful, the Destroyer of Manmata (Cupid), manifested himself as his holy embodiment, as a Śivaliṅgam, on a hill

> known as Vṛṣhācala, located near the Purna River in the Kerala country.[25] Lord Śaṅkara, the blue-necked one, out of boundless love for the welfare of living beings, will incarnate himself.[26]
>
> In the Kerala country in the village of Śaśala, a part of me (Śiva) shall be born with the name of Śaṅkara.[27] In Kālaṭi, the wife of the learned Śivaguru, will bear a son by name Śaṅkara being a part of Śiva.[28]

Advaita's well-known, oft-quoted invocatory verse (*Guru-parampara śloka*) mentions the unbroken lineage of the teachers of Advaita. Dakṣiṇamūrti, the primordial *Guru*, is universally understood and then:

> Nārāyaṇam Padmabhūvaṁ Vaśiṣṭhaṁ Śaktiṁca tatputra Parāśarañca Vyāsaṁ Śukaṁ Gauḍapādaṁ mahāntaṁ Govinda Yogīndra athāsya śiṣyam Śrī Śaṅkarācārya athāsya Padmapādañca Hastāmalakañca śiṣyam taṁ Toṭakaṁ vārttikakāramanyān asmad gurūn santatamānato'smi

It may be observed from this list that the lineage begins with Lord Nārāyaṇa and the line continues from father to son down to Vyāsa's son, Śuka. From Śuka to Gauḍapāda onwards, the lineage is passed from *sannyāsin* to *sannyāsin* and the *Guru* has now become a *parivrājaka*, 'one who wanders' (looking for disciples), instead of the prior passing of the lineage from father to son directly within one's own house. As well, before Gauḍapāda, the teachers were either divine or semi-divine and, commencing with Gauḍapāda, the tradition of human preceptors begins.

Among other things, what this lineage does is to invoke authenticity. Not only does it provide continuity, a direct passage of the truth from the primordial teacher directly to Śaṅkara, but it also invokes the ideal, the norm, the authoritative voice of an authentic tradition coming from an authentic source, and Śaṅkara valued tradition (*saṁpradāya*) as the highest authority.[29] He said:

> A conceited knower might say: I shall reveal the essence of the wheel of birth and death, of bondage, and the essence of liberation; I shall reveal the essence of the scriptures, but he is himself confused and is stupefying others since he rejected the teachers' tradition of deliberation on the essence of the scriptures and came to the refutation of scripture and to mental constructions opposing scripture.[30]

According to tradition, to legend, on the banks of the Periyar River in the small village of Kālaṭi in Kerala, in the extreme south of India, Āryāmbā (Śivatārakā – Śiva's eye or Śiva's falling star) the virtuous wife of a Nambūṭiri *brahmin* named Śivaguru (Śiva the Teacher) gave birth to a son just like Śrī Pārvatī, who begot Lord Subrāhmaṇya. The birth was in an auspicious ascendant (*śubha lagna*) with an auspicious planet both in conjunction and aspected with it. The Sun, Mars, Saturn, and Jupiter were in exaltation.[31] The birth of the child was accompanied by heavenly music and the sweet fragrance of flowers. The body of the child dazzled in its brilliance and on top of his head the sign of Śiva, a crescent moon, could be clearly seen. On his palm was a mark left by Śiva's trident and on his breast was an image of a coiled cobra. On his forehead could be seen his third eye. Once again, for the protection of the good and the destruction of the wicked, the auspicious Lord Śiva had taken birth as an incarnation.[32]

Before Śaṅkara was born, Āryāmbā and Śivaguru had been childless for quite some time. After many years, they decided to go to nearby Trichūr where there was a famous Śiva temple, Vṛṣācala, and seek Lord Śiva's blessings for a child. Time passed, and austerities were performed, and then, one night, Lord Śiva appeared to Śivaguru in a dream and offered him a boon. After hearing of Śivaguru's desire for a child, the Great God said, 'I grant your prayer, but you have to select either of these two alternatives – choose either an all-knowing and virtuous but short-lived son, or one who will live very long but without any special virtue or greatness.'[33] Śivaguru, instead of declaring his preference, replied, 'What do you think? Will you please do whatever is best for humanity.'[34]

This incident is typical of a Śaṅkara story which may or may not be historically accurate. Such occurrences are possible and do occasionally happen, though they probably happen much less in life than in fantasy. However, whether the story is historically accurate or not, it does serve as a very useful teaching tool. Whenever one is confronted with a choice, one can learn from this incident that if the person giving one a choice is much greater than oneself, the best option would appear to be to defer the decision to the boon-giver.[35]

Another such story concerns Śaṅkara's mother. Tradition declares that Śaṅkara's father died before Śaṅkara turned five. This was probably the source for Dvaitins disparagingly referring to Śaṅkara as the son of a widow. As we shall soon see, Śaṅkara promised his mother that he would be with her when her death day approached. In this regard, Śaṅkara declared, 'There may be a bad child but there is no such thing as a bad mother.' What is the logic here? Is it merely a parochial Indian custom, or is there an universal truth involved? Śaṅkara held that a mother, in an incredible act of creation, gives a child its physical body. It is with this body that one is able, not only to seek the ultimate goal of life, e.g., liberation, but also to enjoy the myriad sense objects which all individuals desire and enjoy. Now, how will the child ever repay this gift? Even if the mother were to scold and beat and mistreat the child, there are not enough meritorious acts to counter-balance the merit which a mother receives for giving birth. Thus, even though one may dislike the individual personality and dislike a mother's actions, one must honor, respect, and love one's mother. Reverence and respect for one's mother is the only way to repay one's mother for her grace-bestowing act.

Śaṅkara's early childhood was full of signs and wonders. He was said to have been a precocious child prodigy who learned quickly and retained whatever he heard but once.[36] By the age of three it is said that he could speak and read Sanskrit. At five he was invested with a sacred thread and by the age of eight he had mastered the *Vedas* and *Vedāṅgas*.[37] At the age of seven he was said to have written his first book, the *Balabodha Samgraha*.

Numerous miraculous stories are told about Śaṅkara's childhood. There is no agreement among the traditional biographies, either in regards to individual events or even among particular incidents for a given event. Some of the more commonly related incidents include the actual partaking of a ritual offering by the goddess when he was five;[38] the shower of gold coins for the poverty-stricken woman who gave him an *āmalaka* fruit in the absence of any other possession;[39] the diversion of the Cūrṇā (Pūrnā) River for the convenience of his mother;[40] at the age of eight, his declaration to his mother that a crocodile had caught his leg while bathing in the river and her subsequent blessing for him to become a renunciant (*sannyāsin*).[41]

The eight-year-old *sannyāsin* walked north[42] until he reached the banks of the Narmadā River. There, he encountered his guru, Govinda Bhagavatpāda, who asked him, 'Who are you (*kas tvam*)?'[43] Tradition declares that Śaṅkara burst into the hymn, 'Six Stanzas on Liberation',[44] which begins, 'I am neither the mind nor the intellect, neither the ego nor the mind-stuff . . . I am consciousness and bliss; I am Śiva, I am Śiva!' Legend also says that he composed the 'Hymn of Ten Verses' on one's true identity. 'That ultimate reality is not even One, then how can it be dual? It is neither aloneness nor the opposite. It is neither void nor the opposite. It is pure Advaita. In fact, words cannot encompass its meaning.'[45]

Hagiographical accounts vary as to how long the young Śaṅkara spent with Govinda. During his stay of two, three, or four years, Śaṅkara supposedly composed a number of hymns, philosophical treatises, and commentaries. Tradition also claims that Śaṅkara wrote the *Vivekacūḍāmaṇi* during this period.[46] There is also a legend that during this period a great flood came and the waters of the Narmadā rose up to the entrance of the cave where Govinda and his disciples were staying. Seeing this, Śaṅkara chanted a particular *mantra* and invoked the waters to enter into his begging bowl (*kamaṇḍalu*), thereby quelling the flood. As this was happening, Govinda remembered Bādarāyaṇa's famous prophecy that the best and greatest commentary on his *Brahmasūtras* would be written by someone who succeeds in taming the raging river.[47]

Śaṅkara's period of residence with Govinda had come to an end and thus Govinda said, 'Now it is time for you to compose your commentaries (*bhāṣya*) on the foundation works of Vedānta (*prasthānatrayī*).[48] Therefore, proceed to Kāśī and do what you are ordained to do.'[49]

During his four-year stay in Kāśī, a tale is told of an encounter Śaṅkara had with an outcast (*cāṇḍāla*).[50] While walking with his disciples in one of the narrow lanes of the city, Śaṅkara suddenly and expectedly encountered the *cāṇḍāla* and, as the social custom of the day required an outcast to move aside so as not to pollute a *brahmin*, Śaṅkara asked the *cāṇḍāla* to move aside. The reply was an unexpectedly surprising rebuke. 'O distinguished ascetic, best among the twice-born. You have established that the Absolute is everywhere. Who or what are you asking to move aside? This body, like yours, built up of food, is inert and cannot move by itself. If you are asking the omnipresent pure Consciousness of which I am the apparent manifestation to move from blocking your way, that too is not possible. In brief, we are the same. Thus, whom are you asking to clear the way for whom?'

Śaṅkara immediately bowed to the *cāṇḍāla* and, having acknowledged the truth of the outcaste's words, composed a poem on the spot.

> O best among men. What you have said is true. One gets a clear experience of that pure Consciousness during waking, dreaming, and deep sleep. That pure Consciousness is present in all bodies, from Brahma to small ants and insects. It witnesses all that happens in this universe. That pure Consciousness alone exists. I am not matter in the form of this body or sense organs. He who has such a complete understanding, whether that person be a cāṇḍāla or twice-born, he is my guru. This is my understanding.

Time passed and Śaṅkara knew that his mother, Āryāmbā, was on her death bed.[51] He sat comforting her and assured her that she would be liberated. She asked him about liberation and Śaṅkara explained to her the four-fold prerequisites of spiritual discipline (*sādhana catuṣṭaya*).[52] Tradition says that Śaṅkara tried to teach her the essence of Advaita, but, finding that he wasn't succeeding, he chanted hymns to Śiva and Viṣṇu and enabled his mother to meet death with courage and calmness. Then, although his *sannyāsin* vows, in principle, should have prevented him from performing her last rites, he thought to himself, 'I have given her my word and besides my body grew out of hers. How can that connection be severed even if I am a sannyāsin?' The traditionalists were infuriated and would not let Śaṅkara proceed. Thus, Śaṅkara decided to cremate his mother in the back yard of her house. Since the *brahmins* refused to give him fire to light the pyre, Śaṅkara used his yogic powers, and, chanting vedic *mantras*, lit the pyre and cremated his mother.

The tale goes on, as is now well known, of the things that were done at that time, of the things that are yet to be known, of the mysteries long unforeseen, and of the victory looked for. Legends abound. Tales are told of Śaṅkara meeting Vyāsa;[53] of his life-span being extended to thirty-two years;[54] of his visit to Bādarikāśrama;[55] of his meeting with Lord Siva;[56] of Govinda's passing away (*mahāsamādhi*);[57] of his victory tour (*digvijaya*);[58] of his meeting with the Kāpālikas;[59] of his meeting his four main disciples, Padmapāda,[60] Hastamalaka,[61] Sureśvara,[62] and Toṭaka;[63] of his debate with Maṇḍana;[64] of his ascending the Sarvajñā Pītha;[65] of his establishing his monasteries (*maṭha*);[66] of his visit to Mount Kailāsa and his receiving the five *liṅgas*;[67] and finally his *mahāsāmadhi*.[68]

The Works of Śaṅkara

The lion of Vedānta roared;
the universe of duality disappeared

During Śaṅkara's relatively short life, more than four hundred works including commentaries and sub-commentaries (*bhāṣya* and *vārttika*), independent works (*prakaraṇa*), and hymns, poetry, and praises of deities (*stotra*, *stava*, *stuti*) have been attributed to him.[69] It is generally agreed that the majority of these works are apocryphal. In all likelihood this list grew to such proportions because, in order to give a book authenticity, it has long been a common practice in India to attribute it to a famous author. Further, all the heads (*maṭhādipati* or *jagadguru*) of the various Śaṅkara monasteries have borne the title 'Śaṅkarācārya' and thus any works which they wrote could easily be mistaken for, and legitimately called, a work of Śaṅkarācārya.[70]

The question of determining the authenticity of which works are truly Śaṅkara's is controversial and vexing.[71] One of the early criteria considered by critical scholarship for determining Śaṅkara's authorship of a given work was whether it was commented upon or quoted in one of the early commentaries.[72] However, this criteria of subsequent commentaries or mention therein is as easily doubtable as to doubt Śaṅkara himself. Certainty is still lacking.

The German scholar Paul Hacker was one of the first modern scholars to formulate the problem of authorship clearly and to propose methods of investigation thereon.[73] He proposed three main principles for determining the validity of a work: Check the colophon of a work and observe whether it is attributed merely to 'Śaṅkarācārya' or, more authentically, to 'Bhagavat' or any of its versions such as 'Bhagavatpāda' and 'Bhagavatpūjyapāda'; check for references in the works of his immediate disciples; and analyze the contents and/or special use of terminology in the work in question. However, it must be noted that Śaṅkara's authorship cannot be *conclusively* solved by an analysis of a particular work's contents, table of categories, terminology, or colophon. Further, the plethora of ascribed poetical works neither contain strict philosophical terminology, logical argumentation, nor colophons. Thus, the debate rages on.

The question of determining the authenticity of the writings attributed to Śaṅkara is a complicated issue. The fact that he allegedly lived such a short life coupled with the plethora of works of such diverse character attributed to him makes the issue all the more difficult. Which ones are genuine? Tradition wants to accept them all. Modern critics tend to be at the other extreme and be reluctant to accept more than three or four of the possibilities.

It is beyond the scope of this book to examine further the details of the debate concerning the authenticity of the works ascribed to Śaṅkara – a subject which has been dealt with by other scholars in great detail. However, I will take up this issue with regard to whether or not Śaṅkara was the author of the *Vivekacūḍāmaṇi*.

The Vivekacūḍāmaṇi

Within Indian philosophy there are a number of types of sourcebooks. The *Vedas* and *Upaniṣads* comprise the primary scriptures (*śruti*). The Epics (*Itihāsa*) including the *Bhagavadgītā*, the *Purāṇas*, the Law Books (*Dharmaśāstra*), and the philosophical literature (*darśana*) comprise the secondary scriptures (*smṛti*). Among the philosophical literature, Vedānta recognizes the *prasthānatraya* (*Upaniṣads*, *Bhagavadgītā*, and *Brahmasūtras*) as foundational. However, to study these three foundational sourcebooks requires not only a qualified teacher, but also a profound knowledge of Sanskrit and a proficiency in grammar, logic, investigation, and vedic lore.[74] Śaṅkara, knowing that not all people would be qualified to study the foundational sourcebooks, compassionately wrote what are known as independent philosophical treatises (*prakaraṇa grantha*).[75] A *prakaraṇa* treatise has four indispensable elements (*anubandha catuṣṭaya*): the determination of the fitness of a student for the study of the treatise (*adhikāri*); the subject matter (*viṣaya*); the mutual relationship between the treatise and the subject matter (*sambandha*); and the object to be attained by the study (*prayojana*).[76]

Though the *Upadeśasāhasrī* (*A Thousand Teachings*) is the only independent treatise which modern scholars have unequivocally ascribed to Śaṅkara,[77] tradition claims that among the more important independent works which Śaṅkara wrote are *Ātmabodha*, *Aparokṣānubhūti*, *Pañcīkaraṇa*, *Śataślokī*, *Sarva Vedāntasāra Saṅgraha*.

The *Vivekacūḍāmaṇi* is one such independent philosophical treatise and is perhaps the most popular of the *prakaraṇas* ascribed to Śaṅkara.[78] It is a dialog between a teacher (*guru*) and student (*śiṣya*) expounding the quintessence of Advaita Vedānta. As its name indicates, *cūḍāmaṇi* or crown jewel[79] of *viveka* or discrimination, discrimination is of paramount importance in one's quest for liberation.

In a recent article,[80] Francis Clooney describes the *Vivekacūḍāmaṇi* as a 'pedagogical masterpiece exclusively for male *brahmins*'. I take issue with this claim, as my commentary on V. 2 states. This entire issue has been well documented in a recent book by Roger Marcaurelle.[81]

Ingalls declares that there are four texts which are indubitably Śaṅkara's on the evidence of his direct disciples.[82] He then states that, 'if we then find a single occurrence of some distinctive theory on a problem of Vedānta philosophy (which does not appear in his *Brahmasūtra-bhāṣya*), whatever the traditional ascription of this other work may be, we have *prima facie* evidence that it is not by Śaṅkara'.[83] Thus, he concludes with absolute certainty that Śaṅkara definitely did not write the *Vivekacūḍāmaṇi* for, the author of it has (1) made an absolute equation of the waking and dream states, and (2) employed the theory of indescribability (*anirvacanīya*). On the other hand, Hacker, who pointed out that Śaṅkara uses the word 'anirvacanīya' in quite a different sense from that found in the *Vivekacūḍāmaṇi*,[84] still accepts the work as genuine based on the colophon.[85]

All this being given, a strong case can be made that the *Vivekacūḍāmaṇi* is a genuine work of Śaṅkara's and that it differs in certain respects from his other works in that it addresses itself to a different audience and has a different emphasis and purpose. There is no rule that insists that a *prakaraṇa* treatise should be consistent with a commentary. Indian philosophical works must conform to a prescribed form, setting forth, in an ordered manner, their leading concepts and doctrines. *Prakaraṇa* works, on the other hand, are short manuals which confine themselves to some essential topics of a given theme.

In the case of the *Vivekacūḍāmaṇi*, it is a manual for spiritual disciplines (*sādhana*). Further, it places an emphasis on spiritual practices which purify the mind;[86] it emphasizes the horrors of the world;[87] it makes numerous precise lists with very fine distinctions; it prolifically mentions 'wise men' and expands the scope as to who and what a wise man is.[88] Obviously, one of the consequences of these latter references is to draw attention to, and invoke, tradition, lineage, and authority. Gussner claims this is a blatant attempt to claim legitimacy, but it may just be an attempt to inspire the spiritual aspirant. The *Vivekacūḍāmaṇi* advises the spiritual aspirant to revere and worship the teacher as a means of progressing in one's spiritual life.[89] Thus, in all likelihood, the numerous references to 'wise men' is not only a ploy to invoke authority but is also an encourager of inspiration.

Some of the tests Hacker proposed to determine whether or not a work was authentically Śaṅkara's or not include:[90]

1. The term *avidyā* means superimposition (*adhyāsa*) and not as synonymous with such terms as *jaḍa*, *bhāvarūpa*, *āvaraṇa*, *vikṣepa*, *anirvacanīya*
2. The term *māyā* being infrequently used in comparison with *avidyā*
3. Reluctance or refusal to accept the term *ānanda* as a positive property of *Brahman*
4. The waking and dreaming states are not equated (as in Gauḍapāda)
5. A work concludes with the colophon, 'Bhagavatpāda or Bhagavatpūjyapāda'.[91]

Then, there are two other issues: the use of *prāgabhāva* and *jīvanmukti*. Let us examine these points, one by one.

Avidyā

It would appear that for Śaṅkara, *avidyā* is a term which is fundamentally a description of an affliction of the psyche, an existential description of a state of being, an experiential realm of ignorance. It is a 'given', an existential fact in each and everyone's experience. The moment a person is born, ignorance is there. Thus, it is not, first and foremost, a metaphysical entity, a full-blown philosophical concept, so much as it is a useful tool and description. If this is so, and it should be, as it would be in keeping with the feeling that Śaṅkara was first and foremost concerned with an individual's liberation and not with philosophy *per se*, then I believe a case may be made that Śaṅkara was the author of the *Vivekacūḍāmaṇi* or, if that is too strong, there are at least some reasonable replies to the objections that he was not.

Śaṅkara defined ignorance (*avidyā*) in his *Brahmasūtrabhāṣya* as 'Ignorance is the mutual superimposition of subject and object, the mutual transposing of Self and nonself, the unacceptable combining of true and false.'[92] In the same place he also said that 'learned men regard this superimposition (*adhyāsa*) thus defined as *avidyā*'[93] and that superimposition is the imposition of a thing on what is not that thing (*atasmiṁs-tad-buddhiḥ*).[94] He also said, '*Avidyā* is *parameśvarāśraya*, that is, it depends upon *Brahman*. And in it (*avidyā*) the individuals, having lost their identity with *Brahman*, rest.'[95]

As a philosophical term, *avidyā* (*māyā*) is the key concept of Advaita (see verse 45 onwards).[96] Since Śaṅkara did not differentiate between *avidyā* and *māyā*, as post-Śaṅkarite Advaitins did, in the present context the two terms may be viewed as one key concept. This entails elaboration in order that a misunderstanding does not result. Critics sometimes label Advaita Vedānta as '*māyā-vāda*' and Advaitins are called '*māyā-vādins*'. These terms are used disparagingly and yet there is a grain of truth in the matter. *Avidyā/māyā* cannot exist or function independent of *Brahman* and it ceases to be when *Brahman* is realized. Still, *avidyā/māyā* is the device by which the Advaitin explains how the One Reality appears as multitudinous. Strictly speaking, *Brahman* is the be-all and end-all of Advaita and, if anything, Advaita should be called '*Brahma-vāda*'. This is so because Advaita, and Śaṅkara, never lose sight of the central doctrine that *Brahman* is Real, the world is non-real, and the individual is non-different from *Brahman*. And yet, the concept of *avidyā/māyā* may still be said to be central to Advaita.[97] What the critics have done is to mistake the means for the end. The reality of *Ātman/Brahman* is Śaṅkara's sole concern. Śaṅkara is not interested in proving the existence of *avidyā/māyā*. Nonetheless, though *avidyā/māyā* is not ultimately real, its importance cannot be exaggerated for the role that it plays.

Hacker claims that Śaṅkara (in his BSBh) does not raise *avidyā* to an eternal, metaphysical entity in the way his successors do.[98] This seems acceptable. In this context, the *Vivekacūḍāmaṇi* constantly uses the word 'beginningless' (*anādi*) in conjunction with *avidyā*.[99] Does this imply that Śaṅkara did not write the *Vivekacūḍāmaṇi*? Not necessarily, for it should be noted that Śaṅkara himself, in his most unquestionable work, does call *adhyāsa* 'beginningless'.[100] And as he equates *adhyāsa* with *avidyā*, it logically follows that *avidyā* is beginningless. How many instances make a case?

Interestingly, Hacker says that the fact 'that Śaṅkara equates *avidyā* with the basic error of all worldly existence distinguishes him from all later Advaitins who considered *avidyā* a factor which causally conditions all error insofar as it is, so to speak, the stuff out of which every false idea is formed.' For Śaṅkara, *mithyājñāna* or false knowledge occurs like a synonym for *avidyā* while for post-Śaṅkara writers *avidyā* is the cause of *mithyājñāna*.

In V. 199, 'Individualness exists only so long as delusion persists, as it is born of false knowledge. The rope is mistaken for a snake only as long as the delusion lasts; there is no more a snake once the delusion is destroyed.' In V. 203, 'The relation of the Self and the intellect is due to false knowledge.' In V. 348, 'So too, the removal of illusory knowledge and suffering produced by false projections withdraws.' We can observe that the three instances in which *mithyājñāna* occurs in the *Vivekacūḍāmaṇi*, the term is used as a synonym for *avidyā*. However, this being said, it is true that the *Vivekacūḍāmaṇi* does describe *avidyā* as the material source of the world[101] and this goes against Hacker's criterion that *avidyā* should not be materialized. Yet, Śaṅkara does speak of *avidyā-bīja*[102] and *avidyātmaka*[103] in terms which suggest a relationship of material causality.

Again, Hacker claims that the sequence of terms like '*avidyā-kāma-karma*' distinguishes Śaṅkara's use of *avidyā* from that of his successors.[104] He contends, and in this he appears to be correct, that Śaṅkara uses *avidyā* as a general term equated with the basic error of all worldly existence, while his successors defined it much more precisely, especially its role as the material cause of the empirical world as well as of all errors. This is to be expected since his successors had to reply to specific philosophical challenges. However, on the one hand, Advaita is not a house divided against itself for the concept of *avidyā* is central to Advaitin's in spite of their individual uses and, second, it is strange that V. 58 reads '*avidyākāmakarmādi*'; V. 98 reads '*avidyāpi ca kāmakarmāṇī*'; and V. 334 reads '*avidyākāryaduḥkham*'. Again, how many instances do there need to be to make a case? Whether this series of terms seems to coincide with the Yoga system's similar series, as Hacker speculates,[105] does not affect the point at hand.

Anirvacanīya

In the *Vivekacūḍāmaṇi* (V. 111), *māyā* is described as, 'neither real nor unreal nor both; It is neither undifferentiated, nor different, nor both; It neither has parts nor is partless nor both. It is supremely wonderful and of an inexpressible, undeterminable (*anirvacanīya*) form.' This is the only occurrence of *anirvacanīya* in the *Vivekacūḍāmaṇi*. Hacker claims that Śaṅkara never calls *avidyā anirvacanīya*. Yet the *Vivekacūḍāmaṇi* does not draw any technical distinction between *avyakta*, *avyākṛta*, *anirvacanīya*, and *avidyā*. The falsity of the empirical world consists in its being misunderstood as other than *Ātman/Brahman*. Superimposition is ignorance. Even if Śaṅkara did not spell out the characteristics of *avidyā* in any detail in his unquestioned works, this does not mean that he could not, or did not, in others. The idea logically extrapolated implies 'what is other than the real nor unreal and so on.' Śaṅkara himself used the term *tattvānyatvābhyām*, while later writers employed *sadasadbhyām* or *sattvāsattvābhyām*.[106] The first term means 'that or other than that'; the second term means, 'either real/being or non-real non-being'. *Anirvacanīya* means indeterminable or unspecifiable. All these terms mean 'indeterminable either as real or unreal'. Hacker's analysis of these terms is certainly open to interpretation, and, as the traditional commentators did not explain them, one is left to one's own insight.[107]

Māyā

Over the centuries, as we earlier noted, Advaita has been known as *māyāvāda*. Śaṅkara never called his thought that and Hacker believes that were one to select a catchword, it would hardly be that.[108] But, as myself and many many others state, *māyā* is the key-concept of Advaita and the one term which opponents of Advaita need to both exploit and demolish if they are to erect their own systems of thought. Personally, I think that the one catchword for Śaṅkara's thought should be the Self (*ātman*), as it is the be-all and end-all of Advaita. I am the Self. You are the Self, he/she/it is the Self. That is the Truth. But that is another matter.

In the *Vivekacūḍāmaṇi*, the word '*māyā*' occurs fifteen times and the word '*avidyā*' sixteen times. Those who count words say that Śaṅkara, in his uncontested works, employed these two terms in a 1:5 ratio. But what does that prove? Especially since it has often been noted that Śaṅkara did not make a distinction between these two terms. In one place, Hacker seems to imply that these two terms are not synonymous since they are being compared and not equated, but I cannot accept this interpretation.[109] In the sentence, 'The one Parameśvara . . . appears in manifold manifestations through *avidyā*, as the magician through *māyā*' (BSBh 1.3.19), the manifestation of the world appears through ignorance just as a magician's magic appears through illusion. There *is* a similarity of concepts; there *is* a resemblance; they *are* synonymous.

This being said, whether in Śaṅkara's accepted works or in the *Vivekacūḍāmaṇi*, *māyā* is employed to mean either imagination or magic[110] (especially in conjunction with a magician); illusion[111] (especially in comparison); concealment;[112] or the magical power of God[113] (Viṣṇu's special power). Thus, it is not logical to draw the conclusion that Śaṅkara is not the author of the *Vivekacūḍāmaṇi* from the use of *avidya/māyā* found therein. In this day and age it should be well understood that Śaṅkara could easily have used a variety of terms in a variety of ways without being pinned down to one usage or being accused of inconsistency if he did. Consistency is important, yet, perhaps the only real inconsistency which would destroy Śaṅkara's Advaita is if he uses a term which denotes the ontological reality of duality. After all, he surely spoke to a number of different audiences, each with its own qualifications, at various times, in various places, and for various purposes. In this, he was truly within the Upaniṣadic fold and employed Upaniṣadic techniques.

Ānanda

In V. 107, 109, 153, 213, 227, 240, 301, 307, and 352 the Self is described as ever-blissful (*ānanda*). Śaṅkara did not or could not deny that *Ātman/Brahman* is of the nature of bliss. This is both obvious and convincing from his commentary on the *Brahmasūtras*.[114] What he was careful not to do was to give the impression that this 'bliss' was some sort of empirical happiness, that it was an attribute, that it was an experience, that it involved some sort of change and duality. But, without a doubt, Śaṅkara is in agreement with the *Taittirīya Upaniṣad* which declares that bliss is part of the nature (*svābhāvika*) of the Self.[115] In the BSBh. context, Śaṅkara says that 'bliss is the Highest Self' (*tasmād ānandamayaḥ paramātmeti siddham*). Yet, because the argument is neither perfectly clear nor rigorous in this context, at the end of the discussion, Śaṅkara points out that in the *Taittirīya Upaniṣad* 2.1–5, if the *mayaṭ* suffix indicates abundance in the sheath of bliss (*ānandamaya kośa*), the same will have to be accepted for the four other/outer sheaths, and this is not acceptable to any Advaitin. Thus, he explains that the Absolute cannot literally be a part of the bliss sheath and that the Absolute is really the foundation of it. In his BSBh. 1.3.8–9, Śaṅkara accepts bliss as an important attribute of Īśvara. In this regard, the *Vivekacūḍāmaṇi* is in perfect accord with Śaṅkara's other works.

The *Taittirīya Upaniṣad* enumerates five sheaths from the food sheath to the sheath of bliss, which are arranged inside each other, with the food sheath outermost and the sheath of bliss innermost. When superficially viewed, it appears as though the text speaks of each subsequent inward sheath as the self of its outward sheath, i.e., the sheath of vitality as the self of the food sheath and so on. Śaṅkara, however, ultimately rejects the idea that the sheath of bliss is the Self. On various grounds, he rejects the idea that the self, consisting of bliss, cannot be the Self but only the conditioned self. This view is also put forth in his BSBh.[116]

Waking and Dreaming

A doctrinal point which is dramatically raised in support of the claim that Śaṅkara is not the author of the *Vivekacūḍāmaṇi* is its seeming equation of the waking and dream states in the manner of Gauḍapāda while Śaṅkara is said to carefully distinguish the two.[117] However, while V. 172 says that, 'there is no difference is the waking and dream states', V. 100 says, 'Dream is a state different from the waking state'. Before leaping to conclusions, however, V. 172 draws a parallelism between dreaming and waking to illustrate the power of the mind and to point a way to spiritual equanimity. It states that 'the mind creates everything' and this is true for both the waking and dreaming states.

This very point is made in the *Upadeśa Sāhasrī*:

> Just as it is experienced in this world that a snake superimposed upon a rope does not exist, nor water in a mirage, and the like, unless they are apprehended, so it is reasonable that duality in the waking and dreaming states also does not exist unless it is apprehended.[118]

How does one know that one is awake? No matter what one may claim as proof that one is awake, the charge may always be made that one is merely dreaming. Dreams and dream objects are real so long as one is dreaming. It is only when one 'wakes' up that one knows such objects were mind-made. The *Māṇḍūkya Upaniṣad*[119] makes an analysis into the three states of experience to show the non-duality of the Self. What is at issue is the use that one makes of the analysis. It is true that Śaṅkara has made distinctions between the waking and dreaming states as well as between empirical (*vyāvaharika*) and illusory (*prātibhāsika*) objects. But this does not necessarily imply that he could not or did not equate these two states when making another point. The discipline of an enquiry into the three states of existence (*āvastha-traya-vicāra*) may also be for the explicit purpose of liberation and not just for establishing ontological theories.

Colophon

It is a wonder that, in spite of the *Vivekacūḍāmaṇi* failing to meet Hacker's criterion for declaring a particular work as genuinely by Śaṅkara, it is declared by Hacker as genuine on the basis of its colophon.[120] Śaṅkara was called 'Śaṅkara', 'Bhagavat', 'Bhagavatpāda', and 'Bhagavatpūjyapāda' by his direct disciples.[121] In later Advaita literature, Śaṅkara is called 'Bhagavatpāda' and 'Bhagavatpūjyapāda'.

It is a curious phenomena that in none of the ancient works was Śaṅkara called Śaṅkarācārya, the name by which he is best known today. Of his direct disciples, Padmapāda once calls him 'Śaṅkara' (*Pañcapādikā*, *Maṅgalācaraṇa*, V. 3) but usually designates him as 'the Commentator' (the Bhāṣyakāra). Sureśvara calls him 'Śaṅkara' twice (*Naiṣkarmyasiddhi* 4.74,76) as well as 'Bhagavatpāda' (*Naiṣkarmya-siddhi* 4.19) and 'Bhagavatpūjyapāda' (*Naiṣkarmyasiddhi* 4.43). He was also known as 'Bhagavatpāda – Toṭakācārya's teacher',[122] 'Bhagavān Bhāṣyakāra' by Vācaspati-miśra,[123] and 'Bhāṣyakāra, Bhagavatpādācārya, Bhagavatpūjyapādācārya' by Jñānottama.[124]

Research has revealed that Śaṅkara was generally known as either just plain 'Śaṅkara' without any title or else 'Bhagavat' (either with or without -pāda or -pūjyapāda). Using this as a definitive criterion of the genuineness of a work, Hacker thus concludes that, like the *Upadesasāhasrī*, since the *Vivekacūḍāmaṇi* concludes with the colophon 'Śaṅkara-Bhagavat', it must be genuine.

Finally, in addition to Hacker's points, there is the issue of the use of the term 'prior non-existence' (*prāgabhāva*) found in the *Vivekacūḍāmaṇi*.

Prāgabhāva

According to Pande, 'The major argument against the authenticity of the *Vivekacūḍāmaṇi* is its use of the term *prāgabhāva* (prior non-existence)[125] which as Belvalkar had pointed out, Śaṅkara had rejected in his *Brahmasūtrabhāṣya*.'[126] According to Indian philosophy, there are four types of non-existence that can be known through non-cognition: *prāgabhāva*, *pradhvamsābhāva*, *anyonyābhāva*, and *atyantābhāva*.[127] *Prāgabhāva* is defined as 'The non-existence of an object before it comes into being'.

In the *Vivekacūḍāmaṇi*, this term is used as a typical example or illustration (*dṛṣṭānta*) to illustrate the destruction of ignorance (*avidyā*) as something which never was. In this verse, Śaṅkara is not advocating the possibility of something (any- and every-thing) existing. There has never really been an object. To illustrate this, the water in a mirage doesn't exist now, it did not exist in the past, nor will it exist in the future. The author of the *Vivekacūḍāmaṇi* is not using the term in the context of a real causality (*satkāryavāda*). The world illusion seemingly appears and then disappears and ceases. It is only in this context that the term is being employed.

Jīvanmukta

Verses 318, 419, 429–441, and 552 of the *Vivekacūḍāmaṇi* mention the concept of liberation-while-living (*jīvanmukti*). This idea is one of the most original and inspirational ideas that India has contributed to the world. Of all the Indian philosophical systems which propound this concept of *jīvanmukti*, Advaita Vedānta is unique in that it is the only school which must *necessarily* embrace the concept.[128] That is, doctrinally, Advaita's metaphysics has a built-in necessity which *demands* the concept. If one grants Advaita's presuppositions, *jīvanmukti* is not only a logical consequent, but necessarily so. However, modern scholars contend that Śaṅkara never employed the term and thus it follows that Śaṅkara is not the author of the *Vivekacūḍāmaṇi*.

This being said, the final position (*siddhānta*) of Śaṅkara states that the Self (*Ātman*) and liberation (*mukti*) have the same meaning.[129] This implies that the term '*jīvanmukti*' is both relative and redundant. The qualifier '*jīvan*' is unnecessary. A *mukta* is a *mukta*, with or without a body.[130] It may be said that a knower of the Self with a body is a *jīvanmukta* and when that person sheds the body, he attains *videhamukti*. But this difference exists only for the onlooker, not the *mukta*.

Obviously this does not prove that Śaṅkara wrote the *Vivekacūḍāmaṇi* but his numerous references to 'mukti' demonstrate conclusively that he was aware of the meaning of the concept. Without other evidence, this alone is not enough to deny he employed the term in other work.

The distinctive insight of Śaṅkara is simple to state and even more devastating in its implications: 'The Absolute is Real; the world is neither real nor unreal; the individual is not different from the Absolute.'[131] To unpack this *sūtra*-like insight is to make explicit what is implied in the central teachings of Śaṅkara. In other words, the individual is the Absolute,[132] the seeker is the sought . . . not sometime later, in a place above and beyond, but here and now.[133] Thus, liberation-while-living (*jīvanmukti*). Any seeking obviously manifests a denial of the presence of the sought and necessarily implies ignorance of what-is. As the *Vivekacūḍāmaṇi* says, 'It can be neither thrown away nor taken up.'[134]

The word '*jīvanmukti*' itself does not occur in the canonical texts of Vedānta. It is not found in the *Vedas*, nor in the earlier *Upaniṣads*, the *Bhagavadgītā*, or the *Brahmasūtras*. However, the concept or idea of liberated-while-living can be found scattered throughout the literature. Below are a few references:

> Verily, while we are here we may know this – BṛhUp 4.4.14

> A mortal becomes immortal, attains *Brahman*, even here, when the knots of the heart are destroyed – KaUp 2.3.14

He who knows that which is set in the cave of the heart, he, here on earth, cuts the knot of ignorance – MuṇḍUp 2.1.10

Whosoever, O Gārgi, in this world, without knowing this Imperishable . . . departs from this world is pitiable – BrhUp 3.8.10

There is truth if a person knows it here and if not there is a great loss – KenaUp 2.5

When, to one who knows, all beings have, verily, become one with his own Self, then what delusion and what sorrow can be to him who has seen the oneness? Īśa Up 1.7

While I (Vāmadeva) was in the womb I realized (the Self and subsequently lived a long and productive life) – AitUp.2.1.–5–6

Śaṅkara's commentary on Bṛhad. Up. 4.4.6 – The man free from desires realizes *Brahman* even here (*sa ca vidvān āpta-kāmaḥ ātma-kāmatayā ihaiva brahmabhūtaḥ*)

The BG 5.23, 28 says, "Before he is released from the body (*prāk śarīra vimokṣaṇāt*), if a *yogi* has perfect control over his mind and attains identity with *Brahman*, he is eternally liberated (*yaḥsadāmukta eva saḥ*)."

Brahman-knowledge takes place even in this life – BS 3.4.51

On the realization of *Brahman*, non-attachment and the destruction of both prior and subsequent actions occurs – BS 4.1.13

Having reached the Self, the soul attains liberation – BS 4.1–3

Those who have a mission to fulfill continue in the physical state as long as the mission demands – BS 3.3.32

Thus, a case can be made that it is unlikely that Śaṅkara was unaware of the term 'jīvanmukti' and also that he was unaware of what it stood for. To declare that because he did not use this exact term in his BSBh does not necessarily imply that he may not have employed it in another place. To be fair, however, it also does not necessarily imply that he ever did employ the term either.

Conclusion

Was Śaṅkara the author of the *Vivekacūḍāmaṇi*? His thought has been, and continues to be, described, defined, and interpreted in different ways depending upon one's point of view. In other words, there are seemingly many Śaṅkaras. His thought is a 'philosophy' to the scholar who desires conceptual consistency; it is 'words to live by' for the spiritual aspirant who is interested in personal experience; it is a 'methodological tool' or a 'thunderous silence' for the *sadguru* who 'speaks' about the Unspeakable.

On the one hand, these points of view are most appropriate. A distinction between Absolute (*pāramārthika*) and relative (*vyāvahārika*) points of view can be found in Śaṅkara's writings.[135] On the other, an incorrect understanding regarding perspectives has led to gross misconceptions resulting in misinterpretations where critics have accused Śaṅkara of doctrinal inconsistencies, contradictions, and absurdities. Here are three examples:

1. While Śaṅkara is prepared to admit a plethora of distinctions at the empirical level, all distinctions are denied from the Absolute point of view. What is true from one point of view or level of reality is not from another. However, this does *not* mean that there are two realities, two truths. There is one Truth, one Reality as seen from two different perspectives.[136] Śaṅkara avers that one perspective is from the point of view of ignorance; it is relatively true (the sun seemingly rises and sets), while the other point of view is from the perspective of wisdom. The pluralism that is experienced at the empirical level, and with which philosophical enquiry commences, is not the final Truth.

   Śaṅkara avers that anything which is experienced is real, in some sense or other.[137] Therefore, his epistemology is realistic and posits that every cognition points to an objective reference – whether veridical or erroneous. The question is: Exactly *how* real are the things that are experienced in the empirical world? What is their ontological status? Śaṅkara replies that the things of the empirical world are real only so long as the empirical order lasts:

   > The division of real and unreal depends upon knowledge or experience: That is real whose knowledge does not miscarry; the unreal on the contrary, is the object of a knowledge which fails or goes astray.[138]

   Thus, according to Śaṅkara, the Real is that which lasts, which suffers no contradiction, which is eternal and unsublatable (i.e., unchangeable). The unreal is that which never appears, not even in one's wildest imagination (i.e., a square circle or the child of a barren woman). Things of the world may be said to be (provisionally) real until they suffer sublation. Thus they are called illusory (*mithyā*). Since they are cognized, they cannot be called unreal. Since they are sublated, they cannot be called Real. What a mystery! The sun is *seen* to traverse across the sky and, yet, everyone knows that it does not move! Water is *seen* in a mirage and yet there never has been water there, nor will there be, nor is there now. By this criterion, *Ātman/Brahman* alone is the absolutely Real. All else is called 'real' only by courtesy. The distinction between one individual and another, distinctions regarding a single individual, all multiplicity is but a concession to the Truth made from the relative point of view.

   However, to bring out the full implications of this, it should be noted that such expressions as 'Absolute', 'Real', 'absolutely Real', or 'from an Absolute point of view' are merely contextual.[139] They are used only by way of contrast with all that is not real. For example, in no other sense can the Self (*Ātman*) or the Absolute (*Brahman*) be called Real. If one accepts (even provisionally) the empirical world of plurality, then such expressions are meaningful. But to one who has realized the Self, these expressions lose their significance. For such a one, '*Veda* is no longer *Veda*'.[140]

2. There are those who pit Advaitin against Advaitin. Śaṅkara's systematic exposition of Advaita has been explained, expounded upon, and interpreted by a number of Advaitins either by way of subcommentaries, glosses, or independent treatises.[141] Because of the various subtle and not so subtle doctrinal variations found therein, some scholars aver that Advaita Vedānta is not only not a single, uniform system of thought, but a house divided against itself. It must be stressed again and again that these differences are only *exegetical* and not doctrinal. Such differences have arisen in the course of an elucidation of a particular point of view, in the clarification of an issue, in the answering of a critic's objection, in the presentation of another avenue for experience for a spiritual aspirant, and so on. All these subtle and not so subtle differences take place *only from within* the framework of Advaita Vedānta. Every perspective, every mode of interpretation, which are all no doubt significant and insightful, are relative to, and are intended only to help a spiritual aspirant realize the inward Self.[142] As such, these differences are not irreconcilable within the framework of Advaita. No Advaitin ever takes his eyes off their central theme regarding the absolute non-difference of *Ātman* with *Brahman* and all that that implies.
3. The radical mark of Śaṅkara's writing is that it stands for a plenary experience of non-duality. This experience, he claims, is the culmination of all thought, of all systems of philosophy. Non-duality can be, and has been, expounded systematically – but strictly speaking it is not a system of thought nor a school of philosophy. Teachings are methodological tools devised primarily as an instrument employed to shift one's focus from the unreal to the real. Acknowledging this, a teacher will employ whatever means are suitable for the awakening of an individual.

Was Śaṅkara the author of the *Vivekacūḍāmaṇi*? The answer depends upon whom one asks. Modern scholars tend to reject its authenticity as a work by Śaṅkara. Traditionalists tend to accept it. The arguments and counter-arguments are unending. However, whether or not one accepts Śaṅkara as the author of the *Vivekacūḍāmaṇi*, the discussion does have the positive benefit in that it helps one to better understand some often overlooked aspects of Advaita. Discussions seem unending. Disputes continue and show no signs of abating. What is obvious is that the value of this discussion, no matter one's ultimate conclusion, is that it helps one to distinguish and define and become clearer on the doctrine itself. I have attempted to strengthen the case that there is still a likelihood that Śaṅkara is the author of the *Vivekacūḍāmaṇi*.

The Philosophy of Śaṅkara

Indian philosophy has traditionally been classified in terms of six orthodox (*āstika*) and three heterodox (*nāstika*) schools.[143] In common parlance within India today, a '*nāstika*' means an 'atheist'. But in this philosophical context, the division into *āstika* and *nāstika* only means an acceptance of, or rejection of, the Vedic corpus as an authority. It is not an exaggeration to say that of these schools, Vedānta in general and Advaita Vedānta in particular have captured the cultural, philosophical, and spiritual imagination of India to an extent unparalleled in Indian thought. Of all the Indian philosophical systems, Advaita has been given pre-eminence.

By the beginning of the twentieth century, Advaita Vedānta in general and Śaṅkara in particular had begun to receive considerable attention in Europe. This was primarily due to the pioneering work of F. Max Muller and Paul Deussen.[144] Following them, Western studies into Advaita Vedānta's doctrines have received an impetus from the work of such scholars as Paul Hacker, Tillmann Vetter, Hajime Nakamura, Eliot Deutsch, Sengaku Mayeda, and Wilhelm Halbfass.

Śaṅkara is undoubtedly the greatest exponent and consolidator of Advaita.[145] Because it is frequently called the 'Advaita of Śaṅkara', this leads to a misunderstanding and one is likely to assume that Śaṅkara was the founder or originator of Advaita.[146] Such an impression is false, although there is no doubt Śaṅkara was the greatest expounder of Advaita. In practice, Advaita speaks of no *founder* in the sense in which one speaks of the founders of other schools, e.g., Gautama as the founder of the Nyāya school, Kaṇāda as the founder of the Vaiśeṣika school, Kapila as the founder of the Sāṅkhya school, Jaimini as the founder of Mīmāṃsā and so on.

However, this is not to deny that Śaṅkara, as the author of the commentaries (*bhāṣyakāra*), gets the credit for consolidating Advaita and making clear beyond doubt the basic doctrine of Advaita.

> The doctrine advocated by Śaṅkara is, from a purely philosophical point of view, and apart from all theological considerations, the most important and interesting one which has arisen on Indian soil; neither those forms of the Vedānta which diverge from the view represented by Śaṅkara, nor any of the non-Vedāntic systems can be compared with the so-called orthodox Vedānta in boldness, depth, and subtlety of speculation.[147]

There is no doubt that Advaita takes its distinctive position vis-à-vis the contribution of its predecessors. Advaita developed its 'vocabulary' not only from the Indian scriptures, but also from the Pūrva Mīmāṃsā, Sāṅkhya, Yoga, Buddhist, and Jain philosophies. Advaita developed, at least partially, by polemicizing against other systems and in defending its own position. Still, in order to have an insight into Advaita's insights, one needs to look at Advaita's relationship with the *Vedas*. As Natalia Isayeva recently wrote:

> This method revealed some important inner tenets of Advaita, precisely because attention was brought to the role of sacred scripture in Śaṅkara's teaching. 'It turned out that Vedic texts play a serious theoretical part in securing an inner intellectual balance to his system, valid for every specific problem arising in course of the polemics.[148]

Adherents of Advaita Vedānta's message would therefore claim it to be eternal and impersonal. Śaṅkara never seemed to tire of teaching that the *Ātman*, one's inner Self, is wholly non-different from *Brahman*. This was not only the starting point of his thought, but also its goal. This truth he claimed to have found in the *Upaniṣads*. As well, Śaṅkara used philosophy, not as his aim, but the weapon with which to fulfill his aim of rescuing individuals from their 'seeming' bondage.

Vedānta is both a name for the *Upaniṣads* as well as a philosophy whose primary concern is 'an enquiry into the nature of the Absolute (*Brahman*), into the nature of the Self (*Ātman*)' and, as the *Upaniṣads* declare, 'I am the Absolute' (*Ayam Ātman Brahman*).[149]

The word '*vedānta*' is directly traceable to India's primary scripture, the *Vedas*, specifically that part of the *Vedas* known as the *Upaniṣads*. The *Upaniṣads* are known as '*Vedānta*' = *veda* (wisdom) + *anta* (end/essence) for two reasons, one literal/physical, the other conceptual/philosophical: (1) Because the *Upaniṣads* are literally found at the back of the *Vedas* (i.e., at the end of the book) they are said to form the concluding portion of the *Vedas*. (2) Besides expressing the fact that the *Upaniṣads* form the concluding part (*avasānabhāga*) of the *Vedas*, the term also expresses the idea that the *Upaniṣads* represent the *essence* or *goal* of the *Vedas*. As such, the *Upaniṣads* are known as the crown or summit of the *Veda* (*śruti-śiras*). See:

> *sarva-vedānta-siddhānta* – the culmination of all wisdom (V. 1)
>
> *vedāntārtha-vicāreṇa jāyate jñānam-uttamam* – supreme wisdom arises from an enquiry into the meaning of the Vedānta (V. 47)

Thus, the term 'vedānta' is a most apt term for the *Upaniṣads*. Like most Sanskrit terms, there is a *śleṣa* or rhetorical figure involved. Sanskrit roots are multi-significant. The Sanskrit '*anta*', like the English word 'end', means both 'terminus' and 'aim', (i.e., 'the end/essence of practice is proficiency'). This transparent multiplicity of meanings permeates the philosophy of Vedānta. Vedānta brings knowledge of the Truth. The '*anta*' of Vedānta means last, or final. It can signify the last section which comes after the three *Vedas*, or it can mean last in the sense that there is nothing beyond it: *Veda-anta*, the last/final knowledge, beyond which no one can speak. What does the final part of Vedānta say? *Aham brahmāsmi*, 'I am the Absolute.' This is the end of Vedānta, the final word.

Since Vedānta arose from the *Veda*, especially that portion of the *Veda* known as the *Upaniṣads*, it behooves us to situate the Vedānta vis-à-vis the *Veda*. First and foremost, one should take note of the fact that the word *Veda* (from the Sanskrit root *vid*, 'to know', meaning 'knowledge' or 'knowledge *par excellence*' i.e., divine wisdom) has different referents (which need not necessarily be exclusive). Its most ancient meaning referred to a 'direct, inner intuitive knowledge of the Truth'. In this first usage, 'knowing is being'.[150] Later Vedānta philosophy invoked this insight to interpret the statement, 'the knower of *Brahman* becomes *Brahman* (*brahmaveda brahmaiva bhavati*)',[151] to mean that 'knowing is being'. The Sanskrit root '*bhū*' from which '*bhavati*' (becomes) is derived, means both 'being' and 'becoming'. In the present context it refers to 'being'. One is what one always is. To attain the unattained, action is necessary. But to attain the already attained, no action is required. Knowledge of the fact will dispel the darkness of ignorance which covers it. Thus, there is no means for attaining the Self because Vedānta says that the Self is always you. One has to liberate that which is already liberated; one has to attain that which is already attained.

To bring out the full implication of this usage, *Veda* as-a-direct-inner-intuitive-knowledge-of-the-Truth is merely a contextual expression. To one who lives in a state of duality, the empirical world of plurality is meaningful. To one who lives in a state of non-duality, such an expression loses its power to delude. For such a one, '*Veda* is no longer *Veda*.'[152] The *Upaniṣad* declares,

> What is that which once known, all things are known? Reply: There are two types of knowledge: Higher (*parā vidyā*) and lower (*aparā vidyā*). *Rgveda*, *Sāmaveda*, *Yajurveda*, and *Atharvaveda*, and so on are all *aparā*. *Parā* is that by which the Imperishable is known.[153]

Second, the word *Veda* refers to 'the entire body of Vedic revelation'. This usage refers not only to the content or subject matter of the *mantras*, but also the form of expression that they assume. Further, in this usage, the word *Veda* refers to a single body of revelation, irrespective of whether that revelation is known directly or indirectly. Later Vedānta will draw upon this usage to present a body of teachings, of spiritual practices, which will be used as external and internal aids for self-realization.

Third, the word *Veda* refers to revealed knowledge which has been divided into four collections: *Rgveda*, *Yajurveda*, *Sāmaveda*, and *Atharvaveda* (along with their numerous recensions – *śākhā*) and divisions into *samhitā* (*mantra*) and *brāhmaṇa* (*brāhmaṇa*, *āraṇyaka*, *upaniṣad*) sections. This paradigm will later manifest itself as the 'philosophical system known as Advaita Vedānta.'

Thus, depending upon one's point of view, this three-fold schemata may be applied to Advaita Vedānta as: (1) the 'thunderous silence' which 'speaks' about the Unspeakable non-dual state; (2) 'words to live by' for the spiritual aspirant who is interested in personal experience; (3) a 'philosophy' for the scholar who desires conceptual consistency. In other words, there are seemingly several Advaitas. Or one could say that Advaita may be approached from a position of non-duality, a position of qualified non-duality, or a position of duality.

The *Veda*(s) themselves contain references to a remote past.[154] They must have had a long formative period before they finally assumed their present classification according to families of authors. Tradition informs us that the *Veda* once existed as a single body of divine wisdom. For whatever reason, over the course of time it became necessary to collect and classify the various *mantras* that must have been existing in a scattered, unorganized condition.

We are told that the ancient sage Kṛṣṇa Dvaipāyana, better known as Vedavyāsa[155] (literally 'the compiler of the *Veda*) arranged the *Veda* into four collections (*saṁhitā*): *Rk*, *Yajuḥ*, *Sāma*, and *Atharva*, each of which came to be called a *Veda*.[156] For our interest, this same Vyāsa is attributed with writing the *Vedāntasūtras*.

Whether Vedavyāsa's collection was made for the purposes of preserving the *Veda*, for propagating the *Veda*, for facilitating rituals, for remembering and honoring the various Vedic *ṛṣis* who fashioned the *mantras*, for noting and recording the historical consciousness which was developing as family lineages grew, or for homogeneity of subject matter is not our concern here. Each of these reasons points to the fact that transmission from teacher to disciple, from generation to generation, was taking place. Further, the various standpoints support the well-documented phenomena that there are different teachings for different levels of a student's competency.

The point this is that in whatever way one conceives of, or interprets, the *Veda* (Vedānta), one cannot escape the fact that there exist hymns (teachings) which convey something, and, whatever that something may be or mean, it has been, and is being transmitted from seer to seeker. Advaita always commences its teachings by establishing the *adhikārin*, the level of the seeker and, depending upon one's qualifications, thus the teaching imparted.[157]

What is Advaita Vedānta?

Advaita Vedānta,[158] derives its name '*Vedānta*' from the fact that it founds its thought upon the *Upaniṣads*. The Vedānta (the *Upaniṣads*) are the foundation for the Vedānta (philosophical systems).

> In its widest sense, the term '*Vedānta*' means: The *Upaniṣads*, the source of right knowledge, and the *Śārīrakasūtras*, and the *Bhagavadgītā* (and the commentaries on the *Upaniṣads*, the *Śārīrakasūtras*, and the *Bhagavadgītā*).[159]

The sourcebooks foundational to all Vedāntic systems alike are The *Upaniṣads*, the *Bhagavadgītā*, and the *Brahmasūtras*.[160] Together these three are known as the *prasthāna-traya*, the triple canon of Vedānta. '*Prasthāna*' means 'foundation' and thus these three constitute the three foundations known as Primary Scripture (*śruti*), the *Śruti-prasthāna* (*Upaniṣads*), Remembered Tradition (*smṛti*), the *Smṛti-prasthāna* (*Bhagavadgītā*), and Reason (*nyāya* or *tarka*), the *Nyāya-prasthāna* (*Brahmasūtras*).

The *Vedas* are called *śruti* (that which is 'heard')[161] and, since the *Upaniṣads* form part of the *Vedas*, their name *Śruti-prasthāna* is apt. The *Bhagavadgītā* stands next to the *Upaniṣads* in authoritativeness and importance. As the *Bhagavadgītā* forms part of the Indian epic, the *Mahābhārata*,[162] which is a remembered text (*smṛti*), it is called *Smṛti-prasthāna*. The *Brahmasūtras* represent the standpoint of reason because therein the Vedāntic teachings are set forth in a logical order. Thus, we see that the basic sourcebooks of Advaita, and therefore its basic doctrine, are based upon scripture (*śruti*) and supported by tradition (*smṛti*) and reason (*nyāya*).

The central question for Vedānta concerns the nature of *Brahman*. The *Brahmasūtras*, which philosophically string together the central concepts of the *Upaniads* in an ordered manner, begins: '*Athāto brahma jijñāsa*' – 'Now, therefore, the enquiry into *Brahman*.'[163] And this enquiry is not only intellectual, but also practical. Advaita's thought circles around the theme, '*Ātman* is *Brahman*'.[164] Its approach is self-enquiry. Its concern is for individuals, here and now. Its goal is that which is eternally present, immediate, and accessible.

To reveal the Self is the be-all and end-all of Advaita. This experience, Advaita further claims, is within the reach of all. The same method does not suit everyone. The average person may have no knowledge of the particular combination of factors that is necessary to bring to completion the hitherto neglected factors of one's being. Thus, it is not really theory that Advaita advocates, so much as experience. As Mayeda said, 'Philosophy is not his (Śaṅkara's) aim but is rather a vital weapon with which to fulfill this aim, which is to rescue people out of transmigratory existence.'[165] Advaita means the truth of 'non-duality'. The prefix 'non' applies not only to duality but also to 'isms' and 'systems of thought'. The goal of Advaita is not so much to 'know about' the Self, as it is to 'personally experience' the Self.

Literally, *Advaita Vedānta* means: 'Non-duality (*a-dvaita*) (is the) end/essence (*anta*) (of) wisdom (*veda*)'. Succinctly put, 'The Absolute is Real; the world is non-real; the individual human being and the Absolute are not different'.[166] (See V. 20 '*brahma satyam, jagan mithyā*'). This insight is simple to state and even more devastating in its implications. What-is is 'I am That' or, to turn the phrase, 'There is nothing which exists which is not That'.

The most distinguishing features of Advaita Vedānta are: (1) the non-difference of the individual human being (*Ātman*) with the Absolute (*Brahman*); (2) the distinction between the absolute (*pāramārthika*) and relative (*vyāvahārika*) standpoints; (3) the doctrine of ignorance (*māyā/avidyā*); (4) and the conception of liberation here and now (*jīvanmukti*). The next sections deal with there are by one.

The non-difference of the individual human being The quintessence of Advaita is its doctrine that the individual human being is non-different from the Absolute. This essential identity is expressed in the four great sayings (*mahāvākya*)[167] of the *Upaniṣads*: 'The Absolute is Consciousness',[168] 'The Self is the Absolute',[169] 'That thou art',[170] and 'I am the Absolute',[171] (see V. 162, 204, 251–65, 270, 281, 284, 305, and 334). The implications of this are not that nothing exists (as some aver) but that 'All this, whatsoever, in whatever way, is only *Ātman/Brahman*' (*ekaṁ eva advitīyam*). In other words, That in which there is no question of form or formlessness, that is beyond name and form and attributes, transcending even the beyond, That alone I am.

The essence of Advaita is simple to state: 'You are That, here and now.' To the person who objects, 'But is not my search proof of my having become lost?' The reply is, 'No, it only shows that you *believe* you are lost. For, what are you in search of? How can you find that which you already are?' Or, to word it another way, 'Any seeking is a denial of the presence of the sought.' To paraphrase Śaṅkara, 'Why are you looking for the Self or God in city after city, temple after temple? God dwells in the heart within. Why look in the East and in the West. Don't look for God, look for the *Guru*. God dwells within you, in truth, you are God. You don't need to find God, you need to find a *Guru* who will guide you to yourself.'

Throughout history, individuals have found themselves tossed between the twin banks of pleasure and pain, gain and loss. They are seemingly alienated from themselves, alienated from others, and alienated from the Absolute. From such a perspective, it makes sense to ask, how is it possible for a finite, relative, mortal individual human being to be identical to an infinite, immortal Absolute?

Each of the *mahāvākyas* imparts a three-fold knowledge which Advaita seizes upon as the key to self-realization. First, they remove a person's deep-seated misconception that they are a finite, bound, imperfect mortal being, and conversely, they reveal that the true Self of each individual is infinite, ever-free, ever-perfect, immortal. Second, they remove the deep-rooted misconception that the supreme Reality is remote, hidden, unattainable, and declare that it is immediate, direct, the innermost Self of all. Third, they reveal that there are not separate individuals *and* an Absolute *and* that each individual is somehow part of the whole. Instead, they declare, unequivocally, that, here and now, 'You are That', without an iota of difference. In other words, Advaita rejects all three types of difference: 'There is nothing similar to *Brahman*; there is nothing dissimilar to *Brahman*; and there is no internal variety.'[172]

When individuals mistakenly superimpose various qualities (e.g., mortal, imperfect, male/female, intelligent/stupid, and so on) upon themselves and the opposite qualities (e.g., immortal, perfect, omniscient, far away) upon the Absolute, Advaita resorts to a series of negations (*neti-neti*) to correct this misunderstanding.[173] Śaṅkara, commenting on this says, 'The Absolute can never be properly denoted by any words, including the word "Absolute" (*Ātman/Brahman*).'[174]

Thus, in the Advaita tradition, although there are passages like 'Everything is *Brahman*',[175] *Brahman* is Existence-absolute, Knowledge-absolute, Infinitude-absolute[176] (see V. 154, 227, 395, 413, 466, 475), 'The Self is all this',[177] 'The world is an unbroken series of perceptions of *Brahman* and hence nothing else but *Brahman*',[178] until one's ignorance is destroyed, such statements will not be correctly understood. Thus, for spiritual aspirants, Advaita emphasizes 'not-this, not-this', which is given, not to say that appearances are not applicable to the Absolute, as to indicate the impossibility of attributing any conceptualization to It. *Brahman* is too great for words to adequately describe, for the finite mind to fathom. Reality is called '*a-dvaita*' to point to the fact that there is nothing with which it may be compared.

It is the thesis of Advaita that the Self is ever-present and, yet, one does not realize it. The problem for each individual can be reduced to the simple question of 'knowing' or 'not-knowing'. With Vedānta there is nothing to be done; it is only a matter of understanding, but that understanding has to be very *accurate* and *refined*.

The purpose of Advaita, of the *mahāvākyas*, of the *Guru*, of spiritual disciplines, is to kindle an awakening to this ever-present, already established Self. It does this by utilizing the knowledge that appearances cannot appear independent of a reality which upholds them. But we are getting ahead of ourselves.

To realize that one is the Self, one must make an enquiry into the nature of the Self, the content of the notion 'I'. The Self is not a hypothetical postulate. It is the most immediate, direct, and certain perception of all. Because one believes in oneself, the thinker, seer, hearer, and so forth, one has faith that what one thinks, sees, and hears is 'real'. Instead, why not doubt the things which come and go, for example, thoughts, sights, and sounds, and hold onto that which is always there and is foundational to it all, your Self. The 'I am' can never be changed into an 'I am not'. What is experienced, as well as its meaning, is always open to doubt. But that *someone* experienced it is certain.

Is there a truth, anywhere, which is so certain that no one could possibly doubt its veracity? Advaita avers that the only thing which one can never logically doubt is one's own Self, the doubter him- or herself. No matter where one finds oneself, one is *always* there. Why, the very act of doubting oneself is but an affirmation of oneself, for, one can always ask, 'Who exactly is doing the doubting?' To say that 'I do not exist' is to affirm the 'I' who will do the doubting.[179]

Advaita asks one to enquire into exactly who this 'I' is. How do you refer to yourself? Only as 'I'. This one single syllable. Every person says 'I', but who makes an effort to know what this 'I' exactly is? One usually refers to the physical body when one speaks of 'I', but a little reflection will reveal that the 'I' cannot be the physical body. The body itself cannot say 'I', for it is inert.[180]

One says, 'This is *my* coat, this is *my* hair, this is *my* body'. What is 'mine' belongs to me. What belongs to me is not me. I am separate from it, I possess it. Whatever I possess I can dispense with and still remain who I am.

On a deeper level, when one says 'I', one is referring to the faculties of thinking, feeling, and willing. Yet the same analysis applies. These are *my* thoughts, *my* feelings *my* emotions – they come and they go. I know them. I am the knower and they are the known. No one says, 'I am this shirt' or 'I am this house'. Likewise, it is a mistake to superimpose one's body, one's thoughts, one's feelings, upon the 'I'.[181]

Then what is the 'I'? Advaita avers that a little reflection will reveal that upon awakening from sleep, the first thought which arises is the 'I' thought. One thinks, '*I* slept well last night' or '*I* am still tired' or '*I* am going to the bathroom'. First the 'I', and then the drama of one's life. Further, there is not a single thought, at any time, which does not first invoke this 'I'. One has never, and will never, have a thought or experience without this 'I' being present. It is the pillar around which each and every thought clings. Every thought relates to the 'I', either directly or in connection with other individuals, objects, things, events, opinions, and so on. The 'I' is the basis for everything else – the entire myriad universe of second and third persons, the universe of he, she, and it. Everything, inclusive, is rooted in one's 'I'.

Before anything can come into existence, there must be someone to whom it comes. All appearance and disappearance presupposes a change against some changeless background. The 'I' is that support. One is not 'what happens' to oneself, but to whom things happen. Who am I? It is enough to know what you are not. The 'I' is not an object to be known. Truly, all one can say is that 'I am not this, not that'. The 'this' and 'thats' of the world come and go. But the 'I' persists. If one can point to something, one cannot meaningfully say, 'I am (only) that'. If one can point to it, one is more than that. One is not 'something else' and yet, without you, nothing can be perceived nor imagined either.

All of a person's existence is encompassed by the three states of waking, dreaming, and deep sleep.[182] If one enquires into these three states of experience, one will discover that the waking state teaches one that (1) I am there; (2) there is an external world revealed by an external light that is experienced through the sense organs; (3) what is experienced is taken as real; (4) there is a reality. The dreaming state teaches one that (1) I am there; (2) one can create a world by their own inner light; (3) the world one experiences may be a dream, or to put it differently, the Self does not necessarily act and is unattached even though it may appear otherwise (one dreams that one is in Paris when in fact one has gone nowhere); (4) the waking state may have no more reality than the dream state. Finally, the deep sleep state teaches one (1) I am there; (2) one may exist quite happily without any desires, imperfections, limitations, even a world; (3) the Self is beyond desires, relations. Even the feeling, 'I am the body' does not arise. It shows that the Self is beyond desires; is fearless; is blissful; and is relationless.

Throughout the three states of existence, the Self ('I') persists. Everyone has the same intuition that it is the same 'I' who appears in all the three states. Further, the three states alternate and differ from one another, but the Self, which underlies them, is unaffected and unattached throughout. Surely this reveals that the Self is beyond the changing modes of existence. It is the underlying invisible substrate. It is not the content of any experience but is that which allows every experience to happen.

The distinction between the absolute and relative standpoints To understand, let alone appreciate, any philosophical system demands that one comprehend its (unique) perspective. In Advaita Vedānta, it is crucial that one comprehend the distinction made between the absolute (*pāramārtika*) and the relative (*vyāvahārika*) points of view.[183] This distinction pervades the entire system and what is true from one point of view is not so from another.

Without being absolutely clear in regards to this distinction, it is likely that one will not only misinterpret Advaita's doctrine, but accuse the Advaitin of inconsistencies, contradictions, and absurdities.

To put this in simple terms, from the sun's perspective, the sun neither rises nor sets; there is neither darkness nor concealment nor varying shades of light. By definition, darkness cannot be where light is. However, from the perspective of an individual upon the Earth, the sun rises and sets; there are both light and darkness and varying shades in between, and it is valid to label the sun an enemy of darkness. These are two seemingly contradictory propositions, both equally valid, and true, once their particular perspectives are correctly understood. Nevertheless, note that what is valid from one perspective *is not* from another. From the sun's perspective, 'all is light'. From darkness' perspective, there is relative light and relative darkness and every shade in between. The question becomes, 'Who do you identify with?'

While the Advaitin acknowledges that distinctions *appear* distinctly individual at the empirical level, all distinctions, while perceived, lose their distinct individuality from the Absolute point of view. That is, 'All this is *Brahman*' is absolutely true while 'all this is individually separate and distinct' is relatively true. What is true from one point of view or level of reality is not from another. However, this does *not* mean that there are two realities, two truths. There is one Truth, one Reality, as seen from two different perspectives.[184] Śaṅkara avers that one perspective is from the point of view of ignorance, it is relatively true (the sun seemingly rises and sets), while the other point of view is from the perspective of wisdom (I am the Light).

Advaita's insight is that there are not two types of being nor two truths, but one reality, one truth, as seen from two different perspectives. This is the crux of the matter and precisely the point which is most misunderstood.

> *Brahman* is known in two forms as qualified by limiting conditions owing to the distinction of name and form, and also as the opposite of this, i.e., as what is free from all limiting conditions whatever . . . thus many (*śruti*) texts show *Brahman* in two forms according to as it is known from the standpoint of *vidyā* or from that of *avidyā*.[185]

From the point of view of ignorance, Advaita admits to numerous distinctions. Metaphysically, there is the riddle of the One and the many. Individuals are different from one another and there exists a seeming plurality of things. Epistemologically, there is the subject–object dichotomy, as well as the problem of truth and error. Ethically, there is the problem of bondage and freedom. Yet, from the Absolute point of view, there is only *Brahman/Ātman* – One and non-dual.[186]

Either a person is bewitched by multiplicity (and thus said to be under the sway of ignorance) or one is Consciousness Absolute, firmly established beyond all modifications, eternal, pure, and ever-steady. The pluralism that is experienced at the empirical level, and with which philosophical enquiry commences, is not the non-dual vision.

Merely because one imagines that one is a distinct limited physical being, a finite entity in a universe of infinite entities, does not make it so. Advaita avers that there is the Self – not 'my self', 'his self', 'her self', and 'itself'. Because one is misled by the seeming diversity of names and forms, minds and bodies, one imagines multiple selves. The body or mind may be like a room – it is there, but one need not live in it all the time. There is space within a jar and outside the jar. To identify with the space within the jar and then to declare that one is limited is a false view of what space is. Merely because one identifies with something does not make it so.

The consequence of this 'distinction between standpoints' is simple to state and devastating in its implications: At the Absolute level, '*Ātman* is *Brahman*.'

> Where verily there is, as it were, a duality, there one knows another. But when to the Knower of *Brahman* everything has become the Self, what should one know and through what? Through what should one know That owing to which all this is known – through what, O Maitreyi, should one know the Knower?[187]

The doctrine of ignorance The cornerstone of any philosophical system is that 'key concept' upon which the system revolves. The key concept of Advaita is *avidyā/māyā*[188] (see V. 67, 110–112, 125, 245, 406, 497, 574). This entails elaboration so that a misunderstanding does not result. Critics sometimes label Advaita Vedānta as '*māyā-vāda*' and Advaitins are called '*māyā-vādins*'. These terms are used disparagingly and yet there is a grain of truth in the matter. *Avidyā/māyā* cannot exist or function independent of *Brahman* and it ceases to bewitch when *Brahman* is realized. Still, *avidyā/māyā* is the linguistic device by which the Advaitin explains how the non-dual Reality appears as multitudinous. Strictly speaking, *Brahman* is the be-all and end-all of Advaita and, if anything, Advaita should be called '*Brahma-vāda*' This is so because Advaita never loses sight of its central doctrine that *Brahman* is real, the world is non-real, and the individual is non-different from *Brahman*.

What the critics have done is to mistake the means for the end. The reality of the Self is Advaita's sole concern. The Advaitin is not interested in proving the existence of *avidyā/māyā*. Nonetheless, though *avidyā/māyā* is not ultimately real, its importance cannot be exaggerated for the role that it plays. No one can deny that individuals perceive multiplicity and distinctions. How does this happen?

> *Ātman*, the self-luminous, through the power of one's own *Māyā*, imagines in oneself, by oneself (all the objects that the subject experiences within or without).[189]
>
> This unborn (changeless, non-dual *Brahman*) appears to undergo modification only on account of *Māyā* illusion) and not otherwise.[190]

According to Advaita, the real is that which lasts, which suffers no sublation; which is eternal. Appearances are perceived and thus they are not unreal (*asat*). According to Advaita, the unreal can *never* appear, not even in one's wildest dreams, e.g., a square circle or the child of a barren woman. The real (*sat*) never changes and thus appearances cannot be called real. Yet, miraculously, mysteriously, inscrutably distinctions, all that is perceived as 'other than you' (*seemingly*) *is perceived*. Thus, appearances are called 'what is other than the real or the unreal' (*sadasatvilakṣaṇa*), 'illusory' (*mithyā*), 'indescribable' (*anirvacanīya*), *māyā*. How wonderful!

It is by means of this concept that Advaita will delineate its epistemology, metaphysics, and practical teachings. For instance, epistemology presupposes a subject who knows, the object which is known, and the resulting knowledge. The justification and elucidation of this triple form (*tripuṭī*) is accounted for by *avidyā*. Similarly with error, *avidyā* is its material cause.[191] Superimposition (*adhyāsa*) and the theory of illusory appearance (*vivartavāda*), which both help to explain the problem of error, presuppose *avidyā*. An inert, material mind needs the help of consciousness for knowledge to arise. Knowledge exists in and through a conscious experience of multiplicity. And it is *avidyā* which is the cause of all these empirical distinctions. The Advaitin contends that the very possibility of empirical distinctions rests upon the existence of *avidyā*.

According to the metaphysics of Advaita, the Absolute is one and non-dual. Thus arises the apparent problem of the One and the many. What is the relationship between the One and the many, between the Absolute and the relative? The Advaitin must account for the seeming plurality of the universe if the Reality is One and non-dual. An explanation is also called for in regard to the distinction which the Advaitin makes between the Reality with form (*saguṇa*) and the formless Reality (*nirguṇa*). The seeming difference between the individual self and the Absolute needs to be explained. The place of God (*Īśvara*), as well as the creation of the world, must be accounted for. Every Indian metaphysical system endeavors to explain these three entities, i.e., the Reality, the individual self, and the physical universe. Advaita must explain how these three entities are really only one. And this Advaita does by elucidating how the concept of *avidyā* is presupposed in each of these issues.

Finally, the entire practical teachings of Advaita presuppose the concept of *avidyā*. The bondage of the individual, as well as its liberation, hinge upon *avidyā*. *Avidyā* is the root cause of bondage, and knowledge is the direct means of its removal. Ethics, aesthetics, and values all have meaning only within the context of *avidyā*. Likewise, all disciplines prescribed for attaining release only become meaningful within the context of *avidyā*.

By this criterion, *Brahman* alone is absolutely real; never being subject to contradiction. All else will be called 'real' only by courtesy. The distinction between one individual and another, the existence of a plurality of things, the attribution of attributes to the Absolute are all concessions to the Truth made from the relative point of view.

The concept of liberation here and now Next, it must be understood that the metaphysics of Advaita is immanent and not transcendent. This is a key point because it has several far-reaching consequences. Advaita is primarily and foremost an enquiry into the Self – a Self which is involved in, and is the basis of, every individual's every experience. The Self is here and now; not something to be obtained from outside, at a later time. Nor is *Brahman* a God, above and beyond. That (*Brahman*) thou art – here and now.

However, though the Self is radically enmeshed in one's experience, it is not consciously present to one's awareness in the way that sense objects are. An individual must make an earnest enquiry and divine the Self through discrimination. Although the Self is not something to be gained afresh, it does need to be discriminated from the not-self. Such a search is not divorced from experience, nor is it outside one's personal experience. It comes through self-enquiry. This means that at any given time, an aspirant's qualifications and readiness determine how meaningful religious discourse statements will be.

The teachings of Vedānta is that one *is* the Self, here and now. Why one doesn't realize this ever-present fact and suffers is due to ignorance.[192] The human being claims, 'I am deficient, inadequate, incomplete, right now.' The evidence for this appears overwhelming. 'Isn't it a fact that I am compulsively pursuing pleasure and security; I am full of desires, wants, and needs?' Further, the fulfillment of these desires is so incredibly important precisely because they are the means of one's fulfillment. Human beings feel incomplete and the means to escape this incompleteness, which inherently brings with it feelings of sorrow and suffering, is to acquire that which one presently does not have.

A person seeks liberation the moment one realizes that one is inadequate and that this inadequacy is not dependent upon the presence or absence of things. The teacher (*Guru*) arrives informing one (*śruti*) that inadequacy is centered in one's imagination, in one's incorrect view of who they really are. Armed with the liberating knowledge that one is complete, here and now, the next stage commences – that of practising spiritual disciplines.

Teachings involve revealing who one is. What teachings accomplish is the removal of incorrect knowledge. Completeness is completeness. Nothing can be added to it to make it complete. Adequacy does not come in degrees. To be perfect is to be completely perfect. Any and every experience is, by definition, inadequate. It comes and it goes. It has a beginning and it will have an end. Thus, if there is truly something called the Self, something called completeness, it must either be present, here and now, or it cannot be at all.

Vedānta declares that one is already *Brahman*. There is no such thing as attainment or non-attainment. The one who seeks liberation is already liberated. The Self has no bondage or liberation. If freedom from inadequacy is already achieved, it means I, who want to be free from inadequacy, *am the very one* who is adequate. The seeker is the sought, here and now. It also means that I have discovered that pursuit of desires/pleasures/security will never achieve completeness. I now understand what means are available to gain my goal, to destroy my ignorance. Seek the Self within, seek the *Sadguru* who will guide me to myself.

It is only when the individual is identified with the body, when he/she considers the body and soul to be him or herself, that they experience pleasure or pain. It is only in the state of identification with the body and the mind, the state in which one considers the eyes to be 'my eyes', the ears to be 'my ears', the mind to be 'my mind', that one experiences pleasure or pain. The experience of pleasure or pain belongs neither to the body nor to the Self. Both are free from it. The Self is without any stain, and so is the body. It is only the intermediary who joins the two in a wrong connection who experiences pleasure or pain. This is the state of ignorance, or the state of delusion. The real teaching of Vedānta is that the ignorance which is destroyed never really existed. To destroy ignorance and attain bliss is to destroy what never was and to attain what we have always had.

This is the case with the false 'I'. It poses as a friend of both the Self and the not-Self. It appears to possess existence, consciousness and bliss as the 'I' (which is the nature of the Self), and at the same time, it is limited to a particular name and form (which is the nature of the not-Self).

Why does this false 'I' disappear when enquired into? It exists only by posing as that which it is not. Without names and forms it cannot endure. All names, all forms, all knowledge, all thought belong to the 'other'. They are mere appearances which are 'added onto', 'assumed by' this 'I'. This 'I' has no form of its own. Thus, when it attends to itself, it loses strength, it begins to subside until it finally disappears. What has disappeared is the superimposed imagination that it was 'something special', 'something particular and distinct' in opposition to all else. Thus, it remains as it always was, is, and will be – regardless of whether it thinks 'the tenth man is missing or not'. There is no incompleteness during *sādhana* and completeness upon liberation; there is no duality during spiritual practices and non-duality during liberation. There is only the ocean of the Self, before, during, and after.

The real purpose of Vedānta is to reveal the bliss of the Self. Suffering comes from the sense of duality, from the idea of I and yours. If you could see that you pervade everything, you wouldn't suffer. The Vedāntin knows only the basic reality, he doesn't bother too much about names and forms. There are infinite names and forms, but they all arise from the nameless One, the formless One.

This leads us to Advaita's conception of the nature of achievement.

The most important question raised in Vedāntic philosophy is this: Can you attain what you haven't attained, or do you attain what you already have? If you are going to get something which you didn't have before, what good is it? Since you didn't have it before and get it now, there is every possibility that you'll lose it some time. And the question of getting what you already have is ridiculous, isn't it?

There are said to be two types of attainment: attainment of the not-yet-attained and attainment of the already attained. What has not-yet-been-attained, say the attainment of a new automobile, is achieved in space and time. It may be attained by a limited effort and will produce a limited result, i.e., a new car. This type of attainment always involves both gain and loss. One gains a new condition and loses their old condition.

However, Vedānta also talks about another type of attainment. Some call it 'obtaining the already obtained' or 'getting rid of what you haven't got'.

To obtain the already obtained, there is neither space nor time involved. One can obtain only that which one does not already have. Since one always is the Self, when one realizes this fact it is designated as 'obtaining the already obtained'.

We should observe, however, that though Vedānta sometimes drastically denied one's most cherished beliefs, it did not advocate a denial of the various spiritual tools which are indispensable for liberation. Of these, as we shall note in a moment, the *Sadguru* is indispensable.

Even as an individual's attachment to the non-self was being severed, positive prerequisites like the cultivation of the virtues, selfless service, chanting, meditation, and purification of the mind were being advocated.[193] Because Advaita puts an emphasis on the Self, most of its philosophical works do not spend much time on an independent, exhaustive treatment of the prerequisite spiritual practices. One should take note, however, that they are there in Advaita and that it is left to one's *Guru* to reveal them as the occasion demands.

The heart of Vedānta is the Self. This means that a spiritual aspirant must discriminate between the Self and the not-self.[194] Obviously Vedānta's voice is perfect for conveying this idea, as it emphasizes, 'Don't take the world so seriously; beware the not-self.' Its emphasis on 'not-this, not-this' (*neti-neti*) is a wonderful check against desires, worldliness, and imagination, the enemies of ignorance, lust, anger, greed, delusion, and so on.

The question arises, 'How does one go about discriminating between the Self and the not-self?' To declare the existence of the Self is one thing; to realize it is another. For this, one needs to take note of the components which comprise the world of Vedānta. In this context we may note the final instructions (*upadeśa*) of Śaṅkara: 'Meet the Master (*Sadguru*). Ceaselessly, selflessly, serve his feet. Learn from him knowledge of *Brahman*; digest the Great Sayings of the *Upaniṣads*.'[195] Within this instruction are aphoristically contained Vedānta's secret of the Self, a teaching which hinges upon service, surrender, the great redeeming *mantra* and, first and foremost, the necessity of a *Sadguru*.

If the *Guru* is the grace-bestowing power of the Absolute (*sa gurur matsamaha prokto mantravīrya prakāśakaha*), *what* the *Guru* bestows is the direct personal experience that 'I am the Absolute (*aham brahmāsmi*)'. It is the *Guru's* spiritual power (*śakti*) which is transmitted by the *Guru* and which awakens the disciple's own inner power. Obviously, as both tradition and the texts reveal, the *Guru* plays a major role in Vedānta. And yet, even if one intellectually understands that one is the Self, the senses may still lead one astray. One needs some instrument, some device, whereby one can overcome the pull, the tyranny of the senses. That instrument is the *Guru*.

For the *Guru* to awaken the disciple, there must be a link between the two. This link is called, in Vedānta, grace (*anugraha*). It is like the wire which connects the power station with the lightbulb that shines in one's home. Or, it is like the original flame which can then light an infinite number of candles without diminishing itself. The *Taittirīya Upaniṣad* says, 'The teacher is the first letter; the student is the last letter; knowledge is the meeting place; instruction is the link.'[196]

'Who am I? Where am I going?' In order to answer these questions, in order to put an end to sorrow and suffering, the Self assumes a name and a form. How else would communication be possible? To express Itself, to reveal Itself, to know Itself, the Self concretizes, as it were, as this world clothed in the twin characteristics of name (*nāma*) and form (*rūpa*).

According to Vedānta, what has a name must have a form, and vice versa. Every appearance in the universe has these two characteristics. The wonder and power of the physical *guru-parampara* is in the special qualities inherent in its names and forms. The *Guru's* name and form is filled with Bliss. The *Guru's* name and form possess a special power.[197] Somehow the mind must be made to sink into the heart. How can one do this? Attach the name and form of the *Guru* to the mind and it will automatically sink, for, the word '*guru*' literally means 'heavy', 'weighty', and thus it will enable the mind to journey from the name to the Nameless, from the form to the Formless, from the relative to the Absolute.

A disciple finds that spiritual disciplines are many and varied. Much will depend upon the capacity of a seeker to understand the guidance which the *Guru* provides. While the *śakti* is pulling the disciple from within, the *Guru* is pushing the disciple from without. In order to turn one's mind inwards and discover the inner Self, a number of spiritual aids and disciplines are provided.

Generally, the human being directs all one's thoughts and actions outwards. This is because the sense organs are turned outwards and attuned to contacting things from the outside. To turn inwards is the first requirement regarding the question 'Who am I?' An individual whose attention is turned outwards, by that very act, excludes any possibility of discovering who they really are. An object, the known, will never be the knower. Yet strangely, even in the act of turning outwards, the divine consciousness within one is not excluded. It is merely unnoticed.

Whether an individual knows it or not, Vedānta says that they are this divine inner consciousness. That which conceals this truth from an individual's conscious experience is one's ignorance, one's age-old habit of clinging to externals. If one were to dive deep within, one would find the so-called secret heart-cave, the ocean of consciousness, the mysterious Self, the source of one's very being. God dwells within you as you. I am the Absolute. One understands such scriptural declarations when one comes to experience, first hand, the divine essence which is within one, which one really is and always has been.

Advaita regards the Absolute as that which is foundational to all experience, although it is in no sense a substance. It is considered to be that which is different from the phenomenal, the spatial, the temporal, and the sensible. It is not to be located in space, though seemingly it is everywhere – since all things imply and depend upon it. It is seemingly nowhere since it is not a thing which has spatial relations to anything. Its nature is inexpressible since to say anything about it is to make it into a particular thing.

Advaita's tradition declines to characterize the Absolute in any terms other than in the sense of 'secondless', 'non-dual'. It is in this sense that the terms 'Absolute' and 'non-dual Reality' are used in this work. There is no English equivalent of the terms '*Ātman*' or '*Brahman*'. To translate them as 'Spirit' or 'Self' or 'Absolute' can be extremely misleading for these terms, in the English language, are loaded with different meanings and connotations from various Western religious and philosophical contexts which do not resemble or equal Advaita's intention.

The Legacy of Śaṅkara

To reveal the Self is the be-all and end-all of Advaita. This experience, Śaṅkara further claims, is within our reach. The Self, which is Consciousness, is ever free and never bound. It is the sole Reality. However, seemingly the formless becomes embodied. Thus, the basic problem is to answer how it is possible for the Self, which is essentially different from everything, gets involved in the things of the world. Śaṅkara stated the problem:

> It is a matter not requiring any proof that the object and the subject which are signified by the terms *yuṣmad* (not-self) and *asmad* (Self) and which are opposed to each other like light and darkness, cannot be identified. In the same way, their respective attributes also cannot be identified. Hence, it follows that it is wrong to superimpose upon the subject, which is of the nature of Consciousness and which is referred to as *asmad*, the object which is spoken of as *yuṣmad*, and the attributes of the object; it is also wrong to superimpose the subject and the attributes of the subject on the object. In spite of this, it is quite natural, owing to wrong knowledge, not to distinguish the two entities and their respective attributes . . . and carry on the worldly life by saying, 'That I am' and 'That is mine.'[198]

The method that Śaṅkara proposes consists of a rigorous enquiry into the Self as well as an enquiry into the world. Again Śaṅkara says,

> The Self within is one only; two inwards Selfs are not possible. But, owing to its limiting adjunct, the one Self is practically treated as if it were two, just as a distinction is made between the space of a jar and universal space. Hence, there is scope for scriptural texts which set forth the distinction between the knower and the known, for perception and other means of knowledge, for the experience of the empirical and for scripture which contains injunctions and prohibitions. Thus the scriptural text, 'Where there is duality, as it were, there one sees another', declares that the whole empirical world exists only in the state of ignorance; while the text 'But when the Self only is all this, how should one see another?' (Bṛh. Up. 4.5.15) declares that the empirical world vanishes in the sphere of true knowledge.[199]

Śaṅkara's truth is simple to state. Self-realization is not something that can be captured in words or actions. It is not outside the seeker. He spoke words only to point to That, to celebrate That. Truly, he had nothing to teach. The

Self is not about learning. The Self is not about obtaining something new. It is only about realizing that which one already is. That which one yearns for, that which one hungers for, is that which is always present, here and now, as who you truly are.

Notes

1 There are three supposedly lost biographies: Padmapāda's *Vijayaḍiṇḍima*, Citsukha's *Bṛhatś aṅkaravijaya*, and Ānandagiri's *Prācīnaśaṅkaravijaya*. There are twenty extant biographies: Mādhava (Mādhavācārya-Vidyāraṇya) *Śaṅkaradig-vijaya* (a.k.a. *Śrīmādhaviyaśaṅkaravijayam* or *Samkkshepasankaravijaya*) with its two commentaries, Dhanapati Sūri's *Diṇḍima* and Acyutarāya Moḍaka's *Advaitarājyalakṣmī*; Vyāsācala's *Śaṅkaravijaya* (a.k.a. *Śrī Vyāsacalīyam*); Brahmānandīya's *Bṛhacchaṅkaravijaya*; Anantānandagiri's *Śaṅkaravijaya* (a.k.a. *Guruvijaya* or *Acāryavijaya*); Sarvajña Sadāśivabodha's *Puṇyaślokamañjarī*; Sarvajña Sadāśivabrahmendra's *Jagadgururatnamālāstava*; Atmabodha's *Paris śiṭa, Makaranda*, and *Suṣamā*; Govindanātha's *Śaṅkarācāryacarita* (a.k.a. *Keralīyaśaṅkaravijaya*); Cidvilāsa's *Śaṅkaravijayavilāsa* (a.k.a. *Cidvilasiyaśaṅkaravijayam*); Rājacūḍāmaṇi Dīkṣita's *Śaṅkarābhyudaya*; Tirumala Dīkṣita's *Śaṅkarābhyudaya*; Parameśvara Kavi Kaṇṭhīrava's *Ācāryavijayacampū*; Purusottama Bhāratī's *Śaṅkaravijayasaṁgraha*; Sadānanda's *Śaṅkaradigvijayasāra*; Kāśī Lakṣamaṇa Śāstrī's *Guruvaṁśakāvya*; Nīlakaṇṭha's *Śaṅkarābhyudaya*; Nīlakaṇṭha's *Śaṅkaramandārasaurabha*; Kṛṣṇabrahmānanda's *Śaṅkaravijaya*; Vallīsahāya's *Śaṅkaravijaya (a.k.a. Ācāryavijayacampū)*; Bālagopālayati's *Śaṅkarācāryamahima*. There are also what seem to be biographical references in the Purāṇic literature (*Mārkaṇḍeyasaṁhitā* 72.7.10, *Śivarahasya* 9.16, *Liṅga Purāṇa* 1.40.20–22, *Kūrma Purāṇa* 28,32.35, *Bhaviṣyottara Purāṇa*, *Skanda Purāṇa*, *Saura Purāṇa*, and *Padma Purāṇa*. Finally, there are monastic records such as *Mahānusāsana*, *Guruparamparāstotras*, *Maṭhāmnāyopaniṣad*, *Maṭhāmnāya* or *Amnāyestu*.

2 This is stated neither as praise nor condemnation. The modern deterministic tendency governing what constitutes history is a product of its own times, with its own presuppositions and expectations, even as ancient India had its own milieu, style, and vision. For a discussion about Śaṅkara and myth, see Jonathan Bader, *Meditation in Śaṅkara's Vedanta*, pp. 15–24.

3 Numerous modern writers have given thought to this problem. Some of the more recent summaries of the materials available include G.C. Pande, *Life and Thought of Śaṅkarācārya*; Bader, *Conquest of the Four Quarters: Traditional Accounts of the Life of Sankara*; S. Vidyasankar, 'Conflicting Hagiographies and History: The Place of Sankaravijaya texts in Advaita Tradition', *International Journal of Hindu Studies*, forthcoming. Another interesting attempt of note is W.R. Antarkar 1961, PhD dissertation from the University of Poona entitled, 'Śaṅkara Vijayas: A Comparative and Critical Study'.

4 Ingalls, 'The Study of Saṁkarācārya', *Annals of the Bhandarkar Oriental Research Institute*, vol. XXXII (1952) p. 4, first enumerated these three approaches. Also see Pande's *Life and Thought of Śaṅkarācārya*, pp. 41–54; Bader's *Meditation in Śaṅkara's Vedānta*, pp. 7–24; A. Kuppuswami's *Sri Bhagavatpada Sankaracarya*, pp. 20–35; and so on.

5 Notable modern exponents of this approach include Ingalls, Hacker, Nakamura, and Vetter.

6 Exponents of this method include Radhakrishnan, P.T. Raju, D.M. Datta, Belvalkar, Ingalls, Hacker, Mayeda, Vetter, Nakamura, and Gussner.

7 BG 13.12.

8 BSBh 1.i.4. *Svābhāvikapravṛttiviṣayavimukhīkaraṇārthānīti brūmaḥ.*

9 See Hacker, 'Distinctive Features of the Doctrine and Terminology of Śaṅkara: Avidyā, Nāmarūpa, Māyā, Iśvara', in *Philology and Confrontation*, ed. Wilhelm Halbfass, pp. 57–100.

10 Ibid. 'Śaṅkarācārya and Śaṅkarabhagavatpāda: Preliminary Remarks Concerning the Authorship Problem', pp. 41–56.

11 See Robert E. Gussner, 'Śaṅkara's Crest Jewel of Discrimination: A Stylometric Approach to the Question of Authorship', *Journal of Indian Philosophy* 4 (1977), pp. 265–278.

12 Because they are directly quoted either by Śaṅkara's contemporaries or those who came after him.

13 See US and V. 14–17 (i.e., who is competent to know the Self); V. 18–32 (the four-fold prerequisites) and so on.

14 See K.B. Pathak, 'The Date of Samkaracarya', *Indian Antiquary*, Vol. 2 (Bombay, 1882, p. 175), K.T. Telang, *Sankaracarya, Philosopher and Mystic* (Adyar, 1911), N.K. Venkatesan, *Sankaracarya and His Kamakotipitha* (Kumbhakonam, 1915), N. Venkataraman, *Sankaracarya the Great and His Successors in Kanchi* (Madras, 1923), H. Nakamura, *Early Vedanta Philosophy* (Tokyo: Iwanami Shoten, 1950), C.N. Krishnasvami Iyer, *Sankaracarya – His Life and Times* (G.A. Nateshan, Madras), S.S. Suryanarayana Sastri, *Sankaracarya* (G.A. Netesan, Madras), Bhasyacharya, *Age of Sankara* (Adyar Library Series), N. Ramesan, *Sri Sankaracarya* (Ponnur, 1959), Baldeva Upadhyaya, *Sri Sankaracarya* (Allahabad, 1963), T.M.P. Mahadevan, *Adisankara – His Life and Times* (National Book Trust, 1960), K.G. Nateshan Shastri, *Sri Sankaracarya* (Tiruchirapalli, 1980), K.K. Raja, 'On the Date of Sankaracarya and Allied Problems', *Adyar Library Bulletin* (Vol. XXIV, pts. 3–4, 1960, pp. 125–148), P. Hacker, *Philology and Confrontation: Paul Hacker on Traditional and Modern Vedanta*; L. Renou, *Journal Asiatique*, vol. CCXLIII (1955), no. 2, pp. 249–251, D.H.H. Ingalls, *Philosophy East and West*, Vol. 3 (1954), p. 292, n. 2, F. Max Muller, *Three Lectures on the Vedanta Philosophy* (London, 1894), A.B. Keith, *The Karma-Mimamsa* (London, 1921), M. Winternitz, *Geschichte der indischen Literatur*, vol. III (Leipzig, 1913), G.C. Pande, *Life and Thought of Sankaracarya* (Delhi: Motilal Banarsidass, 1994), A. Nataraja Iyer, *The Traditional Age of Sri Sankaracarya and the Maths*, Pranab Bandyopadhyay, *Shankaracharya* (Calcutta: United Writers, 1990), S.K. Belvalkar, *Vedanta Philosophy* (Poona, 1929), D.R. Bhandarkar, 'Can We Fix the Date of Sankaracarya More Accurately?' *Indian Antiquary*, Vol. XLI, p. 200), N. Bhashyacharya, *The Age of Sankaracarya* (Madras: Adyar Library, 1915), T.R. Chintamani, 'The Date of Sankara', JOR, Vol. III, pp. 39ff.), T.R. Chintamani, 'The Date of Sankaracarya', IA Vol. XIII, pp. 95ff.), V.A. Devasenapathi, *Kāmakoṭṭam, Nāyanmārs, and Ādi Sankara* (Institute of Traditional Cultures, University Buildings, Madras, 1975), F.J. Fleet, 'A Note on the Date of Sankaracarya' (Indian Antiquary, Vol. XVI, pp. 41ff.), Paul Hacker, 'Sankaracarya and Sankarabhagavatpada', *New Indian Antiquary* (Vol. IX, pp. 175ff.), D.H.H. Ingalls, 'The Study of Sankaracarya',

ABORI, Vol. XXXIII, pp. 1–14), T.K. Balasubramania Iyer, *Guruvaṁśa-kāvya* (Sri Vani Vilas Press, Srirangam, 1928), S.D. Kulkarni, *Adi Sankara: The Saviour of Mankind* (Shri Bhagavan Vedavyasa Itihasa Samshodhana Mandira Bombay, 1987), A. Kuppuswami, *Sri Bhagavatpada Sankaracarya* (Varanasi: Chowkhamba, 1972), Swami Mukhyananda, *Acharya Shankara* (Sri Ramakrishna Advaita Ashrama, Kalady, Kerala, 1987), N. Ramesam, *Sri Sankaracharya* (M/s Bhavanarayanaswami Temple, Ponnur, A.P. 1971), N.M. Sastri, *A Study of Sankara* (Calcutta, 1942), T.S. Narayana Sastri, *The Age of Sankara* (Madras: M/s B.G. Paul and Co: Madras 1971), K.A. Nilakanta Sastri, 'A Note on the Date of Sankara', JOR, Vol. XI, p. 285), Udayavira Sastri, *Age of Sankara* (Gaziabad, 1981), K.T. Telang, 'The Date of Sankara', JOR, Vol. III, pp. 39ff. and 'The Date of Sankaracarya', IA, Vol. XIII, pp. 95ff.), R.M. Umesh, *Shankara's Date*, Madras, and Natalia Isayeva, *Shankara and Indian Philosophy*.

15 I.e., once, long ago, the virtuous wife of Śivaguru, Aryamba, gave birth to a son. It was noon on a Sunday, on the 15th day of the bright half of the month of Vaiśākha when the Sun was in Aries. The year was 2631 of the Yudhiṣṭhira era (805 CE?), in the auspicious cycle known as Nandana. The constellation was Punaravasu (Ardrā?) in the zodiac sign of Cancer. The Sun, Mars, Jupiter, and Saturn were in exhaltation with the Sun in Aries, Mercury and Mars in the seventh house, Capricorn in the fourth house in Libra, Jupiter in the first house in Cancer, and Venus in Pisces. See *Bṛhatśaṅkaravijaya*, '*ṣaḍviṁśe śatake śrīmad yaudhisthira śakasya vai ekatriṁśe thavarṣe tu hāyane nandane śubhe meṣa rāśiṁ gate sūrye vaiśākhe māsi śobhane śuklapakṣe ca pañcamyāṁ tithyāṁ bhāskara vāsare*' (quoted in T.S. Narayana Sastri, Age of Śaṅkara, p. 223. The *Bṛhatśaṅkaravijaya* itself is no longer available); also see *Gurumaṁśāvali* (*Jagadgururatnamālā*) of the Dvārakā Maṭha; Atmabodha's *Suṣamā*; *Vimarśa*; *Prācīnaśaṅkaravijaya*; *Jinavijaya*; *Puṇyaślokamañjarī* of Sarvajña Sadāśiva Bodha; *Śivarahasya; maṭhāmnāyas*. As an interesting side note, if examined astrologically over the last 3000 years, the positions of the planets as set out above occurs only once, in 805 CE. At no other time are these five planets in this state of exaltation.

16 See Nīlakaṇṭha Bhaṭṭa, Kṛṣṇabrahmānanda, Yajñeśvara Sāstri, K.P. Thiele, K.B. Pathak, F. Max Muller, A. Macdonell, A.B. Keith, and M. Winternitz, who all accepted this date. Hajime Nakamura proposed 700–750 CE which was accepted by L. Renou and D.H.H. Ingalls.

17 These dates are based on information provided in the *Bṛhatśaṅkaravijaya*, *Prācīnaśaṅkaravijaya*, *Puṇyaślokamañjarī*, *Jagadgururatnaamālā*, and the *Suṣamā*. Those who uphold this view include T.S. Narayana Sastry, A. Nataraja Iyer, S. Lakshminarasimha Sastry, Kota Venkatacalam, and D.S. Triveda.

18 See D.H.H. Ingalls, 'Śaṅkara's Arguments against the Buddhists', *Philosophy East and West*, Vol. 3, January 1954, no. 4, p. 292, note 2; K.B. Pathak, 'Bhartṛhari and Kumārila', *Journal of the Bombay Branch of the Royal Asiatic Society*, Vol. 18, p. 213; and V. Bhattacharya, 'Śaṅkara and Diṅnāga,' *Indian Historical Quarterly*, Vol. 6, p. 169.

19 See G.C. Pande, *Life and Thought of Śaṅkarācārya*, p. 52. Also see Nakamura, *A History of Early Vedanta Philosophy*, I., pp. 68–72. The *Darśanaprakāśa*, quoting the *Śaṅkarapaddhati*, states that Śaṅkara was born in 686 CE and died in the Śaka year 642 which corresponds to 720 CE. The Śṛṅgerī Maṭha claims to have some palm-leaf manuscripts which declare that Śaṅkara was born

in the 14th year of king Vikramāditya. If this Vikramāditya was Badami Cālukya Vikramāditya I, son of Pulakesin II, a disputed point, Śaṅkara's dates would be 668–700 CE. It may also be noted that the Śṛṅgerī Maṭha is the one monastical tradition which eschews the legendary and highly mythical stance of the other monasteries.

20 Recent modern studies include those by G.C. Pande and S. Vidyasankar.

21 See Pande, pp. 73+.

22 See *Mārkaṇḍeya Saṁhitā khaṇḍa* 72, *parispanda* 7 (*lokānugraha tatparaḥ paraśivaḥ samprārthito brahmaṇā cārvākādi mata prabheda nipuṇām buddhim sadā dhārayan kālaṭyākhya purottame śiva gurur vidyādhināthaśca yaḥ tat patnyaṁ sivatārake samuditaḥ śrī śaṅkarākhyāṁ vahan*) *Skandapurāṇa*, *Kūrmapurāṇa* 27.31–32 (*kalau rudro mahādevo lokānām īśvaraḥ paraḥ/tadeva sadhayen nṛāṁ devatānāṁ ca daivatam// kariṣyatyavatāram svaṁ Śaṅkaro nīlalohitaḥ/śrauta smārta pratiṣṭhārthār the bhaktānāṁ hita kāmyayā*), *Saurapurāṇa*, *Bhaivṣyottarapurāṇa*, and *Śivarahasya* 9th *aṁśa*, 16th chapter (*varṇāś rama paribhraṣṭān adharmapravaṇān janān/kalyabdhau majjamānān stān dṛṣtvānukr-ośatombike/madaṁśa-jāto deveśi kalāvapitapodhanam/keralesutadā vipraṁ janayāmi maheśari// jainā bauddhā buddhiyuktā mīmāṁśāniratāḥ kalau/ vedabodhaka-vākyānām anyathaiva praprocakāḥ/ . . . teṣām utpāṭanārthāya sṛjāmīśe madaṁśataḥ*).

23 See David Lorenzen, 'Śaṅkara', in Mircea Eliade, ed. *The Encyclopedia of Religion*, XIII (New York: Macmillan, 1987) pp. 64–65 who posits that this followed an essentially *vaiṣṇava* conception of divine incarnation (*avatāra*). However, note that Vidyasankar 1 (p. 27) believes that the Śaṅkara literature is not responsible for this view, but is merely an amplification of it into a full-fledged story. It is common feature of Hinduism for devotees to declare great souls as divine incarnations.

24 See *Dakṣināmūrti stotra* (Aesthetic Rapture), J.L. Masson and M.V. Patwardham (Poona: Deccan College, 1970), 2 vols. *Dakṣiṇamūrti* is the name for Lord Śiva as the grace-bestowing *Guru*. See *Dakṣiṇamūrti Upaniṣad* wherein, as the gracious Lord, he is depicted not only as the first *Guru* but also as *the* Guru.

25 Opening lines to the *Sankara Digvijaya: The Traditional Life of Sankaracharya* by Madhava-Vidyaranya.

26 *Kūrma Purāṇa* 27 (*kariṣyati avatāram svam Śaṅkaro nīlalohitaḥ*). See also *Bhaviṣyottara Purāṇa* 36.

27 *Śivarahasya* 9.16 (*keralaśaśalagrāme viprapatnyām madāṁśajaḥ, bhaviṣyati mahādevi śaṅkarākhya dvijottamaḥ*).

28 *Mārkaṇḍeya Saṁhitā* 72.7 (*kālaṭākhyapurottame śivaguru vidyādhi-nāthasyaca yaḥ, tatpatnyām śivatārakaṁśamuditaḥ śrīśaṅkarākh-yām vahan*).

29 See KenaUpBh 1.4: 'Indeed, *Brahman* can be grasped only through the instructions of teachers, transmitted from one to the other, and not owing to reasoning, nor through intelligence or many heard/texts/ascetic practices,. sacrifices, etc.' Also see V. 13, 'The goal of life is seen to arise from an inquiry in accord with the words of the wise and never by taking sacred baths or performing acts of charity or by hundreds of breathing exercises' (*arthasya niścayo dṛṣṭo vicāreṇa hitoktitaḥ| na snānena na dānena prāṇāyāma-śatena vā*); V. 15, 'Therefore, that person who desires to know the nature of the Self, correctly and completely, should perform an earnest inquiry after duly approaching a Master who is a supreme knower of the Absolute and an ocean of compassion (*ato vicāraḥ kartavyaḥ jijñāsor ātma-vastunaḥ| samāsādya dayāsindhuṁ guruṁ*

brahma viduttamam); V. 26, 'Acceptance, with firm conviction, of the scriptures and the words of the Master as conveying the Truth is called faith by the wise. By this does reality become apprehended (*śāstrasya guruvākyasya satya-buddhyāvadhāraṇa*l *sā śraddhā kathitā sadbhiḥ yayā vastūpalabhyate*).

30 See Śaṅkara's BGBh 13.2 (*evaṁ manvāne yaḥ sa paṇḍitāpasadaḥ saṁsāramokṣayoḥ śāstrasya ca arthavattvaṁ karomītyātmahā, svayaṁ mūḍhaḥ anyāṁśca vyāmohayati śāstrārtha-saṁpradāyara-hitatvāt śruta-hānimaśrutakalpanāṁ kurvan*).

31 See *Mādhavīya Śaṅkara Digvijayam* and. *Vyāsācalīyam*. Tradition is not unanimous in respect of the different astrological charts of Śaṅkara's birth. The *Prācīna-Śaṅkaravijaya* says Śaṅkara was born in the fourth (*Karkata*) *lagna* under the constellation of *Punarvasu*, in the month of Vaiśākha in the year Nandana. See T.S. Narayana Sastri, *Age of Sankara*, pp. 217, 237, 239, 256, 265, 273.

32 Compare Kṛṣṇa's words in the BG 4.7, 'Whenever there is a decay of righeousness and a rise of unrighteousness, then I embody myself, O Bharata' (*yadā yadā hi dharmasya glānir bhavati bhārata abhyutthānam adharmasya tadā'tmānyaṁ sṛjāmy aham*). Also BG 4.1–2, 'This yoga formerly I taught to Vivasvān. A long time has elapsed since then. If the persons who receive the teaching are supremely eligible, they will preserve it forever. Since those who came after had diminishing eligibility, there was damage done to the teachings. This yoga which came done as a tradition began to decay because those who came later were not supremely eligible. I hae now come to resuscitate it.' Legend says that Śiva, while sitting atop Mt. Kailāsa, gives the gods a solemn promise to descend to earth in order to reinstate the shattered foundations of true wisdom, of Vedānta.

33 *Śaṅkara Digvijaya*, p. 14.

34 In some versions of this story, Śivaguru himself chooses the brilliant child.

35 Hinduism is rift with stories of those individuals who think they can outwit fate, destiny, God, and so on; For example, Hiranyakasipu, Ravana, Dharmaraja.

36 Such a one is known as an *eka śruti dhara*. The survival of Padmapāda's *Pañcapādikā* is attributed to this ability of Śaṅkara.

37 There are four *Vedas*: *Ṛg-veda*, *Yajur-veda*, *Sāma-veda*, and *Atharva-veda*, and the *Vedāṅga* or limbs of the *Vedas* are phonetics (*sikṣā*), prosody (*chandas*), grammar (*vyākaraṇa*), etymology (*nirukta*), astronomy (*jyotiṣa*), and ceremonial (*kalpa*).

38 See Kulkarni, p. 97; Pande, p. 81. A line (*tava stanyam manye*) in the *Saundaryalaharī* has been interpreted by commentators as referring to this incident. A similar incident has been spoken of in the life of the Maratha saint, Nāmadeva (see Callewaert and Lath, p. 17) and in regards to the Hindu deity, Gaṇeśa, in 1995 (see Subramaniya, Sivaya: *Lord Ganesha: Benevolent Deity for the Modern World*). Tradition declares that Śaṅkara composed the *Devībhujaṅga-stava* on this occasion.

39 See Kulkarni, p. 98; Pande, p. 81. Tradition declares that Śaṅkara composed the *Kaṇaka-dhārā-stotra* on this occasion.

40 See Kulkarni, p. 101; Pande, p. 81.

41 See Kulkarni, p. 102; Pande, p. 81, Isayeva, p. 75. Śaṅkara was supposed to live for just eight years but by becoming a renunciant, it was like a new birth and thus his life span doubled. On the day that Śaṅkara left home at the age of eight, he promised his mother that he would return before her death, in order to console her, liberate her, and perform her funeral rites.

42 See Kulkarni, p. 106, 113; Pande, p. 83, Isayeva, p. 75. On the way, at the place where Ṛṣyaśṛṅga once had an *āśrama*, he saw a cobra spreading its hood to protect a frog from the sun. He thought this would make a great place for an āśrama. Ten years later he is reputed to have established his first monastery (Śṛṅgerī) here.

43 See Kulkarni, p. 114. Once, many years ago, I had a chance meeting with an Indian monk. He asked me, 'Who you?' Having lived in India and being used to this type of English and being young and polite I began to answer him, 'I am John Grimes' but just as I reached the 'G' of Grimes, he said, '*Bas*, family name, who you?' ('*bas*' is Hindi for 'stop, enough'). Again, since I had lived in India and studied Indian thought, I very confidently and boldly began to reply, 'I am the immortal *Ātman*' but just as I reached the 'A' of *Ātman*, again he stopped me with another '*Bas*, who you?' With the first 'stop', he wiped out the idea that I am my physical body. With the second 'stop', he wiped out my entire mental universe. What was left? With two small words he had succeeded in conveying to me that I was neither my physical body nor my mental knowledge. How to answer him? So I said, 'I do not know'. Quick as a wink, he responded, 'Find out'. I replied, 'How?' He responded, 'Not how, find out'. Again I asked, 'How?' He was holding a handkerchief in his hand and he opened his fingers and let the handkerchief drop to the ground and, as it fell, he said, 'Let go'. Again I asked, 'How (to let go)?' He responded, 'Not how, let go'. And then he turned and left the room.

44 *Nirvāṇaṣaṭkam*. This hymn is also known as the *Ātmaṣataka* – Six Verses On the Self: '*manobuddhyahaṁkāra cittāni nāham . . . cidānandarūpaḥ śivo'ham śivo'ham*'.

45 *Daśaśloki* (*na caikam tadanyad dvitīyam kutaḥ syāt, na vā kevalatvam na cākevalatvam; na śūnyam na cāśūnyamadvaitakatvam, katham sarvavedānta-siddham bravīmi*).

46 See Kulkarni, p. 116. The invocatory verse of the *Vivekacūḍāmaṇi* is: 'I offer my salutations to Govinda, the Divine Master, the embodiment of the highest bliss, who is beyond thought and speech, and who is the culmination of all wisdom' (*sarva-vedānta-siddhānta-gocaraṁ tam agocaram govindaṁ paramānandaṁ sadguruṁ praṇato'smyaham*).

47 See Kulkarni, p. 119–20; Pande, p. 83. During this incident Śaṅkara is said to have composed the hymn 'Narmadā Aṣṭaka.'

48 The three source-books are: The *Upaniṣads*, the *Bhagavadgītā*, and the *Brahmasūtras*. Together these three are known as the *prasthānatraya*, the triple canon of Vedānta. '*Prasthāna*' means 'foundation' and thus these three constitute the three foundations of: Primary Scripture (*śruti*), Remembrance (*smṛti*), and Reason (*nyāya*). These three are respectively called the *Sruti-prasthāna* (*Upaniṣads*), the *Smṛti-prasthāna* (*Bhagavad gītā*), and the *Nyāya-prasthāna* (*Brahmasūtras*).

49 See *Sankara Digvijaya* 5.162+; Kulkarni, p. 122+; Pande, p. 85+; Isayeva, p. 77.

50 See Kulkarni, p. 128–31+; Isayeva, p. 81.

51 See Kulkarni, p. 140–41; Isayeva, p. 81.

52 See V. 17, 'That person alone is considered qualified to inquire into the Absolute who possesses discrimination, detachment, the virtues such as tranquillity and so on. and an intense-longing-for-liberation' (*vivekino viraktasya samādi-guṇa-sālinaḥ mumukṣor eva hi brahma-jijñāsā-yogyatāmatā*); also see V. 19–29.

53 See Kulkarni, p. 131; Pande, p. 89. The account claims that Śaṅkara had a debate with Vyāsa over some of Śaṅkara's commentary on the *Brahmasūtras*. Padmapāda, recognizing that this was a debate between Śiva and Viṣṇu, suggested that the debate end.

54 See Kulkarni, p. 133; Pande, p. 89. Tradition declares that Śaṅkara was originally destined to live but eight years. Due to his taking *sannyāsa*, his life-span was extended to sixteen years. Then, after his debate with Vyāsa, at the request of Vyāsa, Brahmā gave Śaṅkara another sixteen years.

55 See Kulkarni, p. 134.

56 See Kulkarni, p. 136. When Śaṅkara met Śiva at Kailāsa, he composed his famous hymn on Dakṣināmūrti. Tradition says that Śaṅkara saw Lord Śiva, as a young child, sitting under a banyan tree teaching ancient sages through silence.

57 See Kulkarni, p. 151. Just before performing the last rites of his mother, Śaṅkara heard that Govinda was about to pass from this earth and that Govinda desired to see Śaṅkara one last time. Thus, Śaṅkara went to visit him and at that time composed the Hymn in Praise of the Guru ('Guruaṣṭaka') which contains the famous refrain, 'Of what use is (anything and everything) if your mind is not attached to the lotus feet of your *guru*?' (*tataḥkim* 4×).

58 See Kulkarni, p. 153.

59 See Kulkarni, p. 155–58, 221.

60 See Kulkarni, p. 127. Padmapāda was a *brahmin* named Sanandana from Ahobilam before he became Śaṅkara's first disciple. He was noted for his devotion to Śaṅkara.

61 See Kulkarni, p. 163. Hastāmalaka was deaf and dumb from the age of five. When the boy was brought to Śaṅkara, he put his hand on his head and asked him, 'Who are you my body?' The child spontaneously sang thirteen verses known as the Hastāmalakīyam which begin, 'I am neither a man, nor a divine being, nor a demon. I do not belong to any of the castes nor do I belong to any of the four stages of life. I am the Absolute, Consciousness, Being.'

62 See Kulkarni, p. 176–206; Isayeva, p. 78–80. Maṇḍana, doing his departed father's *śraddha* ceremony, was taken aback seeing a young lad in ochre robes descending from the sky. 'From where are you, O clean shaven one?' Śaṅkara replied, 'Shaven up to the neck only'. Pricked by this clever answer, Maṇḍana says, 'I am asking your way' (I want to know what spiritual path you follow). Śaṅkara replied, 'Well, what did my way tell you?' Losing his temper, Maṇḍana says, 'The way said that your mother is a widow.' Śaṅkara replies, 'It might be true' with a shrug. Infuriated, Maṇḍana relies, 'Are you drunk?' Śaṅkara twists this to mean, 'Is the liquor yellow in color?' and replies, 'The liquor is whitish in color.' Maṇḍana replies, 'So I see you know the color.' Śaṅkara replies, 'I know the color, but perhaps you know the taste.' Thus, a debate was scheduled to settle the issue. For eighteen days the debate raged on. Finally Maṇḍana's garland faded and thus he became Sureśvara.

63 See Kulkarni, p. 217. Toṭaka distinguished himself by his selfless service to Śaṅkara. By merely thinking of the boy, Giri, Śaṅkara awakened him (*manana śaktipata*) and spontaneously Giri began to compose verses in the *toṭaka* meter. It was thus that Śaṅkara initiated him into *sannyāsa* and gave him the name Toṭakācārya.

64 See Kulkarni, p. 167–206; Isayeva, p. 78–80.

65 See Kulkarni, p. 206–208. The 'all-knowing throne or seat of learning' is in Śṛnagar, Kāsmīr.

66 See Kulkarni, p. 209–225. There are four well-known monasteries established by Śaṅkara: Jyothir Maṭha at Badarikāśrama, Kalika Pīṭha at Dwāraka, Vimala Pīṭha at Jagannātha and Śarada Maṭha at Śṛṅgeri.

67 See Kulkarni, p. 212–216; Isayeva, p. 77; *Śivarahasya* 9.16 verse 47 (*tad yoga bhoga vara mukti sumokṣayoga liṅgarcana prāptajayaḥ svakāśramam tān vai vijitya tarasā kṣataśāstravādaiḥ miśrān sa kāñcyām atha siddhim āpa*). Tradition says that Śaṅkara received five crystal (*sphatika*) *liṅgas* from Lord Śiva who said: 'Take these five *liṅgas* and by applying sacred ash to your body and wearing a garland of *rudrākṣa* beads, worship these five with *bilva* leaves and other suitable items and rites. Always repeat the five-syllabled *mantra om namaḥ Śivaya*. These five are *mukti-liṅga* at Kedarnātha; *vara-liṅga* at Nilakanta kṣetra in Nepal; *mokṣa-liṅga* at Chidambaram; *bhoga-liṅga* at Śṛṅgeri; *yoga liṅga* at Kañcī.

68 See Kulkarni, p. 253; Isayeva, p. 82. Some sources say Śaṅkara died in Kedārnātha, others in Kāñcī. There are other, less likely possibilities, that Śaṅkara died at Vṛṣācala or Śṛnagar.

69 This is a convenient and traditional way to divide Śaṅkara's works. See S.K. Belvalkar (*Sri Gopal Basu Mallik Lectures on Vedanta Philosophy*, Part 1, Poona, 1929, pp. 222ff.); Isayeva, *Shankara and Indian Philosophy*, p. 91; Pande, *Life and Thought of Sankaracarya*, p. 104. For lists of Śaṅkara's works see: Th. Aufrecht, *Catalogus Catalogorum*, 3 vols, Leipzig, 1891–1903.

70 There is at least one text, the *Vākyasudhā* (*Dṛgdṛśyaviveka*), which has been ascribed to Śaṅkara, to Bhāratītīrtha, and to Vidyāraṇya. Both of the later were heads of the Śṛṅgeri monastery.

71 Hacker believed that Śaṅkara wrote only the *Brahmasūtrabhāṣya*, commentaries on the ten principal *Upaniṣads* and subcommentaries on the *Yogasūtra* and *Dharmasūtra* (known as the *Adhyātma-paṭala-vivaraṇa*). Potter, surveying the analyses available to him, concludes that only the *Brahmasūtrabhāṣya*, the *Bṛhadāraṇyakopaniṣadbhāṣya*, the *Taittirīyopaniṣadbhāṣya*, the *Muṇḍakopaniṣadbhāṣya*, and the *Praśnopaniṣadbhāṣya* are authentic. According to him, everything else is merely speculation (Potter, p. 116). Mayeda (p. 6) includes as reliably certain the *Bhagavadgītābhāṣya* and the *Upadeśasāhasrī*. Other scholars who have discussed this issue include H. Jacobi, V. Bhattacharya, G.N. Kaviraj, Baldev Upadhyaya, T.R. Chintamani, and S.K. Belvalkar.

72 Thus, because of Sureśvara's commentaries on the TaittUpBh and the BṛhUpBh and quotations from the US in the *Naiṣkarmyasiddhi*, they are considered authentic works of Śaṅkara's.

73 See Hacker, 'Śaṅkarācārya and Śaṅkarabhagavatpāda', *New Indian Antiquary* (vol. IX, pp. 175ff.), and 'Eigentumlichkeiten der Lehre und Terminologie Śaṅkara's', *Zeitschrift der Deutschen Morgenlandischen Gesellschaft*, 100 (1950), pp. 246–286.

74 *Guru*, *vyākaraṇa*, *nyāya*, *mīmāmsā*, and *veda-adhyayana*.

75 A *prakaraṇa grantha* is an independent treatise or introductory work in which the elements of philosophy are set forth according to the logic of the views themselves, rather than in an order determined by that of scriptural authority. A *prakaraṅa* treatise is defined as: *śāstraikadeśamasa bandham śāstra kārayāntaresthitam, āhuḥ prakarañam nāma granyabhedam vipascitaḥ*.

76 Grimes, *A Concise Dictionary of Indian Philosophy*, p. 235.

77 Hacker, and Mayeda, and Ingalls are unanimous on this point.

78 English translations of the *Vivekacūḍāmaṇi* include *Śaṅkara's Crest Jewel of Discrimination*, trans. by Swami Prabhavananda and Christopher Isherwood.

Vivekacūḍāmaṇi of Śrī Śaṅkarācārya, trans. by Swami Turiyananda. *Vivekacūḍāmaṇi*, trans. and Commentary by the Śaṅkarācārya of Sṛṅgeri. *Vivekacūḍāmaṇi of Śrī Śaṅkarācārya*, trans. by Swami Madhavananda.

79 On her wedding day, Sītā was given a crown jewel to signify her marriage to Rāma. It was this jewel which she gave to Hanumān so that he could take it back to the mainland and convince Rāma that the whereabouts of Sītā were known and that she was alive.

80 'To Be Heard and Done, But Never Quite Seen', Francis X. Clooney, *The Human Condition*, ed. Robert C. Neville, SUNY Press, 2001, pp. 73–99.

81 Roger Marcaurelle, *Freedom Through Inner Renunciation*, SUNY Press, 2000.

82 Ingalls, 'The Study of Saṁkarācārya', *Annals of the Bhandarkar Oriental Research Institute*, vol. XXXII (1952) p. 6. These are BSB, BṛhadUpBh, TaittUpBh, and US.

83 Ibid, pp. 6–7.

84 Hacker, *Philology and Confrontation*, p. 65, 71. Mayeda ('Śaṅkara's *Upadeśasāhasrī*: Its Present Form') says, 'It is impossible to regard the *Vivekacūḍāmaṇi* as authentic since it uses some technical terms foreign to Śaṅkara: for example . . . *anirvacanīya* as a qualification of *avidyā*.'

85 It should be pointed out that Hacker mentions in two places in his other writings that he does not accept the V. as an authentic work of Śaṅkara: see pp. 30 and 128 in Hacker's *Philology and Confrontation*.

86 See V. 138, 150, 276, 315, 336, 361–63.

87 See V. 79, 81–84, 89, 143, 257, 273, 288, 298, 303, 308, 325, 332–33, 378, 397, 519.

88 V. variously terms the wise: *buddha, guru, paṇḍita, muni, mahātma, mahāpuruṣa, prajñavān, satām, sudhiya, viduṣa, vidvān, vipaścitā, vipratā*, etc.

89 V. 1, 15, 33–39, 477.

90 See Hacker, 'Distinctive Features of the Doctrine and Terminology of Śaṅkara' in *Philology and Confrontation*.

91 See Hacker, 'Śaṅkarācārya and Śaṅkarabhagavatpāda,' in *Philology and Confrontation*.

92 BSBh 1.1.1 (*itaretarādhyāsa viṣayin viṣaya ātman anātman satyānṛte mithunīkṛtya*) Also BSBh 1.1.1 where Śaṅkara defines superimposition as the appearance, in the form of remembrance of one thing previously perceived, in another (*smṛtirūpaḥ paratra pūrvadṛṣṭāvabhāsaḥ*).

93 BSBh 1.1.1 (*tam etam evaṁlakṣaṇam adhyāsaṁ paṇḍitā avidyeti manyante*).

94 BSBh 1.1.1; also *Upadeśasāhasrī* 2.2.51.

95 BSBh 1.4.3 (*avidyātmika hi bījaś akthi avyaktaś abdanirdeśāy māyāmayī mahāsuṣuuptiḥ, yasyāṁ śerate svarūpapratibodharahitāḥ saṁsāriṇo jīvāḥ*); also see BṛhUp 3.8.12; BGBh 13.2.

96 See Radhakrishnan, *Indian Philosophy*, Vol. II, p. 565. Also see R. Balasubramanian in *Perspectives of Theism and Absolutism in Indian Philosophy*, p. 48. The extensive scholarship over the philosophical differences between '*avidyā*' and '*māyā*' arose only after Śaṅkara's time.

97 Paul Hacker voiced other ideas about the role of *māyā* in Advaita.

98 Hacker, 'Distinctive Features of the Doctrine and Terminology,' p. 65. Hacker notes that Śaṅkara characterizes *avidyā* as beginningless *once* in the BSBh, but feels that this is not enough and that it was left to later post-Śaṅkara Advaitins to make the concept into a metaphysical term.

99 V. 85, 98, 110, 200, 367.

100 BSBh 1.1.1.
101 V. 110, 'It is compacted of the three *guṇas* . . . She gives birth to this entire world'.
102 BSBh 1.1.1; 2.3.31.
103 BSBh 1.4.3; 2.3.31.
104 Hacker, 'Distinctive Features of the Doctrine and Terminology,' p. 59.
105 Ibid.
106 BSBh 1.1.5 (*tattvānyatvābhyām anirvacanīye nāmarūpe avyākṛte*).
107 See Hacker, 'Distinctive Features of the Doctrine and Terminology,' pp. 71–73.
108 Ibid. p. 78.
109 Ibid. p. 83
110 V. 111, 406, 497, 574.
111 V. 112, 125, 406.
112 V. 67, 245.
113 V. 110, 245.
114 BSBh 1.1.12–19 wherein *ānandamaya* is said to be the Highest Self (*ānandamayo'bhyāsāt, vikāra-śabdān neti cen na prācuryāt, taddhetu vyapadeśāc ca, māntra-varṇikaṁ eva ca gīyate, netaro'nupapatteḥ, bheda-vyapadeśāc ca, kāmāc ca nānumānāpekṣā, asminn asya ca tad yogaṁ śāsti*).
115 TaitUp 2.5; 2.8–9; 3.6. He also declares such in his BṛhUpBh (acknowledging that *Brahman* is bliss, while arguing that one should not say that *Brahman* has bliss as it is found in relative existence, that is, through the mode of relationship.
116 Radhakrishnan holds the view that Śaṅkara gives a two-fold explanation of this position. In the first he contends that Śaṅkara holds that the Self is bliss. However, since this interpretation goes against the unqualified character of the Self, Radhakrishnan contends that the sheath of bliss is a vesture of the Self. See Radhakrishnan, BS, p. 257 and 261.
117 See Ingalls, 'The Study of Śaṅkarācārya,' p. 7, 'The improbable becomes impossible . . . (when) the author of the V. makes the absolute equation of the waking and dream states after the fashion of Gauḍapāda. Śaṅkara may liken the two to each other, but he is careful to distinguish them.'
118 US II.2.109 (also see Mayeda, pp. 43–45).
119 See also ChānUp 8.6.3 & 8.11.1.
120 See Hacker, 'Śaṅkarācārya and Śaṅkarabhagavatpāda.'
121 See Padmapāda, *Pañcapādikā*, *Maṅgalācaraṇa*, v. 3 and *Pañcapādikā*, Viz. S.S. edition, p. 29 line 9 and p. 39 line 4; Sureśvara, *Naiṣkarmyasiddhi* 4. 74 and 76.
122 See Saccidānanda Yogīndra in his commentary on *Śrutisārasamuddharaṇa* 178 (*tān gurūn bhagavatpādākhyān yāvadāyur namāmi*).
123 *Bhāmatī*, pp. 8, 27 (Nirnayasagar edition, ed. by Mahadeva Shastri Bakre, 2nd ed., Bombay, 1909.
124 Commentary on *Naiṣkarmyasiddhi* 1.6, 4.20; 4.22; 4.23.
125 See V. 201. According to Advaita, there are four kinds of non-existence: *prāgabhāva*, *pradhvaṁsābhāva*, *anyonyābhāva*, and *atyantābhāva*. *Prāgabhāva* is defined as 'The non-existence of the effect in its material cause previous to its coming into existence'.
126 Pande, p. 119.
127 Datta, *Six Ways of Knowing*, p. 175.
128 Exactly when and how the term '*jīvanmukti*' originated is debatable. The most commonly accepted designation has post-Śaṅkara Advaita Vedānta propounding the concept with Sāṅkhya-Yoga, Śaiva Siddhānta, and Kāśmīrī

Śaivism following thereafter. However, the concept itself, if not the term, has ancient roots.

129 There are numerous references to this, e.g., BSBh 1.1.4, *brahmabhāvaś ca mokṣaḥ*; US 2.57.

130 See BSBh 3.4.52. Śaṅkara defines embodiedness not as a physical state so much as a matter of false knowledge (*na saśarīratvasya mithyājñānanimittatvāt* – BSBh). BSBh 1.3.19 states, 'Unembodiedness or embodiedness for the Self follows respectively from the fact of discrimination or non-discrimination'. See KaUp 1.2.22 and BG 13.31.

131 *Brahma satyaṁ, jagan mithyā, jīvo brahmaiva nā'paraḥ*. Compare V. 20 where two-thirds of this verse occur. The former verse is an oft-quoted definition of Advaita Vedānta, though its original source is unknown.

132 MāṇḍUp 1.2.7, *ayam ātmā brahma*. Also see: BṛhUp 2.5.19, This Self, the lord of everything, is *Brahman* (*sa vā ayam ātmā sarveṣām bhūtānām adhipatiḥ*) and BṛhUp 1.4.10, I am *Brahman* (*aham brahmāsmi*).

133 'That which is absolutely real, immutable, eternal, all-penetrating like space, exempt from all change, ever-satisfied, impartite, self-luminous; in which neither good nor evil nor effect, nor past nor present nor future has any place – this incorporeal state is called liberation.' *Brahmasūtrabhāṣya*. The word 'all-pervading' (*sarvavyāpīti prāpya-karmatāmapākaroti*) denotes that liberation is not a remote goal someplace else. Nor is it subject to time (*nityatṛptam* and *kālātīte vilasati pade svātmakantīravo naḥ*).

134 V. 240.

135 BSBh. 1.1.11. *Brahman* is known in two forms as qualified by limiting conditions owing to the distinction of name and form, and also as the opposite of this, i.e., as what is free from all limiting conditions whatever . . . thus many (*śruti*) texts show *Brahman* in two forms according as it is known from the standpoint of *vidyā* or from that of *avidyā*. Also see *Vedāntaparibhāṣā* 4, p. 150.

136 '. . . *śruti* speaks of *Brahman* in two forms according as it is known from the standpoint of knowledge or from that of ignorance', BSBh 1.1.11.

137 See *Vedānta-paribhāṣā*, p. 7. 'Just as the notion of one's identity with the body is assumed to be valid knowledge exactly so is this ordinary knowledge – until the Self is true known.'

138 BGBh 2.16. See also BSBh 2.2.11 and 3.2.4.

139 *Māṇḍūkya-kārikā* 4.74, *ajaḥ kalpitasaṃvṛtyā pāramārthena nāpi ajaḥ*.

140 BṛhUp 4.3.22, *yatra vedā avedāḥ*.

141 Within Advaita arose two distinct schools or ways (*prasthāna*) to interpret his thought: the *Vivaraṇa-prasthāna* and the *Bhāmatī-prasthāna*.

142 BṛhUpBhVār 1.4.402.

143 Āstika: Nyāya, Vaiśeṣika, Saṅkhya, Yoga, Mīmāṃsā, and Vedānta, who all accept the authority of the *Veda* and Nāstika: Cārvāka, Jainism, and Buddhism – who all deny the authority of the *Veda*. Thus, in some sense or other, the *āstika* schools all accept *śruti* as a valid means of both empirical and trans-empirical knowledge while the *nāstika* schools do not.

144 Europeans first became acquainted with Advaita in the 1800s. There was a Latin treatise written by F.H. Windischmann (*Sancara sive de theologumenis Vedanticorum*, Bonn, 1833); G.C. Haughton's *The Exposition of the Vedānta Philosophy*, London, 1835; T. Foulkes' *The Elements of the Vedantic Philosophy*, Madras, 1860; and J.R. Ballantyne's *Christianity Contrasted with Hindu*

Philosophy, Madras, 1860. For Muller, see *Three Lectures on the Vedanta Philosophy*, London, 1984, and *The Six Systems of Indian Philosophy*, New Delhi, 1973. For Deussen, see *Das System des Vedanta*, Leipzig, 1883; *Vedanta und Platonismus im Lichte der Kantischen Philosophie*, Berlin, 1922; *The System of the Vedanta*, London, 1972; and *The Philosophy of the Vedanta*, Calcutta, 1957.

145 Setting the date of Śaṅkara's birth is one of the most controversial problems in the history of Indian philosophy. See Sengaku Mayeda's *A Thousand Teachings*, pp. 3–5.

146 Regarding Śaṅkara being the founder of Advaita, see his references to Gauḍapāda in the BSBh. 2.1.9, 1.1.14 as: 'one who knows the traditional way of interpreting the Vedānta or Upaniṣads' (*annoktam dedāntasampradāyavi*).

147 Thibaut, *Vedānta Sūtras* with Śaṅkara's Comm., p. xiv.

148 Natalia Isayeva, *Shankara and Indian Philosophy*, p. 17.

149 MāṇḍUp 2.7.

150 In this usage, *Veda* is synonymous with *mantra* which is called *Brahman*. *Mantra* was called *brahman* (fr. *bṛh* 'to grow, expand, be great') because it is through *mantra* that *brahman* is manifested. *Rgveda* 10.114.8 identifies *brahman* with *vāc*. Also see *Taittīriya Brāhmaṇa* 2.8.8.5; *Rgveda* 1.164. 39, 45.

151 MuṇḍUp 3.2.9.

152 BṛhUp 4.3.22, *yatra vedāḥ avedāḥ*.

153 MuṇḍUp 1.1.3. The sage Śaunaka to Aṅgiras.

154 See RV 1.1.27 where it refers to the works of earlier (*pūrvaiḥ*) and later (*nūtanaiḥ*) authors, and to RV 10.98.9 where it refers to *Agni* being worshipped in bygone ages (*pūrve*) by *ṛṣis*.

155 Indian tradition ascribes this collection and classification to him. That one individual really did such a work is open to doubt, though Advaita Vedānta tradition clearly accepts him as a single individual.

156 Tradition declares that, because the vigor, energy, and strength of human beings had become so deficient with the passage of time, Vedavyāsa divided the entire corpus of the *mantra* literature into four parts called *saṁhitās* for the good of all creatures and taught them to his disciples Paila, Vaiśampāyana, Jaimini, and Sumantu. These four parts developed 144 textual variations (*śākhā*). See *Viṣṇu Purāṇa* 3.2.18; 3.3.4 ff.; 3.4.1 ff.; *Vāyu Purāṇa*, section 60; *Bhāgavata Purāṇa* 1.14–25.

157 V. 13.

158 Vedānta is a name used by many schools of philosophy which have founded their teachings upon the *Upaniṣads*. Because Advaita was the first philosophical school to do this, it is very often referred to as 'the Vedānta'. Besides Advaita, other major schools include: Rāmānuja's (1017–1137) Viśiṣṭādvaita Vedānta, Madhva's (1199–1276) Dvaita Vedānta, Vallabha's (1479–1531) Śuddhādvaita Vedānta, and Caitanya's (1485–1533) Acintyabhedābheda Vedānta.

159 *Vedāntasara*, Chapter 1.3. Compare Baba Muktananda's 'I have nothing new to teach. I wish to bring home to you the same Truth that is revealed through the *Vedas*, the *Upaniṣads*, the *Gītā* and ancient and modern seers. I wish to make it a matter of direct and personal experience in your daily life', *A Search for the Self*, p. 106.

160 The *Brahmasūtras* are also known as: *Śārīrakasūtras*, *Vedāntasūtras*, *Bhikṣusūtras*, and/or the *Uttaramīmāṃsāsūtras*.

161 The *Vedas* are called *śruti* because they were 'heard' by *ṛṣis*.

162 *Mahābhārata, Bhīṣma parvā*, Chapters 25–42.
163 BS 1.1.1. Every *sūtra* of the BS is based upon an Upanisadic passage. The Upaniṣadic verse (*viṣayavākya*) upon which BS 1.1.1 is based comes from the BṛhUp where Yajñavalkya tells Maitreyī, 'The Self ought to be known'.
164 MāṇḍUp 2.7, *Ayam ātma brahma.*
165 Mayeda, *A Thousand Teachings: Upadeśasāhasrī*, pp. 11–12.
166 *Brahma satyam, jagan mithyā, jīvo brahmaiva nā 'paraḥ.*
167 According to Advaita, a *mahāvākya* is an identity statement; that is, a statement which directly declares the essential identity between the individual and the Absolute. Any other types of statement is, at best, an indirect account (e.g., to say that *Brahman* is great does not directly reveal one's own identity with *Brahman*). The *mahāvākya* is the essence of the *Upaniṣads* precisely because of its unique purport.
168 AitUp 3.1.3 of RV, '*prajñānam brahma*'.
169 MāṇḍUp 2.7 of AV, '*ayam ātmā brahma*'.
170 ChānUp 6.8.7 of SV, '*tat tvam asi*'.
171 BṛhUp 1.4.10 of YV, '*aham brahmāsmi*'.
172 *Pañcadaśī* 2.20, *sajātīya vijātīya svagata bhedara hitam.*
173 See BṛhUp 2.3.6; 3.8.8; KaUp 1.3.15; US 1.17.70; *Ātmabodha* 29.
174 BṛhUp Bh.2.3.6, 'There is no other and more appropriate description than this 'not-this.'
175 ChānUp, 3.14.1, *sarvam khalvidam brahman.*
176 TaittUp, 2.1, *satyam, jñānam anantam brahman.*
177 ChānUp, 7.25.2.
178 V. 521. Perception of the Self is radically empirical, for it is not mediated by the sense organs. Ordinary empirical sense perception is always mediated, never all-encompassing. Ordinary sense perceptions are, also, always open to doubt – the Self never is.
179 V. 240; US 1.2.1.
180 V. 87–92; *Ātmabodha* 10–11.
181 V. 93–96; *Ātmabodha* 12.
182 V. 88–107.
183 Throughout Advaita works, the seemingly apparent difference between the individual and the Absolute is explained by invoking ignorance (*avidyā* / *māyā*).
184 '. . . *śruti* speaks of *Brahman* in two forms according as it is known from the standpoint of knowledge or from that of ignorance', BSBh. 1.1.11.
185 BSBh. 1.1.11.
186 ChānUp 6.2.1, *ekam eva advitīyam.*
187 Ibid., II.4.14.
188 BSBh. Preamble; V. 108. See Radhakrishnan, *Indian Philosophy*, vol. II, p. 565. Also see R. Balasubramanian in *Perspectives of Theism and Absolutism in Indian Philosophy*, p. 48. The extensive scholarship over the philosophical differences between '*avidyā*' and '*māyā*' arose only after Śaṅkara's time.
189 Māṇḍ. Up. with Gauḍapāda's *Kārikā* and Śaṅkara's *Commentary*, 2.12, p. 97.
190 Ibid., 3.19, p. 166.
191 Mahadevan, *The Philosophy of Advaita*, p. 79.
192 BSBh. 1.1. Preamble; V. 55; 137; 192.
193 See US 2.1.4–6; V. 9–11; 22–27; *Ātmabodha* 1. Advaita's well-known fourfold requirement (*sādhana catuṣṭaya*) sets forth numerous qualifications required in a seeker before one is finally initiated into the knowledge of the Self.

194 *Nitya-anitya vastu viveka*, V. 21. This idea is so prevalent in Vedānta literature, that numerous examples could be quoted from any book chosen.

195 *Upadeśa Pañcakam, sadvidvān upasṛpyatām, pratidinam tatpāduke sevyatām*||
brahmaikākṣaramarthyatām śrutiśiro vākyam samākarṇyatām.

196 Taitt. Up. 1.3.3.

197 The great sage Vālmīki was liberated even though he uttered the name of God backwards. Furthermore, it enabled him to tell the life story of Rāma. By meditating on the name, Prahlāda was protected again and again. The outcast Ajāmila was made holy by the name. Rukmini balanced the scales against Satyabhama. Hanuman lept over the ocean and the monkeys built a bridge using Rāma's name. The lists are endless. Even the great God *Śiva* has been relieved from the torments of poison by the power of the name. Therefore, chant the name continuously.

198 BSBh 1.1.1.

199 BṛhUpBh 1.2.20.

PART TWO
The Crown Jewel of Discrimination

sarva-vedānta-siddhānta-gocaraṁ tam agocaram |
govindaṁ paramānandaṁ sad-guruṁ praṇato'smy aham ||1||

I offer my salutations to Govinda, the Divine Master, the embodiment of the highest bliss, who is beyond thought and speech, and who is the culmination of all wisdom.

Traditionally, Indian philosophical treatises begin with an invocation to God and/or to one's Guru. Śaṅkara, in this invocation, ingeniously, insightfully, and subtly reveals the non-duality of Advaita even as he offers his obeisance simultaneously to both God and Guru. He was able to do this because one of the names for God is Govinda and the name of Śaṅkara's Guru was also Govinda. Intriguingly, this stanza simultaneously admits both interpretations. Underlying this play of language is the insight that God, Guru, and the goal of life for the individual are not different; they are the same.

The Vedic injunction, 'Only that person who obeys, can command' provides the rationale for first invoking God and Guru. Why are you looking for God in town after town, temple after temple? God dwells in the heart within. Why look in the East and in the West? Don't look for God, look for the Guru. God dwells within you; in truth, you are God. You don't need to find God; you need to find a Guru who will guide you to yourself. By offering reverence to God and the Guru, one pays respect to: (1) the Creator of all that is created; (2) one's tradition, which is both ancient and authoritative; (3) the time-honored prerequisites for a spiritual life, e.g., humility, devotion, respect, and discipline.

In this introductory verse, Śaṅkara affirms the time-honored wisdom that from the ultimate point of view, God has no name: 'Words return along with the mind, not attaining It' (TaittUp 2.4.1). This is representative of numerous Upaniṣadic passages which echo this wisdom, 'The eye does not go there, nor speech, nor mind. The Absolute is not to be known as such and such' (KenaUp 1.3–5). And yet, mysteriously, these same *Upaniṣads* declare, 'Name is the Absolute' (BṛhUp 4.1.2); 'This Absolute indeed shines forth, when one speak with language' (KauṣUp. 2.13); 'The ultimate abode of language is the Absolute' (RV 1.1.164).

govinda = (from *go* + *vid* = 'speech' + 'knower', i.e., Knower of the scriptures) or (from *go* + *inda* = 'cows' + 'master', i.e., cowherd). Govinda is an epithet for Śrī Kṛṣṇa as well as one of Lord Viṣṇu's names; **gocaram tam agocaram** = beyond the range of the sense organs, especially the range of the eye; **pranām; namaḥ** = *namaḥ* literally means 'to bow, to salute, to make obeisance to'. It is a corrupt form of '*na-mama*' ('this is not mine') and indicates, 'O Lord, whatever I am about to think, say, plan, and do is "not-mine" but yours.' To emphasize this, it is customary to *pranām* or prostrate oneself or, at the very least, to put one's hands together in a gesture of humility; **sadguru** = (from *sat* + *guru* = 'truth, Reality, Existence, Being, Essence' + teacher, preceptor, great, 'heavy,' weighty, venerable, from the root *gṛ* = 'to invoke or to praise'); *sadguru* has been translated as Divine Master throughout this book; **paramānandaṁ** = highest or supreme bliss; **sarva-vedānta-siddhānta** = culmination of all wisdom; or, the essence of all the *Upaniṣads* (*veda* + *anta* = '*Vedas*; wisdom; knowledge' + 'end of; culmination; essence). The word *vedānta* was initially a synonym for the *Upaniṣads* and derivatively, a name for various philosophical schools of thought which base their teachings upon the *Upaniṣads*.

jantūnāṁ nara-janma durlabham ataḥ puṁstvaṁ tato vipratā
tasmād vaidika-dharma-mārga-paratā vidvattvam asmāt param |
ātmānātma-vivecanaṁ svanubhavo brahmātmanā saṁsthitiḥ
muktir no śata-koṭi-janma sukṛtaiḥ puṇyair vinā labhyate ||2||

For all things subject to birth, birth in a human body is rare. Even rarer to obtain are strength[1] of body and mind. Rarer still is purity. More difficult than these is a desire to live a spiritual life. Rarest of all is to have an understanding of the scriptures. As for discrimination between the Self and the not-self, direct Self-realization, continuous union with the Absolute, final and complete liberation are not to be obtained without meritorious deeds done in a hundred billion well-lived lives.

How many myriad things are there in the universe! Think of the billions of stars and specks of dust and grains of sand and microbes beyond count. Innumerable are the drops of water and leaves on trees and atoms beyond count. Of all the entities in the universe, those with a human body are very rare! This is not speculation but an obvious objective observation. And, what is rare and difficult to obtain is generally considered to be precious, valuable.

The physical body is precious. Why? Ignoring for the moment spiritual realization, it is because one has a physical body with which one has been able to enjoy all the pleasures that have come one's way throughout one's life. All of the delicious foods and wonderful sights and relationships, colors and fragrances and sounds beyond compare, everything that has been experienced is only because one has a physical body. The body is the vehicle by which and through which a person is able to enjoy all that one deems enjoyable. Thus, birth in a physical body is rare, valuable and precious.

According to Śaṅkara, the individual soul is a conscious living being. The individual is singled out as the principal being because individuals have eligibility for action and knowledge. He said in his commentary of the AitUp 3.2.3, 'The *ātman* is expanded only in human beings. They, indeed, are most endowed with intelligence. They give expression to what is known. They see what is known. They know what is to come. They know the visible and the invisible. They perceive the immortal through the mortal. Thus are humans endowed. But with other animals, eating and drinking alone constitute the sphere of their knowledge.'

Even rarer and more difficult to obtain than the physical body is a strong, inwardly inspired or awakened (*vipratā*) body and mind. The word 'vipratā' has, in common parlance, come to mean 'the rank or condition of a priest (*brāhmaṇa*)' and, combined with the word 'puṁstvaṁ' meaning 'strength, masculinity,' this verse is usually translated as 'more difficult to obtain than a human body is to be born as a male member of the priestly caste'. Orthodox interpreters have generally interpreted this verse to mean that the act of a male birth in a *brahmin* family is an indispensable prerequisite for Self-realization. Commentators, scholars, and apologists have gone to great lengths in an attempt to expound this interpretation. To mention but a few: Women are (declared to be) not fit to realize the Self because of their involvement in domestic duties, child-bearing, child-rearing, and/or sense-pleasures; rulers and warriors (*kṣatriya*), business people (*vaiśya*), and laborers (*sūdra*) are unfit to realize the Self because their activities are directed outwards; renunciation (*sannyāsa*) is said to be reserved for *brahmins*. However, there is another interpretation of the word '*vipratā*'. A possible interpretation is that this verse is describing the stages of self-development. And in regards to the Self, *vedāntic* spiritual practice does not pertain to the physical body, male or female. Enquiry and reflection are categorically declared to be the means to Self-realization. Thus, the word '*vipratā*' can be interpreted as describing

[1] See MuṇḍUp 3.2.4, 'This Self cannot be attained by one without strength'. Śaṅkara, commenting on this, said, 'Strength is at the root of all great achievements.' Also see BṛhUp 5.14.4, 'Truth is based on strength'.

qualifications and qualities and not gender or caste. *Vipra* literally means 'stirred; quivering; inwardly inspired or excited; wise; learned; a sage or seer'. A qualified aspirant, a seeker of the Self, must be able to discriminate the Real from the unreal; must be able to be detached and dispassionate; must be intellectually strong and tranquil; must possess a sharp intellect which is able to vigorously reflect and tirelessly and unceasingly meditate on the Self. Firmness of determination, steadiness of composure, detachment and discipline, and a burning desire to know the inner Self are required – not merely a male *brahmin* body. A substantial portion of the Vedic hymns themselves were either given by female seers (*ṛṣi*) or were addressed to females by male *ṛṣis*. To exclude females from being qualified seekers of the Self is to blindly ignore both the subject matter of Vedānta as well as a whole host of knowers of the Self such as Maitreyī, Gārgī, Romaśā, Lopāmudrā, Apālā, Kadrū, Viśvavārā, Ghoṣā, Juhū, Vāgāmbhṛinī, Paulomī, Jaritā, Urvaśī, Yamī, Indrānī, Sāvitrī, and so on. Thus, to have *vipratvam*, birth in a family need be neither necessary nor sufficient, while recognizing, as in all cases, hereditary and environment do play a role. Perhaps birth and gender used to play a significant role in the interpretation of certain doctrines and in the admission to a *gurukula*, and there are those who perpetuate this type of thinking, though it is possible that a broader meaning may be found herein.

A strong and sharp intellect is necessary in order to determine and digest the illusory nature of names and forms. To conclude that the sand is sand and the rope is a rope and not to be deluded into thinking there is water in a mirage or a snake underfoot takes a strong and sharp intellect. To remain quiet and reason out that what was not there before and what will pass away in the morning must therefore be merely fleeting appearances is the work of a (strong) intellect. In regards to the necessity of strength, see verse 343.

narajanma = human birth; **durlabham** = rare, scarce, seldom found; **vipratā** = 'stirring, excited, to tremble, shake, quiver;' sage, learned, priest (*brāhmaṇa*) see above commentary; **puṁstvaṁ** = strength; virility; masculinity; **vaidika dharma mārga** = the path of righteousness as pertaining to the Vedas; **ātmānātmaviveka** = discrimination between the Self and not-self; **svanubhavo** = Self-realization (*sva* = one's own; *anubhava* = direct, immediate experience); **brahman** = the Absolute, supreme Reality (from the root *bṛh* = 'to expand; greater than the greatest'); **ātma** = the Self (from the root *at* = 'to breathe' or the root *āp* = 'to pervade'. One can breathe because of the Self. One can search for the Self only because of the Self. One can think only because of the Self. Without the Self, the body is a worthless corpse); **puṇya** = meritorious actions.

durlabhaṁ trayam evaitat daivānugraha-hetukam |
manuṣyatvaṁ mumukṣutvaṁ mahā-puruṣa-saṁśrayaḥ ||3||

Rare and difficult to obtain are these three: a human birth, a burning-desire-for-liberation, and association with great-beings. They are the results of divine grace.

This is an oft-quoted verse of Śaṅkara's which delineates three boons that are the results of divine grace. To obtain a human body, which is so rare and precious, involves grace. To have a burning desire for liberation is even rarer and more precious. Out of all the human beings in the world, there are very few who are seriously, earnestly, continuously seeking either God or the Self. This is a simple fact. Look around. There are few people at any given time, who are completely consumed with the spiritual quest. And of all those individuals who both possess a human body and who are earnestly seeking the divine, even fewer have the great good fortune to have the association with a Divine Master, with a knower of the truth. As well, according to Advaita, divine grace, though absolutely necessary for the removal of ignorance, is not something to be acquired. It is there all along. It is the innermost Self of everyone. All that is necessary is to know of its existence. Thus, grace has been compared to the sun, always present and eternally shining, but one must turn one's eyes in its direction and look at it.

Mumukṣu is defined as '*mokṣam ikṣasu yasya sah*' – one who has a burning desire for liberation is a *mumukṣu*. For references to *mumukṣutva* see V. 19, 28, 29, 30, 31, 44, 84, 120, 178, and 576.

See V. 29, 42, 50, 138, 149, 477, 489, 518, and 519 for references to grace.

trayam = three; **daivānugraha** = divine grace. There are said to be three types of grace: *sādhana* or the grace of self-effort; *guru* or the grace of a Master; and *divya* or divine grace. **manuṣyatvaṁ** = human birth; **mumukṣutvaṁ** = an earnest burning desire for liberation; **mahāpuruṣa** = great person; spiritual giant; **saṁśrayaḥ** = associated with, connected.

labdhvā kathaṁcit nara-janma durlabhaṁ
tatrāpi puṁstvaṁ śruti-pāra-darśanam I
yassvātma-muktyau na yateta mūḍhadhīḥ
sa ātmahā svaṁ vinihanty-asad-grahāt II4II

That person, having somehow obtained a rare human birth, together with bodily and mental strength and a correct understanding of the scriptures, who does not strive for liberation, is a fool.[1] Verily, such a person commits suicide,[2] clinging to things unreal.

Is it not strange that whatever it is that one wants, desires, thinks about, or ponders over is *something other* than the one who is wanting/desiring/thinking/pondering? One is continually seeking that which one is not. A person not only wants to maintain, but also to sustain and nourish, him or herself with things other than themselves. Because one believes in oneself, the thinker, seer, hearer has faith that what one thinks, sees, and hears is real. Instead, why not doubt the things which come and go – thoughts, sights, sounds – and hold on to that which is always there and is foundational to it all – yourself. Find out if you are the body. Find out if you are the mind. Enquire.

Is it not ironic that the general definition of a renunciant is a person who has given up the things of this world? But who is the true renunciant? Is it a person who has renounced the things of the world (for the Self) or is it a person who has renounced the Self (for the things of the world)? The *Upaniṣads* declare that one who knows the Self, obtains all, and that one who does not know the Self, knows nothing. If this is so, then who is the greater fool?

---

1 See V. 4, 5, 77, 162, 163, 220, and 549 for fools (*mūḍhadhīḥ*). Also see MuṇḍUp 1.2.8, 'Fools, abiding in the midst of ignorance, wise in their own esteem, thinking themselves to be learned, afflicted with troubles, go about like the blind leading the blind'; also KaUp 1.2.5; MaitrīUp 7.9; BG 17.5–6.

2 See IśāUpBh 3, 'Because a person neglects his ever-present Self through the ignorance, he is called one who commits suicide'.

labdhvā = one who has obtained, gained, received; **śruti** = primary scripture, i.e., Vedas (lit. 'that which is heard'); **mūḍhadhīḥ** = fool; one with a foolish mind; **vinihanti** = calamity, destruction, suicide; asat = unreal, what is not real.

itaḥ konvasti mūḍhātmā yas tu svārthe pramādyati |
durlabhaṁ mānuṣaṁ dehaṁ prāpya tatrāpi pauruṣam ||5||

What greater fool[1] is there than a person who, having obtained this rare human birth, together with bodily and mental strength, fails, through delusion, to realize their own highest good?

KaUp 1.2.1 declares, 'Different is the good (*śreyas*), and different, indeed, is the pleasant (*preyas*). These two, with different purposes, bind a person. Of these two, it is well for one who takes hold of the good; but that person who chooses the pleasant, fails in their aim.' Naciketas has just asked Lord Yama about immortality for his third boon. Yama replied that there are two paths: the good and the pleasing. He says, 'I can tell you about them, but, you will have to make this discovery yourself. I will be your guide and I will bestow my blessings upon you, but you must choose; you must do the spiritual practice.' All people are born with a capacity to make choices. Every moment choices must be made, in regards to thoughts, words, and deeds. No one can avoid this. And, both the good and the pleasing promise the same thing: happiness and satisfaction. Both come to one whether one wants them or not. The moment one encounters the pleasing, the moment it is experienced, one likes it and wants it. It appeals directly to the senses and provides immediate gratification. It gives instant pleasure. However, it doesn't care about the future. The good, on the other hand, makes no reference to pleasure or displeasure. It merely fosters what is spiritually uplifting. It demands a disciplined approach and promises eternal bliss, even if its fruits are not readily apparent. It demands a one-pointed determination. It is true that everything one experiences, somehow involves the Self. Thus, all things are worthy of respect. But, a proper attitude is necessary. To handle fire, one should use tongs. To look at the sun requires protective glasses. BṛhUp 1.4.7 declares that what one knows empirically is true of the Self, but incomplete and hence imperfect ('the Self they see not for, as seen, it is incomplete'). So long as a person thinks of him/herself as a physical body, possessing natural functions and thinking, seeing, hearing, and so on, they do not know the Self in its fullness.

See MuṇḍUp 3.1.1: 'Two birds, companions always united, cling to the self-same tree. Of these two, one eats the sweet fruit and the other looks on without eating.' See also MuṇḍUp 3.1.2–10; RV 1.164.20; ŚvetUp 4.6; KaUp 1.3.1.

prāpya = attaining, reaching, arriving at, finding; **tatrā** = in that place, on that occasion.

paṭhantu śāstrāṇi yajantu devān
kurvantu karmāṇi bhajantu devatāḥ |
ātmaikya-bodhena vinā vimuktiḥ
na siddhyati brahma-śatāntare'pi ||6||

---

[1] See V. 4, 77, 162, 163, 220, and 549 for fools (*mūḍhātmā*). See MuṇḍUp 1.2.8, 'Fools, abiding in the midst of ignorance, wise in their own esteem, thinking themselves to be learned, afflicted with troubles, go about like the blind leading the blind'; also KaUp 1.2.5; MaitrīUp 7.9; BG 17.5–6.

Individuals may read and recite the scriptures, sacrifice to the gods, perform rituals, worship deities. Still, liberation will not occur, even after hundreds of millions of years, without a personal experience of one's identity with the Self.

What one is seeking for is the one who is seeking. Individuals practice spiritual disciplines, read, recite, sacrifice, worship, because they have some destination in mind, something to attain which they feel they presently lack. Śaṅkara declares that what is eternal is here and now; what is eternal is the Self. Where could you go to get it; what could you do? If there was somewhere the Self was not, one could go there. But as the Self is ever-present; there never has been a time or place when one was not the Self. For spiritual practice, there is the obvious and necessary requirement of somebody to practice, something to practice, and some intention for practicing. Practices come and go. However, you, the practicer, are present whether you are practicing or not. Find out who this seeker is. Śaṅkara declares that spiritual practices are not for self-realization but for purifying the intellect and removing old habits, especially identification with the body. As Mayeda (*A Thousand Teachings: Upadeśasāhasrī*, pp. 11–12) said, 'Philosophy is not his [Śaṅkara's] aim but is rather a vital weapon with which to fulfill this aim, which is to rescue people out of transmigratory existence.' When one is performing spiritual practices, the Self is there all along.

The Self must be realized first-hand. Second-hand information is not ultimately satisfying. If it has not been directly realized, it is only something that one hopes is true, or wants to be true, or tries to make true. These may be comforting, but comfort is not ultimately adequate. When one is hungry, it is not enough, it is not satisfying merely to hear about food. Nor is it enough to merely see food or for someone else to eat. What is required in order to satisfy one's hunger is that one must actually eat oneself.

See BrhUp 1.4.15, 'If a person does not know this, performs even a grand and holy rite, it is sure to fade away after their death. It is the Self alone that a person should venerate'; Also MuṇḍUp 1.2.8–10; 1.7.7–11; 3.2.3; BṛhUp 4.4.23; KaUp 1.2.11 'the endless fruit of rites'.

paṭha = to read or recite; **śāstra** = scripture; teaching (from the verb root *śās* = 'to rule, teach'). The sacred books of Indian thought are divided into four categories: primary scripture (*śruti*), secondary scripture (*smṛti*), historical/mythological (*purāṇa*) and epics (*itihāsa*), and religious treatises (*tantra*); **yajña** = sacrifice, sacrificial ceremony; **deva** = god; celestial being; one who shines (from the verb root *div* = 'to shine'); **kurvantu karmāṇi** = perform rituals; **bhajantu devatā** = worship the gods; **vimukti** = liberation.

amṛtatvasya nāśāsti vittenetyeva hi śrutiḥ |
bravīti karmaṇo mukteḥ ahetutvaṁ sphuṭaṁ yataḥ ||7||

The scriptures declare that there is no hope of immortality by means of wealth. Hence, it is clear that actions cannot be the cause of liberation.

The reference is to the Yājñavalkya-Maitreyī dialogue in BṛhUp 2.4.2 (Then said Maitreyī), 'If indeed, venerable sir, this whole earth filled with wealth were mine, would I be immortal through that?' 'No,' said Yājñavalkya. 'Like the life of the rich even so would your life be. Of immortality, however, there is no hope through wealth.' Note the vedic saying, 'Neither by rituals, nor by progeny, nor by riches, but by renunciation alone is immortality attained.' Nachiketas declares, 'Humans are not contented with wealth' (KaUp 1.1.27); see also BṛhUp 4.5.6; KaUp 1:2.1; 1.2.10.

Actions take innumerable forms, both secular and spiritual. Immortality, or eternal bliss, cannot be obtained by impermanent, momentary actions. Actions may certainly give moments of happiness, but to recognize that one is happy requires that one give up all thoughts of obtaining something new. Who one really is has no need of, no desire for, anything. The concept of liberation points solely to this fact. Liberation is simple and this simplicity is the deepest secret. All striving, all practicing, are seen as irrelevant in the vastness of this utter simplicity.

Wealth (*vitta*), in this verse, implies not only material wealth but also the wealth of experiences. One's sense organs convey a myriad of experiences, all of which come and go, begin and end. Thus, wealth of all types, being transitory, can never convey liberation which is eternal.

amṛta = lit., 'not death' (from the verb root *mṛ* = 'to die' + the prefix *a* = 'not'), immortality; elixir; **vittam** = wealth.

ato vimuktyai prayateta vidvān
saṁnyasta-bāhyārtha-sukhaspṛhaḥ san ।
santaṁ mahāntaṁ samupetya deśikaṁ
tenopadiṣṭārtha-samāhitātmā ॥8॥

Therefore, giving up all desire[1] for pleasures coming from external objects, let the wise person[2] strive for liberation. Let such a person, in the prescribed manner, approach[3] a Great One, who by their realization is to be equated with Truth,[4] and become absorbed whole-heartedly in the Truth taught by him.

The quest for enlightenment begins when one gives up desiring external pleasures. Eternal satisfaction, permanent happiness, is not possible from temporary, impermanent

[1] See BṛhUp 4.4.7, 'When all desires that dwell in the heart are given up, then does the mortal become immortal'. Also see KaUp 2.3.14; BG 2.55–71.

[2] See BG, 'Whatever pleasures are born from sense-object contact are only sources of sorrow for they have a beginning and an end. The wise do not delight in such.'

[3] See MuṇḍUp 1.2.12, 'For the sake of this knowledge, let him only approach, with sacrificial fuel in hand, a teacher who is learned in the scriptures and established in the Absolute'; also MuṇḍUp 1.2.13 says, 'To that student of tranquil mind and calm disposition, who had come to the Master in the right manner, that learned one faithfully imparted knowledge of the Absolute.' Also see KaivUp 1.5 '. . . bowing with devotion to the Master'; See Satyakāma Jābāla's approach and Gautama's ultimate acceptance in ChānUp 4.4.1–5. KaUp 1.2.8. says, 'Unless taught by one who knows It, one cannot gain access to it.' See also BṛhUp 2.1.14; ChānUp 4.14.1–4, 6.14.1, 7.1.1; TaittUp. 1.2.3., 1.3.3., 1.9.1., 3.1.1; KaUp 1.2.7. There are also the well-known phrases, 'One obtains knowledge from a teacher (*ācāryavān puruṣo veda*)'; 'Knowledge obtained from a teacher has the greatest efficiency'; and Śaṅkara's frequent use of '*gurum eva*' (only by the grace of the *guru*).

[4] See ChānUp, 'If a person knows that the Absolute exists (has realized the Absolute), they are called a *san*.'

The characteristics of a Great One are given in V. 35.

sensory indulgence. The objects which the five senses record can, at best, give a momentary fulfillment. Though even there, it is said that it is not the object itself which gives one happiness, but the fulfillment of the desire for it. When the desire is present, while there is still a wanting to achieve, to obtain something, there is no happiness. The desire disappears only at the moment of fulfillment. What is obvious from this is that objects and the desire for them is transitory; they come and go. Whatever comes and goes is not permanent, and to expect permanent happiness from a temporary thing is foolishness.

A person is wise (*vidvān*) when they understand and fully accept that the pleasures which spring from external objects are transitory and therefore ultimately a source of sorrow. A wise person understands that the very act of reaching out causes both desire and suffering to arise. For a wise person, the world and all its things will still be there, but they will no longer cause trouble or suffering because the desire to obtain pleasure and happiness through them will no longer arise.

When a seeker begins to strive for liberation and when he begins to understand that permanent happiness cannot be gained through the pursuit of worldly pleasures, a true teacher must be sought. One should then look for a perfect being, someone who has permanently established him/herself in the state of permanent bliss. This is so because the Self, the supreme reality, is infinitely subtle and not to be known through argument, reasoning, hearsay, or thought. Because a Great One knows this truth, the Great One can point towards it. Such is the case even in the world of objects, e.g., the road to a place has to be learnt from one who knows it, knowledge of a science must be learnt from one who knows the science.

The Great One, the knower of the truth, is here spoken of as a '*san*'. *Sat* means 'existent, real, true'. The famous BG verse 2.16, 'Of the real there is no nonbeing and of the non-real there is no being' declares that that which exists, exists forever and that that which does not exist, never is. One who knows this truth is 'existent, real, true', and it is only from one who knows this that this truth can be learned. Further, such a being is described as Great (*mahān*). A Great One is one who is not limited. To be great, greater than the greatest, is also the root meaning of the word '*Brahman*' (the Absolute).

A Great One gives spiritual instruction or *upadeśa* to the seeker. *Upadeśa* literally means 'restoring an object to its proper place'. That is, the seeker thinks that he or she is different from the Self, their true and natural state, and pursues objects of sense-gratification. The Master restores the seeker's thoughts to their natural place. Or, a spiritual instruction can be understood as 'presenting an apparently distant object to close proximity'. The Master reveals that what the seeker had thought was far away, distant and different from oneself, is really immediate and identical with oneself.

vidvān = wise, learned. In this context, a wise person is more than just a scholar, learned in book knowledge and grammar. It implies a person who is able to discriminate between the Real and the unreal, the permanent and the transitory. **bāhyārtha** = 'coming from external objects'; **sukha** = pleasant, happy, agreeable, joyful (from *su* = 'good, fine' + *kha* = 'state'); **san(tam)** = Truth, Real, Existence. That (or he) which (or who) exists. A Great One Is (*sat*), i.e., the verse *santam mahāntam*. **mahān** = great, neither divided nor limited; **deśika** = one who gives instructions or teachings (*upadeśa*) to a student; **samupaiti** = to come together, to approach, to have recourse to; **tenopadiṣṭārthasamāhitātmā** = with a mind (*ātma*) which is concentrated on the meaning (*ārtha*) of his teachings.

uddhared ātmanātmānaṁ magnaṁ saṁsāra-vāridhau |
yogārūḍhatvam āsādya samyag-darśana niṣṭhayā ||9||

By attaining a state-of-detachment-and-desirelessness, by firm knowledge of the Absolute, let one disentangle oneself from the ocean of worldly existence.

The explicit purport of what is implied in this verse will be explained in the next seven verses. The means for becoming firmly established in the Absolute begins with detachment and desirelessness or what is technically known as the state of *yogarudha*. When perfect in this, when firmly established therein, success is achieved and there is a correct understanding or vision (*darśana*) of the truth.

Worldly existence (*saṁsāra*) has been compared to the ocean in this verse. Just as the ocean is vast and deep and cannot be crossed without the aid of a ship, so too is worldly existence. If one does not know how to swim and one ventures into the ocean where there are waves and whirlpools and dangerous creatures, one will suffer and eventually drown. In the *Lakṣmīnṛsiṁha stotra*, Śaṅkara says, 'O Lord! Extend Thy helping hand so as to rescue me from the vast ocean of *saṁsāra* beset with the all-devouring monster of time and the mounting waves of passions.'

Śaṅkara, in his BSBh 1.1.4. also says, 'Their aim (knowledge of the Absolute) is to be the means of detachment from the objects towards which one is naturally attracted.'

saṁsāra = (from the verbal root *sṛ* = 'to flow' and *sam* = 'together') empirical existence; the wheel of birth and death; transmigration; the flux of the world; worldly illusion; **vāridhau** = ocean; **yogārūḍha** = BG 6.4, 'one has attained a state of detachment and desirelessness when one does not get attached to sense objects or to works, and has renounced all purposes'; **niṣṭhayā** = grounded or resting in; firmly established; **samyagdarśana** = right or correct understanding, right vision.

saṁnyasya sarva-karmāṇi bhava-bandha-vimuktaye |
yatyatām paṇḍitair dhīraiḥ ātmābhyāsa upasthitaiḥ ||10||

For release from the bonds of empirical existence, the wise and learned person completely gives up all desire-motivated actions[1] and commences an unceasing contemplation of the Self.

Simply put, if you set aside your ego for a moment you will realize that you, the traveler, are that which you are seeking. Everything is within you. The supreme inner stillness is your destination. Or, to put it another way, any seeking is a denial of the presence of the sought.

Fulfilled desires only breed more desires. Unfulfilled desires lead to anger, frustration, and confusion. Desires distract one from making a direct Self-enquiry. A quiet mind is what is required for this enquiry. Why? Because, compared to the body, to things, the mind is subtle. And the mind, although subtle, is gross compared to the Self. Even though one is beyond the mind, one knows with the mind. Thus, if one improves one's instrument, one's knowledge improves.

---

[1] Actions are done with a view to achieve one of four results: production, purification, transformation, or attainment. In regards to attaining liberation, action is of no use for liberation is eternal, not something to be produced. Liberation has no qualities or impurities and thus is not something to be purified. Since it is immutable, it is not something to be transformed. Since it is always attained as the Self of everyone, it is not something to be attained.

See BṛhUp 3.5.1, 'Wise seekers of the Absolute, having known that Self, having overcome desire for progeny, wealth, worlds, live the life of a renunciant'; also BG 5.26.

saṁnyasya sarva-karmāṇi = completely giving up all actions which are desire-based; **bhava-bandha-vimuktaye** = freedom from the bonds of worldly life (*bhāva* = existence, state of being, from the verb root *bhū* = 'to become, exist); **paṇḍita** = learned, scholar, one who has second-hand knowledge; **dhīraiḥ** = one who has control of their intellect. See KaUp 2.1.1, 'The Self is not to be sought through the senses . . . The wise, in search of immortality, turn their sight inward and see the Self within (*kaścid dhīraḥ pratyag ātmānam aikṣad āvṛtta cakṣur amṛtatvam icchan*); also KaUp 1.2.24, 'Not he who has not a concentrated mind (*nāsamāhitaḥ*)'; **ātmābhyāsa** = perpetual contemplation or continuous and constant practice (of the mind) on the Self.

cittasya śuddhaye karma na tu vastūpalabdhaye |
vastusiddhir vicāreṇa na kiṁcit karma-koṭibhiḥ ||11||

Actions help to purify the mind; not to perceive reality. Reality is attained through enquiry and never in the slightest degree by even a hundred million actions.

When a person makes an effort or employs a method to achieve something, it implies that thing is not present now and will come into being at some future time. But the reality, according to Śaṅkara, is ever-present. To obtain that which is already obtained, no effort is necessary. This is technically known as *prāptasya prāptiḥ* or the attaining of the aleady attained. Only to achieve that which is not already achieved will effort prove efficacious. Actions can never get one to that which one already is. Further, the idea of doing something or not doing something are both impediments. What one *is* does not involve what one does, doing something.

See KaUp 1.2.23, 'This Self cannot be attained by instruction, nor by intellectual power, nor even through much hearing'; also MuṇḍUp 3.1.5 and 3.1.8; BṛhUp 1.4.15; 4.4.23. See V. 138, 150, 177–78, 183, 276–77, 315, 336, 361–63, 367, 370–71, 384, and 408 for purification of the mind.

citti śuddhi = pure mind; **vastu** = reality, essence, the real, object, thing; **vicāra** = enquiry, reflection, investigation, introspection, discernment; **karma** = action.

samyag-vicārataḥ siddhā rajju-tattvāvadhāraṇā |
bhrāntodita-mahāsarpa-bhava-duḥkha-vināśinī ||12||

Proper enquiry establishes a conviction about the true nature of the rope and removes the great suffering of worldly existence caused by the delusory snake.

A proper discernment is the recognition that it is folly to chase impermanent, transitory things in the hope that they will give permanent, eternal happiness. Appearances can never be trusted. Anything that comes and goes, changes, ultimately vanishes, cannot be trusted to do anything except come and go. For one who has seen the rope as a rope, there will never be a mistaken impression that it is a snake. Delusion comes from ignorance of the rope, from an ignorance of what is real and what is appearance. Having been bitten by the serpent of ignorance, one suffers the agony of a snake bite. If left alone, one will exhibit the effects of poisoning too.

See V. 63, 112, 140, 199, 237, 248, 303, 388, 405, 407, and 550 where Śaṅkara makes references to a snake.

rajju = rope; **tattvādhāraṇā** = conviction of the true nature; **siddha** = complete, established, perfect, accomplished; **sarpa** = snake; **mahā** = great; **duḥkha** = suffering, pain, sorrow, grief, unhappiness (from *dur* = 'bad' + *kha* = 'state').

arthasya niścayo dṛṣṭo vicāreṇa hitoktitaḥ |
na snānena na dānena prāṇāyāma-śatena vā ||13||

The goal of life is seen to arise from an enquiry in accord with the words of the wise and never by taking sacred baths or performing acts of charity or by hundreds of breathing exercises.

How to gain conviction of the truth? First, one must hear the truth from the lips of one who is established therein. Traditionally, the student goes to the Master and says, 'Please, Master, rescue me as I am drowning in worldly existence.' The Master declares, 'You are That. Your involvement in the bondage of worldly life is due to ignorance.' Thus, in order to overcome the darkness of ignorance, the Master's knowledge is essential for one who wants knowledge of the Self.

When a person knows the false as false, then no action is necessary at all. One is free. Any idea of doer-ship, that things happen because you do something, disappears when the truth is clearly seen. Once, through enquiry, the snake has been perceived to be nothing but a rope, nothing more need be done. And if this enquiry has not been performed, no amount of action will ever transform the snake.

See BṛhUp 1.4.15, 'Even if one performs a great and holy work, but without knowing this, that work is exhausted in the end'.

arthasya = aim, purpose, goal; **niścayo** = enquiry, ascertainment; **dṛṣṭo** = seen; **hitokti** = words of the wise, of a beneficient person; **snāna** = sacred ritual bath; **dāna** = gift, charity, alms-giving, generosity; **prāṇāyāma** = breath control.

adhikāriṇam āśāste phala-siddhir-viśeṣataḥ |
upāyā deśa-kālādyāḥ santy asmin saha-kāriṇaḥ ||14||

Success depends chiefly upon the qualification of the seeker. Place, time, and other such circumstances are merely auxiliaries.

In ChānUp 8.7, the demon king Virocana went to Brahmaloka to obtain knowledge of the Self. He was taught by the best of teachers, Prajāpati. Yet, he did not realize the Self. This demonstrates that an individual's qualification, and not place and time, are of primary importance. All time is God's time and all places are God's places. The unknown variable is the state of the seeker. Water which falls on barren soil merely evaporates. Water which falls on well-prepared soil produces a bountiful crop.

What is happening today was begun thousands and thousands of years ago. If you think a thought, it must reach its goal. Do you think that it stops just because you go away or because you stop thinking? It catches up to you, sometime, someplace . . . it always catches up. Nothing remains unfinished. Everything is connected. And then happiness, joy without limit, unbounded bliss. When one has that, then everything is finished. Whether one comes, whether one goes, joy permeates everything. Never again the pangs of separation, of fear. You may hurry forward, you may run backwards, you may plan your little dramas, but know that these are all mere auxiliaries to the one which is you.

adhikārin = qualified aspirant; eligible person; **phala siddhi** = success, fruitfulness, results accomplished; **deśa** = place; **kāla** = time; **upāyā** = to come near, towards, approach.

ato vicāraḥ kartavyaḥ jijñāsor ātma-vastunaḥ |
samāsādya dayāsindhuṁ guruṁ brahma-vid-uttamam ||15||

Therefore, that person who desires to know the nature of the Self, correctly and completely, should perform an earnest enquiry after duly approaching a Master who is a supreme knower of the Absolute and an ocean of compassion.

When one's *jijñāsa*, one's desire to know, is solely to know the Self, correctly and completely, then one's attention is in the right place. Phenomena come and go. Thoughts come and go. Experiences come and go. Good and bad, pleasures and pains, all come and go. An earnest seeker will perform an earnest enquiry after having met the Master and heard the truth that the Self dwells within. Attend to That. Surrender to That.

A Master, a Guru, is declared to be a supreme knower of the Absolute. That is, a Master is one who is established in the Self. Such a one knows the Self because they are the Self. This is not something they teach nor is it something the disciple learns. There is no possible way to learn who one is. The message the Master gives is simply that in the heart of awareness, one recognizes without a shadow of a doubt the truth of one's own Self. In other words, the Master shines light on the disciple's ignorance and the truth stands revealed. In the *Guru Gītā* 23, the etymological derivataion of the word '*guru*' is given as, 'The root *gu* stands for darkness; the root *ru* stands for its removal – the syllable *gu* is darkness and the syllable *ru* is light. There is no doubt that the Guru is indeed the supreme knowledge that swallows the darkness of ignorance)'. The *Pāṇinisūtras* also declare, '*gu saṁvaraṇe, ru hiṁsane*' (*gu* indicates concealment and *ru* its annulment. Thus, by the Master's spiritual teaching, the ignorance which conceals the truth is annuled).

See MuṇḍUp 1.2.12, 'For the sake of this knowledge, let him only approach, with sacrificial fuel in hand, a teacher who is learned in the scriptures and established in the Absolute' (*tad vijñānārthaṁ sa gurum evābhigacchet samit pāṇiḥ śrotriyam brahma niṣṭham*); MuṇḍUp 1.2.13 says, 'To that student of tranquil mind and calm disposition, who had come to the Master in the right manner, that learned one faithfully imparted knowledge of the Absolute.' See KaivUp 1.5; '. . . bowing with devotion to the Master' (*bhaktyā svagurum praṇamya*) See Satyakāma Jābāla's approach and Gautama's ultimate acceptance in ChānUp 4.4.1–5. See also BṛhUp 2.1.14; ChānUp 4.14.1–4, 6.14.1., 7.1.1.; TaittUp 1.2.3., 1.3.3., 1.9.1., 3.1.1; KaUp 1.2.8.

ataḥ = therefore. *Ataḥ* implies that something must have come before and in this case that something is 'approach a Master after an earnest enquiry into the nature of the Self' has been performed; **kartavyaḥ** = what must be done; jijñāsoḥ = one who has an earnest desire to know; **brahmaviduttama** = best or supreme knower of the Absolute; **dayāsindhu** = ocean of compassion; **guru** = Master.

medhāvī puruṣo vidvān ūhāpoha-vicakṣaṇaḥ |
adhikāryātma-vidyāyām ukta-lakṣaṇa-lakṣitaḥ ||16||

That person who has an excellent memory, is learned, possesses great powers of comprehension and the ability to reason properly is alone considered qualified for the knowledge of the Self.

This verse delineates the characteristics of a person competent to learn of the Self. Such a one is known as an *ātmavidyā adhikārī* or a qualified aspirant for the knowledge of the Self. One's mind has the potential for leading to liberation. But these qualities have been temporarily obscured. The future depends on the quality of one's mind, on an excellent mind.

medhāvī = a person who has an intellect (*dhi/buddhi*) which has the capacity to retain the meaning of what has been heard; **ūha** = positive reasoning, conjecture; **apoha** = negative reasoning, exclusion.

vivekino viraktasya śamādi-guṇa-śālinaḥ |
mumukṣor eva hi brahma-jijñāsā-yogyatā matā ||17||

That person alone is considered qualified to inquire into the Absolute who possesses discrimination, detachment, the virtues such as tranquillity and so on, and an intense longing for liberation.

These are the famous four-fold prerequisites (*sādhana catuṣṭaya*) that comprise the proximate aid to liberation. They will be individually expounded in verses 19–29.

yogyatā = being qualified, special fitness; **jijñāsa** = enquiry, desire to know; **vivekino** = discrimination; **viraktasya** = detachment.

sādhanāny atra catvāri kathitāni manīṣibhiḥ |
yeṣu satsu eva san niṣṭhā yad abhāve na siddhyati ||18||

Regarding this, the sages have spoken of four qualifications for attainment. The experience of Reality is possible only if they exist, and impossible in their absence.

The desire to be free implies a certain readiness to renounce all that is not the Self. Such a desire is rare and arises only after considerable experience and evolution of character. There is nothing dogmatic about this. Even to learn of things of the world, be they science or mathematics or whatever, require certain prerequisites. The Self is not an object to be seen. Thus, there is the necessity for an ability to discriminate. When left to oneself, the world of objects exherts a powerful pull to secure what is pleasing and avoid what is painful. In due course one discovers that no lasting, permanent satisfaction may be derrived from such a course of action. Śaṅkara, in his BSBh 1.1.1, points to this necessity of qualification with the word '*atha*' (then).

manīṣibhiḥ = sage; one who has knowledge of the import of the scriptures; **kathitāni** = said to be, spoken of; **abhāva** = non-existent; **sat** = existence.

ādau nityānitya-vastu-vivekaḥ pariganyate |
ihāmutra phala-bhoga-virāgas tad-anantaram ||19||
śamādi-ṣaṭka-sampattiḥ mumukṣutvam iti sphuṭam |

First is enumerated discrimination between the eternal and the non-eternal. Next comes detachment from the enjoyment of the fruits of action, both here and elsewhere. Then, the collection of six treasures of virtue beginning with tranquillity.[1] Last, undoubtedly, is an earnest desire for liberation.

From the reference to discrimination (*viveka*), detachment (*vairāgya/viraktasya*), the virtues (*śamādi guṇa*), and a burning desire for liberation (*mumukṣutva*) in verse 17, follows this elucidation. Each qualification follows its predecessor according to the logic that 'what precedes is the cause of what follows'. Thus, detachment cannot be secured in the absence of discrimination. Until one is able to discriminate between what is real and what is unreal, what is permanent from what is impermanent, detachment will not arise. Likewise, the virtues will naturally flow from a person when one is dispassionate.

See KaUp 5.13, 'He is the eternal in the midst of the non-eternals' (*nityo'nityānaṁ*). For references to *mumukṣutva* see V. 3, 28, 29, 30, 31, 44, 84, 120, 178, and 576.

Note: from verse 19 through verse 24, the critical edition breaks the verses into odd pairs. I have divided them as follows for translation purposes.

nitya = eternal, permanent; **anitya** = non-eternal, transient, impermanent; **viveka** = discrimination; **virāga** = detachment, renunciation; **phala** = results, fruits; **bhoga** = enjoyment, pleasure; **iha** = here, in this world; **amutra** = there, in the life to come, in the other world; **tad anantaram** = after that, next, that which follows; **śama** = calmness, tranquillity, control of the inner sense organs; **ādi** = and so on, etc; **mumukṣutva** = burning desire for liberation.

brahma satyaṁ jagan-mithyety evaṁrūpo viniścayaḥ ||20||
so'yam nityānitya vastu-vivekaḥ samudāhṛtaḥ |

The unwavering conviction that the Absolute alone is real and that the empirical world is non-real is well-spoken of as discrimination between the eternal and the non-eternal.

To discriminate between the Real and the non-real is a good beginning. It is important. Discriminating wisdom makes the distinction between what is permanent and what is impermanent. However, eventually one must experience that there is no boundary between in and out, Real and non-real. Thus, this is but the first of the preliminary aids to liberation.

What is meant by discrimination between the eternal and the non-eternal? Śaṅkara accepts as 'real' only that which neither changes nor ceases to exist. No object, no knowledge, can be said to be absolutely real if its existence is only temporary. Absolute reality implies permanent existence. Thus, discrimination between the eternal and the non-eternal is the conviction that the Absolute alone is eternal (*nitya*) and all else is ephemeral (*anitya*), bound by time, transitory. One must be absolutely clear that thoughts are impermanent. They appear and disappear. Forms are impermanent.

[1] The paradigm for the six treasures is BṛhUp 4.4.23 (*śānto dānta uparatas titikṣuḥ samāhito*). Advaita tradition usually depicts these as tranquillity (*śama*), self-control (*dama*), withdrawal of the sense objects from the sense organs (*uparati*), forbearance (*titikṣā*), the perfect establishment of the intellect in the Absolute (*samādhāna*), and faith (*śraddhā*). These will be explained in the following verses.

They appear and disappear. Even the most sublime experiences come and go. No form can be held onto. One must recognize the impossibility of holding onto anything: one's body, one's thoughts, one's experiences.

This verse contains two-thirds of what has become an oft-quoted verse said to encapsulate Advaita in a nutshell: *Brahman satyam, jagan mithyā jīvo brahmaiva nā'paraḥ* (the Absolute is real; the world is non-real; the individual and the Absolute are not different). Note that Śaṅkara describes the world as non-real, not as impermanent. The logic is, if the world were merely thought to be impermanent, it would still hold some sort of attraction. But if the world is known to be non-real, then true dispassion arises. Many individuals seek that which is impermanent, but few seek that which is non-real.

See MuṇḍUp 1.2.12, 'When he perceives the worlds as won by actions which are transitory, let a *brahmin* resort to renunciation. He sees, there is nothing here which is not the result of action.'

See KaUp 5.13, 'He is the eternal in the midst of the non-eternals' (*nityo'nityānaṁ*).

brahma = the Absolute; **satya** = real, true, existing; **jagat** = world, cosmos; **mithyā** = non-real, false, neither real nor unreal, illusory; incorrect; **viniścaya** = unwavering conviction; **samudāhṛtaḥ** (*samyak udāhṛtaḥ*) = well explained; spoken of.

tad vairāgyaṁ jugupsā yā darśana-śravaṇādibhiḥ ||21||
dehādi-brahma-paryante hy anitye bhoga-vastuni |

Detachment is aversion for all things seen, heard, and so on, as well as for all transient objects of enjoyment ranging from the physical body up to the creator's highest form.

What is dispassion, detachment? Dispassion or detachment is the absence of any desire to enjoy the fruits of one's efforts, either here in this life or in any other life anywhere else. This dispassion arises out of discrimination and not despair or despondency. It is the natural result of a vigorous discrimination by which the seeker recognizes that the pleasures which result from gain are transitory, fleeting, impermanent and therefore cannot fulfill one's deepest longing for eternal bliss. See V. 9, 17, and 373–74 on detachment.

Darśana-śravaṇādibhiḥ may also be translated as the giving up being effected through all the enjoying organs and faculties.

vairāgya = detachment, dispassion, renunciation, non-attachment; **jugupsā** = dislike, disgust, aversion, revulsion; **brahmā** = the creator of the universe.

virajya viṣaya-vrātāt doṣa-dṛṣṭyā muhur muhuḥ ||22||
svalakṣye niyatāvasthā manasaḥ śama ucyate |

Tranquility[1] is said to be detaching the mind from the myriad sense objects by continuously perceiving their defects and resting the mind permanently on one's objective.

Perfect equality. To detach the mind from all objective, transient things by continually seeing their imperfections and limitations and to direct it steadfastly toward the Absolute.

---

[1] See TaittUp 1.6.2, 'the Absolute is complete tranquillity'.

śama = tranquillity, calmness, control of the internal sense organs.

viṣayebhyaḥ parāvartya sthāpanam sva-sva-golake ||23||
ubhayeṣām indriyāṇām sa damaḥ parikīrtitaḥ |

Self-control is said to be the retention of both kinds of sense organs in their respective centers, withdrawing them from all sense objects.

Perfect self-control is control over the external sense organs of perception such as the eyes, ears, skin, tongue, and nose and over the sense organs of action such as the voice, hands, feet, organs of excretion, and organs of generation.

dama = self-control, restraint, control of the external sense organs; **parā-vartya** = turning away from; **sthāpana** = maintaining, preserving, fixing, establishing, causing to stand firm; **ubhaya** = both, two-fold; **indriya** = sense organs.

bāhyānālambanaṁ vṛtter eṣoparatir uttamā ||24||

The best self-withdrawal is when thought-waves cease to be supported by external objects.

Once the sense organs have been restricted, one must ensure that they may not once again be tempted towards worldly objects. Self-withdrawal is sometimes said to be the strict observance of one's own duties (*svadharma*).

uparati = self-withdrawal; **vṛtti** = mental mode, modification of the mind, fluctuation; **uttamā** = highest, best.

sahanam sarva duḥkhānām apratīkāra pūrvakam |
cintā-vilāpa-rahitam sā titikṣā nigadyate ||25||

Forbearance is said to be the endurance of all afflictions without caring for redress or revenge while always being free from anxiety or lament.

Forbearance is that frame of mind in which one is able to endure all the opposites such as heat and cold, pleasure and pain, sickness and health, and so on, with a blissful disposition. It involves knowing that whatever is destined to happen must happen, that events will take their own course, and thus one should remain content. As well, it involves accepting that whatever happens is welcome.

See BG 2.14, 'Contacts with their objects, O Kaunteya, give rise to heat and cold, pleasure and pain. They come and go and do not last forever; these learn to endure, O Bhārata.'

titikṣā = forbearance, endurance of opposites, tolerance; **duḥkhānām** = afflictions, all the causes of suffering such as all the dualities in the world, i.e., heat, cold, pleasure, pain, and so on.

śāstrasya guruvākyasya satya-buddhyāvadhāraṇam |
sā śraddhā kathitā sadbhiḥ yayā vastūpalabhyate ||26||

Acceptance, with firm conviction, of the scriptures and the words of the Master as conveying the Truth is called faith by the wise. By this does reality become apprehended.

The Master's grace is always there. It is for all, always complete, ready for the taking. There is no rule, no law which says now is the time, now you are ready. All that the Master can do is to point to that which we are. If there are no obstructions, like doubt, intellectual vanity, or attachment, one sees it immediately.

The BG 4.39 says, 'He who has faith, obtains knowledge.' If one does not have faith, a whole-hearted commitment, a burning zeal, then one does not achieve one's desired goal. To the extent that one has faith, progress is made. True faith is defined as acceptance with a firm conviction, when one's mind is given wholly to the ideal.

See Nārada's *Bhaktisūtra* 2 in regards to faith.

śraddhā = faith; **śāstra** = scripture, teaching, doctrine (from verb root *śās* = 'to rule, teach'); **satya** = truth; **buddyāvadhāraṇa** = firm conviction.

samyagā-sthāpanam buddheḥ śuddhe brahmaṇi sarvadā |
tat samādhānam-ity uktam na tu cittasya lālanam ||27||

One-pointedness is said to be the perfect establishment of the mind forever in the pure Absolute; not through any indulgence of the mind.

Single-pointedness (*samādhi*) is when the mind is absorbed in a chosen flow of thought. It is the process of diving into deeper layers of one's consciousness. The mind is perfectly concentrated and cut off from the world yet is dynamic, alert, under complete control of the will. See V. 342–43, 354–55, 358, 361, 363–67, 376, 408–411, and 474 on *samādhi*.

samādhāna = one-pointedness of the mind, absorption, profound contemplation (from *sam + ādhi* = putting together, joining, combining, union); **buddhi** = mind, intellect; **lālanam** = indulgence, giving in to whatever one wants.

ahaṅkārādi-dehāntān bandhān ajñāna-kalpitān |
sva-svarūpāvabodhena moktum icchā mumukṣutā ||28||

An intense longing for liberation is the desire to be free from the bonds of ignorance, extending from the ego-sense and so on, down to the physical body itself, through the realization of one's true nature.

An intense longing for liberation has liberation as its only objective; nothing else. True desire is desire for reunion with one's own Self, a desire to end suffering, a desire to be free. Such a true desire lies at the core of all other distorted and misplaced desires. One longs for the Self because one *is* the Self. If this intense longing for liberation is not recognized, then all the distorted imitations of this longing arise and lead to suffering.

See V. 3, 19, 29–31, 44, 84, 120, 178, and 576 for references to *mumukṣutva*.

mumukṣutva = intense longing for liberation; **ahaṅkāra** = egoism, the 'I'-maker; **bandha** = bondage, bonds; **ajñāna** = ignorance; **kalpitā** = imagination.

manda-madhyama-rūpāpi vairāgyena śamādinā |
prasādena guroḥ seyam pravṛddhā sūyate phalam ||29||

Even though this longing for liberation may be present in only a slight or moderate degree, through detachment, self-surrender, and so on and by the grace of a Master it will bear fruit.

Longing for liberation is within each individual. Before it is recognized, one remains at the whim of society, culture, family, and all the other myriad conditioning agents. When this desire is intense, one will follow it no matter whether it means losing one's reputation, one's status, one's family, one's happiness, even one's life. Everyone wishes to be happy and no one desires suffering. This hardly needs to be said. However, on the one hand, a person does not know what they should do or avoid in order to secure happiness. On the other hand, because one's negative tendencies are so strong, one engages in negative actions even though one knows they are wrong. See V. 3, 19, 28–31, 44, 84, 120, 178, and 576 for references to *mumukṣutva*.

Prasāda means grace, a gift from God or the Guru. It is also known as *kṛpā* (there are three types of grace: *sādhana kripā* or the grace of self-effort; *guru kripā* or the grace and guidance of a living master; and *divya kripā* or divine grace) and *anugraha*. Ajāmila is the paradigm example of a person rescured by God's grace. He was a *brahmin* who fell from his life of pure conduct when he was aroused by passion for a woman. But by invoking the name of God at the time of his death, he was redeemed, and was taken to heaven by messengers of Viṣṇu. His life shows that even the most wicked person can attain liberation by God's grace. See V. 3, 42, 50, 138, 149, 477, 489, 518, and 519 for references to grace.

prasād = grace; **manda** = inferior, slight; **madhyama** = middling, moderate.

vairāgyaṁ ca mumukṣutvaṁ tīvraṁ yasya tu vidyate |
tasminn evārthavantaḥ syuḥ phalavantaḥ śamādayh ||30||

Only when one's detachment and longing for liberation are intense will the practice of tranquillity and so on become meaningful and bear fruit.

This intense longing for liberation, for the Self, whether small or great, whether smoldering or blazing, is burning within each individual. When it is recognized for what it is, and becomes a raging fire, it will burn everything, all the falsehoods, disguises, hopes, and ignorances completely, leaving only that which was eternally, beautifully, nakedly there all along. See V. 3, 19, 28, 29, 31, 44, 84, 120, 178, and 576 for references to *mumukṣutva*.

etayor mandatā yatra viraktatva-mumukṣayoḥ |
marau salilavat tatra śamāder bhāna-mātratā ||31||

Where detachment and a desire for liberation are weak, tranquillity and the other virtues are merely appearances like the water in a mirage.

The water in a mirage will not quench one's thirst. Likewise, even if one believes that one is virtuous, if their detachment and desire for liberation are weak, then their virtuousness is likewise weak and will not produce any real happiness. Lasting happiness comes only from a realization of the Self. Bliss is experienced when one experiences the truth of one's own nature. Thus, it cannot be said that virtues are the ultimate goal of life. Yet, it is also true that no one ever reaches their goal without them.

See V. 3, 19, 28, 29, 30, 44, 84, 120, 178, and 576 for references to *mumukṣutva*.

viraktatva = detachment, renunciation; **salilavattatra** = flowing, fluctuating, unsteady; **maru** = wilderness, sandy waste.

mokṣa-kāraṇa-sāmagryām bhaktir-eva garīyasī |
sva-svarūpānusandhānam bhaktir ity abhidhīyate ||32||

Among all the means to liberation, devotion is supreme. Continuous contemplation of one's own essential nature is said to be devotion.

Nārada, in his *Bhaktisūtra* 2, defined devotion as being 'of the nature of extreme love for Him'. Devotion is when nothing stands between God and one's love for Him. In this context, Śaṅkara has equated God and the great inner Self and thus, devotion is when nothing stands between one's own Self and love for that Self.

mokṣa = liberation, freedom; **kāraṇa** = cause, means to, instrument; **sāmagrī** = resources; **eva** = alone, only; **bhakti** = devotion; **sva-sva-rūpānusan-dhānam** = vontemplation of one's own essential nature.

svātma-tattvānusandhānaṁ bhaktir ity apare jaguḥ |32½|

Others maintain that devotion is the continuous contemplation of the Truth of one's own self.

Devotion is the melting of the ego in its source. Although the world with all its myriad names and forms does not in reality exist, or exists for the individual established in the Self as identical with his own Self, to the individual struggling with delusion, contemplation has its use from that standpoint.

svātma = one's own individuality; **apare jaguḥ** = others say; **anusan-dhānaṁ** = continuous contemplation; **tattva** = truth.

ukta-sādhana-sampannaḥ tattva-jijñāsur ātmanaḥ ||33||
upasīded gurum prājñam yasmād bandha-vimokṣaṇam |

That person who desires to know the truth of the Self and who possesses the above-mentioned qualifications should approach a Master, a knower of the Self, who confers freedom from bondage.

As soon as a Master is satisfied that the prospective student is sincere, ardent, well-behaved, and possesses all the necessary prerequisites, the teacher must begin instruction. A teacher could observe a prospective student for six months to a year, but after that they are bound to start instructions. If the student wants knowledge of the Self, it may take longer, i.e., see *Tantrarāja Tantra* 2.37–38 (5 years) or ChanUp 8.7.2.3. (32 years).

See MuṇḍUp 1.2.12, 'For the sake of this knowledge, let him only approach, with sacrificial fuel in hand, a teacher who is learned in the scriptures and established in the Absolute'; MuṇḍUp 1.2.13 says, 'To that student of tranquil mind and calm disposition, who had come to the Master in the right manner, that learned one faithfully imparted knowledge of the Absolute.' See KaivUp 1.5; ChānUp 4.4.1–5; KaUp 1.2.8; BṛhUp 2.1.14; ChānUp 4.14.1–4, 6.14.1., 7.1.1.; TaittUp 1.2.3., 1.3.3., 1.9.1., 3.1.1.

sādhana = spiritual disciplines; **prājña** = knower; **yasmāt** = by nearness, by approaching (such a Master).

śrotriyo'vṛjino'kāma-hato yo brahma-viduttamaḥ ||34||
brahmaṇyuparataḥ śānto nirindhana ivānalaḥ |
ahetuka-dayā-sindhuḥ bandhur ānamatām satām ||35||

A Master is one who is well-versed in the scriptures, taintless, desireless, a perfect knower of the Absolute; continually established in the Absolute, calm like the flame when its fuel is consumed; a boundless ocean of spontaneous compassion for which there is no reason, a friend to all good people who surrender to him.

There are countless teachers, known and unknown, human and otherwise. However, a Master is that teacher who points to the absolute end of separation and the pain it entails. The Master is one who will ruthlessly destroy one's sufferings. Such a one is as relentless as life itself. Being absolutely loving yet wanting nothing from anyone, the Master is one who will search out any and all identification with the not-self and rip it out wherever such is found. Anything else is mere deception, playing at what is sacred business. What the Master conveys, and all that the Master conveys, is that the truth of the Master and the truth of the seeker are the same.

To be well versed in the scriptures means that the Master is one who is established in the source, stillness, pure consciousness unmediated by conditioning. Their thoughts and thus words come directly from emptiness and thus are spontaneously insightful, revelatory, original and pure. Scripture is but the union of a pure mind with its source. From that union flows beauty, truth, insight, and revelation.

See ŚvetUp 6.19, 'To him who is without parts, without activity, tranquil, irreproachable, without blemish, the highest bridge to immortality like a fire with its fuel burnt.' See MuṇḍUp 1.2.12, 'For the sake of this knowledge, approach . . . a Master who is . . . established in the Absolute' (*brahma niṣṭham*).

śrotriyaḥ = one who has studied the scriptures; **avṛjinaḥ** = without defect, pure; **akāma** = desireless; **brahmaviduttamaḥ** = perfect or highest knower of the Absolute; **brahmaṇyuparataḥ** = one whose mind has found rest in, is established in the Absolute; **śānta** = calm, tranquil, at peace; **ahetuka** = without reason; **bandhur** = one who destroys afflictions; **ānamatām** = those who make obeisance, surrender; **satām** = good or wise people.

tam ārādhya guruṁ bhaktyā prahvaḥ praśraya-sevanaiḥ |
prasannaṁ tam anuprāpya pṛcchet jñātavyam ātmanaḥ ||36||

Worship that Master with devotion[1] and when the Master is pleased[2] with your humble[3] speech and service, approach and ask for whatever is required to be known.[4]

The teacher alone can initiate a student into knowledge of Self. Thus, the teacher is indispensible. The teacher is qualified, equipped. Thus, the teacher is revered. This makes the teacher responsible to teach. It puts a demand upon the student. The student must seek the *guru*'s grace and favor in order to learn. The teacher may or may not admit the student. When admitted, the teacher may still withhold certain teachings.

---

1 See KaivUp 1.5, '. . . bowing with devotion to the Master'.
2 See MaitrīUp 2.1, 'Then, the revered Sākāyanya, well pleased'.
3 See MuṇḍUp 1.2.12, 'For the sake of this knowledge, let him only approach, with sacrificial fuel in hand, a teacher who is learned in the scriptures and established in the Absolute'; also MuṇḍUp 1.2.13; KaivUp 1.5; ChānUp 4.4.1–5; KaUp 1.2.8; BṛhUp 2.1.14; ChānUp 4.14.1–4, 6.14.1, 7.1.1; TaittUp 1.2.3, 1.3.3, 1.9.1, 3.1.1.
4 See MaitrīUp 1.4, 'Be pleased, therefore, to deliver me. In this world I am like a frog in a waterless well. Revered Sir, you are our way, you are our way'.

The teacher has authority over the pupil. Some examples of a teacher examining a pupil's qualifications include ChanUp 4.4.9 (Satyakāmạ Jābāla and Hāridrmata Gautama); ChanUp 4.1.3 (Jānaśruti Pautrāyaṇa from Raikva); ChanUp 7.7.12 (Indra, Virocana and Prajāpati); and BrhUp 3.6 (Yājñavalkya and Gārgī).

prahvaḥ = humble, modest, reverent; **praśraya** = speaking with humility; **seva** = selfless service; **prasanna** = clear, bright, pure, gracious, kindly disposed towards, showing favor.

svāmin namaste nata-loka-bandho
kāruṇya-sindho patitam bhavābdhau |
mām uddharātmīya-kaṭākṣa-dṛṣyā
ṛjvyāti-kāruṇya-sudhābhivṛṣṭyā ||37||

O Lord, friend of all who surrender to you. I offer my obeisance to you. O ocean of boundless compassion. I have fallen into the sea of worldly existence. Shower on me the nectar of your direct and supremely compassionate glance and rescue me.

The meeting with the Master comes about when an individual finally cries out in all humility for help. To truly ask for help implies that one has finally surrendered, one has finally given up providing possible solutions. In this exquisite embrace everything is put aside – all that one has learned and all that is yet to be learned, all that one has done and all that one is yet to do. In this magical, mysterious moment, a seeker-after-liberation becomes open, absolutely still, and therefore humble and ready to receive.

See note to V. 29 for grace.

svāmin = lord; **namaste** = I offer my obeisance to you, I bow to you, salutation, (lit. *na* = 'not' + *ma* = 'mine'); **nata loka bandho** = the destroyer of the afflictions of those who bow to him; **kāruṇya-sindho** = ocean of compassion; **patitam** = fallen, descended; **māmuddharātmīya** = rescue me; **ṛjvvā** = direct, straight; **atikāruṇya** = utmost, supreme compassion; **sudhā** = nectar.

durvāra-saṁsāra-davāgni-taptaṁ
dodhūyamānam duradṛṣṭa-vātaiḥ |
bhītam prapannam paripāhi mṛtyoḥ
śaraṇyam anyad yad ahaṁ na jāne ||38||

I am burning in the unquenchable fire of the world-forest. I am violently shaken by the winds of misfortune. I am full of fear.[1] I seek refuge in you. Save me from death, for I know of no other refuge.

There are those who declare that they want a Master, but what they really want is someone powerful enough to do what they want done. When such a person prays to the Master that, thy will be done, what is really meant is, 'my will be done'. However, when one is fortunate enough to find the Master in the core of one's own being, one stops being a plaything of society, culture, family, or desires. When one

---

1 See BṛhUp 1.4.2, 1.5.3, 3.9.26, 4.2.4, 4.3.20, 4.4.22, 4.5.15; ChānUp 1.3.1, 8.9.1, 8.10.1, 8.11.1; TaittUp 2.4, 2.7–8; KaUp 3.2, 6.2–3 on freedom from fear.
See V. 41, 43, 178 on the forest.

has surrendered within, the external Master appears and the impossible becomes possible.

The wheel of birth and death (*samsāra*), otherwise known as the empirical world, is commonly compared to a wilderness on fire.

durvāra = hard to be restrained, irrepressible; **davāgni** = forest fire; **taptaṁ** = inflamed, hot; **dodhūyamānam** = shaken again and again, trembling constantly; **duradṛṣṭavātaiḥ** = winds of misfortune; **bhītam** = frightened, terrified, afraid; **prapannam** = come for protection; **mṛtyoḥ** = death; **śaraṇyam** = surrender, refuge, protection.

śāntā mahānto nivasanti santo
vasantavat lokahitaṁ carantaḥ |
tīrṇāḥ svayaṁ bhīma-bhavārṇavaṁ janān
ahetunānyān api tārayantaḥ ||39||

There exist great and peaceful individuals who, like the season of Spring, are ever doing good to the world. Having themselves crossed the frightful ocean of worldly existence, they help others to cross it for no reason of their own.

A Master wants nothing from anyone except their own happiness. How could they not? They know that everyone and everything is only one's own Self. The Self is that which is totally, permanently present and always has been so. The Self cannot be given. No one possesses it to give it to another. How could someone give you that which you already are?

This verse compares the spontaneous joy which a Great One gives to the world to the season of Spring which brings forth flowers and new life. Even as a flower spreads its fragrance to one and all, equally, without distinction, so does the Great One spread love and joy equally to all. (The next verse follows up this idea.)

śāntā = one who is calm, peaceful; **mahānto** = a great person; **vasanta** = spring; **lokahitaṁ carantaḥ** = doing good to the entire world; **tīrṇāḥ** = one who has crossed, one who has gone over; **bhīma-bhavārṇavaṁ** = the ocean of worldly life is frightful; **ahetunā** = with no reason.

ayam svabhāvas svata eva yatpara
śramāpanoda-pravaṇaṁ mahātmanām |
sudhāṁśur eṣa svayam arka-karkaśa
prabhābhitaptām avati kṣitiṁ kila ||40||

Indeed, it is the very nature of these Great Ones, of their own accord, to remove the ills of others. Does not the moon, of its own accord, cool the earth when it is scorched by the fierce rays of the sun?

This sounds wonderful and appears to be the case, however, though a Great One may see what looks like people, what looks like trees, what looks like the earth and the myriad things of the earth, at the core of these experiences is the Self, as it has always been. Thus, from one perspective it appears that the Self pervades everywhere, overflowing, and thus gives solace to all that come in contact with it, but, from another perspective, there is nothing which is not the Self. It is only because the ignorant individual believes afflictions are happening that solace is spoken of. It is not the sun that speaks of illumination, but the earth.

In the previous verse, the spontaneous compassion of the Great One was compared to the season of Spring.

svabhāva = self-nature, essence; **śramāpanoda** = distressed with weariness, ills; **pravaṇaṁ** = removal; **mahātmanām** = Great One; **arka** = sun; **kila** = signifies what is well known.

brahmānanda-rasānubhūti-kalitaiḥ pūtaiḥ suśītaiḥ sitaiḥ
yuṣmad vākkalaś ojjhitaiḥ śruti-sukhaiḥ vākyāmṛtaiḥ secaya |
santaptam bhava-tāpa-dāva-dahana-jvālābhir enaṁ prabho
dhanyās te bhavad-īkṣaṇa-kṣaṇa-gateḥ pātrīkṛtāḥ svīkṛtāḥ ||41||

O Lord! I am tormented by worldly afflictions as by the flames of a forest fire. Sprinkle your cool words upon me, issuing from your lips as from the mouth of a pitcher, your words which have been sweetened by the ambrosial bliss of the Absolute. They are purifying, soothing, delightful to the ear. Blessed are those on whom your glance rests for even a moment, accepting them as your own.

Here commences the dialog between the Master and the student, a dialog instigated by the student who, in essence, says, 'Have compassion for me and teach me the way to end suffering.'

See V. 38, 43, and 178 on the forest.

brahmānanda = bliss of the Absolute; **rasānubhūti** = experience of immortality, of nectar, of elixir; **pūtaiḥ** = pure; **susītaiḥ** = cool; sitaiḥ = stainless; **śruti sukhaiḥ** = give delight to the ear; **prabho** = lord; **kṣaṇa-gateḥ** = even for a moment obtaining (your) glance, or, being connected with it; **pātrīkṛtāḥ** = those on whom it falls; **svīkṛtāḥ** = fortunate ones.

kathaṁ tareyaṁ bhava sindhum etaṁ
kā vā gatir me katamo'styupāyaḥ |
jāne na kiñcit kṛpayā'va māṁ prabho
saṁsāra-duḥkha-kṣatim ātanuṣva ||42||

How to cross this ocean of worldly existence? What should be my goal? What means should I adopt? Of these I know nothing. O Lord! Save me by your grace. Tell me how to uproot the grief of worldly life.

A sharp intellect is a wonderful tool. But a point comes when one is no longer satisfied with second-hand information. Then arises a tremendous resolve to 'find out'. It involves a willingness to surrender. One surrenders all ideas of who one is, where one is, how one is, and humbly prays, 'teach me'.

What 'means' should I adopt refers to which, of all the various and seemingly conflicting means prescribed in the scriptures, should the disciple adopt.

See ChānUp 7.1.3, 'It has been heard by me from those like you that he who knows the Self crosses over sorrow. Such a sorrowing one am I, venerable sir. Do you, venerable sir, help me to cross over to the other side of sorrow?'

See V. 3, 29, 50, 138, 149, 477, 489, 518, and 519 for references to grace.

kathaṁ = how; **tareyam** = how shall I cross; **bhavasindhum** = ocean of worldly existence; **kṛpa** = grace; **prabho** = Lord; **saṁsāra** = ocean of worldly life.

tathā vadantam śaraṇāgataṁ svaṁ
saṁsāra-dāvānala-tāpa-taptam |
nirīkṣya kāruṇya-rasārdra-dṛṣṭya
dadyād abhītim sahasā mahātmā ||43||

Scorched by the flames of the world-forest and seeking protection, the disciple speaks thus. The Great One looks at him with the tender eyes of compassion and immediately promises him relief.

The moment a disciple earnestly asks for relief from the flames of the world-forest, the Great One promises such. This is a universal law and if one thinks that one has asked for help, and help has not appeared, one should look deep within oneself and see where the fault lies. The saying is true, 'Ask and ye shall receive.'

See V. 38, 41, and 178 on the forest.

tathā vadantam = he who speaks thus; **śaraṇāgati** = absolute self-surrender; **nirīkṣya kāruṇya-rasārdra-dṛṣṭya** = seeing him with tender eyes of compassion; **mahātmā** = Great One, great individual; **sahasā** = immediate; **dadyād abhītim** = promise of comfort, relief.

vidvān sa tasmā upasattim īyuṣe
mumukṣave sādhu yathokta-kāriṇe |
praśānta-cittāya śamānvitāya
tattvopadeśaṁ kṛpayaiva kuryāt ||44||

Out of compassion the knower of the Absolute should give the knowledge of the Truth to that student who, thirsting for liberation, has sought his protection, who duly obeys the injunctions, who observes the prescribed austerities, who is of serene mind and who is endowed with calmness[1] and the virtues.

As soon as the Master is satisfied that the prospective student is sincere, ardent, well-behaved, and possesses all the necessary prerequisites, the Master must begin instruction. In olden times, the teacher observed a prospective student for a lengthy period. ChānUp 8.7.3 mentions that Virocana and Indra lived a disciplined life for 32 years before Prajāpati began instructing them. The *Tantrarāja Tantra* mentions a five-year preparatory period.

See MuṇḍUp 1.2.13: 'Unto him who has approached in due form, whose mind is tranquil and who has attained peace, let the knowing teacher teach in its very truth that knowledge about *Brahman* by which one knows the Imperishable person, the true.'

See V. 3, 28, 29, 30, 31, 84, 120, 576 for references to *mumukṣutva*.

vidvān = knower (of the truth); **upasattimīyuṣe** = has approached in the proper and prescribed manner; **sādhu** = an aspirant practicing spiritual disciplines, an ascetic; virtuous, good; **prasānta cittāya** = serene mind; **śamānvitāya** = one who possesses the six virtues beginning with tranquillity.

śrī gurur-uvāca
mā bhaiṣṭa vidvan tava nāstyapāyaḥ
saṁsāra-sindhos taraṇe'styupāyaḥ |
yenaiva yātā yatayo'asya pāraṁ
tam eva mārgaṁ tava nirdiśāmi ||45||

[1] See BṛhUp 4.4.23, 'having become calm, self-controlled . . .'.

The auspicious Master said:
Fear not, O learned one. For you there is no danger. There is a means to cross the ocean of this fluctuating worldly life. I shall reveal to you that very way by which those who have striven in the past have reached the other shore.

The gift of fearlessness (*abhayadāna*) is, in one sense, the only gift that a Master can give to a student. What more can a Master say than, 'Have no fear, be happy.' For the student is actually the great inner Self and all that the student need do is to realize this truth. Thus, the first teaching given is the knowledge, 'Have no fear', and then, once the student is no longer frightened and a certain amount of composure and concentration are present, the student is qualified to receive further instruction.

See BṛhUp 4.2.4 wherein Janaka and Yājñavalkya speak of fearlessness. Also see BṛhUp 1.4.2, 1.5.3, 3.9.26, 4.3.20, 4.4.22, 4.5.15; ChānUp 1.3.1, 8.9.1, 8.10.1, 8.11.1; TaittUp 2.4, 2.7–8; KaUp 3.2, 6.2–3 on freedom from fear.

śrī gurur = auspicious Master (*śrī* is used as an honorific prefix to indicate holiness); **mā** = not; **bhaya** = fear; **nāstyapāyaḥ** = there is no danger; **saṁsāra-sindhostaraṇe'styupāyaḥ** = there is a means to cross the ocean of fluctuating worldly life; **mārgaṁ** = path.

astyupāyo mahān kaścit saṁsāra-bhaya-nāśanaḥ |
tena tīrtvā bhavāmbhodhiṁ paramānandam āpsyasi ||46||

There is a great means which will destroy the fear of worldly existence. By it you may cross the ocean of worldly life and attain[1] the supreme bliss.

astyupāyo mahān = there is a great means, path, technique; **nāśa** = to destroy; **bhaya** = fear.

vedāntārtha-vicāreṇa jāyate jñānam uttamam |
ten *ātyantika-saṁsāra-duḥkhanāśo bhavatyanu* ||47||

Supreme wisdom arises from an enquiry into the meaning of the Vedānta. This is followed by the complete destruction of the sorrows born of relative existence.

Again and again one hears Vedānta proclaim the necessity, and greatness, of 'enquiry' (*vicara*). In order to begin to have an insight into the Self, it appears that one must question one's most cherished presuppositions, i.e., Was I born? Am I my physical

[1] Again, both for emphasis and for fixing the teachings securely in the student's mind, as well as for increasing the student's ardor, the Master repeats that there is a means, and, that means is 'great', by which one may destroy fear and attain supreme bliss. Embedded in this teaching (*upadeśa*) is the idea that all one must do is to destroy fear (Advaita is fond of declaring that liberation is nothing more than the destruction of ignorance – *avidyānāśa*) and that which was always the case, liberation/eternal bliss, will spontaneously manifest itself. Śaṅkara said in his BSBh 1.1.4, 'All the scriptures do is to aim at the removal of difference imagined through ignorance'. Thus, the 'attainment' of the Self is but a 'discovering,' a realization of what has actually always been the case. Being eternally attained, where is the need for action ('being already released, he is released' (KaUp 5.1); 'being already the Absolute, he attains the Absolute' (BṛhUp 4.4.6))?

body? Am I my thoughts? Am I really so and so? How do I know that I exist? Who were my parents? Have they created me or have I created them? Who am I?

See KaivUp 1.4, 'The ascetics who have ascertained well the meaning of the Upaniṣadic knowledge . . . are all liberated'.

vedānta = the *Upaniṣads* (see Introduction.); **artha** = meaning, purpose, aim; **vicāra** = enquiry; **jñāna** = knowledge or wisdom depending on the context; **uttama** = highest or supreme; **anu** = followed by.

śraddhā-bhakti-dhyāna-yogān mumukṣoḥ
mukter hetūn vakti sākṣāt śruter gīḥ |
yo vā eteṣveva tiṣthatyamuṣya
mokṣo'avidyā-kalpitād deha-bandhāt ||48||

The scriptures declare that faith, devotion, meditation,[1] and yoga are the direct means to liberation. That person who stands established in them is liberated from the bondage of the body which is due to ignorance.

In the Introduction to his BSBh, Śaṅkara said, 'Superimposition (of the not-self on the Self) is considered by the learned to be ignorance. And the realization of the nature of the real entity by separating the superimposed from it is called knowledge/liberation.'

Bondage of the body means the false superimposed identification of the body upon the Self which is solely due to ignorance.

śraddha = faith (see v. 26, 120); **bhakti** = devotion (see v. 32–33, 36, 120); **dhyāna** = meditation; **yoga** = a path(s) leading to oneness with the divine or one's Self (YS 1.2 defines yoga as 'destruction of the mind's fluctuations – *yogaś citta vṛtti nirodhaḥ*), this verse may also be translated as *bhakti-yoga* and *dhyāna-yoga*; **tiṣṭhatya-muṣya** = one who is established in them; the word *amuṣya* = 'belonging to the family of such a one', indicates that such a person is very rare.

ajñāna-yogāt paramātmanas tava
hy anātma-bandhas tata eva saṁsṛtiḥ |
tayor vivekodita-bodha-vanhiḥ
ajñāna-kāryaṁ pradahet samūlam ||49||

In reality you are the supreme Self but due to your association with ignorance, you appear to be in bondage to the not-self which alone is the sole cause of relative existence. The flame of knowledge, kindled by discrimination between the Self and not-self, completely burns away the effects of ignorance and its roots.

This verse encapsulates the entire teaching of Śaṅkara. The Master, out of compassion, instructs the seeker that, in reality, he is the supreme Self. However, out of ignorance, the seeker imagines himself to be a body and in his imagination, he is now frantically seeking the secret to the liberation. Yet, one cannot find liberation by doing anything. What a surprise to hear that liberation comes by knowledge and not by action. That which is, is self-evident. It needs no one's help to be.

See V. 11 which says that one must discriminate between the Self and the not-self.

---

[1] See KaivUp 1.2, 'Seek to know the Absolute by faith, devotion, meditation, and concentration'.

paramātma = supreme Self; **anātma-bandha** = bondage to the not-self; **bodha** = knowledge.

śiṣya uvāca:
kṛpayā śrūyatāṁ svāmin praśno'yaṁ kriyate mayā |
yad uttaram ahaṁ śrutvā kṛtārthaḥ syāṁ bhavan-mukhāt ||50||

The student said:
Master, please be compassionate and listen to the question I wish to ask. By hearing an answer from your lips, I shall feel gratified.

There are two points implied in this verse. First, tradition declares that a student should never address the Master until and unless he or she has first received the Master's grace (*kṛpayā śrūyatām*). Regarding behavior, a student should show respect; rise to answer when spoken to; approach the teacher only when told to; speak only when spoken to; speak only as much as necessary. One is either a student or a teacher. A student should not behave like a teacher nor should the teacher act like a student. To be a student necessarily entails that one has an attitude of, 'I do not know, please teach me.' Humility is the foremost quality and hallmark of a student. Humility implies, 'I do not know, please teach me.' Thus, a student, first and foremost, listens. The phrase 'from your lips' implies not only that the student acknowledges his studentship, but also that there is nowhere else to turn other than to the Master. The KaUp 1.2.8 states, 'Unless taught by one who knows, one cannot gain access to it.' The second point is that tradition declares that one should not instruct another until and unless one is asked to do so. Thus, even were it the case that God or the Master knows everything, it is still incumbent upon the student to ask for instruction.

See Satyakāma Jābāla's approach and Gautama's ultimate acceptance in ChānUp 4.4.3, 'I wish to become a student of sacred knowledge. May I become your pupil, venerable Sir.' See also BṛhUp 2.1.14; MuṇḍUp 1.1.3; ChānUp 4.14.1; 4.2.2, 4.9.2, 6.14.1, 7.1.1; TaittUp 1.2.3, 1.3.3, 1.9.1, 3.1.1; MuṇḍUp 1.2.12–13; KaivUp 1.5; KaUp 1.2.8.

See V. 3, 29, 42, 138, 149, 477, 489, 518, and 519 for references to grace.

kṛpayā = grace; compassion. In this context, what is being asked for is *gurukṛpā* or the grace of the Master; **svāmin** = lord; master; teacher; spiritual preceptor (from the verb root **sva** = 'own' or 'self' + *asmi* = 'I am'; thus the only independent one, i.e., the Lord or Master); **praśno** = question.

ko nāma bandhaḥ katham eṣa āgataḥ
kathaṁ pratiṣṭhā'sya kathaṁ vimokṣaḥ |
ko'sāvanātmā, paramaḥ ka ātmā
tayor vivekaḥ katham etad ucyatām ||51||

What, indeed, is bondage? How did it begin? How does it continue to exist? How is one freed from it? What is this non-self? What is the supreme Self? How is one to discriminate between them? Please speak to me about all these.

In verse 49, the Master declared that the student is, in reality, the supreme Self (*paramātman*) and it is an apparent association with ignorance which produces the not-self (*anātman*) and bondage. Thus, after hearing this, the student reverently asks a series of seven questions beginning with the seemingly experiential predicament of bondage. The Master begins by answering the fourth question first, namely 'how is liberation achieved?' This he does in verse 71 after first making sure the disciple clearly understands that liberation is not merely book-learning nor second-hand knowledge nor something that is outside of the disciple.

katham = what; wherefore; by what reason; how; **bandha** = bondage (from the verb root *bandh* = 'to bind'); **pratiṣṭhā** = standing still; resting; existing for a long time; persevering; **vimokṣaḥ** = cessation; set free; liberated; freedom; **anātmā** = not-self; **paramaḥ ātmā** = supreme Self; **vivekaḥ** = discrimination.

śrīgurur-vāca:
dhanyo'si kṛta-kṛtyo'si pāvitam te kulam tvayā |
yad avidyā-bandha-muktyā brahmī-bhavitum icchasi ||52||

The beneficent Master said:
Blessed are you. You have done what needed to be done. Through you your entire family has been purified because you desire to attain the Absolute by becoming free from the bonds of ignorance.

By speaking so compassionately and with such high praise, the student will naturally, and at least for the time being, lose whatever anxiety was present and begin to seek the Self with confidence and earnestness. As in all explanations, many perspectives are simultaneously possible. The student is blessed for, from the Master's perspective, the student is the Self, here and now. The student has done what needed to be done or, as Advaitins say, 'accomplished the already accomplished' (*prāptasya prāptiḥ*) From another perspective, because the student has begun to seek the Self, success is assured; it is just a matter of time now. Once one has begun the quest, one will not stop until victory is gained. The BG 2.40 declares, 'In this path, no effort is ever lost and no obstacle prevails.' Because one is the Self, bliss absolute, one will never cease searching until one discovers that which one really is. This is true for everyone but especially for those who are consciously seeking the Self. And not only oneself, but also one's biological family benefits. However, the word family (*kula*) has an incredible variety of meanings, all of which may be subsumed under the concept of 'grouping together, implying manifestation', including condensation, solidification, that which binds or contracts; whatever has name and form; any unit of manifestation; human body; abode; residence; family; world; universe; embodied cosmos; all of creation; divine creative energy; God's body; philosophical systems characterized by certain principles. Thus, the family, from many perspectives, will be purified.

One's treasure (*dhana*) is that-which-one-holds-dear. The Master implies, 'because you desire to attain the Absolute . . . you and your entire family have become pure . . . thus are you blessed, thus do you deserve the treasure.' Worldly people believe that sense objects constitute one's treasure, one's fortune. But sense objects, truly speaking, are not enjoyed and consumed by individuals so much as they enjoy and consume individuals. When sense organs come into contact with sense objects, after some time, and a fleeting moment of happiness, one becomes tired and worn out. Eventually even the body itself wears out. If sense objects really gave bliss absolute one would not become tired and seek solitary rest in sleep. True good fortune, to the spiritual aspirant, is detachment from sense objects.

Note that '*bhavitum*' in *brahmī-bhavitum icchasi* indicates a reference implying that the realization of the Absolute happens in a future time. In other words, realization is something that has not yet occurred. Yet, according to the Advaita dictum 'whatever is produced is impermanent' (*yat janyam tadanityam*), it follows that realization must also be impermanent. This is not so. Though the individual is the Self, here and now, it is not known. What is the Reality which one is attempting to speak about? Is it somewhere else? Is it not (somehow/some way) the very light by which one asks the question and goes in search of the answer? The seeking itself must be That. Non-duality implies that the seeker, the sought, and the act thereof are not different. One can never meaningfully say, 'I am this'. It is not possible to know what the Self is, but one can know what it is not. Whatever is pointed out as 'this' is not all of oneself. Can there ever be a perception or act of imagination without you? Experiences belong to you. Experiences come and go. Thus, the Self need not be obtained. One is already the Self. What is 'other', alone can be obtained. Though the 'I', as the constitutive Being of the individual, is continually and eternally manifesting itself and is known as the content of the 'I'-notion, for it to be consciously known a philosophical/religious enquiry is necessary. The fruit of this enquiry is immediate realization. The MuṇḍUp 3.2.9 statement, '*Brahmaveda brahmaiva bhavati*', (the knower of *Brahman* becomes *Brahman*), does not mean a change of state or an attainment. The Sanskrit root '*bhū*' from which '*bhavati*' (becomes) is derived, means both 'being' and 'becoming'. In the present context it refers to 'being'. One is what one always is. To attain the unattained, action is necessary. But to attain the already attained, no action is required. Knowledge of the fact as-it-is will dispel the darkness of ignorance which covers it.

dhanya = fortunate; auspicious; blessed; treasure; one who deserves the prize or treasure; **pāvitam** = purified; cleansed; **kulam** = family.

ṛṇa-mocana-kartāraḥ pitus santi sutādayaḥ |
bandha-mocana-kartā tu svasmād anyo na kaścana ||53||

There are sons and others to discharge the debts of the father. However, there is no one other than oneself to free one from one's own bondage.

According to the TaittSaṁ 6.3.10.5, a *brahmin* is born with three debts: to the seers, to the gods, and to the forefathers. Also see BDh. 2.11.9–33. In the second stage (*āśrama*) of one's life, that of the householder (*gṛhastha*), one pays back these three debts. The debt to one's ancestors is repaid by marrying and having children, especially male children. In a patriarchal society, it is the male children who keep the family line alive. The debt to one's teachers is repaid by educating the next generation. The debt to the gods is repaid by performing sacrifices. The point of this verse is that, even were a father not to repay these three debts, or any others that he may have contracted, it is always possible for another to repay them for him. But, no one can free another besides that person themself. This verse and the following verses emphasise that direct realization is the only means of removing ignorance.

See V. 54–58, and 68 on freeing one's own self.

ṛṇa = debt; **mocana** = to free; **pitā** = father; **pitṛ** = forefather, ancestor; **suta** = child, offspring; **bandha** = bondage; **mocana** = freedom from.

mastaka-nyasta-bhārādeḥ duḥkham anyair nivāryate |
kṣudhādi-kṛta-duḥkhaṁ tu vinā svena na kenacit ||54||

The suffering caused by a load on the head can be removed by others. But the suffering caused by hunger and the like can only be relieved by oneself.

A person may enter a restaurant and remain there year after year, from morning until evening, reading the menu. They may speak with the waiters and make friends with the cook. But until and unless one orders the food and eats it, one's hunger will not be appeased. What is necessary is a direct, personal experience. And once one has had the experience, one need not go to another restaurant. It is one's hunger which brought one to the restaurant. Once appeased, its purpose is finished.

See V. 53–58, and 68 on freeing one's own self.

masta = the head; **nyasta** = placed, deposited; **bhāra** = load, burden, trouble; **duḥkha** = suffering, pain, unhappiness, sorrow; **kṣudha** = to be hungry.

pathyam auṣadha-sevā ca kriyate yena rogiṇā |
ārogya-siddhir-dṛṣṭā'sya nānyānuṣṭhita-karmaṇā ||55||

A patient alone regains health by taking medicine and observing dietary rules, but not by the efforts of another.

Śaṅkara's slogan is: 'To one's Self; to Self-experience.' The Real is involved in, and is the basis of, one's everyday experience. Immanently here and now, the quest begins and ends. Where could Reality be but right here, right now? To search means that one is really looking for comfort, which one wants to last forever. But no state of mind can last forever. Nothing in space and time lasts. In the 'realm' of non-duality, everything is complete, right now. Where there is One, no support or proof is needed. Reality need not be pointed at. It can't be said to be 'here' or 'there'. It is not the result of a concerted effort. It is here and now. It is nearer than the nearest. It is not seen because one looks far away from oneself (outside, in names and forms, in objects and in that which is not one's Self).

See BGBh. 18.50, 'Though quite self-evident, easily knowable, quite near and forming the very Self, *Brahman* appears to the unenlightened, to those whose understanding is carried away by the differentiated phenomena of names and forms created by ignorance, as unknown, difficult to know, very remote, as though he were a separate thing.'

See V. 53–58, and 68 on freeing one's own self.

pathyam = suitable, proper, 'belonging to the way'; **auṣadha** = medicine; **rogiṇā** = sick, ill; **ārogya-siddhir** = healthy.

vastu-svarūpam sphuṭa-bodha-cakṣuṣā
svenaiva vedyaṁ na tu paṇḍitena |
candra-svarūpaṁ nija-cakṣuṣaiva
jñātavyam anyair avagamyate kim ||56||

The true nature of Reality should be apprehended by oneself through the eye of clear knowledge and never through another, though he may be a scholar. The nature of the moon is to be known through one's own eyes. Can others make one know it?

Once, many years ago, I had a chance meeting with an Indian monk who asked me, 'Who you?' Having lived in India and being used to this type of English and being young and polite I began to answer him, 'I am John Grimes' but just as I reached the 'G' of Grimes, he said, '*Bas*, family name, who you?' ('*bas*' is Hindi for 'stop, enough'). Again, since I had studied Indian thought, I very confidently and boldly began to reply, 'I am the immortal *Ātman*' but just as I reached the 'A' of *Ātman*, again he stopped me, '*Bas*, book name, who you?' With the first '*bas*' he wiped out the idea that I was my physical body. With the second '*bas*', he wiped out my entire mental universe. What was left? With two small words he had succeeded in conveying to me that I was neither my body nor mind. How to answer him? So I said, 'I do not know.' Immediately he responded, 'Find out'. I replied, 'How?' He responded, 'Not how, find out'. Again I asked, 'How?' He was holding a handkerchief in his hand and he opened his fingers and let the handkerchief drop to the ground and as it fell he said, 'Let go'. Again I asked, 'How (to let go)?' He responded, 'Not how, let go'. And then he turned and left the room.

See BṛhUp 2.4.5, 'The Self is to be seen'.

See V. 53–58, and 68 on freeing one's own self.

vastu-svarūpam = the true nature or essence of reality; **sphuṭa-bodha-cakṣuṣā** = known through the clear, undefiled eye of knowledge; **svenaiva vedyaṁ** = become the object of one's own comprehension; **paṇḍit** = scholar; **candra** = moon.

avidyā-kāma-karmādi-pāśa-bandhaṁ vimocituṁ |
kaḥ śaknuyād vinātmānaṁ kalpa-koṭi-śatair api ||57||

Who but one's own self, even after the lapse of hundreds of millions of years, could destroy the bonds of ignorance, desire, action, and so on?

The question is, 'Who is the Self; what is knowledge?' Certainly it is not information. It is not about things, people, places, ideas, externals outside of oneself. Knowledge is wisdom which is the Self, within. Knowledge is not a prize for passing some tests. Knowledge is not a reward for good behavior. One is eligible for knowledge because one is knowledge. One need not merit knowledge, it is one's own. Because one sees 'the other' as physical, as a body, one is quick to look elsewhere. The question is, 'Why begin with others?' Begin with yourself. Advaita declares that the world is non-real and that one's Self is real. Isn't it strange? One says one thing and another hears another. Though the words are the same, there appears to be a gap between speaker and listener, between scriptural injunctions and religious aspirants. How to close the gap? Give up the idea of being what you think yourself to be and there will be no gap. When one imagines one as separate, a gap is created. Such a gap need not be bridged – just don't create it. *Ekam evādvitiyam* – 'one only without a second.' How very strange! The very same words which seem true to the sage, to me appear immanently false. 'There is no other,' how obviously untrue! Thus, the injunction of qualification. To find the Self it is imperative that one look in the right place: i.e., within. Looking outside just won't do it.

A *kalpa* is a cycle of time of an extremely long duration. It is a 'day' of Brahmā and is divided into a number of lesser periods called *manvantara*. Four *yugas* makes a *mahāyuga* (or *manvantara*) and one-thousand *mahā-yugas* make a half-*kalpa* or 4,320,000,000 years, which is the duration of one day or one night of Brahmā. Two half-*kalpas* make a *kalpa* which is One Day of Brahmā (i.e., a day and a night).

See V. 53–58, 68 per freeing one's own self.

avidyā = ignorance; **kāma** = desire, lust; **karma** = action; **ādi** = 'and so on', which includes birth, life, death, happiness, unhappiness, etc.; **pāśa** = bonds, rope; **kalpa** = an extremely long cycle of time, 8,640,000,000 years; **koṭi-śatair** = hundreds of millions.

na yogena na sāṁkhyena karmaṇā no na vidyayā |
brahmātmaikatva-bodhena mokṣaḥ siddhyati nānyathā ||58||

Neither by Yoga, nor Sāṅkhya, nor action, nor learning is liberation achieved but only by the realization of the oneness of the Absolute and the Self and in no other way.

The Sāṅkhya and Yoga philosophical systems both postulate dualism. As well, they both postulate that the supreme goal of life is to be achieved by action and/or discriminative knowledge (*puruṣa prakṛti viveka*). Both systems postulate a plurality of individuals. All of this is in conflict with the oneness of the Absolute as presented by Śaṅkara. As the BṛhUp declares, 'Liberation, which is not a product since it is ever-existent, cannot be produced by action.'

The saint Tayumanuvar said, 'Why all these *mahāyogas*? You are already the Self. Why don't you remain established in your own natural state? Don't forget who you are, don't cease to be aware of it, and don't concern yourself with all these exotic practices.'

See V. 6, 7, 10, 11, 13, 57, 60–61, and 149 on 'action will never produce liberation'.

See ŚvetUp 3.8, 'Only by knowing the supreme person does one pass over death. There is no other path for going there'; also ŚvetUp 6.15.

yoga = a philosophical school expounding mind control founded by Patañjali; **sāṁkhya** = a philosophical school expounding dualistic realism founded by Kapila; **brahmātmaikatva bodhena** = realization of the oneness of the identity between the Absolute and the Self; **siddhyati** = is revealed or realized; **nānyathā** = not otherwise, in no other way.

vīṇāyā rūpa-saundaryam tantrī-vādana-sauṣṭhavam |
prajā-rañjana-mātraṁ tan na sāmrājyāya kalpate ||59||

The beauty of a vīṇa's form and the skill of playing on its strings serve only to please others; but they do not suffice to confer sovereignty.

Practice is needed only when one has a goal; something to attain. The eternal is here and now. Advaita calls this 'the attainment of the aleady attained'. Examples given include 'finding a necklace around one's neck which was thought to be lost' or 'a man who thought he was a thief but discovers that he is really a prince', or 'the discovery of the seemingly lost 10th man'. This is called 'obtaining the already attained' (*prāptasyaprāptiḥ*). In other words, one is already the Self and thus no amount of action will render one what one already is. One is *born* a prince; one need not *become* a prince.

See TaittUp 1.6.2, 'In this space of the heart lies the immortal . . . he obtains sovereignty'.

See ChānUp 8.28, 'If a person is desirous of the world of song and music, out of one's mere thought, song and music arise. Possessed of that world of song and music, one is happy.'

vīṇā = the Indian lute; **saundarya** = beautiful; **sāmrājya** = sovereignty.

vāg-vaikharī śabda-jharī śāstra-vyākhyāna-kauśalam |
vaiduṣyaṁ viduṣāṁ tadvad bhuktaye na tu muktaye ||60||

Erudition, articulate speech, proficiency in explicating the scriptures, scholarship of the learned, these give enjoyment but not liberation.

A wave is only water. Forgetting what it really is, and thinking itself to be a name and a form, it endlessly goes in search of its own identity. When a wave first enquires into who it is, it initially thinks that it is a part of the whole. Big, little, good, bad, action, inaction seem to rise up, mere froth of ignorance. Yet these waves will never find out who they really are if they restrict their enquiry to what is other than what they are. Looking at names and forms can never take one back to one's essence.

See KaUp 1.2.9, 'One cannot grasp this by reasoning'.

Generally four stages of speech/sound are distinguished: supreme sound (*parā*); visible sound which can be heard as '*om*' (*paśyantī*); middle sound which refers to a variety of basic sounds (*mātṛkā*) which are very subtle (*madhyama*); and manifest sound (*vaikhāra*) which is the grossest level of sound and which is heard in ordinary speech.

vāg vaikharī = erudition, speech made of easy words; **śabdajharī** = fluent speech, articulate words; **kauśalam** = skillfulness, proficiency; **bhukti** = enjoyment.

avijñāte pare tattve śāstrādhītis tu niṣphalā |
vijñāte'pi pare tattve śāstrādhītis tu niṣphalā ||61||

Study of the scriptures is fruitless if the supreme Truth is not known and, when the supreme Truth is known, study of the scriptures is equally fruitless.

Who is it that desires to study? The Truth is here and now. It has always been here and now. It is only because one has an idea that one has to perform some action, to obtain something new, that one studies, one searches. Yet, that which is prompting one to search is already present. The desire for Truth arises from Truth itself. Study is but the mind working on the mind. But the Truth is somewhere where the mind cannot go.

An oft-noted consequence is that, prior to self-realization, mere book-learning is useless unless it is accompanied by discrimination and detachment, and, to a person of self-realization, it is useless since that person has already achieved the ultimate goal of life.

Compare BṛhUp 4.3.22, 'the Vedas are not the Vedas' (*yatra vedāḥ avedāḥ*).

Compare KenaUp 3, 'It is other than all that is known, and It is also beyond the unknown'.

pare tattve = superior or supreme truth; **niṣphala** = fruitless, without results.

śabda-jālaṁ mahāraṇyaṁ citta-bhramaṇa-kāraṇam |
ataḥ prayatnāt jñātavyaṁ tattvajñat tattvam ātmanaḥ ||62||

The flowing together of many words is like a great forest which causes the mind to wander confused. Therefore, those who know this Truth should earnestly endeavor to know the true nature of the Self.

Words, like trees in a forest, proliferate and increase unceasingly. However, they also tend to obscure what is of utmost importance.

See ChānUp 7.1.3, 'But, venerable sir, I am only like one knowing the words and not a knower of the Self.' See V. 64–65, 399, and 474 on mere words.

mahāraṇyaṁ = great forest; **bhramaṇa** = wandering, roaming about; **ataḥ** = therefore.

ajñāna-sarpa-daṣṭasya brahma-jñānauṣadhaṁ vinā |
kimu vedaiś ca śāstraiś ca kimu mantraḥ kim auṣadhaiḥ ||63||

For one who has been bitten by the serpent of ignorance, the only remedy is knowledge of the Absolute. To such a one, of what avail are the Vedas and scriptures, sacred syllables and medicines?

Knowledge of the Absolute is that which removes ignorance. This has nothing to do with the body, the mind, the senses. One is the Self, here and now. There is no relationship, no cure. This has nothing to do with anything that is destructible or impermanent. One is the lion of Truth and wherever a lion roams it cuts its own path.

When a person has been bitten by a snake, one does not ask irrelevant questions like, 'How large was the snake? When was it born? How fast was it moving?' and so on. If one does, one will die before one is saved. What is of utmost importance is to remove the poison. Likewise, the only antidote for the poison of ignorance is knowledge of the Absolute. See V. 12, 112, 140, 199, 237, 248, 303, 388, 405, 407, and 550 for references to a snake.

See BṛhUp 4.3.22, 'Here a father is not a father, a mother is not a mother, worlds are not worlds, gods are not gods, and the Vedas are not the Vedas'.

ajñāna-sarpa-daṣṭasya = bitten by the snake of ignorance; **mantra** = sacred syllables, a sacred word or phrase of spiritual significance and power; **auṣadha** = medicine.

na gacchati vinā pānaṁ vyādhir auṣadha-śabdataḥ |
vinā'parokṣa anubhavaṁ brahma-śabdair na mucyate ||64||

A disease is not cured by the mere repetition of the word 'medicine'. One must imbibe it. Similarly, without direct realization, liberation does not arise merely by uttering the word 'Brahman'.

A dream ends only when one awakens. A disease is cured only when one imbibes the medicine. Hunger ceases only when one consumes food. Arise! Awake! A merely mechanical repetition of a *mantra* will not, by itself, produce liberation. When one is suffering from a headache, the mere repetition of the word 'aspirin' will not remove the headache. In fact, it may increase it! The only cure is to take the medicine, assimilate it, become one with it.

See KaUp 3.14, 'Arise, awake! Pay attention, when you've obtained your wishes! A razor's sharp edge is hard to cross; that, poets say, is the difficulty of the path.'

See ChānUp 7.1.3, 'But, venerable sir, I am only like one knowing the words and not a knower of the Self.' See V. 62, 65, 399, and 474 on mere words.

vinā = without, except; **aparokṣānubhava** = direct experience.

akṛtvā dṛśya-vilayam ajñātvā tattvam ātmanaḥ |
brahma-śabdaḥ kuto muktir uktimātraphalair nṛṇām ||65||

Without effecting the dissolution of the seen, and without knowing the Truth of the Self, how can one achieve liberation by the mere repetition of the word 'Brahman?' The result is merely noise.

It should be obvious that one can learn to chant the *mantras*, and even to learn what they mean, and still remain unenlightened. Surely this shows that the *mantras* must have some deeper meaning which does not appear to the intellect. Inner enlightenment is based upon intuition and not intellect. 'Only he who has seen can properly speak about the One' (AV 2.1.1; RV 1.164.6); 'It is not understood by those who understand. It is understood by those who do not understand' (KenaUp 2.3). See also BṛhUp 4.3.30; 2.4.14; 3.4.2; 3.7.23.)

dṛśya = whatever is seen; **kutaḥ** = whence?

akṛtvā śatru-saṁhāram agatvā akhila-bhū-śriyam |
rājā aham iti śabdād no rājā bhavitum arhati ||66||

A person does not become a king merely by saying: 'I am king', but by killing one's enemies and taking possession of the splendor and wealth of the entire kingdom.

Though it may be true that a person is already the Self, unless one ceases to be under the spell of the delusion of ignorance and directly, personally realizes the Self, it is as if one is not the Self. Further, it is not merely by declaring oneself a king that one is so. It is by possessing the necessary requirements.

śatru = enemy; **rājā** = king.

āptokiṁ khananaṁ tathopariśilāpākarṣaṇam svīkṛtiṁ
nikṣepaḥ samapekṣate na hi bahiḥ śabdais tu nirgacchati |
tadvad brahma-vidopadeśa-manana-dhyānādibhir labhyate
māyā-kārya-tirohitaṁ svamamalaṁ tattvaṁ na duryuktibhiḥ ||67||

A buried treasure hidden underground requires the words of a reliable person, excavating, removal of the stones and earth covering it, and actually possessing it. Merely calling its name will never bring it forth. Similarly, the pure Truth of the Self, which is hidden by the obscuring power of illusion (māyā),[1] can be obtained only through the teachings of a knower of the Absolute followed by reflection,[2] meditation, and so forth; but never by perverted reasoning.

In the last few verses, Śaṅkara has been trying to point to the absolute necessity for certain prerequisites to be present. These prerequisites require effort. Even if eventually Śaṅkara will declare that it is not by action that the Self is realized, there are still

[1] According to Śaṅkara, *māyā* meant either the veiling power of Viṣṇu, magic, or illusion. In the BS itself, the term only occurs once (BS 3.2.3) and there the implied meaning is illusion ('But the dream creation is mere *māyā*, because of its nature of not being a complete manifestation of the totality of attributes').

[2] See BṛhUp 2.4.5, 4.5.6, '. . . to be heard, to be reflected on, to be meditated upon'. See V. 70, 72, 342, 365 on reflection, meditation and so on.
See V. 110–112, 125, 245, 406, 497, and 574 for *māyā*.

certain conditions which must be established before the liberating word will achieve its magic. One must know where to look, and what to look for.

āptokiṁ = words of a reliable person; **khananaṁ** = the act of digging, excavating; **brahma-vidopadeśa** = comprehensive spiritual instruction by a knower of the Absolute; **manana** = reflection; **dhyāna** = meditation; **māyā** = illusion; **tirohitaṁ** = hidden; **na duryuktibhiḥ** = not obtained by perverted reasoning.

tasmāt-sarva-prayatnena bhava-bandha-vimuktaye |
svaireva yatnaḥ kartavyo rogāder iva paṇḍitaiḥ ||68||

Therefore, the wise themselves should, as in the case of disease and the like, personally strive by every means to experience liberation from the bondage of worldly existence.

The word 'therefore' signals that the discussion of the previous nine verses is now being concluded. 'By every means' means that, having acquired the four-fold pre-requisites, the wise disciple should seek and approach a *sadguru* and strive diligently to achieve realization.

tasmāt = therefore, hence (one must get rid of one's bondage oneself); **sarvprayatnena** = by every means; **svaireva** = by themselves; **rogādi** = from disease and so on (hunger, thirst, etc); **paṇḍitaiḥ** = by the wise (this context implies not so much a scholar as a wise person).

yas tvayā adya kṛtaḥ praśno varīyān śāstravin mataḥ |
śūtra-prāyo nigūḍhārtho jñātavyaś ca mumukṣubhiḥ ||69||

The question that you have asked today is excellent. It is approved by those well-versed in the scriptures. Like an aphorism, it is brief, well-formed, and pregnant with meaning. All who seek liberation should know this question.

In verse 51, the disciple asked, 'What is bondage? How did it arise? How does it continue to exist? How is one to get rid of it? What is the not-self? Who is the Self? How to distinguish between the two?' Instead of immediately answering the first question, the teacher spoke at length about the futility of mere words without an accompanying earnest desire for liberation and the understanding that this seeking requires real self-effort. After thus forewarning the student and rendering absolutely clear what is involved, once again the teacher praises the disciple for his intelligent question. Today, with gossip at such a premium, it should be noted that the disciple did not ask about the teacher or other needless pieces of information. In a few words, all that was asked was all that is necessary. This, itself, reveals the student's worthiness.

An aphorism (*sūtra*) is defined as: 'It must be brief; with the words not further reducible; clear; comprehensive; penetrate the essence meant; and faultless grammarwise.'

praśno = question; **sūtra** = aphorism; thread (from the verb root *siv* = 'to sew'); terse, pithy, extremely condensed; **nigūḍhārthaḥ** = words are few.

śṛṇuṣvāvahito vidvan yan mayā samudīryate |
tad-etad-śravaṇāt sadyo bhava-bandhād vimokṣyase ||70||

Listen attentively, O learned one, to what I say. By listening[1] you will immediately be freed from the bonds of worldly existence.

Listening, carefully listening, is essentially an investigation determining the meaning of scriptural words or declarations, especially the great sayings (*mahāvākya*). Listening, for a supremely qualified aspirant, will immediately enlighten that aspirant. Otherwise, listening and subsequently study, reflection and contemplation orient one's mind to what is to be sought and provide a framework, grounded in the sage's experience, by which an aspirant's own subsequent realization will occur. Listening, in this context, does not mean merely hearing the sounds, but carefully imbibing the meaning putting it into practice.

śṛṇuṣvāvahito = listen attentively; **vidvan** = learned one; **bhava-bandhād vimokṣyase** = immediately freed from the bonds of worldly existenc.

mokṣasya hetuḥ prathamo nigadyate
vairāgyam atyantam anitya-vastuṣu |
tataḥ śamaścāpi damas titikṣā
nyāsaḥ prasakta akhila-karmaṇām bhṛśam ||71||

The first step in the means to liberation is declared to be a complete absence of desire[2] for all things impermanent. Then comes tranquillity,[3] self-control, forbearance, and the complete relinquishment of all desire-prompted actions.

Because one believes in oneself, the thinker, the seer, the hearer, etc., one has faith that what one thinks, sees, and hears is real. Instead, why not doubt the things which come and go – thoughts, sights, and sounds – and hold on to that which is always there and is foundational to it all – yourself. The *I am* can never be changed into *I am not*. *What* is experienced is always open to doubt. The *meaning* of what is experienced can always be doubted. But, that *someone* experienced it is certain. Attachment to the body is what produces bondage and thus the first step one must take is to cultivate detachment.

'Absence of desire for all things impermanent' was defined in verses 21–25.

mokṣa = freedom, liberation; **hetu** = means to; **prathamo** = first step, initially; **vairāgya** = detachment (see verse 21); **anitya** = impermanent, transitory; **śama** = tranquillity (see verse 22); **dama** = self-control (see verse 23); **titikṣā** = forebearance (see verse 25).

tataḥ śrutis tan mananaṁ satattva-
dhyānaṁ ciraṁ nitya-nirantaraṁ muneḥ |
tato'vikalpaṁ parametya vidvān
ihaiva nirvāṇa-sukhaṁ samṛcchati ||72||

---

1 See BṛhUp 2.4.5, 4.5.6, '. . . to be heard, to be reflected on, to be meditated upon'. See V. 67, 72, 342, and 365 on 'hearing'.

2 See KaUp 2.1–11 regarding transient joys to be abandoned.

3 See BṛhUp 4.4.23, '. . . tranquil, self-controlled, withdrawn, patient, collected. See V. 21, 29, 30, and 31 on detachment.

Then one must hear[1] the Truth, reflect upon it, and finally, as a wise one does, meditate long upon it constantly, continuously, uninterruptedly. Thus, the learned one attains the supreme state in which there is no subject-object dichotomy[2] and experiences the bliss of liberation in this very life.[3]

A qualified spiritual aspirant shall resort to the hearing of texts (*śravaṇa*), reflection thereon (*manana*), and meditation (*nididhyāsana*) which are considered the principal proximate means (*mukhya antaranga sādhana*) to liberation.

tataḥ = then, after that; **śruti** = to hear, listen; **manana** = reflection; **dhyāna** = meditation; **ciram** = long (time); **nitya** = constantly, permanently; **nirantara** = uninterruptedly, without break; **muni** = wise, sage; **nirvikalpa** = indeterminate, without parts; **nirvāṇa** = liberation, perfection; **ihaiva** = here and now, in this very life.

yad boddhavyaṁ tavedānīm ātmānātma-vivecanam |
tad ucyate mayā samyak śrutvātmany avadhāraya ||73||

Now I will tell you about that which you must know in the matter of discrimination between the Self and the not-self. Listen, and then decide about it in your mind.

The disciple asked about the discrimination between the Self and the not-self in V. 51. Now, the Master says he will tell him about it. See V. 2 and 11 on discrimination between the Self and the not-self.

yad boddhavyaṁ = that which you must know (before one attains knowledge which will destroy ignorance and produce liberation, one must first learn to **ātmānātma viveka** = discriminate between the Self and the not-self); **avadhāraya** = decide, put into.

majjāsthi-medaḥ pala-rakta-carma-
tvagāhvayair dhātubhir ebhir anvitam |
pādoru-vakṣo-bhuja-pṛṣṭha-mastakair
angair upāṅgair upayuktam etat ||74||

---

[1] See BṛhUp 2.4.5; 4.5.6, 'Verily, *Maitreyī*, by the seeing of, by the hearing of, by the thinking of, by the understanding of the Self, all this is known'; also BṛhUp 4.5.6. See, on 'hearing, reflection, meditation', V. 67, 70, 342, and 365.

[2] See BṛhUp 4.4.19, 'In it there is no diversity'; also BṛhUp 2.4.14; 4.5.15.

[3] While the concept of liberated-while-living does not occur in the *Upaniṣads*, there are many references which, directly or indirectly, allude to the idea. See BṛhUp 4.4.14, 'Verily, while we are here we may know this'; KaUp.2.3.14, 'A mortal becomes immortal, attains the Absolute even here, when the knots of the heart are destroyed'; MuṇḍUp 2.1.10, 'He who knows that which is set in the cave of the heart, he, here on earth, cuts the knot of ignorance'; BṛhUp 3.8.10, 'Whosoever, O *Gārgi*, in this world, without knowing this Imperishable . . . departs from this world is pitiable'; KenaUp.2.5, 'There is truth if a person knows it here and if not there is a great loss'; ĪśaUp 1.7, 'When, to one who knows, all beings have, verily, become one with his own Self, then what delusion and what sorrow can be to him who has seen the oneness?' AitUp 2.1.5–6, 'While I (Vāmadeva) was in the womb I realized (the Self and subsequently lived a long and productive life)'; Śaṅkara's commentary on BṛhUp 4.4.6, 'The man free from desires realizes the Absolute even here'.

For liberated-while-living-in-a-body (*jīvanmukti*) see V. 72, 318, 419, 429–441, and 552.

Marrow, bone, fat, flesh, blood, skin, and epidermis are the seven substances the body is composed of. The body also consists of the legs, thighs, chest, arms, back, and the head.

The physical body is described as consisting of seven substances. If one takes a cross-section of the body, one would see, at the center, the marrow which lies at the innermost core. In a progressive exteriorization the marrow is surrounded by bone, bone by fat, fat by flesh and blood. The outermost covering consists of skin and the epidermis.

majjāsthi = marrow, bone; **medaḥ** = fat; **pala** = flesh; **rakta** = red-colored, blood; **carma** = skin; **tvagāhvayair** = outer layer of the skin, epidermis, cuticle; **pādoru** = legs; **vakṣo** = back; **bhuja** = arms; **pṛṣṭha** = back; **mastakair** = head; **angair** = limbs of the body.

ahaṁ mameti prathitaṁ śarīraṁ
mohāspadaṁ sthūlam itīryate budhaiḥ |
nabho-nabhassvad-dahanāmbu-bhūmayaḥ
sūkṣmāṇi bhūtāni bhavanti tāni ||75||

The body, which is the basis for the delusion of 'I' and 'mine', is called by the wise 'the gross body'. The sky, air, fire, water, and earth are the subtle elements.

Because one thinks that one is their body, delusion arises. All delusions and all troubles are based upon the body. There is not a single problem in the world which is not dependent upon the body. Think about it. The body is the basis for delusion.

The five great elements (*mahābhūta*) are space (*ākāśa*), which emerges from sound (*śabda*), air (*vāyu*) which emerges from touch (*sparśa*), fire (*tejas*) which emerges from color (*rūpa*), water (*ap*) which emerges from taste (*rasa*), and earth (*pṛthivī*) which emerges from smell (*gandha*). These five gross elements emerge from the subtle essences of the elements (*tanmātras*). The TaittUp 1.7 speaks of the five-fold division (*pañcīkaraṇa*). See V. 90. It is the theory that every physical object contains all the five elements in various proportions. Each of the five elements is divided into two equal parts. One half is reserved for that element and the other half is again split into four parts and associated with each of the others. Also see BS 2.4.22.

ahaṁ = 'I'; **mama** = mine; **prathitaṁ** = manifested; **śarīraṁ** = body, that which perishes; **sthūlam** = gross body; **nabho** = sky; **nabhassvad** = air; **dahanāmbu** = water; **bhūmayaḥ** = earth; **sūkṣmāṇi** = subtle; **bhūtāni** = elements.

parasparāṁśair militāni bhūtvā
sthūlāni ca sthūla-śarīra-hetavaḥ |
matrās tadiyā viṣayā bhavanti
śabdādayaḥ pañca sukhāya bhoktuḥ ||76||

Having united with parts of one another, the elements combine to become gross and form the gross body. Their five subtle essences, such as sound and the rest, constitute the sense objects which contribute to the enjoyment of the enjoyer.

The subtle essences (*tanmātra*) are sound (*śabda*), touch (*sparśa*), sight (*rūpa*), taste (*rasa*), and smell (*gandha*). The five elements (*mahābhūta*) are derived from the *tanmātras* as follows: from sound comes space; from touch comes air; from sight comes fire; from taste comes water; and from smell comes earth. The *tanmātras* are said to evolve from the *tāmasa* aspect of egoity according to Sāṅkhya.

parasparāṃśair = like one another, mutually; **militāni** = unite, combine, mix; **sthūla-śarīra** = gross body; **mātrāḥ** = made of sense objects (*tanmātra*); so called in the scriptures because of its root form '*mīyante*' or 'they are made of the sense objects too because they are enjoyed'; **viṣayā** = bind (from the verb root *ṣinj* + *vi* = 'to bind'; **śabdādayaḥ** = sound and the rest (touch, form, taste, smell); **pañca** = five; **sukhāya** = enjoyment; **bhoktuḥ** = enjoyer.

ya eṣu mūḍha viṣayeṣu baddhā
rāgorū-paśena su-durdamena |
āyānti niryānty adha ūrdhvam uccaiḥ
sva-karma-dūtena javena nītāḥ ||77||

Those fools, who are bound to the sense objects by the strong chord of attachment which is difficult to break, come and go, carried up and down by the powerful emissary of their own past actions.

See MuṇḍUp 1.2.8, 'Wallowing in ignorance, but calling themselves wise, thinking they are learned, the fools go around, hurting themselves badly, like a group of blind men, led by a man who is himself blind.'

See KaivUp 1.14, 'Again, the individual, on account of his connection with the deeds of his past life wakes up and sleeps'.

See V. 4, 5, 162, 163, 220, and 549 for fools (*mūḍha*). See also MuṇḍUp 1.2.8; KaUp 1.2.5; MaitrīUp 7.9; BG 17.5–6.

mūḍhaḥ = fools; **paśa** = cord, rope, bond; **rāga** = attachment, greed, passion; **sudurdamena** = difficult to break; **dūta** = messenger, ambassador, negotiator.

śabdādibhiḥ pañcabhir eva pañca
pañcatvam āpuḥ svaguṇena baddhāḥ |
kuraṅga-mātaṅga-pataṅga-mīna-bhṛṅgā
naraḥ pañcabhir-añcitaḥ kim ||78||

The deer, the elephant, the moth, the fish, and the black bee each meet death through their bondage to only one of the five senses. What, then, is the condition of the human being who is attached to all five?

The deer meets death through its attachment to sound. The elephant is caught by its desire for touch. The moth meets death due to its fascination for a sight. The fish meets death due to its relationship with taste. The black bee meets death due to its fascination for smell. A deer can be caught by enticing it with sweet sounds like those of a flute. Upon hearing the flute, a deer stands motionless, entranced; an elephant, during the mating season, is easily lured by the touch of a female elephant; a moth is attracted to the light of a flame not knowing that if it falls into it it will burn; a fisherman baits a hook, and a bee is attracted to the odor of a flower.

śabdādibhiḥ = sound and the rest; **kuraṅga** = deer; **mātaṅga** = elephant; **pataṅga** = moth; **mīna** = fish; **bhṛṅgā** = black bee; **naraḥ** = human being, person, people.

doṣeṇa tīvro viṣayaḥ kṛṣṇa-sarpa-viṣād api |
viṣaṁ nihanti bhoktāraṁ draṣṭāraṁ cakṣuṣāpyayam ||79||

Sense objects are even more deadly than the poison of a king cobra. The latter is fatal to one who swallows it, but the former kills by merely looking at it.

A cobra can kill by its injection of poison into its victim. How much deadlier are sense objects, which kill upon sight. Sense objects are pleasing, they give instant gratification. The moment one comes into contact with a sense object, liking, attachment, and desire arise. Sense objects appeal directly to the senses and hold out the promise of pleasure. There is no consideration for what the consequences will be. In this verse, 'looking' implies all the sense organs, not only sight.

tīvro = strong, intense, excessive; **viṣayaḥ** = sense obects; **kṛṣṇa-sarpa-viṣād** = poison of a king cobra.

viṣayāśā mahāpāśād yo vimuktaḥ su-dustyajāt |
sa eva kalpate muktyai nānyaḥ ṣaṭśāstra-vedy api ||80||

Only one who is completely free from the great binding chord of sense-attachment, so difficult to renounce, is fit for liberation and none else, even though they be versed in the six schools of philosophy.

The six orthodox (*ṣaḍ-āstika-darśana*) schools of Indian philosophy are Nyāya, Vaiṣeśika, Sānkhya, Yoga, Mīmāmsa, and Vedānta.

sudustyajāt = very difficult to relinquish; **viṣayāśāmahāpāśāt** = desire for sense objects itself is the great binding cord; **vimuktaḥ** = completely free; **sa eva kalpate muktyai** = that person alone has the capacity, competence, possibility for liberation; **ṣaṭsāstra** = six schools of philosophy.

āpāta-vairāgyavato mumukṣūn
bhavābdhi-pāraṁ prati yātum udyatān |
āśāgraho majjayate'ntarāle
nigṛhya kaṇṭhe vinivartya vegāt ||81||

The crocodile of desire catches by the throat those seekers-after-liberation who are attempting to cross the ocean of worldly existence while having only an apparent detachment and, violently snatching them away, drowns them in the middle of the ocean.

The Self, although always attained, is unattained, as it were, through ignorance; when that (ignorance) is destroyed, as it were, it becomes manifest as if attained, like the ornament round one's own neck.

Sense objects are like a monster that devours one. This should be obvious when one notices that a human being is worn out, becomes exhausted after exercising one's sense organs and gorging them with sense objects. After an hour or a day of enjoyment, one is tired and wants to go to sleep to recharge one's energy. If one devoured sense objects, instead of vice versa, one should gain energy from them. But that is not the case.

āpāta vairāgyavataḥ = those of superficial or apparent detachment; **graha** = crocodile; **āśā** = hope, expectation; **majjayate** = drowns.

viṣayākhya-graho yena suvirakty-asinā hataḥ |
sa gacchati bhavāmbhodheḥ pāraṁ pratyūha-varjitaḥ ||82||

One who has destroyed the crocodile of sense objects with the sword of steadfast detachment attains the other shore of worldly existence, thoroughly freed from all passions.

This verse and the preceding one convey the essence of the KaUp text, 'He who is unlearned, unmindful, always impure, he does not attain that state; he does not cross over the ocean of birth and death. He who is learned, mindful, always pure, he, however, reaches that state; he is not born again.'

graha = crocodile; **suviraktyasinā** = by the steadfast sword of detachment; **gacchati bhavāmbhodheḥ pāraṁ** = gone to, attains the other shore of worldly life; **varjita** = without; **pratyūha** = obstacle.

viṣama-viṣaya-mārgair gacchato'naccha-buddheḥ
prati-padam-abhighāto mṛtyur apyeṣa siddhaḥ |
hita-sujana-gurūktyā gaccataḥ svasya yuktyā
prabhavati phala-siddhiḥ satyam ity eva viddhi ||83||

Know that obstacles and death plague at every step a person of impure mind who travels the dangerous path of sense-pleasures. Whereas one who lives according to the advice of well-meaning friends and of the Master, along with his or her own reasoning, spontaneously achieves success. Know this to be the Truth.

The English word 'friend' can be derived from an etymology which means 'those who foster the spirit'. A proverb says that God is one's only friend; for everyone, acquaintances, wife, husband, children, will all leave one, if not before at least at one's death. A friend is someone who will advise one to seek the highest and never deviate from that path. The ChānUp says, 'The learned person who is clever ultimately reaches the Gāndhāra country; so, too, here he who is guided by a *guru* is able to realize the Supreme.'

viṣama = uneven, inconstant, difficult; **viṣayamārga** = path of sense-pleasures; **anaccha buddhiḥ** = of one whose mind is impure; **mṛtyu** = death; **siddhi** = success; **abhighāta** = infliction of injury; **hitasujana** = those who have others' spiritual welfare at heart, friends; **prabhavati** = arises, spontaneously spring forth; **satyamity-eva** = know this to be the truth, without any doubt.

mokṣasya kāṅkṣā yadi vai tavāsti
tyajātidūrād viṣayān viṣaṁ yathā |
pīyūṣavat toṣa-dayā-kṣamārjava-
praśānti-dāntīr bhaja nityam ādarāt ||84||

If indeed you ever have a burning aspiration for liberation, abandon all desires for sense objects as if they were poison. With great reverence, daily and always cultivate the nectar-like virtues of contentment, compassion, forgiveness, calmness,[1] straightforwardness, and self-control.

---

[1] See BṛhUp 4.4.23, 'having become calm, self-controlled . . .'.

In verses 76–82, Śaṅkara explained that only bondage will result from attachment to sense objects. Now he explains what should be cultivated. In order to experience freedom, one must shun sense objects as if they were poison. Sense objects destroy a person.

See IśaUp 1, '. . . do not covet anyone's wealth'.

See BG Ch 16, for a list of the divine virtues and the demonic traits.

See BG 4.17, 'It is needful to discriminate action, to discriminate forbidden action, and to discriminate inaction'.

For references to *mumukṣutva*, see V. 3, 28, 29, 30, 31, 44, 120, and 576.

kāṅkṣā = desire; **viṣaṁ** = poison; **tyajātidūrād** = abandon, renounce them, don't even think of them; **viṣayān** = sense objects; **toṣa** = contentment; **dayā** = compassion; **kṣamā** = forgiveness, patience; **ārjava** = straightforwardness, honesty; **praśānti** = supreme peace, calmness; **dāntiḥ** = self-control; **bhaja** = revere, adore; **nitya** = always, constantly, eternal; **ādarāt** = cultivate, accept.

anukṣaṇaṁ yat parihṛtya kṛtyaṁ
anādy avidyākṛta-bandha-mokṣaṇam |
dehaḥ parārtho'yam amuṣya poṣaṇe
yas sajjate sa sva-manena hanti ||85||

Whomsoever gives up what should continuously and always be pursued, namely, freedom from bondage born of beginningless ignorance, and instead passionately seeks to gratify one's body which is an 'other'-object, destroys oneself.

A person imagines that they are the body, limited and finite. Then, in this imagination, they frantically try to discover how to secure unlimited, infinite happiness from this body. To pursue sense gratification involves acquisition activities. All of these doing-to-obtain activities are related to the body. However, the body cannot be liberated. The physical body is inevitably and necessarily doomed to disappearance, one day or another. Birth, growth, death, decay are the body's fate. Freedom from birth, growth, death, and decay is the meaning of liberation. Freedom from bondage comes when the knowledge that one has been living in ignorance gives way to the thought, 'I want to stop living in ignorance, I want to be free.'

anukṣaṇam = always, every moment; **parihṛtya** = completely giving up, to shun or avoid; **anādyavidyā** = beginningless ignorance; **deha** = body; **parārtho'yam** = an object 'other' than 'I'; **amuṣya** = of such a one; **poṣane** = nurture, support, gratify.

śarīra-poṣaṇārthī san ya ātmānaṁ didṛkṣati |
grāhaṁ dārudhiyā dhṛtvā nadīṁ tartuṁ sa gacchati ||86||

Whomever seeks to realize the Self through the gratification of the body is like one who wishes to cross a river on the back of a crocodile, thinking it is a log of wood.

A person considers that they are an individual because of a mistaken identification with the body. This identification lasts only so long as the body lasts. Yet, once there is a firm conviction that one is not the body, individuality immediately disappears.

śarīra = body; **poṣa** = nurture, support, gratify; **graha** = crocodile; **taru** = wood, tree; **nadī** = river.

moha eva mahāmṛtyuḥ mumukṣor vapur ādiṣu |
moho vinirjito yena sa mukti-padam arhati ||87||

For a seeker-of-liberation, delusion concerning the body is the great death. Those who conquer this delusion deserve liberation.

See BṛhUp 3.5.1, '. . . having overcome the desire for sons, wealth, worlds.'

moha = delusion; **mahāmṛtyuḥ** = great death; **vapur ādiṣu** = in the body and so on, i.e., wife, children, relatives, friends, etc.

mohaṁ jahi mahā-mṛtyuṁ deha-dāra-sutādiṣu |
yaṁ jitvā munayo yānti tad viṣṇoḥ paramaṁ padam ||88||

Destroy your attachment to your body, wife, children, friends, and so on, which is the great death. Conquering these, sages reach the supreme state of Viṣṇu.[1]

Attachments destroy, whether they are to harmful objects or to beneficial ones. Eventually and ultimately, one must not be attached to anything. 'I' and 'mine' have no existence in themselves. They need a body to exist. The body is their point of reference. My wife or my kids are really the body's wife or the body's kids. Who am I?

They know not truth who dream such vacant dreams as father, mother, children, wife and friend. The sexless Self, whose father He? Whose child? Whose friend? Whose foe is He who is but One? The Self is all in all, none else exists, and thou art that.

moha = delusion; **mahāmṛtyuḥ** = great death; **jahi** = destroy; **deha** = body; **dāra** = wife; **suta** = friends; **ādi** = and so on, i.e., children, wealth, etc.; **muni** = sages; **viṣṇu** = Lord Viṣṇu, the All-pervading One; **paramam padam** = highest step.

tvaṅ-māmsa-rudhira-snāyu-medo-majjāsthi-saṁkulaṁ |
pūrṇaṁ mūtra-purīsābhyāṁ sthūlaṃ nindyam idaṁ vapuḥ ||89||

This gross body is abhorrent, for it consists of skin, flesh, blood, arteries and veins, fat, marrow, bones, and is full of urine and faeces.

See MaitrīUp 3.4, 'It is built up with bones, smeared over with flesh, covered with skin, filled with faeces, urine, bile, phlegm, marrow, fat.'

See V. 74, 75, 89–94, 156–157, and 396 on the gross body.

tvaṅ = skin; **māmsa** = flesh; **rudhira** = blood; **snāyu** = arteries; **majjāsthi** = marrow, bone; **medaḥ** = fat; **snāyu** = muscle, tendon, veins.

pañcī-kṛtebhyo bhūtebhyaḥ sthūlebhyaḥ pūrva-karamaṇā |
samutpannam idaṁ sthūlaṁ bhogāyatanan ātmanaḥ |
avasthā jāgaras tasya stūlārthānubhavo yataḥ ||90||

---

[1] See RV 1.22.20–21; 1.154.5; 10.15.3 and KaUp 1.3.9, '. . . that highest step of Viṣṇu'.

This gross body is produced by one's previous actions in past lives and is made up of the gross elements, formed by the combination of the five gross elements, and is the instrument of an individual's experiences. The state in which it experiences gross objects is its waking state.[1]

Pañcikaraṇa is a technical philosophical term to describe the evolution of primordial nature (*prakṛti*) into the physical universe. It consists of a mixture of different parts of the five elements in certain proportions. First, the aggregate of each of the five elements (space, air, fire, water, earth), is divided into equal parts. Then, each half is subdivided into four parts followed by taking one-eighth of the five elements and mixing it with the half part of each of the elements. Thus space, for example, consists of half of that element plus one-eighth of each of the other four elements, and so on. The ChUp 6.3.3 speaks of the admixture of three elements (earth, fire, water) only.

Pūrva karmas are actions performed in previous lives. If there are only purely meritorious (*puṇya*) actions involved, one is born in a divine body; if there are only purely demeritorious (*pāpa*) actions involved, one is born in a subhuman body. If there is a mixture of the two, one is born in a human body.

pañcikaraṇa = quintuplication, the combination of the five gross elements by the admixture of different parts therein; **pūrva-karma** = previous actions; **jāgrat avasthā** = waking state.

bāhyendriyaiḥ sthūla-padārtha-sevāṁ
srak-candana-strī ādi vicitra rūpām |
karoti jīvaḥ svayam etad ātmanā
tasmāt praśastir vapuṣo'sya jāgare ||91||

An individual, identifying himself with the gross body, enjoys gross objects of diverse shapes and forms such as garlands, sandalwood paste, women, and so on by means of the external sense organs. Therefore, the body's importance is in the waking state.

Because one has a physical body, one is able to enjoy all the myriad things of the world. It is due to one's identification with the body that all pleasure and pain arise.

See KaivUp 1.12, 'The same self deluded by *māyā* attains a body and performs all actions.'

bāhyendriyaiḥ = by the external sense organs; **vicitra rūpa** = diverse forms; **srak** = garlands; **candana** = sandalwood; **strī** = women; **ādi** = and so on, etc; **sthūla padārtha sevām** = enjoyment of gross objects; **jīva** = individual; **svayam karoti** = does itself.

sarvo-api bāhyaḥ saṁsāraḥ puruṣasya yad āśraydḥ |
viddhi deham idaṁ sthūlaṁ gṛhavad gṛhamedhinaḥ ||92||

Know that this gross body is the foundation upon which rests an individual's entire interaction with the external world and is like a house to a householder.

The world comes into being only when one is born in a body. It is an fact that if there is no body, there is no world. This is a fact even if it seems to be counter-intuitive.

---

[1] See MāṇḍUp 3; 9 'Perceiving what is outside . . . enjoying gross things Also KaivUp 1.12, 'In the waking state, he attains satisfaction by the varied enjoyments of women, food, and drink.'

Find out if you are the body. Who was born first, you or the world? If one gives first place to the world, one is bound. Of course, one's body remains in the world, but one is not deluded by that. Don't ask the mind to confirm that which is beyond the mind. Birth is merely the idea, 'I have a body'. But I am not the body? A body may be there or not – what difference does it make? The body is like a room. It is there, but one need not live in it all the time.

bāhyaḥ = external; saṁsāraḥ = empirical existence, worldly life, the wheel of birth and death (from the verb root *sṛ* = 'to flow' + *sam* = 'together'); āśraydḥ = foundation; gṛhavad = like a house; gṛhamedhinaḥ = of a householder.

sthūlasya saṁbhava-jarā-maraṇāni dharmāḥ
sthaulyādayo bahuvidhāḥ śiśutādyavasthāḥ |
varṇaśramādi niyamā bahudhāmayāḥ syuḥ
pūjāvamāna-bahumāna-mukhā viśeṣāḥ ||93||

The essential properties of the physical body are birth, decay, and death. It has many states of various kinds, such as fatness, thinness, infancy, youth, and so on. It is subject to the rules and duties of caste, class, stages of life, lineage and so on, as well as to various kinds of afflictions. It is subject to different kinds of worship, honor, dishonor, respect, and so on.

saṁbhava = birth, origination; jarā = old age; maraṇāni = death; dharmāḥ = essential properties, quality; sthaulyādi = excessive growth, fatness, and so on, i.e., thinness, infancy, youth, etc; bahuvidhāḥ = of various kinds; śiśuādya = childhood and so on, i.e., infancy, adult, etc; varṇaśramādi niyamā = the rules of caste or social class. stages of life, family, lineage; bahudhāmayāḥ = various afflictions or ailments; pūjā = worship, honor, ritual; avamāna = dishonor; bahumāna = high esteem, respect.

buddhīndriyāṇi śravaṇaṁ tvag-akṣi
ghrāṇaṁ ca jihvā viṣayāvabodhanāt |
vāk-pāṇi-pādā gudam-apy-upasthaḥ
karmendriyāṇi pravaṇāni karmasu ||94||

The ears, skin, eyes, nose, and tongue are known as the organs of knowledge, for they give knowledge of external objects. The mouth, hands, feet, anus, and genitals are the organs of action for their tendency to work.

The five conative (*karmendriya*) sense organs are the organs of speech (*vāk*), comprehension (*pāṇi*), movement (*pāda*), excretion (*pāyu*), and generation (*upastha*). The five cognitive (*jñānendriya*) sense organs are the organs of knowledge. They are the organs of hearing (*śrotra), touch (tvak*), sight (*cakṣus*), taste (*rasana*), and smell (*ghrāṇa*).

buddhīndriyāṇi = organs of knowledge (*jñānendriya*); śravaṇaṁ = ears; tvag = skin; akṣi = eyes; ghrāṇaṁ = nose; jihvā = tongue; vāk = mouth; pāṇi = hands; pādā = feet; gudam = anus; upasthaḥ = organs of reproduction; karmendriyāṇi = organs of action.

nigadyate'ntaḥkaraṇaṁ mano dhīr
ahaṁkṛtis cittam iti sva-vṛttibhiḥ |
manas tu saṁkalpa-vikalpanādibhiḥ
buddhiḥ padārthādhyavasāya-dharmataḥ ||95||

According to its different functions, the inner organ is known as the mind, the intellect, the ego, and the conscious awareness. The mind is responsible for thinking. The intellect determines, doubts, and imagines in various ways as well as apprehends the real nature of a thing.

The *antaḥkaraṇa* is the internal organ or the inner instrument. It is comprised of the intellect, the mind, the ego and the consciousness (*buddhi*, *manas*, *ahaṅkāra*, and *cit*) according to Advaita Vedānta. It is the seat of the functions of the senses as distinct from their outer organs. It receives and arranges what is conveyed to it through the senses. It reflects objects by its relation to the Self (*ātman*). The perceived variations of different individuals' cognitions are due to the differences in their respective *antaḥkaraṇas*. The inner organ functions by streaming out to an object, illumining it, assuming its shape, and then cognizing it. See also V. 105 on the internal organ.

antaḥkaraṇaṁ = inner ogran (comprised of *manas*/mind, *buddhi*/intellect, *ahaṁkāra*/ego, and *citta*/conscious awareness or apperception); **mano** = mind; **dhīr** = intellect; **ahaṁ kṛti** = egoism; **cittam** = consciousness; **sva-vṛttibhiḥ manas** = the mind is responsible for its own fluctuations; **saṁkalpa-vikalpa-nādibhiḥ** = the intellect determines (*samkalpa*), doubts, and imagines (*vikalpa*) in various ways; **buddhiḥ padārthādhyavasāya-dharmataḥ** = the intellect apprehends (*adhyavasāya*) the real nature (*dharma*) of things, objects of experience (*padārtha*).

atrābhimānād aham ityahaṁkṛtiḥ |
svārthānusandhāna-guṇena cittam ||96||

In this way, the ego brings about attachment to the body. The mind-stuff is that which investigates/illumines things that interest it.

To take one's stand in the mind means that all one sees will be in and of the mind. The mind is often said to be one's enemy and one's friend.

atrā = in this way; **abhimāna** = attachment, pride, egoism; **ahaṁ-kṛtiḥ** = egoism, the 'I'-maker; **anusandhāna** = investigation, enquiry, awareness.

prāṇāpāna-vyānodāna-samānā bhavatyasau prāṇaḥ |
svayam eva vṛtti-bhedāt vikṛti-bhedāt suvarṇa-salilādivat ||97||

Like gold[1] and like water,[2] according to its functions and modifications, one and the same life breath becomes ascending breath, descending breath, diffusing breath, up-breath, and digestive breath.[3]

Different names are associated with the varied mutiplicity which appears as the world. These names appear to distinguish one thing from another. But even as the same individual may be called 'father', 'husband', 'son', 'Devadatta', or 'farmer', etc., so too the Absolute is called by many names. The names change, but the constitutive Reality remains the same. Gold is distinguished by various names and forms like

---

[1] See ChānUp 6.1.5, 'Just as . . . by one nugget of gold, all that is made of gold becomes known.' *loha* originally meant copper or iron, but was later used to mean gold or any metal.

[2] See BṛhUp 4.5.12, 'As the ocean is the point of convergence of all the waters.'

[3] See BṛhUp 1.5.3, 'Out-breath, in-breath, diffused-breath, up-breath, middle-breath, of forms of breathing, they are all simply breath'; see also BṛhUp 3.2.9; ChānUp 5.19–23; PraśUp 4.3–4.

rings, bracelets, and necklaces. But even as the names and forms undergo change, the gold remains as it is.

The breath (*prāṇa*) is thought to have five aspects: *prāṇa* or the vital ascending breath; *apāna* or the descending breath; *vyāna* or the diffusing breath circulating in all the limbs of the body; *udāna* or up-breath which is responsible for eructation, speech, and ascent of higher states of consciousness; *samānā* or the digestive breath.

prāṇa = vital breath; **apāna** = descending breath; **vyāna** = diffusing breath; **udāna** = up-breath; **samānā** = digestive breath; **vṛtti-bhedāt** = fluctuations; **vikṛti-bhedāt** = modifications; **suvarṇa** = gold; **salila** = water.

vāgādi pañca śravaṇādi pañca
prāṇādi-pañcābhra-mukhāni pañca |
buddhyuādy avidyāpi ca kāma-karmaṇī
puryaṣṭakaṁ sūkṣma-śarīram-āhuḥ ||98||

The subtle body[1] is an aggregate of the five beginning with speech, the five beginning with the ears, the five vital airs beginning with inhalation, the five elements beginning with space, the intellect and so on, and ignorance, desire, and action; these eight cities together constitute the subtle body.

The sheaths of vital airs (*prāṇa*), mind (*manas*), and knowledge (*vijñāna*) constitute the subtle body. They are called the *prāṇamayakośa*, *manomayakośa*, and *vijñānamayakośa*. The subtle body consists of the internal organs (*buddhi*, *ahaṅkāra*, and *manas*), the organs of knowledge (*jñānendriya*), the organs of action (*karmendriya*), and the five vital airs (*prāṇa*). It is also called the *liṅga-śarīra* or the astral body. See V. 99, 102, 297–298, and 396 per the subtle body.

vāgādi pañca = the five composed of speech and so on; **śravaṇādi pañca** = the five composed of hearing and so on; **prāṇādi-pañcābhra** = the five-fold breath; **mukhāni pañca** = the five subtle elements; **buddhyuādy** = intellect and so on; **avidyāpi** = ignorance and so on; **kāma** = desire; **karmaṇī** = action; **puryaṣṭakaṁ** = eight cities, towns; **sūkṣma-śarīram** = subtle body.

idaṁ śarīraṁ śṛṇu sūkṣma-saṁjñitaṁ
liṅgam tvapañcīkṛta-bhūta-saṁbhavam |
savāsanaṁ karma-phalānubhāvakaṁ
svājñānato'nādir upādhir ātmanaḥ ||99||

Listen! This subtle body, also known as the 'indicative body', arises from the elements before they have undergone subdividing and combining with each other.[2] It is made up of the residual latent impressions of its past actions. It causes an individual to experience the fruits of one's past actions. Brought about by its own ignorance, it is the beginningless limitation superimposed on the Self.

1 See MāṇḍUp 4, 'The second quarter is *taijasa*, the brilliant one, situated in the dream state, perceiving what is inside, possessing seven limbs and nineteen mouths, and enjoying refined things'; 10, 'The second constituent phoneme or "u" is *taijasa*, situated in the dream state.'

2 See V. 75 and 90 on the subdividing and combining of the elements.

The body is the not-self because it is a product of food (*annakāryatvāt*). Whatever is produced must also decay, and thus the body cannot be the Self. Past actions are said to reside, latent, in the subtle body until their time to manifest arises.

liṅgam = indicative, mark, characteristic (from the verb root *ligi* = 'what reminds'); **anādir** = beginningless; **upādhir** = limitation, adventitious condition, vehicle, limiting adjunct; **savāsanam** = residual latent impressions; **karma phalānu-bhāvakaṁ** = experience the fruits or effects of one's previous actions; **svājñānato** = brought about by one's own ignorance.

svapno bhavaty asya vibhaktyavasthā
sva-mātra-śeṣeṇa vibhāti yatra ।
svapne tu buddhiḥ svayam eva jāgrat-
kālīna nānā-vidha-vāsanābhiḥ ।
kartrādi-bhāvaṁ pratipadya rājate
yatra svayaṁ-jyotirayaṁ parātmā ॥100॥

Dream is a state different from this where the intellect shines by itself, by taking on the role of the agent, and by the various residual impressions of the waking state, while the supreme Self is self-luminous.

The enquiry into the nature of the three states of experience (*avasthā traya vicāra*) is a practice employed by Advaitins to teach the real non-dual nature of the Self. The paradigm for it is found in MaṇḍUp 4.10. The three letters which comprise the *oṁ* (a-u-m) represent the three forms (waking, dreaming, deep sleep) of the Self. In the dreaming state, the Self revels in a world of images, and its experiences are subtle. The Self is said to be dreaming when it creates a world of its own from the impressions of its waking experience. It doesn't need the help of the sense organs nor of external light. The dream state reveals that the Self does not really act and is unattached in dreams, even though the Self appears to roam far and wide and play with many objects. When one awakes, one realizes one hasn't done anything or gone anywhere. Thus, the dreaming state reveals that a person can create an entire universe and does not need the help of an external light to do so.

When a person dreams, he has no use for the external sense organs. There are no chariots there, no roads, no physical objects. The dreamer takes with him impressions from the world of waking and fashions for himself chariots, roads, and so on. He creates a world of his own. The soul goes, as it were, out of its nest (the physical body) and returns to itself, while the breath preserves the body. The objects and enjoyments in dream are all of the soul's own making. The self there is its own light. As a great fish goes along both banks of a river, so does the self go along in both these conditions, i.e., waking and dreaming. As a hawk, having flown around here and there in space, becomes weary, folds its wings and is borne down to its nest, so the soul hastens to that state where, asleep, it desires no desires and sees no dreams. All distinctions then become lost.

See MāṇḍUp 4; 10; also KaivUp 1.13, 'In the dream state, the self experiences happiness or sorrow in the worlds created by its own imaginations'. See V. 100–101, 165, 172, 255, and 456–457 on the dream state.

See US 1.11.11 'Just as it is seen that a sword shines when it is drawn from its sheath, so the Knower, separated in the dreaming state from cause and effect, is seen to be self-effulgent.' See V. 153, 191, 213, 219, 221, 240, 508, and 536 on being self-luminous. 'In the golden space of the heart dwells the Absolute, without parts, without stain. Pure, the light of lights. This light is reflected in all. That shining, everything shines' (MuṇḍUp 2.2.10–11).

svapno = dream; **sva-mātra** = by itself; **jāgrat** = waking state; **vāsanābhiḥ** = residual impressions, latent tendencies, predispositions; **kartrādi-bhāvaṁ** = the attitude of the doer, doership; **pratipadya** = attaining; **rājate** = shines; **svayaṁjyoti** = self-luminous; **parātmā** = supreme Self.

dhī-mātrakopādhir aśeṣa-sākṣī
na lipyate tat-kṛta-karma-leśaiḥ |
yasmād asaṅgas tata eva karmabhir
na lipyate kiñcid upādhinā kṛtaiḥ ||101||

Dream is a state different from this where the intellect shines by itself. In dreams the intellect by itself takes on the role of the doer and so on, owing to the various residual impressions arising from the waking state. In this condition, the supreme Self shines in its own glory, limited only by the intellect. Witness of everything, the Self is not tainted by any action the intellect performs. Since it is entirely unattached, it is never tainted by any action done by the superimposed limitations.

The *sakṣin* and the individual are distinguishable, though not separable. The *sakṣin* is not identical to the Self, because the *sakṣin* is always associated with the *antaḥkaraṇa*. This association is both real and potential. It is real in the waking and dreaming states. It is potential in the deep sleep state (thus the individual loses his individuality in deep sleep). See KaivUp 1.18, 'In the three states of consciousness whatever appears as the object of enjoyment or the enjoyer or the enjoyment, I am different from them, the witness, pure consciousness, the eternal Śiva' (*sākṣī*). See V. 127, 137, 159, 212, 213, 217, 218, 223, 270, 295, 352, 370, 381, 384, 495, 506, 507, and 552 for references to witness (*sākṣī*).

See KaivUp 1.14 , '. . . on account of the individual's connection with the deeds of their past life.'

See V. 100 on the dream state.

dhī = intellect; **sākṣī** = witness; **asaṅgas** = unattached; **na lipyate** = pure or undefiled.

sarva-vyāpṛti-karaṇaṁ liṅgam idaṁ syād cidātmanaḥ puṁsaḥ |
vāsyādikam iva takṣṇaḥ tenaivātmā bhavaty asaṅgo' 'yam ||102||

As the tools of a carpenter are his instruments, so this subtle body is the instrument for all activities of the Self, which is of the nature of consciousness. For this reason only, the Self is perfectly unattached.

What is the nature of this one and non-dual *Brahman*? 'Consciousness is *Brahman*.' (AitUp 3.1.3, *Prajñānam brahma*). Consciousness can assume many forms without endangering its non-duality. Even while being aware of the many, consciousness itself does not cease to be one. Everything is rooted in consciousness. And even after the myriad possible objects are eliminated, consciousness will still remain.

By naming the Absolute *Brahman*, it takes on an appearance to thought of an absolute object – the only thing worth pursuing in a universe of change. But by declaring that 'consciousness is *Brahman*', a radical transvaluation occurs. One's natural tendency is to move towards the supreme object, the other, a transcendent God. By declaring that *Brahman* is one and non-dual, as well as consciousness, a reversal of thought occurs. Where there is no duality, there is no thinker and no thought; there is no knower and no known. One's search for the ultimate object becomes a logical impossibility. And as each individual is already a conscious being, there is nothing 'outside' or lacking to be gained anew. One need only get rid of the superimpositions which cloud the ever-present consciousness.

See V. 98–99, 102, 297–298, and 396 on the subtle body.

liṅgam = subtle body; **cidātmanaḥ** = the Self who is of the nature of consciousness; **tenaiva** = for that reason only; **asaṅga** = devoid of association, unattached.

andhatva-mandatva-paṭutva-dharmāḥ
sauguṇya-vaiguṇya-vaśād hi cakṣuṣaḥ |
bādhirya-mūkatva-mukhās tathaiva
śrotrādi-dharmā na tu vettur ātmanaḥ ||103||

Blindness, weakness, and sharpness are conditions of eyesight due to fitness or defect. Likewise, deafness, dumbness, and so on, belong to the ear, mouth and so on, but never to the Self, the knower.

False knowledge (*mithyā jñāna*) differs from right knowledge (*viveka jñāna*). The four pall-bearers know the heavy weight of the corpse they carry. Discriminatory knowledge knows the real weight of the body versus a false identification of the body which considers it light. The physical body no more belongs to the Self than does blueness belong to the sky. The notions of 'I' and 'mine' are no more properties of the Self than leanness or clothes are. They are objective and subject to cessation. Even as fire does not burn up in its own heat since heat is of its own nature, so, too, if the not-self were the Self it could not be known as an object (since the two would not be distinct). However, the Self knows the not-self as an object and thus the two must be distinct.

See BṛhUp I.5.1–3, *annam brahma.*

andhatva = blindness; **mandatva** = weakness, inflammation; **paṭutva** = sharpness; **dharmāḥ** = conditions, qualities; **sauguṇya** = fitness, good qualities; **vaiguṇya** = defective, absence of qualities; **cakṣuṣaḥ** = eye; **bādhirya** = deafness; **mūkatva** = dumbness; **mukhās** = mouth; **śrotrādi** = ear and so on.

ucchvāsa-niśśvāsa-vijṛmbhana-kṣut-
prasyandanādyutkramaṇādikāḥ kriyāḥ |
prāṇādi-karmāṇi vadanti tajjñāḥ
prāṇasya dharmāvaśanā-pipāse ||104||

Those who know say that inhalation, exhalation, yawning, sneezing, secretion, leaving the body, and so on are physiological functions of the vital breath, and hunger and thirst are qualities of the main vital breath.

These functional properties of the vital breath (*prāṇa*) are known as *upaprāṇas*.

ucchvāsa = inhalation; **niśśvāsa** = exhalation; **vijṛmbhaṇa** = yawning; **kṣut** = hunger; **prasyan** = secretion; **danādyutkramaṇādi** = leaving the body, and so on; **pipāse** = thirst.

antaḥ-karaṇam eteṣu cakṣur ādiṣu varṣmaṇi |
ahamityabhimānena tiṣṭhatyābhāsa-tejasā || 105 ||

The inner organ has its seat in these, the eye and other organs of the gross body and identifies itself with them as 'I', endowed by the reflecting effulgence of the Self in it.

The internal organ is the connecting link between the Self and the not-self; it is that which makes the Self appear as many; it is because of it that the Self, although free of action and attributes, appears to have them; it makes the non-relational Self relational, as it were. The internal organ assumes the form of an external object and, being illuminated by the Self which is reflected therein, then seemingly is a knower. Though it pretends to be the seer, this is a false claim, for the Self alone is the seer and all else is the seen. Every kind of knowledge claim one makes, such as 'I know this' or 'I experience this' reveals the connecting role of the internal organ – on the one hand with objects and on the other with the Self. In the absence of the internal organ, the Self has no relation with anything.

antaḥkaraṇam = inner organ; **cakṣur** = eye; **varṣmaṇi** = in the gross body; **ahamityabhimānena** = identification or conceit, egoism that 'I am'; **ābhāsa-tejasā** = reflection of effulgence.

ahaṁkāraḥ sa vijñeyaḥ kartā bhoktābhimānyayam |
sattvādi-guṇa-yogena cāvasthā-trayam aśnute || 106 ||

Know that, by identifying itself with the body, the ego thinks of itself as the doer, the enjoyer, the experiencer and, in conjunction with the three qualities, *sattva* and so on, it assumes the three states.

See V. 105 in regard to this verse.

See V. 112–121, 176, 181, 279, 303, and 362 on the three qualities.

See ŚvetUp 1.9, 'Indeed, there is another one who is unborn, connected with the enjoyer and the objects of enjoyment.'

ahaṁkāraḥ = ego, 'I'-maker; **kartā** = doer; **bhoktā** = enjoyer; **abhimānyayam** = experiencer, pride, conceit; **sattvādi-guṇa** = the quality of purity (*sattva*, *rajas*, *tamas*); **avasthātrayam** = the three states of existence or waking, dreaming, deep sleep; **aśnute** = attains.

viṣayāṇām ānukūlye sukhī duḥkhī viparyaye |
sukhaṁ duḥkhaṁ ca tad-dharmaḥ sadānandasya nātmanaḥ || 107 ||

When sense objects are pleasurable, one is happy and miserable if they are otherwise. Happiness and misery are characteristics of the ego and not of the Self, which is ever blissful.[1]

Pain is the price of pleasure. Pleasure is the reward of pain. Pleasure is but a moment between two miseries, and misery is but a moment between two pleasures. Both come and go, pass and return, not staying long. Thus, one should accept both with an equal mind and reside in the Self which is ever blissful.

---

[1] See TaittUp, *ānando brahma*; *vijñānamānandam*.

viṣayāṇām = sense objects; **sukhī sukhaṁ** = pleasurable, happy; **duḥkhī duḥkhaṁ** = miserable, unhappy; **sadānandasya** = ever, eternally blissful.

ātmārthatvena hi preyān viṣayo na svataḥ priyaḥ |
svata eva hi sarveṣām ātmā priyatamo yataḥ ||108||

Sense objects are dear only for the sake of the Self; they are not dear by themselves for the reason that the Self alone is dear to all, by its very nature.

See BṛhUp 2.4.5, Yājñavalkya's teaching to his wife, Maitreyī: 'Not for the sake of all things, but for the sake of the Self are things dear.' See also BṛhUp 4.5.7.

tata ātmā sadānando nāsya duḥkhaṁ kadācana |
yat suṣuptau nirviṣaya ātmānando'nubhūyate |
śrutiḥ pratyakṣam aitihyam anumānaṁ ca jāgrati ||109||

The Self is ever blissful and never suffers misery. In dreamless sleep,[1] when there are no sense objects, the bliss[2] of the Self is experienced. This is clearly attested to by the scriptures, perception, tradition, inference, and the waking state.

Śaṅkara declared that Truth must not proclaim something absurd or nonsensical. Ultimately, experience must be the touchstone. Experience (*anubhava*) is the ultimate bedrock for Śaṅkara. Further, Śaṅkara posits that this Truth or Being can only be known through Scripture. However, it is not just any scripture statement that is meant. As Vācaspati said 'It is purportful Scripture that is authoritative, and not Scripture as such' (*Bhāmatī* p. xiv). Scriptural truths are derived from inner experiential truths, and from such insights Śaṅkara expounded the significance of human existence and the world.

'Deep state' is a state wherein there are no experiences, no desires, no objects, no dreams. The Self is one, without the distinction of seer and seen. There is no knower, no knowing, no process of knowledge. The very ideas of within and without have no meaning here. There is no seeing of objects and yet sight remains: 'The sight of the seer is never lost because it is imperishable.'

suṣupti = deep sleep; **śrutiḥ** = primary scripture; **pratyakṣam** = perception; **aitihyam** = tradition; **anumānaṁ** = inference; **jāgrati** = the waking state.

avyakta-nāmnī parameśa-śakthị
anādy avidyā tri-guṇātmikā parā |
kāryānumeyā sudhiyaiva māyā
yayā jagat sarvam idaṁ prasūyate ||110||

That-which-is-not (*māyā*) is called the unmanifest. It is the power of the supreme Lord. It is beginningless ignorance. The three qualities are its constituents. It is superior to their effects and has to be inferred, by the wise whose intellect is in accord with scripture, from the effects it produces. It is this which gives birth to the entire world.

[1] See MāṇḍUp 1.5, 'sees no dreams'.
[2] See MāṇḍUp 1.5, 'consisting of bliss, enjoying bliss'.

This is a controversial verse in the *Vivekacūḍāmaṇi* as it gives a very precise definition of *māyā*. Some scholars maintain that Śaṅkara never gave such a definition in any of his indisputable works (see my Introduction, p. 16). Within the Advaita tradition, *avidyā/māyā* has been defined as having six defining characteristics: it is beginningless (*anādi*); it is terminated by right knowledge (*jñāna-nivartya*); it veils and projects (*āvaraṇa* and *vikṣepa*); it is indefinable (*anirvacanīya*); it is of the nature of a positive existence (*bhāvarūpa*); and it is located either in the individual (*jīva*) or in the Absolute (*Brahman*).

The three qualities (*triguṇās*) are the ultimate building blocks of the material and mental universe. They are the indivisible atoms of everything. They are not merely parts, qualities, properties or ingredients of primordial nature (*prakṛti*). They are the very material of *prakṛti*. There are an almost infinite number of *guṇas* of three different types and, by way of combination and perpetual recombination, they produce multiplicity. This theory is very much like nuclear physics or contemporary field theory with localizations of fields. Nature is like a quivering force field which is undergoing continuous transformations.

The word '*māyā*' may be creatively derived from 'ma-ya' or 'that which is not'. See BG 7.14; 18.61 on *māyā*. See V. 67, 110–112, 125, 245, 406, 497, and 574 on *māyā*.

avyakta = unmanifest; **parameśa-śakthi** = the power of the supreme Lord; **anādi** = beginningless; **avidyā** = ignorance; **triguṇātmikā** = that to which the three qualities pertain; **parā** = superior, highest; **kāryānumeyā** = to be inferred from its effects; **sudhiya** = by the wise, those with a good intellect; **māyā** = the principle of appearance, illusion, 'that which is not'; **jagat** = world; **sarvam idaṁ** = all this; **prasūyate** = to press out, to give birth to.

san-nāpyasan-nāpy-ubhayātmikā no
bhinnāpyabhinnāpyubhayātmikā no |
sāṅgāpyanaṅgāpyubhayātmikā no
mahādbhutā'nir-vacanīya-rūpā ||111||

It is neither real nor unreal nor both; it is neither undifferentiated, nor different, nor both; it neither has parts nor is partless nor both. It is supremely wonderful and of an inexpressible form.

This doctrine has given many the impression that Śaṅkara claims the empirical world is unreal, illusory, non-existent. This impression is in need of a great deal of clarification. Śaṅkara never denied that the physical world of plurality appears real enough to those who live within it. Nor would Śaṅkara deny that it makes sense to say that the waking state of consciousness is a public phenomenon and can be said to be the 'real world' in contrast to the 'private life' of the dreaming state. Further, Śaṅkara would agree that within the physical world individuals may distinguish between what appears to be the case and what is actually the case.

Śaṅkara accepts that a datum, any datum, is a datum or perceived object which is irreducible to the perceiving subject. In this sense, epistemologically, Advaita is a realistic school. Still, if there is a level of experience which transcends the subject–object dualism, then, at that level, duality is transcended or sublated. This in no way alters the fact that the subject and object are correlative terms and one should never think of retaining the subject while also reducing the object to the subject. One should never confuse Advaita with various types of subjective idealism. The Self is not a conglomeration of parts; of subjects and objects somehow reduced to one giant self.

Merely because one imagines that they are one small entity in a universe of infinite entities does not make it so. Śaṅkara avers that there is the Self – not 'my self' and 'his self' and 'her self' and 'itself'. Because one is misled by the diversity of names and forms, minds and bodies, one imagines multiple selves. Simply because there are bodies present does not necessarily mean that one is a body. The body or mind may be like a room – it is there, but one need not live in it all the time. There is space within a jar and outside the jar. To identify with the space within the jar and then to declare that one is limited is a false view of what space is. Merely because one identifies does not make it so.

Śaṅkara avers that anything which is experienced is real, at one level or another. Therefore, Śaṅkara's epistemology is realistic and posits that every cognition points to an objective reference – whether correct or erroneous. The question becomes: exactly how real are the things that are experienced in the empirical world? Śaṅkara replies that the things of the empirical world are real so long as the empirical order lasts. Thus, according to Śaṅkara, the real is that which lasts, which suffers no contradictions, which is eternal and unsublatable. Things of the world may be said to be real until they suffer sublation. Thus, they are called 'what is other than the real or the unreal' (*sadasat vilakṣaṇa*), illusory (*mithyā*), or indescribable (*anirvacanīya*). Since they are cognized, they are not unreal (*asat*). Since they are sublated, they are not real (*sat*). By this criterion, *Brahman* alone is absolutely real, never being subject to contradiction. All else can be called 'real' only by courtesy. The distinction between one individual and another, the existence of a plurality of things, the attribution of attributes to the Absolute are all concessions to the Truth made from the relative point of view. However, to bring out the full implications of the term '*advaita*', it should be noted that such expressions as 'absolutely real' and 'from an absolute point of view' are merely contextual. They are used only by way of contrast with all that is not real. In no other sense can *Brahman/Ātman* be called real. If one accepts the empirical world of plurality, then such expressions are meaningful. But to one who has realized the Truth, these expressions lose their significance.

See ŚvetUp 6.19, 'without parts' (*niṣkalam*); also 6.12.

See V. 67, 110–112, 125, 245, 406, 497, and 574 on *māyā*.

sat = real; **asat** = unreal; **ubhaya** = both; **abhinna** = undifferentiated; **bhinna** = differentiated; **saṅgha** = collection, parts; **asaṅgha** = without parts, indivisible; **adbhuta** = wonderful, marvelous; **anirvacanīya** = inexpressible, inexplicable, ineffable, indeterminable.

śuddhādvaya-brahma-vibodhanāśyā
sarpa-bhramo rajju-vivekato yathā |
rajas-tamas-sattvam-iti prasiddhā
guṇāstadīyāḥ prathitaiḥ svakāryaiḥ ||112||

Māyā can be destroyed by the realization of the pure, non-dual[1] Absolute, just as the illusion of a snake is destroyed by the discriminative knowledge of the rope. Its qualities are well known by their actions and are called *rajas*, *tamas*, and *sattva*.

When one recognizes that the water one sees in a desert is merely a mirage, the water disappears; when one realizes the snake one sees is merely a rope, the snake

[1] See ChanUp 6.2.1; BṛhUp 1.4.17; AitUp 1.1.1.

disappears; when one realizes that the man one sees is merely a post, the man disappears. *Māyā* is inferred from its effects even if those effects are but erroneous superimpositions.

See V. 106, 112–121, 176, 181, 279, 303, and 362 on the three qualities.

See V. 67, 110–112, 125, 245, 406, 497, and 574 on *māyā*.

See V. 12, 63, 112, 140, 199, 237, 248, 303, 388, 405, 407, and 550 on snakes.

śuddhā = pure, stainless; **advaya** = non-dual; **brahma** = Absolute; **vibodhanāśyā** = destroyed by the realization; **sarpa** = snake; **bhramo** = illusion, error; **rajju** = rope; **rajas** = active, energy, passion; **tamas** = darkness, inertia, dullness, that which resists activity; **sattva** = pure, illuminating, joy; **prasiddhā** = well-known; **guṇa** = quality, attribute, characteristic, rope, constituent; the three basic attributes of nature (*prakṛti*).

vikṣepa-śaktī rajasaḥ kriyātmikā
yataḥ pravṛttiḥ prasṛtā purāṇī |
rāgādayo'syāḥ prabhavanti nityaṁ
duḥkhādayo ye manaso vikārāḥ ||113||

Rajas is projecting power. Activity is its nature. From it commences the well-known ancient flow of creation. From this mental modifications such as unhappiness and attachment are continuously produced.

Rajas is energy; activity; stimulation; dynamism. It derives from *raj/ranj* = 'to glow, be brilliant' and it represents the principle of discontinuity or change. See V. 114 on *rajas*.

As was noted earlier, *māyā* is said to have the twin powers of both concealing (*āvaraṇa*) and projecting (*vikṣepa*). First, Reality is concealed (which is the tamasic power) and then, insidiously, that which is not real is projected upon the Reality.

vikṣepa-śaktī = projecting power; **kriyātmikā** = activity; **prasṛtā** = well-known; **purāṇī** = ancient; **rāgād-** = attachment; **duḥkhādi** = unhappiness; **manaso vikārāḥ** = mental modifications.

kāmaḥ krodho lobha-dambhādy-asūyā-
ahaṁkārerṣyā-matsarādyāstu ghorāḥ |
dharmā ete rājasāḥ puṁpravṛttiḥ
yasmād etat tad rajo bandha-hetuḥ ||114||

Desire, anger, greed,[1] pride, jealousy, egoism, envy, miserliness, and so on, are the terrible characteristics of *rajas* and from which an individual's worldly tendencies spring. *Rajas*, therefore, is the cause of bondage.

In Indian thought, the vices are compared to a terrible crocodile. They are the cause of bondage in both this world and the next. They are said to be characteristics of *rajas* since action induces a person to desire.

See BG 14.7, 'Know *rajas* to be of the nature of passion, the source of thirst, desire, and attachment; it binds fast, O Kaunteya, the embodied one by attachment to action.'

---

[1] See BG 14.12, 'Greed, activity, the undertaking of actions, unrest, longing – these arise, O best of the Bharatas, when *rajas* is predominant.'

kāmaḥ = desire, pleasure, lust; **krodho** = anger; **lobha** = greed, covetousness; **daṁbhādy** = ostentation, pride; **abhyasūyā** = jealousy; **ahaṁkara** = egoism; **irṣyā** = envy; **matsara** = selfishness; **ghorāḥ** = terrible, dreadful, frightful.

eṣāvṛtir nāma tamo-guṇasya
śaktir yayā vastvavabhāsate'nyathā |
saiṣā nidānaṁ purusasya samṣṛteḥ
vikṣepa-śakteḥ pravaṇasya hetuḥ ||115||

The power of tamas is a veiling power. It makes things appear to be other than what they are. It is this which is the original cause of an individual's transmigration and is the cause of the origination of the action of the projecting power.

Tamas is inertia, or darkness. It derives from the root *tam* meaning 'to be exhausted, become rigid'. It is that which represents the principle of continuity. See V. 116–118 on *tamas*.

See BG 14.8, 'Know *tamas* to be born of ignorance, deluding all embodied beings; it binds fast, O Bharata, by heedlessness, indolence, and sleep.'

See V. 115–117, 141, 146, 344, 345, and 348 on veiling power.

vastvavabhāsate'nyathā = things appearing other than; **nidānaṁ** = original cause; **purusasya samṣṛteḥ** = individual transmigration.

prajñavān api paṇdito'pi caturo'py-atyanta-sūkṣmārtha-dṛg-
vyālīḍhas tamasā na vetti bahudhā saṁbodhito'pi sphuṭam |
bhrāntyāropitam eva sādhu kalayatyālambate tadguṇān
hantāsau prabalā duranta-tamasaḥ śaktir mahantyāvṛtiḥ ||116||

Even the wise and learned and those who are expert in reasoning and adept in understanding the subtlest meanings of words, if overpowered by *tamas*, do not realize the nature of the Self even if it is repeatedly and clearly explained in various ways. Such individuals consider to be real what has simply been superimposed by delusion and then attach themselves to its attributes. Alas! The dreadful concealing power of *tamas* is great indeed.

See KaUp 2.5, 'Walling in ignorance, but calling themselves wise, thinking themselves learned, the fools go around, staggering about like a group of blind men, led by a man who is himself blind.'

See BG 14.16, '. . . ignorance is the fruit of *tamas*'; BG 14.18, '. . . those abiding in *tamas* go downwards.'

See V. 115–117, 141, 146, 344, 345, and 348 on veiling power.

prajñavān = the wise, a person of wisdom; **paṇdito** = scholar; **caturo** = one who is adept in reasoning; **atyanta-sūkṣmārtha-dṛg** = one who sees (understands) the subtlest meanings of words; **bahudhā** = in many ways or parts or forms, variously; **bhrāntya** = dellusion, misapprehension, error.

abhāvanā vā viparita-bhāvanā-
saṁbhāvanā vipratipattir-asyāḥ |
saṁsarga-yuktaṁ na vimuñcati dhruvaṁ
vikṣepa-śaktiḥ kṣapayaty ajasram ||117||

Incorrect judgment, contrary judgment, doubt,[1] and contrary impressions never leave one who has any connection with this veiling power. Then, the projecting power destroys anyone so afflicted.

See BG 4.40, 'Ignorant and faithless, one with a doubting mind comes to ruin'. See V. 115–117, 141, 146, 344, 345, and 348 on veiling power.

abhāvanā = incorrect understanding, absence of judgment; **viparīta-bhāvanā** = error, opposite stream of thought; **saṁbhāvanā** = doubt; **vipratipattir** = contrary impression.

ajñānam-ālasya-jaḍatva-nidrā-
pramāda-mūḍhatva-mukhās tamoguṇāḥ |
etaiḥ prayukto na hi vetti kiñcit
nidrāluvat stambhavad eva tiṣṭhati ||118||

Ignorance, laziness, dullness, sleep, negligence, stupidity and so on, are the attributes of *tamas*. One tied to these does not know anything but remains like one asleep or like a pillar.

All of these negative traits are the products of *tamas*. Even as a person sound asleep does not know anything, so is a person subject to these qualities. Likewise, a person who is tied to a pillar does not need to exert himself, nor can he do so. Thus, these qualities are serious hindrances to a person's spiritual realization.

ajñānam = ignorance; **ālasya** = laziness; **jaḍatva** = dullness, inertness; **nidrā** = sleep; **pramāda** = negligence, not doing something even when one has the ability to do it; **mūḍhatva** = stupidity, foolishness; **nidrāluvat** = like one asleep; **stambhavad** = like a pillar, post.

sattvaṁ viśuddhaṁ jalavat tathāpi
tābhyāṁ militvā saraṇāya kalpate |
yatrātma-bimbaḥ prati-bimbitaḥ san
prakāśayaty arka ivākhilaṁ jaḍam ||119||

Even if *sattva* is pure like water, yet, in combination with the other two, it generates worldly existence. But, when the original, the light of the Self, gets reflected in *sattva* alone, then, like the sun, it illuminates the entire inanimate world.

Sattva is purity. It is the principle of luminosity and that which represents the principle of existence, of beingness. It may be compared to a perfectly pure glass. Light passes through it unobstructed and undiminished. Whatever is seen through that glass is clearly visible.

Pratibimbavāda is the theory that the individual is a reflection of *Brahman*. This theory compares an original and its reflection in a reflecting medium (such as a mirror). The reflection is non-different from the original (and appears as such due to the mirror). When the mirror is removed, the reflection vanishes and the original alone remains. The original represents the Truth and the reflection represents the appearance. This theory shows how *Brahman* is reflected in the physical body which gives rise to the individual. It also shows how one *Brahman* can appear as many

[1] Doubt (*viparīta-bhāvanā*) is removed by contemplation (*nididhyāsana*), according to Advaita.

individuals, even as one sun can appear in many vessels of water. *Avacchedavāda* is a theory of limitation (the individual is intelligence defined by ignorance). It is based on an example of space (seemingly limited) in a pot in relation to the space outside the pot. In reality, there is no difference between the space inside and outside the pot. See V. 164, 220–21, 289, and 386 on *pratibimbavāda*.

See BG 14.6, '*Sattva*, being stainless, is luminous and unobstructive.' See V. 120–121 on *sattva*.

viśuddhaṁ = very pure; **jalavat** = like water; **tathāpi** = even then; **saraṇāya** = for worldly existence; **kalpate** = generates; **bimbaḥ** = original, prototype; **pratibimbitaḥ** = reflection.

miśrasya sattvasya bhavanti dharmās-
tvamānitādyā niyamā yamādyāḥ |
śraddhā ca bhaktiś ca mumukṣutā ca
daivī ca saṁpattir asan nivṛttiḥ ||120||

The characteristics of mixed sattva are: a total absence of pride and so on; yama, niyama, and so on; faith, devotion, an intense-longing-for-liberation, divine tendencies, and a turning away from everything unreal.

See YS II.29 regarding *yama* and *niyama*: 'The eight limbs of Yoga are abstinence, observance, posture, breath control, sense withdrawal, concentration, meditation, and one-pointed absorption of the intellect'.

See BG 18.9 regarding 'total absence of pride': 'But that person who performs a prescribed duty as a thing that ought to be done, renouncing all attachment and also the fruits, their renunciation is regarded as *sattvic*.'

See BG 16.1–3 regarding 'divine tendencies': 'fearless, pure, steadfast in the exercise of wisdom, giving, self-controlled, sacrificing, study of the scriptures, austerity, upright, non-violent, truthful, peaceful, renunciation, tranquil, free from fault-finding, compassionate, not greedy, gentle, modest, steady, ardent, patient, forgiving, fortitude, not arrogant or proud.'

The first limb of Patañjali's *rāja-yoga* comprised: non-injury (*ahiṁsā*), truth (*satya*), non-stealing (*asteya*), continence (*brahmacarya*), and non-possession (*aparigraha*). The second limb of Patañjali's *rāja-yoga* comprised purity (*śauca*), contentment (*santoṣa*), austerity (*tapas*), study (*svādhyāya*), and devotion to God (*Iśvara-praṇidhāna*).

See V. 3, 19, 28, 29, 30, 31, 44, 84, 178, and 576 for references to *mumukṣutva*.

miśra = mixed, pure and impure; **amānitvam** = absence of pride, humility; **yama** = abstentions, self-control, restraint; **niyama** = observances, discipline; **śraddhā** = faith; **bhakti** = devotion; **mumukṣutā** = burning desire for liberation; **daivī** = divine tendencies; **saṁpattirasan-nivṛttiḥ** = withdrawal from all is not real.

viśuddha-sattvasya guṇāḥ prasādaḥ
svātmānubhūtiḥ paramā praśāntiḥ |
tṛptiḥ praharṣaḥ paramātmaniṣṭhā
yayā sadānanda-rasaṁ samṛcchati ||121||

The characteristics of pure *sattva* are tranquillity of mind, self-realization, supreme peace, contentment, bliss, abiding always in the supreme Self, which always ensures the essence of everlasting bliss.

See BG 13.7–11 for a list of qualities which an earnest spiritual aspirant should possess: 'Humility, modesty, non-injury, forebearance, patience, uprightness, selfless service to the teacher, purity, steadfastness, self-control, and so on'.

viśuddha = very pure; **prasādaḥ** = tranquillity of mind, to become clear; **svātmānubhūtiḥ** = self-realization; **paramā praśāntiḥ** = the highest or supreme peace; **tṛptiḥ** = contentment, satisfaction; **praharṣaḥ** = effortless bliss; **paramātmaniṣṭhā** = abiding always in the supreme Self; **sadānanda** = eternal bliss; **rasaṁ** = enjoyment, essence, delight; **samṛcchati** = ensures, brings about.

avyaktam etat triguṇair niruktaṁ
tat kāraṇaṁ nāma śarīram ātmanaḥ |
suṣuptir etasya vibhaktyavasthā
pralīna-sarvendriya-buddhi-vṛttiḥ ||122||

The unmanifest, already explained as constituting the three qualities, is the causal body of the individual. Deep sleep is its distinct, differentiated state and is characterized by the dissolution of the functioning of all the sense organs and the the mind.

The causal body is the sheath of bliss enveloped in ignorance, according to Advaita Vedānta. It is also called *ānandamayakośa*.

See V. 109, 122–123, 173, 210, 236, and 295 on deep sleep.

avyaktam = unmanifest; **triguṇair** = three qualities; **suṣuptir** = deep sleep; **etasya** = in this context it means 'of the causal body' spoken of as unmanifest; **vibhaktyavasthā** = differentiated state; **pralīna** = dissolved, disappeared into, dissolution; **sarvendriya** = all the sense organs; **buddhi** = mind, intellect.

sarva-prakāra-pramiti-praśāntiḥ
bījātmanāvasthitir eva buddheḥ |
suṣuptiretasya kila pratītiḥ
kiñcin na vedmīti jagat-prasiddheḥ ||123||

All sources of knowledge are absolutely still. The mind remains only in the form of a seed. Indeed, the test of this is the universal verdict, 'I did not know anything while asleep.'

Why does one sleep? Because it gives one rest and peace of mind. If one had no sleep for a number of consecutive nights, one will become restless and eventually the mind will not function. One must sleep. In sleep, one forgets one's name and form. Yet, in the morning one declares, 'I slept very well.' Who was aware of this absence of name and form? Who enjoyed this sleep?

Advaita is fond of saying that the proof of the attributeless Self is the deep sleep state. That 'someone' is there is proven by the fact that upon waking one declares, 'I slept well.' If one was not present there would be neither continuity nor this knowledge.

prakāra praśāntiḥ = absolutely still; **bīja** = seed; **jagat-prasiddheḥ** = universally well-known; **kila** = indeed, assuredly.

dehendriya-prāṇa-mano'hamādayaḥ
sarve vikārā viṣayās sukhādayaḥ |
vyomādi-bhūtānyakhilaṁ ca viśvam
avyakta-paryantam idaṁ hyanātmā ||124||

The body, the sense organs, the breath, the mind, the sense of 'I', all modifications, the sense objects, pleasures, gross elements such as the sky, the entire universe up to the unmanifested, all this is the not-self.

Once an individual has correctly discriminated between the Self and not-self, desire and aversion no longer affect such an individual. Once an individual has understood that the physical body is the not-self, what will such an individual care if others praise or criticize it? Once an individual has known that they are the immutable Self, what does it matter whether others praise or criticize? When this is accomplished, the bondage which derives from 'I' and 'mine' is cut. The physical body no more belongs to the Self than does blueness belong to the sky. The notions of 'I' and 'mine' are no more properties of the Self than are leanness or clothes. Even as fire does not burn up in its own heat since heat is of its own nature, so, too, if the not-self were the Self it could not be known as an object (since the two would not be distinct). However, the Self knows the not-self as an object and thus the two must be distinct.

deha = body; **indriya** = sense organs; **prāṇa** = breath; **mano** = mind; **aham** = 'I'; **sarve vikārā** = all modificatons or changes; **viṣayās** = sense objects; **sukha** = pleasures; **vyoma** = sky; **bhūta** = elements; **anātmā** = not-self.

māyā māyā-kāryaṁ sarvaṁ mahadādi-deha paryantam |
asad idam anātma-tattvaṁ viddhi tvaṁ maru-marīcikā-kalpam ||125||

Know that everything, māyā and all māyā's effects, from the Great[1] down to the gross body, are the not-self and therefore unreal like a mirage in the desert.

See V. 67, 110–112, 245, 406, 497, and 574 on *māyā*.

mahat = the Great, the first evolvement of primordial nature; **maru** = desert, sandy waste; **marīcikā** = mirage.

atha te saṁpravakṣyāmi svarūpaṁ paramātmanaḥ |
yad vijñāya naro bandhān muktaḥ Kaivalyam aśnute ||126||

Now I will tell you of the real nature of the supreme Self, by knowing which a human being is freed from bondage and attains liberation.

Pure Consciousness is the Self – one only, without a second. This Consciousness is revealed as essentially and fundamentally 'consciousness-as' and not 'consciousness-of'. But this One is not merely an abstract remote entity far removed from life. It ultimately concerns each individual as the immediate and immanent core in the depth of each one's being. *Ātman* is *Brahman*. It is not to be found as an ultimate object, located far away and inaccessible. Though one cannot know the knower, one can become the knower. The movement is from an impersonal object to the personal subject. Thus, the enquiry leads to a search for the *Ātman*, the ultimate subject.

---

1 See KaUp 1.3.10–11, 'Beyond the senses are the objects of the senses and beyond the objects is the mind; beyond the mind is understanding and beyond understanding is the Great/Beyond the Great is the unmanifest; beyond the unmanifest is the great Self. Beyond the Self there is nothing. That is the end; that is the final goal.'

atha = now, then; **svarūpaṁ** = real nature, essential nature; **paramātmanaḥ** = supreme Self; **naro** = human being; **bandhān** = bondage; **muktaḥ** = freed; **Kaivalyam-aśnute** = attains liberation.

asti kaścit svayaṁ nityaṁ ahaṁ-pratyaya-lambanaḥ |
avasthā-traya-sākṣī san pañca-kośa-vilakṣaṇaḥ ||127||

There is something which always exists by itself as the substratum of one's 'I'-awareness. It is the witness of the three states and is distinct from the five sheaths.

The three states of existence are waking, dreaming, deep sleep. See V. 100, 128, 213, and 219.

Various methods are employed to effect a discrimination between the Self and the not-self, one of which is an analysis of the five sheaths (*kośa*). This analysis will show that the Self persists in all the five sheaths while they vary and undergo change. This analysis consists of seeing that what is grosser and more external and less pervasive is less real than what is subtler and more internal and more pervasive. By this type of analysis, one will arrive at the Self, which is Real, due to it being the subtlest, inmost being.

The *pañcakośa viveka prakaraṇa* is based on the third chapter of the Taitt Up wherein the Self is described as being hidden in the cavity of the five sheaths. These sheaths veil and hide the Self from one's view. By discriminating one should remove the five sheaths and realize the supreme Self.

The grossest sheath is the *annamayakośa*. It is the physical body made of food, being the product of the physical elements. It is born of food and sustained by food. As it comes into being and changes, and goes out of being, it cannot be the Self. This body cannot be the Self for it does not exist before birth or after death. Subtler than the physical body is the *prāṇamayakośa*. It is made of the vital airs and energizes the entire body. This sheath is devoid of consciousness, intelligence, and thus cannot be the Self. Still subtler is the *manomayakośa*. This is the mental sheath. It gives rise to the ideas of 'I' and 'mine'. It raises the idea of possession. Because it has desires and is moved by pleasure and pain and is subject to delusion, it cannot be the Self. The Self has no desires, being Itself the fulfillment of all desires. The Self is changeless and thus this sheath is not the Self. Subtler still is the *vijñānamayakośa*. It reflects pure consciousness and pervades the entire body in the waking state. But in deep sleep it disappears and thus it too is not the Self, for the Self does not change or disappear. Lastly is the *ānandamayakośa*. This is the bliss sheath or sheath of enjoyment. This sheath is also impermanent and temporal for, even though it turns inwards and reflects *ānanda* or *cit*, it is a passive enjoyer which eventually slips into deep sleep or ignorance. It is only a reflection, not the unconditional Self.

These five sheaths are not the Self since they are not permanent. Still, they are experienced and the Self is not. How can that which is not experienced be said to exist? The answer is that the Self is not an object to be experienced but the very experiencer itself. There is nothing apart for the experience to know it. Nor does it need an experiencer to know it. It is self-luminous and requires no other source of illumination. The knower cannot be the known for then it would become the known, *ad infinitum*.

Thus when we dismiss the objective element from the five sheaths, what remains is pure consciousness, pure awareness, Being, *Brahman*. When one says nothing remains after dismissing all objective names and forms, what remains is the consciousness which witnesses the absence of names and forms and that is the Self. The witness is incapable of being negated. Thus we see that the supreme Self, the innermost element everywhere, subtler than the subtlest, all-pervasive, eternal, unlimited by anything, is infinite, is Existence, Consciousness, Bliss, Infinity. See V. 151, 153, 156, 167–170, 185–187, 189–190, 208–214, and 245.

See KaivUp 1.18, 'In the three states of consciousness whatever appears as the object of enjoyment or the enjoyer or the enjoyment, I am different from them, the witness, pure consciousness, the eternal Śiva' (*sākṣī*) on witnesses. See V. 101, 137, 159, 212, 213, 217, 218, 223, 270, 295, 352, 370, 381, 384, 495, 506, 507, and 552 for references to witness (*sākṣī*).

svayaṁ = by itself; **nityaṁ** = always, eternal; **ahaṁ-pratyaya-lambanaḥ** = substratum of the 'I' awareness; **avasthā-traya** = three states of existence; **sākṣī** = witness; **pañca-kośa** = five sheaths; **vilakṣaṇaḥ** = other than, distinct.

yo vijānāti sakalaṁ jāgrat-svapna-suṣuptiṣu |
buddhi-tadvṛtti-sad-bhāvam abhāvam-ahamityayam ||128||

That which knows everything in the waking, dreaming, and deep sleep states;[1] which knows the presence or absence of the mind[2] and its actions, That is This.

Advaita Vedānta adopts an enquiry into the three states of experience to reveal the real nature of the Self. By analyzing life as a whole, and not merely the waking state as most philosophical systems are prone to, Advaita reveals a comprehensive approach. An analysis of the waking state shows that the individual self resides in a physical body and employs its instruments to enjoy the objects of the external world. But the Self is not the non-self. The former is conscious while the latter is inert. The analysis of the dream state reveals that the Self does not really act and is unattached. In dreams the Self appears to interact with many things. But upon waking, it is realized that there were no dream objects and no interaction. And an analysis of the deep-sleep state shows that the Self is relationless. Here there are no distinctions whatsoever. There is no knowing subject nor known objects. There is no within and no without, as all empirical distinctions have vanished. Objective consciousness has disappeared though pure consciousness remains. Thus, though the three states exist, they and their contents are not persistent. But underlying them and persisting throughout is the Self. The 'I' that was there in the waking state was also there in the dream and deep-sleep states. The states pass and vary, but the underlying consciousness remains the same.

jāgrat = waking; **svapna** = dreaming; **suṣupti** = deep sleep; **buddhi** = mind, intellect.

yaḥ paśyati svayaṁ sarvaṁ yaṁ na paśyati kiñcana |
yaś cetayati buddhyādi na tad yaṁ cetayatyayam ||129||

That which, in itself, perceives everything but which nothing can perceive; that which illumines the mind and so on, but which itself cannot be illumined, That is the Self.

---

[1] See MāṇḍUp 6, 'This is knower of all (*eṣa sarvajñaḥ*).

[2] See KenaUp 1.6; also BṛhUp 3.4.2 and KaivUp 1.17, 'The world which shines in the states of waking, dream, and dreamless sleep, knowing it is the Absolute who I am, one is freed from all bonds.'

Even if the Self escapes objectification, it does not escape certainty. Nothing is more certain than the fact of one's own existence. It is self-evident, immediate and direct. A man may doubt many things; but he can never doubt his own being. This is because the very act of doubting would be an affirmation of one's very own existence. It cannot be proved since it is the basis of all proof and is established prior to all proofs. How can that by which all the means of valid knowledge are established itself be established by the means of valid knowledge?

Śaṅkara was fond of stating that the Self, which is the content of everyone's understanding of the 'I', is the most immediately known entity possible. Preception of the Self is the most immediate, though it is not mediated by the senses. In fact, preception need not always be sense-mediated. The distinguishing character of perception is its immediacy. This immediacy is a oneness of being. Thus, in this manner, knowing is, or becomes, identified with being. An individual knows the Self as the most certain perception of all because one is that Self. And not only is it that the Self of a sentient being is manifested immediately in one's indubitable experience, but even in the perception of an ordinary object the Self is revealed – for the Self is everything.

BṛhUp 3.4.2, 'You cannot see the seer of seeing, you cannot hear the hearer of hearing, you cannot think the thinker of thinking, you cannot understand the understander of understanding. That is your Self which is in all things.' Also see MāṇḍUp 1.7; KenaUp 1.3, 1.7; MuṇḍUp 2.2.11; KaUp 2.5.15; ŚvetUp 6.14; BG 15.6.

paśyati = perceives; **svayaṁ** = in itself; **sarvaṁ** = all, everything; **cetayati buddhyādi** = illumines the mind.

yena viśvam idaṁ vyāptaṁ yaṁ na vyāpnoti kiñcana |
ābhā-rūpam idaṁ sarvaṁ yaṁ bhāntam anubhātyayam ||130||

That by which this universe is pervaded, but which nothing pervades; which shining, all this, which is not of the nature of effulgence, shines. That is the Self.

The *Puruṣa Sūkta* declares, 'A quarter of it are all the creatures; three quarters of it is the divine part in the sky.'

See KaUp 2.2.15, 'Everything shines only after that shining light. His shining illumines all this world.'

viśvam = universe; **vyāptaṁ** = pervaded; **ābhā** = shining.

yasya sannidhi-mātreṇa dehendriya-mano-dhiyaḥ |
viṣayeṣu svakīyeṣu vartante preritā iva ||131||

That by whose very presence the body, the sense organs, the mind, and the intellect keep to their respective functions like servants obeying their master.

See KenaUp 1.1–2, 'By whom impelled, by whom compelled, does the mind soar forth? That which is the ear of the ear, the mind of the mind, speech of speech, breath of breath, eye of the eye.'

yasya = by whose; **sannidhi** = presesnce; **deha** = body; **indriya** = sense organs; **mano** = mind; **dhiyaḥ** = intellect.

ahaṁkārādi-dehāntā viṣayāś ca sukh-ādayaḥ |
vedyante ghaṭavad yena nitya-bodha-svarūpiṇā ||132||

That because of which everything, from the ego to the body, sense objects, and their pleasures and so on is known as clearly as a pot, is of the nature of eternal knowledge.

See V. 156 for an elucidation of this verse.

See BṛhUp 4.3.23, 'Now, he does not see anything here; but although he does not see, he is quite capable of seeing, for it is impossible for the seer to lose his capacity to see, for it is indestructible.'

ahaṁkārādi = ego; **dehāntā** = body; **viṣayāś** = sense objects; **sukhādayaḥ** = pleasures, etc; **ghaṭa** = pot, jar; **nitya-bodha-svarūpiṇā** = of the nature of eternal knowledge.

eṣo'ntarātmā puruṣaḥ purāṇo
nirantarākhaṇḍa-sukhānubhūtiḥ |
sadaikarūpaḥ pratibodha-mātro
yeneṣitā vāg-asavaś caranti ||133||

This is the innermost Self,[1] the primordial One, whose nature is continuously experienced as an unending indivisible bliss while continuously being reflected[2] in every mental modification and by whom[3] speech and the vital airs perform their function.

purāṇa puruṣa = primordial One, ancient person; **antarātmā** = inner Self; **nirantara** = eternal, unending; **akhaṇḍa** = undivided, whole, indivisible; **sukhānubhūtiḥ** = experience of bliss; **yena** = by whom; **vāg** = speech; **asavaś** = vital airs; **pratibodha** = (either) continuously or in every act of cognition (or) continuously as the object of cognition.

atraiva sattvātmani dhī-guhāyām
avyākṛtākāśa uru-prakāśaḥ |
ākāśa uccaiḥ ravivat prakāśate
sva-tejasā viśvam idaṁ prakāśayan ||134||

In this very body itself, in the secret cave[4] of the intellect, which is by nature pure, in the space[5] known as the unmanifest, the supremely radiant Self shines like the sun[6] high in the sky illuminating this entire universe by its innate effulgence.

The Heart within which everything shines gloriously and which is shining everywhere, is the one flashing light, the supreme Heart (*Paratrimsika* 270–71).

Suddenly there was a sudden shift in my perception. I felt as though there was just a 'slight shift' in my consciousness, and yet I went from feeling limited to limitlessness. It began with tears and an awareness of what seemed to be a thumb-sized cave just to the right of the center of my chest. I could observe this thumb-sized cave and noted that, in fact, it was the center of the universe, the center of everything, it was

[1] See BṛhUp 3.4.1, 'This is your Self that is within all things.'
[2] See KenaUp 2.12 on reflecting.
[3] The opening verse of the KenaUp asks 'By whom?'.
[4] Cave of the heart = TaittAran 10.38.1; ŚvetUp 3.11, 3.13, 3.20, 5.8; MaitrīUp 6.38; BṛhUp 4.4.2, 5.3.1; ChānUp 3.1.4.3, 8.1.1–3, 8.3.3; TaittUp 1.6.1, 2.1.1, KaUp 1.2.12, 1.3.1, 2.1.7, 2.1.12–13; BSBh 1.3.24–25. See V. 191, 219, 257, and 267 on the cave/heart.
[5] See BS 1.1.22 wherein the meaning of the word space (*ākāśa*) is discussed.
[6] See BṛhUp 3.7.9, 5.5.2, 5.15.1; ChānUp 3.18.2–5, 3.19.1–4; 4.17.3–4 on the Self being compared to the sun.

everything and yet, how is it possible, it was there in the center of my chest. This sounds contradictory but it was experiential.

Although linked to the body and my surroundings, I found myself expanded in an indescribable manner. I was an all-encompassing consciousness. Not theory – I was That. There was an immediate and direct contact with an intensely conscious universe and I was that universe. I was no longer John, but That, That immensity which was incredibly blissful, seemingly so because it was full, complete. I was immanent in every single part of it. My body, the ground I was sitting on, everything including the earth, the sky, the entire universe appeared to be distinguishable in this real, interpenetrating, and all-pervasive ocean of consciousness which, to explain the most incredible part of it as best I can seemed to be simultaneously unbounded, stretching out immeasurably in all directions, and yet no bigger than a tiny, thumb-sized cave in the right side of my chest. From this tiny cave, the entire universe, of which my body and its surrounding were a part, poured out and yet, somehow, there was not an iota of separation anywhere. The thought appeared that this heart cave was described by some individuals as an ocean (of consciousness) and that this too was an accurate, perfect description. Still, I liked the image of the heart cave better. How strange! Both descriptions fit perfectly, and yet I preferred one.

Tears were pouring down my face and continued to do so for as long as the experience lasted. There was no emotion and not the least bit of an increased pulse or heart rate as the tears flowed. I just observed them falling down my cheeks as if a faucet had been left open. I was overwhelmed with the silence. The silence was immense, overwhelming, all-pervasive. There were no questions and thus no answers. There was no noise. To say the silence was deafening would not do it justice. It was both humbling and enpowering at the same time. There was nothing left to know; nothing separate that was unknown. All was oneself and thus there was silence. It was sweet. So sweet. To say anything, anything at all, seemed stupid. Words could never come close to approximating This. This was full and I was this and I was full. 'That is full and complete; this is full and complete. The full comes out of the full. Taking the full from the full, the full itself remains full and complete'; see also MuṇḍUp 2.2.11, '*Brahman* alone is all this'; ChānUp 6.2.1, 'It is One alone, without a second'; BṛhUp 4.4.19, 'In *Brahman* there is no diversity whatsoever.'

atraiva = here itself; **sattvātmani** = nature of purity; **dhī** = intellect; **guhāyām** = cave, secret; **avyākṛta** = unmanifest; **ākāśa** = space; **urupra-kāśaḥ** = supremely radiant; **uccaiḥ-ravivat** = shines like the sun high in the sky; **sva-tejasā** = self effulgence; **viśvamidaṁ** = all this universe.

jñātā mano'haṁkṛti-vikriyāṇāṁ
dehendriya-prāṇakṛta-kriyāṇām |
ayo'gnivat tān anuvartamāno
na ceṣṭate no vikaroti kiñcana ||135||

The Self is the knower of the modifications of the mind and the ego, the activities of the body, the sense organs, and the breath, and although apparently accompanying them like fire[1] in iron, it neither acts nor changes in the least.

[1] See KaUp 2.2.9, 'As fire which is one, entering this world becomes varied in shape according to the object, so also the one Self within all beings becomes varied according to whatever it enters and also exists outside"; also see MaitrīUp 3.3.

The entire universe exists only in Consciousness. All modifications take place only in Consciousness. Take your stand in the Absolute. The world rises and sets in Consciousness. One need not negate the world – merely see it as appearing in Consciousness. Whatever begins and ends is mere appearance. Pictures come and go, appear on the movie screen. The screen does not move. Fire comes and goes in iron. Iron is not hot, in and of itself. See V. 193, 350, and 507 for fire in iron.

MāṇḍUp 6, 'This is the lord of all, this is the knower of all, this is the inner controller; this is the source of all'.

mano'haṁkṛti = mind and ego; **vikriyāṇāṁ** = modifications; **dehendriya-prāṇakṛta** = activities of the body, sense organs, breath; **ayas** = iron, metal; **agnivat** = fire.

na jāyate no mriyate na vardhate
na kṣīyate no vikaroti nityaḥ |
vilīyamāne'pi vapuṣyamuṣmin
na līyate kumbha ivāmbaraṁ svayam ||136||

It is not born; it does not die; it does not grow; it does not decline; it does not change. It is eternal. Even if this body is destroyed it does not cease to exist, just as the space in a pot does not become extinct when the pot is broken.

The central theme of Gauḍapāda's philosophy is his theory of 'non-origination'. That is, nothing is ever born and nothing ever dies. This is declared, not because 'nothing' is the ultimate truth, but because the great inner Self (*Ātman*) is the only reality. His logic is that anything that is non-existent in the beginning, that is, which originates, and that is non-existent at the end, that is, which is destroyed, is also non-existent in the middle, that is, completely non-existent. According to Gauḍapāda, the ultimate reality is *Ātman-Brahman* alone. It is defined as 'something unseen, beyond empirical practice, impossible to grasp, without any signs, unthinkable, indescribable'. All appearances are illusory, non-real. All empirical distinctions such as subject and object, knower and known, mind and matter, are but seeming appearances due to ignorance. If one sees them, it is like 'seeing the footprints of birds in the sky'.

See MāṇḍUp 7, '. . . neither inside nor outside nor both; unseen (*adṛṣṭam*), can't be spoken of (*avyavaharyam*), ungraspable (*agrāhyam*), without distinguishable marks (*alakṣanam*), unthinkable (*acintyam*), unnameable (*avyapadeśyam*), peaceful (*śāntam*), non-dual (*advaitam*), auspicious (*śivam*).'

See KaUp 1.2.18, 'The knowing Self is never born; nor does it die at any time'. Also see BṛhUp 4.4.20 (*aja dhruvaḥ*); BG 2.20, 'The Self is neither born nor does it die.'

na = not; **jāyate** = born; **mriyate** = die; **vardhate** = to increase, grow, prosper, strengthen; **kṣīyate** = decline, wane, decay, wear or waste away, end; **vikaroti** = change, modify; **nityaḥ** = eternal; **kumbha** = pot, jar.

prakṛti-vikṛti-bhinnaḥ śuddhabodhasvabhāvaḥ
sad-asad-idam-aśeṣaṁ bhāsayan nir-viśeṣaḥ |
vilasati paramātmā jāgrad-ādiṣvavasthāsu
aham-aham-iti sākṣāt sākṣirūpeṇa buddheḥ ||137||

The supreme Self, of the nature of pure knowledge, is different from primordial nature and its modifications. It is without qualities and illumines the real and the non-real, everything with form as well as the formless. It flashes through the waking and other states as their witness and is referred to as the 'I.'[1]

The nature of the Self defies any description in terms of the categories known to thought. There is nothing similar to the Absolute, dissimilar to the Absolute, and there is no internal differentiation within the Absolute. See *Pañcadaśī*, 2.20–21. See also BSBh II.1.14.

See KaUp 2.2.8, 'That person who is awake in those that sleep, shaping desire after desire, that, indeed, is the pure. That is the Absolute, that, indeed, is called the immortal. In it all the worlds rest and no one ever goes beyond it.'

See KaivUp 1.18, 'In the three states of consciousness whatever appears as the object of enjoyment or the enjoyer or the enjoyment, I am different from them, the witness, pure consciousness, the eternal Śiva' (*sākṣī*) on witnesses. See V. 101, 127, 159, 212, 213, 217, 218, 223, 270, 295, 352, 370, 381, 384, 495, 506, 507, and 552 for references to witness (*sākṣī*).

prakṛti = primordial nature; **vikṛti** = transformations, modifications; **bhinnaḥ** = different from; **śuddhabodhasvabhāvaḥ** = of the nature of pure knowledge; sad = real; **asad** = non-real; **aśeṣaṁ** = everything, with form; **bhāsayan** = illuminates; **nirviśeṣaḥ** = formless, without qualities; **vilasati** = to shine, appear, to gleam, flash; **paramātmā** = supreme Self; **jāgradādi** = waking state; **avasthā** = states of existence; **aham** = 'I'; **sākṣāt** = witness.

niyamitamanasāmuṁ tvaṁ svam ātmānam ātma-
nyayam-ahamiti sākṣād viddhi buddhi-prasādāt |
jani-maraṇa-taraṅgāpāra-saṁsāra-sindhuṁ
pratara bhava kṛtārtho brahmarūpeṇa saṁsthaḥ ||138||

By means of a concentrated mind and the grace of a purified intellect, directly realize your self as the Self. Identify with the Self and by this means cross the boundless ocean of worldly existence with its waves of birth and death. Becoming established in the Absolute, you become one who has accomplished everything.

See KaUp 2.1.11, 'By mind alone is this to be obtained.'

See V. 3, 29, 42, 50, 149, 477, 489, 518, and 519 for references to grace.

See V. 11, 150, 177–78, 183, 276–77, 315, 336, 361–63, 367, 370–71, 384, and 408 for purification of the mind.

niyamitamanasāmuṁ = by means of a concentrated mind; **buddhi** = intellect; **prasadat** = grace, clear, pure; **jani-marana** = birth and death; **taraṅga** = waves; **apāra** = shoreless; **saṁsāra-sindhuṁ** = ocean of worldly existence; **pratara** = cross completely; **brahma-rūpeṇa** = the Absolute; **saṁsthaḥ** = established.

atrānātmanyahamiti matir bandha eṣo'sya puṁsaḥ
prāpto'ñānāt janana-maraṇa-kleśa-sampāta-hetuḥ |
yenaivāyaṁ vapur idam asat satyam ity ātma-buddhyā
puṣyatyukṣatyavati viṣayais tantubhiḥ kośakṛdvat ||139||

---

[1] See BṛhUp 1.4.1, 'He first said, "I am". Therefore arose the name of "I".'

Solely believing that the not-self is the Self is the cause of an individual's bondage. This belief arises from ignorance. It is the cause of being completely engulfed by birth, death, the afflictions and so on. It is because of this that one thinks the unreal body is real and, identifying with it, one nourishes, bathes, and protects it by the sense objects, thereby becoming bound like the silkworm by its own woven cocoon.

The word *kośa* (sheath) is also used for the cocoon of a silkworm (see Yajña 3.147). It is also used in Vedānta as a term for the three sheaths which make up the various covers of the body.

See MuṇḍUp 1.2.8, 'Abiding in the midst of ignorance, wise in their own esteem, thinking themselves to be learned, fools, afflicted with troubles, go about like the blind people led by one who is himself blind.' See also KaUp 1.2.5; MaitUp 7.9.

bandha = bondage; **puṁsaḥ** = human being; **janana-maraṇa** = birth and death; **kleśa** = afflictions, defilements, passions; **saṁpāta** = engulfed, immersed, collision, encounter, confluence; **hetuḥ** = reason, cause; **yenaiva** = by which alone; **vapur** = body; **asat** = unreal; **satyam** = real; **puṣya** = nourish; **ukṣa** = bathes; **tyavati** = protect; **viṣaya** = sense objects; **kośa** = sheath, cocoon.

atasmiṅ tad-buddhiḥ prabhavati vimūḍhasya tamasā
vivekābhāvād-vai sphurati bhujage rajju-dhiṣaṇā |
tato'nartha-vrāto nipatati samādātur adhikaḥ
tato yo'sadgrāhaḥ sa hi bhavati bandhaḥ śṛṇu sakhe ||140||

Being confused by ignorance, a person mistakes a thing for what it is not. It is this absence of discrimination which causes one to mistake a snake for a rope. Then, great danger befalls one subject to it. Hence, listen my friend. Taking unreal things to be real is definitely what constitutes bondage.

Superimposition (*adhyāsa*) is defined by Śaṅkara in his BSBh Preamble (*Adhyāsa Bhāṣya*) as 'cognizing something as something else' (*atasmiṅ tadbuddhiḥ*). It is wrong knowledge and is pervasive in everything one knows and in everything one does. As long as one's perspective is empirical, one is a victim of superimposition at every level. For instance, epistemology presupposes a subject who knows, the object which is known, and the resulting knowledge. The justification and elucidation of this triple form (*tripuṭī*) is accounted for by a superimposition of ignorance. According to the metaphysics of Advaita, the Absolute is one and non-dual. Thus arises the apparent problem of the One and the many. What is the relationship between the One and the many, between the Absolute and the relative? The Advaitin must account for the seeming plurality of the universe if the Reality is One and non-dual. An explanation is also called for in regard to the distinction which the Advaitin makes between the Reality with form (*saguṇa*) and the formless Reality (*nirguṇa*). The seeming difference between the individual self and the Absolute needs to be explained. The place of God (*Īśvara*), as well as the creation of the world, must be accounted for. Superimposition is responsible for all these. Lastly, the entire practical teachings of Advaita presuppose the concept of superimposition. The bondage of the individual, as well as its liberation, all disciplines prescribed for attaining release, ethics, esthetics, and values all have meaning only within the context of superimposition.

See V. 39, 181, 269, 271, 279–86, 307, 393, 407, and 462 on superimposition.

See V. 12, 63, 112, 199, 237, 248, 303, 388, 405, 407, and 550 for references to a snake.

atasmiṁ tad-buddhiḥ = recognizing something as something else; **vimūḍhasya** = perplexed, bewildered, confused; **vivekābhāvād** = absence of discrimination; **bhujage** = snake; **rajju-dhiṣaṇā** = thinking it is a rope; **anartha** = misfortune; **vrāto** = multitude, swarm, troop, flock; **nipatati** = settles down, descends upon; **sa hi bhavati bandhaḥ** = becomes bondage.

akhaṇḍa-nityādvaya-bodha-śaktyā
sphurantam ātmānam ananta-vaibhavam |
samāvṛṇotyāvṛti-śaktir-eṣā
tamomayī rāhur ivārka-bimbam || 141 ||

Just as Rahu[1] conceals the sun, the veiling power, whose nature is ignorance, conceals the Self, whose infinite glory, which is eternal, indivisible, and non-dual,[2] luminously manifests itself by the power of knowledge.

The Self is never under the veil of bondage, imposed by ignorance. The Self is pure by nature, enlightened and liberated from the very beginning.

akhaṇḍa = indivisible; **nitya** = eternal; **advaya** = non-dual; **bodha** = knowledge; **śaktyā** = power; **sphurantam** = shining, luminously manifests; **ananta** = infinite; **vaibhavam** = might, power, grandeur, magnificence, glory; **rāhur** = Rāhu.

tiro-bhūte svātmanyamalatara-tejovati pumān
anātmānaṁ mohād aham iti śarīraṁ kalayati |
tataḥ kāma-krodha-prabhṛtibhir amuṁ bandhana-guṇaiḥ
paraṁ vikṣepākhyā rajasa uru-śaktir vyathayati* || 142 ||

When one's own Self of supreme effulgence[3] is concealed, that person, due to delusion, considers the body to be their Self. Then, by the binding qualities of desire, anger, and so on, which are of the nature of the powerful active-attribute[4] which causes wrong projection, one is afflicted by untold misery.

If a person thinks they are their body and they desire something and that desire is thwarted, then anger arises. This is well known.

See BG 16.21, 'Triple is this gate of hell, destructive of the Self, lust, anger, and greed, therefore one should abandon these three' (*kāmaḥ, krodhaḥ, lobhaḥ*).

tirobhūte = concealment; concealing power, to set aside, vanish, hide, to cause to disappear; **svātmani** = one's own nature; **tejas** = luminous, effulgence; **pumān** = human being, the individual; **anātmānaṁ** = not-self; **mohād** = delusion; **śarīraṁ** = body; **kāma** = desire, lust, passion; **krodha** = anger; **bandhana-guṇaiḥ** = binding qualities; **paraṁ** = untold, great, supreme; **vikṣepākhyā** = wrong, incorrect projection; **rajasa** = active-attribute; **vyathayati** = greatly disturbed, tormented, agitated, unhappy.

---

1 Rāhu, in Indian mythology, is conceived of as a demon who periodically conceals the sun by swallowing it. The reference is to a solar eclipse. See ChānUp 8.13.1, 'like the moon from Rāhu's jaws'.

2 See ChanUp 6.2.1 (*ekam evādvitīyam*) and BG 13.12.

* See V. 115–17, 141, 146, 344, 345, and 348 on veiling power.

3 See MuṇḍUp 2.2.10, 'light of lights' (*jyotiṣāṁ jyotiḥ*); also KaUp 2.3.1.

4 See KaivUp 1.12, 'The same self veiled by *māyā* attains a body and performs all work.'

mahā-moha-grāha-grasana-galitātmāvagamano
dhiyo nānāvasthās svayam abhinayan tad-guṇatayā |
apāre saṁsāre viṣaya-viṣa-pūre jalanidhau
nimajjyonmajjyāyaṁ bhramati kumatiḥ kutsita-gatiḥ ||143||

An individual of deluded mind, in the grip of the crocodile of delusion, is thereby prevented from knowing the real nature of the Self. Such a one superimposes the various transformations of the mind upon the Self and, flounders up and down in the boundless ocean of worldly existence which is full of the poison of sense objects, with a mind unable to move towards realization.

See KaUp 2.1.1, 'The Self is not to be sought through the senses'. KaUp 2.1.2, 'The small-minded go after outward pleasures. They walk into the snare of widespread death.'

mahāmoha = great delusion; **grāha** = grip, imprisoned, captured; **grasana** = to seize with the mouth, devour, swallow; **galitam** = lost; **nānāvasthās** = transformations of various kinds; **tad-guṇatayā** = being based on it, arising from it; **apāre** = endless, shoreless; **viṣa** = poison; **kumatiḥ** = one whose mind does not move towards realization.

bhānu-prabhāsañjanitābhra-paṅktiḥ
bhānuṁ tirodhāya yathā vijṛmbhate |
ātmoditāhaṁkṛtir ātma-tattvaṁ
tathā tirodhāya vijṛmbhate svayam ||144||

As a layer of clouds which have been produced by the rays of the sun conceal the sun and appear themselves, so egoism, which arises from the Self, conceals the Self and expands itself.

The sun knows nothing of darkness. From the perspective of the sun, there is no rising, no setting, no darkness whatsoever. It is only from the perspective of the Earth that terms like rising, setting, darkness, the removal of darkness, and so on make any sense.
See KaUp 2.2.11, 'Just as the sun is not defiled by the external faults seen by the eye.'

bhānu = of the sun; **prabhā** = by the rays, effulgent; **sañjanit** = produced; **ābhra** = cloud; **paṅktiḥ** = a row or set, layer; **tirodhāya** = cover, conceal, hide; **vijṛmbhate** = expands, spreads out, blossoms, arises, appears.

kabalita-dinanāthe durdine sāndra-meghaiḥ
vyathayati himajhañjhā-vāyur-ugro yathaitān |
avirata-tamasātmanyāvṛte mūḍha-buddhiṁ
kṣapayati bahu-duḥkhais tīvra-vikṣepa-śaktiḥ ||145||

Just as a person suffers incalculable hardships[1] on a rainy day when the sun is completely hidden behind dense clouds, accompanied by strong cold winds, so, too, the foolish person when the Self is concealed, is subject to manifold suffering from the projecting power, which is the cause of countless griefs.

---

1 The root '*vyatha*' has a secondary meaning, 'to wander', and this is implied here.

Ignorance is that force which presents the unreal as real and that which is temporary and short-lived as eternal and everlasting. It is described as the beginningless cause which brings about the illusion of the world; an indescribable power of the Absolute (*Brahman*), which is neither real nor totally unreal. It is declared to have two powers – an ability to conceal and an ability to project (*āvaraṇa* and *vikṣepa*); it is indefinable (*anirvacanīya*); it is of the nature of a positive existence (*bhāvarūpa*).

kabalita = clouds which obscure the sun; **dinanāthe** = the sun; **durdine** = rainy or cloudy day, bad weather; **sāndra-meghaiḥ** = heavy clouds; **himajhañjhā-vāyur** = cold winds; **ugro** = violent, strong, mighty, terrible, fierce; **mūḍha-buddhiṁ** = foolish-minded one; **kṣapayati bahu-dhuḥ** = many difficulties; **duḥkhais** = suffering, grief; **tīvra** = intense, countless; **vikṣepa-śaktiḥ** = projecting power.

etābhyām eva śaktibhyāṁ bandha puṁsaḥ samāgataḥ |
yābhyāṁ vimohito dehaṁ matvātmānaṁ bhramatyayam ||146||

A person's bondage proceeds solely from these two powers. Deluded by them, a person mistakes the body for the Self and wanders about.

The two powers are *āvaraṇa* and *vikṣepa saktis*. See V. 115–17, 141, 344, 345, and 348 on veiling power.

etābhyām-eva = by these two only; **śaktibhyāṁ** = powers; **bandha** = bondage; **puṁsaḥ** = human being; **samāgataḥ** = proceeds; **vimohito** = eluded, confused, bewitched, beguiled.

bījaṁ saṁsṛti-bhūmijasya tu tamo dehātma-dhīr-aṅkuraḥ
rāgaḥ pallavam ambu karma tu vapuḥ skandho'savaḥ śākhikāḥ |
agrāṇīndriya-saṁhatiś ca viṣayāḥ puṣpāṇi duḥkhaṁ phalaṁ
nānā-karma-samudbhavaṁ bahuvidhaṁ bhoktā'tra jīvaḥ khagaḥ ||147||

Ignorance is the seed for the tree[1] of worldly existence; mistaking the body for the Self is its sprout; desires are its tender blossoms; actions are its water; the body is its trunk; the vital airs are its branches; sense object contact are its tendrils; sense objects are its flowers; miseries born of actions are its fruits; the experiencer is the individual, the bird[2] who eats the fruit.

The wheel of birth and death is being compared to a tree. Its seed is ignorance, its blossoms are desires. Recall earlier the world being compared to a forest.

bījaṁ = seed; **saṁsṛti-bhūmijasya** = tree of worldly existence; **aṅkuraḥ** = sprout, shoot; **rāgaḥ** = desire, passion, lust; **pallavam** = shoot, sprout, twig, bud, blossom; **ambu** = water; **agrāṇi** = tendrils; **puṣpāṇi** = flowers; **duḥkhaṁ** = misery, suffering; **phalaṁ** = fruits, results; **bhokta** = experiencer; **jīvaḥ** = individual; **khagaḥ** = bird.

---

[1] BṛhUp 3.9.28, 'An individual is like a mighty tree . . . hairs = leaves, skin = bark, blood from skin flows as sap from bark, and so on.'

[2] See MuṇḍUp 3.1.1, 'Two birds, companions always unite, cling to the selfsame tree. Of these two, the one eats the sweet fruit and the other looks on without eating'; RV 1.164.20; ŚvetUp 4.6; KaUp 1.3.1.

ajñānamūlo'yam anātma-bandho
naisargiko'nādir ananta īritaḥ |
janmāpyaya-vyādhi-jarādi-duḥkha-
pravāha-tāpaṁ janayatyamuṣya ||148||

Ignorance is the source of this bondage of the not-self. It is natural to everyone and is said to be without beginning and without end. It engenders for the individual a succession of sufferings such as birth, death, disease, old age, and so on.

Ignorance is always there. Upon birth, one finds ignorance present. There has never been a time when it hasn't been there. It is said to be without beginning and infinite or endless (unless it is destroyed by knowledge). It is endless until and unless wisdom destroys it.

ajñānamūlo = ignorance is the source or root; **anātma-bandho** = bondage to the not-self; **naisarga** = natural; **anādi** = beginningless, eternal; **ananta** = infinite, without end; **īritaḥ** = is said, is understood; **janmāpyaya** = birth and death; **vyādhi** = sickness, disease; **jarādi** = old age; **duḥkha** = suffering; **pravāha** = unbroken series, succession, continuous flow; **tāpam** = causes trouble or pain, engenders (instead of *tāpam*, there is another possible reading given: **pātaṁ** = to fall down, descend).

nāstrair na śastrair anilena vahninā
chettuṁ na śakyo na ca karma-koṭibhiḥ |
viveka-vijñāna-mahāsinā vinā
dhātuḥ prasādena sitena mañjunā ||149||

Not by missiles, nor weapons, nor wind, nor fire, nor even by millions of prescribed actions can this bondage be destroyed; by nothing except the great, sharp, beautiful sword of wisdom which comes from discrimination given by the grace of the supreme Lord.

See MuṇḍUp 3.1.6, 'Truth alone conquers, not untruth'. See also KaUp 1.2.23; MuṇḍUp 3.2.3.

See BṛhUp 1.4.16, 'Even if one performs a great and holy work, but without knowing this, that work of his is exhausted in the end.' Also MuṇḍUp 1.2.8; ĪśaUp 10, 13.

See KaUp 1.2.23, 'He is to be obtained only by the one whom the (Self) chooses.'

See KaUp 1.3.14, 'Sharp as the edge of a razor and hard to cross.'

See V. 3, 29, 42, 50, 138, 477, 489, 518, and 519 for references to grace.

āstrair = missiles; **śastrair** = weapons, arrows; **nilena** = wind; **vahninā** = fire; **chettuṁ na śakyo** = cannot be cut off; **karma-koṭibhiḥ** = millions of actions; **viveka** = discrimination; **vijñāna-mahāsinā** = great sword of knowledge or wisdom; **vinā** = without it; **prasādena** = grace; **mañjunā** = wonderful, beautiful.

śruti-pramāṇaika-mateḥ svadharma-
niṣṭhā tayaivātma-viśuddhir-asya |
viśuddha-buddheḥ paramātma-vedanaṁ
tenaiva saṁsāra-samūla-nāśaḥ ||150||

The realization of the supreme Self is possible only for those whose minds have been supremely purified by being firmly established in the observance of one's duty with a firm knowledge that the scriptures are the sole source for determining it. By this alone, worldly existence, with its root, is destroyed.

In order to realize the Self, action (*karma*) is absolutely necessary to purify the mind (*buddhi*), so that one will be qualified/fit. The Self, which has been obscured by the not-self, shines clearly when they are destroyed. In verse 149, action has been declared to be inadequate and unnecessary for destroying the not-self. This verse shows when and why it is necessary to purify the intellect.

Why does discrimination work? Because the mind has a tendency to focus on the gross only and not the subtle. But enquiring, one becomes aware of the mind and its tendencies. It becomes *sattvic* (pure/lucid), dissolving dullness and quieting the restlessness of the mind. It gently but steadily changes the mind's very substance. It is a shift from darkness to light.

Svadharma or one's own duties are those actions which pertain to an individual's own caste and stage of life. They should be obseved, selflessly, without expecting any reward for such.

See V. 11, 138, 177–78, 183, 276–77, 315, 336, 361–63, 367, 370–71, 384, and 408 for purification of the mind.

See BG 16.24, 'Therefore, let the scriptures be your authority in deciding what ought to be done and what ought not to be done.'

śruti = primary scripture; **pramāṇaika-mateḥ** = sole valid means of know-ledge; **svadharma-niṣṭhā** = firmly established in one's own duties; **viśuddha-buddheḥ** = purified intellect; **saṃsāra** = worldly existence; **sa-mūla** = with its root; **nāśaḥ** = destroyed.

kośair-annamayādyaiḥ pañcabhir-ātmā na saṁvṛto bhāti |
nija-śakti-samutpannaiḥ śaivāla-paṭalair-ivāmbu vāpīstham ||151||

The Self does not shine brightly when covered by the food and other sheaths which arise by its own power like the water in a well covered by a collection of moss.

It is the power of the sun which enables darkness to arise. Likewise, it is the power of the Self which enables the not-self to seemingly obscure the Self. Obviously, from the point of view of the sun, there is no such thing as darkness. From the point of view of the Self, there is no not-self. Still, like the water in a well being obscured by the moss which covers it, the Self cannot be perceived due to the sheaths which are superimposed on the Self.

See BṛhUp 5.15.1, 'The face of truth is covered by a golden disc.'

See TaitUp 2.2.1 on the food sheath. See V. 153, 156, 167–70, 185–87, 189–90, 208–14, and 245 for references to the sheaths.

See V. 138, 150, 183, 276, 315, 336, and 361–63 for purification of the mind.

kośair = sheaths, coverings; **annamayādyaiḥ** = food sheath; **nija-śakti-samutpannaiḥ** = rise of its own power; **śaivāla** = moss; algae; **paṭalair** = cover, screen, veil; **ambu** = water; **vāpīstham** = pond.

tac-chaivālāpanaye samyak salilaṁ pratīyate śuddham |
tṛṣṇā-santāpa-haraṁ sadyaḥ saukhya-pradaṁ paraṁ puṁsaḥ ||152||

When the moss is removed, one can see the pure water completely and it removes the pain of thirst and immediately fills individuals with great joy.

Note that the water is already and always present. All that needs to be done is to remove that which hides it. Nothing new need be obtained.

śaivāla = moss; **salilaṁ** = water; **śuddham** = pure; **tṛṣṇā** = thirst; **santāpa** = pain; **haraṁ** = removed, destroyed; **saukhya** = joy, happiness; **paraṁ** = great, highest; **puṁsaḥ** = individual, human being.

pañcānām-api kośānām apavāde vibhātyayaṁ śuddhaḥ |
nityānandaika-rasaḥ pratyag-rūpaḥ paraḥ svayam-jyotiḥ ||153||

When the five sheaths have been negated, this Self, which is pure, the nectar of eternal bliss, indwelling, supreme, and self-effulgent,[1] supremely shines.

An analysis of the five sheaths which cover the Self will reveal that the Self persists in all the five sheaths while they vary and undergo change. This analysis consists of revealing that what is grosser, more external and less pervasive is less real than what is subtler, more internal and more pervasive. Thereby the Self will be revealed as the subtlest, innermost being and therefore the most real. From the physical body, which is the grossest sheath, to the subtlest sheath of enjoyment will be found impermanence and objectification. But the knower of all these is the subtlest, most pervasive of all. The knower cannot be known for then it would become the known *ad infinitum.* The Self is self-luminous and requires no other source of illumination. It is not an object to be experienced. Thus, when the objective element is removed from the five sheaths, what remains is Pure Consciousness, awareness, the *Ātman*. Even to say that nothing remains after dismissing all objective names and forms, requires a consciousness which witnesses the absence of names and forms. The subtlest of all is this witnessing consciousness which is incapable of being negated.

pañcānām = five; **api** = (indicates the five sheaths should be set aside entirely); **kośānām** = sheaths, coverings; **apavāde** = refuted, denied; **vibhāti** = supremely shines; **nityānanda** = eternal bliss; **rasaḥ** = essence, nectar; **pratyag-rūpaḥ** = indwelling, inside everything; **paraḥ** = supreme; **svayam-jyotiḥ** = self-luminous.

ātmānātma-vivekaḥ kartavyo bandha-muktaye viduṣā |
tenaivānandī bhavati svaṁ vijñāya sac-cid-ānandam ||154||

Therefore, to be free of bondage, the wise should make an effort to discriminate between the Self and the not-self. By having understood that which is of the nature of Existence, Consciousness, Bliss, one becomes blissful.

The Self is here described as being of the nature of Existence, Consciousness, Bliss. *Satyam jñānam anantam brahma* conveys only identity. Usually *satyam jñānam anantam brahma* is interpreted in a secondary sense because the Absolute is considered to be beyond all determinations and attributes. Thus *satyam* is used to indicate that the Absolute is not unreal; *jñānam* is used to indicate that the Absolute is not unconscious; and *anantam* is used to indicate that it is not finite. But it can be maintained that anyone who understands the *mahāvākyas* will immediately know that *Brahman, satyam, jñānam*, and *anantam* all refer to the same content. *Brahman* is *satyam* and *jñānam* is *anantam*, etc. The text produces the knowledge asked for, *viz.*, 'What is *Brahman*?'

---

[1] See US 1.11.11; MuṇḍUp 2.2.10–11. Also see V. 100, 191, 213, 221, 240, 508, and 536 on self-luminous.

Vimuktātman, in his *Iṣṭa Siddhi*, subtly shows how '*satyam, jñānam*, and *anantam* can be interpreted in a primary and direct sense' (*Iṣṭasiddhi* pp. 26–32). The terms are not synonymous and thus there is no repetition. But being non-synonymous, the terms don't indicate diverse attributes either. These non-synonymous terms have an impartite sense. The Absolute alone is, and *satyam, jñānam*, and *anantam* are expressions of the same Absolute. They do not express attributes or aspects of the Absolute. They are the Absolute. They do not express attributes or aspects of the Absolute. They are the Absolute. *Sat* is *Brahman. Cit* is *Brahman. Ānanda* is *Brahman. Anantam* is *Brahman.* And *Brahman* is only one, without a second.

See KaUp 1.2.2, 'The wise, pondering over them (both the good and the pleasant), discriminates.'

ātmānātma-vivekaḥ = discrimination between the Self and the not-self; **kartavyo** = acquired with effort; **bandha-muktaye** = freedom from bondage; **viduṣā** = the wise; **sac** = Existence, Truth, Real; **cid** = consciousness; **ānandam** = Bliss.

muñjād-iṣīkām-iva dṛśya-vargāt
pratyañcam-ātmānam asaṅgam akriyam |
vivicya tatra pravilāpya sarvaṁ
tadātmanā tiṣṭhati yassa muktaḥ ||155||

That person is liberated who separates the Self, which is unattached[1] and actionless,[2] from all perceived sense objects, as one separates the tender core of the *muñjā* grass[3] from its covering, and who then remains firmly established in the Self.

muñjād = a type of grass; **iṣīkām** = a delicate reed inside this grass; **pratyañcam** = not in the outgoing way; facing otherwise than outgoing; **asaṅgam** = unattached; **akriyam** = actionless; **vivicya** = separating, eliminating.

deho'yam anna-bhavano'nnamayas tu kośo
hyannena jīvati vinaśyati tad-vihīnaḥ |
tvak-carma-māṁsa-rudhirāṣthi-purīṣarāśir
nāyaṁ svayaṁ bhavitum arhati nitya-śuddhaḥ ||156||

The sheath of the gross body is food. It originated from food, is sustained by food, and perishes without food.[4] It is a composite of skin, flesh, blood, and excreta.[5] Never can it be the self-existent, eternally pure Self.[6]

---

[1] See BṛhUp 3.9.26, 'It is unattached' (*asaṅgaḥ*). Also BṛhUp 4.4.22.

[2] See ŚvetUp 6.19, 'actionless' (*niṣkriyaṁ*).

[3] See KaUp 2.3.17 (the Self), 'one should draw out with firmness, from the body, as the wind from the *muñja* grass.'

[4] See TaittUp 2.2.1, 'From food, verily, are produced whatsoever creatures dwell on the earth. Moreover, by food alone they live and then also into it they pass at the end.'

[5] See MaitrīUp 3.4, 'It is built up with bones, smeared over with flesh, covered with skin, filled with faeces, urine, bile, phlegm, marrow, fat.'

[6] See KaUp 1.2.18, 'unborn, eternal' (*ajo nityaḥ*); IśaUp 8 'pure, untouched by anything inauspicious.'

anna-bhavano = that which originated from food; **tvak** = skin; **carma** = skin; **māṁsa** = flesh; **rudhira** = blood; **purīṣa** = excrement.

pūrvaṁ janer-api mṛter atha nāyam-asti
jāta-kṣaṇaḥ-kṣaṇa-guṇo'niyata-svabhāvaḥ |
naiko jaḍaśca ghaṭavat paridṛśyamānaḥ
svātmā kathaṁ bhavati bhāva-vikāra-vettā || 157 ||

In both cases, it does not exist before its birth or after its death. Every moment it is subject to origination and destruction and its qualities are fleeting. Its nature is impermanent. It is diverse. It is inert and is seen like a pot. How can it itself be the knower of its own changes?

That which is seen cannot be totally unreal and that which changes and ultimately disappears cannot be called real. It cannot be called both real and unreal, for that is a contradiction. Thus, it is called indescribable (*anirvacanīya*) See V. 110–11.

See MaṇḍUp, 'That which is not in the beginning and at the end, is non-existent also in the present.'

pūrvaṁ janer = before birth; **api** = in both cases; **mṛter atha** = after death; **jāta-kṣaṇaḥ** = origination and destruction; **aniyata-sva-bhāvaḥ** = its nature is impermanent; **jaḍa** = inert; **ghaṭa** = pot.

pāṇi-pādādimān deho nātmā vyaṅge'pi jīvanāt |
tat-tacchakter anāśāc ca na niyamyo niyāmakaḥ || 158 ||

The body, consisting of hands, feet, and so on, cannot be the Self because one lives even without these limbs and it continues to function. The controlled cannot be the controller.

See KaUp 2.2.4–5, 'When the embodied self that dwells within the body slips off and is released from the body, what is there that remains? This, verily is that. Not by the outbreath or inbreath does any mortal whatever live, but by another do they live on which these both depend.'

There are five inferences which may be put forth to demonstrate that the Self is not the physical body. The body is the not-self because it is a product of food (*annakāryatvāt*). Whatever is produced must also decay, and thus the body cannot be the Self. Again, the body is the not-self because it is of the nature of food (*āgantugatvāt*). Before food is eaten and after it is rejected by the body, food is known to be other than the self. Thus, even in its in-between state, food should be recognized as being other than the self. Even as a garland or sandal paste is something which is different from oneself, so too is the body other than the Self. Again, the body is the not-self because upon death it ceases to be (*apāyitvāt*). So long as one dwells in one's body, one feels that one is the body. But once your body becomes a corpse and the dogs begin to fight over its remains, the body becomes an object of contempt. That which eventually dies, ceases to be, has an end. Thus, the body must be other than the Self. Again, the body is the not-self because it is seen (*dṛsyatvāt*). Like a jar, the body is an object of perception. What is seen is different from the seer who sees it. Therefore, the body must be other than the Self. Again, the body is the not-self because it does not persist (*anavayāt*). This is a variation of the third inference. The body is perceived as an external object, like a pot, and its perceived continuity is broken (like dream-bodies which come and go).

pāṇi-pādādimān = hands, feet, and so on; **vyaṅge'pi jīvanāt** = even if one is without these, one lives; **niyāma** = to control, to govern, rule.

deha-tad-dharma tat-karma tad-avasthādi sākṣiṇaḥ ǀ
sata eva svataḥ siddhaṁ tad-vailakṣaṇyam ātmanaḥ ǁ159ǁ

The Self is different from, and the witness of, the body, its qualities, its activities, and its states of being and so on. Being self-established, the Self is other than all these.

The body is continually changing. A person says, 'This is my ear, my nose, my body.' That which belongs to oneself is not oneself – it is one's possession. Simarily for such states as childhood, the teen years, sickness, old age, death, and so on.

See KaivUp 1.18 on witness. See V. 101, 127, 137, 159, 212, 213, 217, 218, 223, 270, 295, 352, 370, 381, 384, 495, 506, 507, and 552 for references to witness (*sākṣī*).

deha = body; **dharma** = qualities; **karma** = actions; **avasthādi** = states of existence and so on; **sākṣiṇaḥ** = of the witness; **svataḥ siddhaṁ** = self-established.

śalya-rāśiḥ māṁsa-lipto mala-pūrṇo'ti-kaśmalaḥ ǀ
kathaṁ bhaved ayaṁ vettā svayam-etad-vilakṣaṇaḥ ǁ160ǁ

How can the body, consisting of bones, covered with flesh, full of defects, and extremely impure, be the Self, the knower, who is always other than them?

śalya = bones; **māṁsa** = flesh; **mala-pūrṇo** = full of defects; **kaśmalah** = extremely impure; **kathaṁ** = how; **vilakṣaṇaḥ** = other than.

tvaṅ-māṁsa-medo'sthi-purīṣa-rāśau
ahaṁ-matiṁ mūḍha-janaḥ karoti ǀ
vilakṣaṇaṁ vetti vicāra-śīlo
nija-svarūpaṁ paramārtha-bhūtam ǁ161ǁ

A foolish person identifies with their skin, flesh, fat, bones, and excreta.[1] **A person of discrimination, however, knows their true nature to be the supreme reality and other than the body.**

See V. 74, 89, 94, 156, and 163 on the consitutents of the body.

mūḍha-janaḥ = a fool who does not enquire; **paramārtha** = absolute, supreme reality.

deho'ham ityeva jaḍasya buddhiḥ
dehe ca jīve viduṣas-tvahaṁ-dhīḥ ǀ
viveka-vijñānavato mahātmano
brahmāham ityeva matiḥ sadātmani ǁ162ǁ

A fool thinks, 'I am the body'. An intelligent one knows of the 'I' in the body and the individual. However, the Great One, a person who has knowledge born of discrimination, always experiences 'I am the Absolute'.

---

[1] See MaitrīUp 3.4, 'It is built up with bones, smeared over with flesh, covered with skin, filled with faeces, urine, bile, phlegm, marrow, fat.'

The ChānUp 3.14.1 declares, 'All this is the Absolute' (*sarvam khalvidam brahma*). This is the great knowledge of Vedānta which boldly declares the identity of the individual and the Absolute (*mahāvākya*, the Great Sayings of the *Upaniṣads*. Traditionally they are four in number: *prajñānam brahma* which occurs in the *Aitareya Upaniṣad* of the *Ṛg Veda; ayam ātma brahma* which occurs in the *Māṇḍūkya Upaniṣad* of the *Atharva Veda; tat tvam asi* which occurs in the *Chāndogya Upaniṣad* of the *Sāma Veda*; and *aham brahmāsmi* which occurs in the *Bṛhadāraṇyaka Upaniṣad* of the *Yajur Veda*).

See BṛhUp 1.4.1, 'This is I' (*aham ayam ity*) and BṛhUp 1.4.5, 'I indeed am this creation for I produced all this'.

See V. 4, 5, 77, 163, 220, and 549 for fools (*mūḍha*). Also see MuṇḍUp 1.2.8; KaUp 1.2.5; MaitrīUp 7.9; BG 17.5–6.

deho'ham = I am the body; **viveka-vijñāna** = knowledge born of discrimination; **mahātmano** = Great One; **brahmāham** = I am the Absolute.

atrātma-buddhiṁ tyaja mūḍha-buddhe
tvaṅ-māṁsa-medo'sthi-purīṣa-rāśau |
sarvātmani brahmaṇi nirvikalpe
kuruṣva śāntiṁ paramāṁ bhajasva ||163||

You with the foolish intellect! Cease to identify yourself with this body comprised of skin, flesh, fat, bones, and excreta.[1] Instead, identify with the Absolute, the one Self of all, which is not subject to change, and enjoy supreme peace.[2]

See V. 4, 5, 77, 162, 220, and 549 for fools (*mūḍha*). Also see MuṇḍUp 1.2.8; KaUp 1.2.5; MaitrīUp 7.9; BG 17.5–6.

mūḍha-buddhe = you with the foolish intellect; **sarvātmani** = Self of all; **brahmaṇi** = the Absolute; **nirvikalpe** = impartite, without changes; **śāntiṁ paramāṁ** = supreme peace; **bhajasva** = enjoy.

dehendriyādāvasati bhramoditāṁ
vidvān-ahaṁtāṁ na jahāti yāvat |
tāvan na tasyāsti vimukti-vārtā
apyastveṣa vedānta-nayānta-darśī ||164||

So long as the scholar does not give up his erroneous identification with the body, sense organs, and so on, which are not real, there can be no talk of his liberation, even if he is supremely proficient in Vedānta philosophy.

There will never be liberation merely from book knowledge. Śaṅkara's famous *Bhaja Govindam* declares, 'Worship Govinda O ignorant fool. When the time to die is near, memorizing grammatical verses will not protect you.'

See V. 119, 220–21, 289, and 386 on *pratibimbavāda*.

---

1 See MaitrīUp 3.4, 'It is built up with bones, smeared over with flesh, covered with skin, filled with faeces, urine, bile, phlegm, marrow, fat.'

2 See BG, 'Attains to the peace abiding in Me (Kṛṣṇa) which culminates in liberation.'

dehendriyādāvasati bhramoditāṁ = erroneous identification with the body, senses and so on; **vidvān** = scholar; **vedānta** = Vedānta; **nayānta** = end of or goal of the scripture; **darśī** = to have sight of, to understand.

chāyā-śarīre pratibimba-gātre
yat svapna-dehe hṛdi kalpitāṅge I
yathātma-buddhiḥ tava nāsti kācit
jīvac-charīre ca tathaiva māstu II 165 II

Just as you do not identify yourself with your body's shadow, or your reflection, or your dream body, or when you imagine it in your heart, so too, do not identify yourself with your living body.

Why does one think that the bodies they identity with are real? They come and go. It is an imaginary world. It is personal, intimately one's own and no one can enter it. Such a person is truly alone and truly deluded. No wonder there is pain and loneliness.

See KaUp 3.1, 'Knows of the Absolute, men with five fires, and with the three fire-altars of Naciketas, they call these two "Shadow" and "Light", the two who have entered – the one into the cave of the heart, the other into the highest region beyond, both drinking the truth in the world of rites rightly performed.'

See V. 414, 431, and 505 on shadow.

chāyā = shadow; **pratibimba** = reflection; **svapna-dehe** = dream body; **kal-pita** = imagination; **hṛdi** = heart.

dehātmadhīr-eva nṛṇām-asaddhiyāṁ
janmādi-duḥkha-prabhavasya bījam I
yatas-tatas-tvaṁ jahi tāṁ prayatnāt
tyakte tu citte na punar bhavāśā II 166 II

For those whose mind rests on the unreal, the belief that the body alone is the Self is the seed which produces the series of sorrows from birth and so on.[1] Therefore, with great effort, destroy this notion. Once the mind is detached, there is no possibility of being born again.

See BSBh, 'He who has in the Self the same idea which he ordinarily, firmly holds that the body is the Self and which cuts at the root of this false identification, such a person is liberated even if he still lives in the world.'

dehātmadhīr = belief that the body is the Self; **eva** = alone; **asaddhiyāṁ** = one whose mind rests on the unreal; **janmādi** = birth and so on; **duḥkha** = sorrow, grief; **bījam** = seed; **jahi** = destroy, give up; **punar bhavāśā** = born again.

karmendriyaiḥ pañcabhir-añcito'yaṁ
prāṇo bhavet prāṇa-mayas-tu kośaḥ I
yenātmavān annamayo'nupūrṇaḥ
pravartate'sau sakala-kriyāsu II 167 II

---

[1] See ChānUp 8.12.1, 'O Maghavan, mortal, verily, is this body. It is held by death. But it is the support of that deathless, bodiless self. Verily, the incarnate self is held by pleasure and pain. Verily, there is no freedom from pleasure and pain for one who is incarnate. Verily, pleasure and pain do not touch one who is bodiless.'

The vital air, in combination with the five organs of action, constitutes the vital air sheath, and pervaded by which the food sheath gets its life and performs all its activities

The vital air sheath is the second sheath encasing the body, with its instrumentality of vital airs and the nervous system. It is located within the physical sheath. It is permeated by the mental, consciousness, and bliss sheaths.

See V. 128, 151, 153, 156, 167–70, 185–87, 189–90, 208–14, and 245 on the five sheaths.

See TaittUp 2.3.1 for a description of the vital air.

karmendriyaiḥ pañcabhir = five organs of action; **añcitaḥ** = made up of, constitutes; **prāṇa** = vital airs; **kośaḥ** = sheath; **annamaya** = food sheath.

naivātmāyam prāṇamayo vāyu-vikāro
gantāgantā vāyuvad antar-bahir-eṣaḥ |
yasmāt kiñcit kvāpi na vettīṣṭam-aniṣṭaṁ
svaṁ vānyam vā kiñcana nityaṁ para-tantraḥ ||168||

The vital air sheath cannot be the Self because it is a modification of air and, like air, it goes in and comes out. It never knows what is agreeable or disagreeable, anywhere, at any time, either of itself or of others, being eternally dependent upon the Self.

The Self is distinguished from the vital air sheath because unlike this sheath, the Self is eternal, immutable, blissful and independent while the vital air sheath undergoes change, is inert, and is dependent.

See V. 128, 151, 153, 156, 167–70, 185–87, 189–90, 208–14, and 245 on the five sheaths.

prāṇamaya = vital air sheath; **vāyu-vikāro** = modification of air; **gantā-gantā** = comes and goes; **antar** = inside; **bahir** = outside; **nityaṁ** = eternal; **para-tantraḥ** = other-dependent.

jñānendriyāṇi ca manaśca manomayaḥ syāt
kośo mamāham iti vastu-vikalpa-hetuḥ |
saṁjñādi-bheda-kalanā-kalito balīyān
tatpūrva-kośam-anupūrya vijṛmbhate yaḥ ||169||

The organs of knowledge, along with the mind, form the mental sheath[1] which is the cause of the sense of 'I' and 'mine' and of the diversity of things. It is powerful and creates differences of name and so on. It pervades the previous[2] vital air sheath.

The mind is declared to be of the nature of both determination and doubt. It distinguishes all modifications and thus makes knowledge possible. The world is dependent upon the mind in the sense that it would not be cognized without it. Yet, the mind is dependent upon the Self.

See V. 128, 151, 153, 156, 167–70, 185–87, 189–90, 208–14, and 245 on the five sheaths.

---

1 See TaittUp 2.3.1 for a description of the mind.
2 See TaittUp 2.2.1, 'By that this is filled' (*sa vā eṣa . . .*).

jñānendriyāṇi = organs of knowledge; **manomayaḥ** = mental sheath; **ma-māham** = 'I' and 'mine'; **vastu-vikalpa-hetuḥ** = cause of the diversity of things; **saṁjñādi** = names and so on; **bheda** = difference; **balīyān** = powerful; **tatpūrva-kośam** = earlier sheath.

pañcendriyaiḥ pañcabhir-eva hotṛbhiḥ
pracīyamāno viṣayājya-dhārayā I
jājvalya-māno bahu-vāsanendhanaiḥ
mano-mayāgniḥ dahati prapañcam II170II

The mental sheath is the sacrificial fire which is fed with the fuel of residual impressions. The five sense organs serve as the sacrificing priests who pour into the fire the oblations of the sense objects.[1] The burning of this mental sheath fire brings about the physical universe.

The sacrificial fire confers on the person or couple (*yajamāna*) who perform the sacrifice, the enjoyments of the heavenly realms. So, too, the mind confers on the individual, the pleasures of the empirical world.

See TaittUp 2.3.1; 2.4.1 for a description of the mind and mental sheath.

See V. 128, 151, 153, 156, 167–70, 185–87, 189–90, 208–14, and 245 on the five sheaths.

pañcendriyaiḥ = five sense organs; **hotṛ** = sacrificial priests; **pracīya-māno** = made to grow; **ājya** = offerings; **vāsana** = residual impressions; **mano-mayāgniḥ** = fire of the mental sheath; **pra-pañcam** = physical universe.

na hy-asty-avidyā manaso'tiriktā
mano hy-avidyā bhava-bandha-hetuḥ I
tasmin vinaṣṭe sakalaṁ vinaṣṭaṁ
vijṛmbhite'smin sakalaṁ vijṛmbhate II171II

Clearly, there is no ignorance apart from the mind. Because the mind is ignorance, it is the cause of the bondage of worldly existence. When that is stilled, everything is stilled. When it is active, everything manifests.

The mind is the cause of bondage and the cause of liberation. However, the word 'mind' itself is vague, incapable of a clear definition. No one can point to the mind and say, 'this is what I mean by the word "mind".' It is a bundle of faculties: cognition/perception/will/imagination/judgment/reason/understanding/memory/etc. It is ever rotating and fluctuating.

See MaitrīUp 6.34, 'Mind, in truth, is the cause of bondage and liberation'; also see AmṛtabinduUp 2. See V. 176–77.

See YS 1.2, 'The cessation of the modifications of the mind is Yoga' (*yogaś citta vṛtti nirodhaḥ*).

hi = (in the first line, indicates conclusiveness); **avidyā** = ignorance; **manaso'tiriktā** = apart from the mind; **hi** = (in second line, indicates because); **bhava-bandha** = bondage of worldly existence; **hetuḥ** = cause; **vinaṣṭe** = stilled, lost; **vijṛmbhite** = active, expanding.

---

[1] See BG 4.26, 'Some offer hearing and the other senses into the fires of restraint; others offer sound and the other sense objects into the fires of sense'; also BG 4.27–30.

svapne'rtha-śūnye sṛjati svaśaktyā
bhoktrādi viśvaṁ mana eva sarvam |
tathaiva jāgratyapi no viśeṣaḥ
tat sarvam-etan manaso vijṛmbhaṇam ||172||

In the dream state, in which there is an absence of external objects, the mind alone creates everything, the enjoyer and so on, by its own power. Similarly, there is no difference in the waking state. All that is but an expansion of the mind.

Dreaming is the state wherein the Self revels in a world of images and its experiences are subtle. The Self is said to be dreaming when it creates a world of its own from the impressions of its waking experiences. It doesn't need the help of the sense organs. It doesn't need the help of external lights. See V. 100–101, 165, 255, and 454–57 on dreams.

svapna = dream state; **artha** = objects; **śūnya** = devoid of, total absence; **sṛjati** = creates; **bhoktrādi** = the enjoyer and so on; **viśvaṁ** = everything, all this; **jāgrat** = waking state; **manas** = mind; **vijṛm-bhaṇam** = expansion, active.

suṣupti-kāle manasi pralīne
naivāsti kiñcit sakala-prasiddheḥ |
ato manaḥ-kalpita eva puṁsaḥ
saṁsāra etasya na vastuto'sti ||173||

It is well known that, in deep sleep when the mind is still, nothing exists. Therefore, worldly existence is but a creation of the individual's mind. In reality it does not exist.

The sleep state is wherein there are no experiences, no desires, no dreams. It is one mass of consciousness and remains as bliss enjoying bliss. Here there is no knower, no known, no process of knowing. See V. 109, 122–23, 210, 236, and 295 on deep sleep.

Has the world ever come to you and said, 'Why am I here? Am I deluded?' No. Think about last night when you were deeply asleep. There was no world, no thoughts, no feelings of delusion or imperfection. This should lead us to conclude that the world is in us, we are not in the world. If one solves the riddle of the 'I', the riddle of the world will also be solved. Which is dependent upon which, the world upon 'I' or 'I' upon the world?

suṣupti = deep sleep; **manas** = mind; **pralīne** = dissolved, reabsorbed into, disappeared; **naivāsti** = nothing exists; **prasiddheḥ** = well-known; **manaḥ-kalpita** = mental imagination; **eva** = but, merely, only; **puṁsaḥ** = individual; **saṁsāra** = worldly existence.

vāyunā nīyate meghaḥ punas tenaiva nīyate |
manasā kalpyate bandhaḥ mokṣas tenaiva kalpyate ||174||

The winds gathers clouds together and again the wind disperses them. Similarly, the mind creates bondage and again it creates liberation.

See MaitrīUp 6.34, 'Mind, in truth, is the cause of bondage and liberation'; see also AmṛtabinduUp 2.

vāyu = wind; **meghaḥ** = clouds; **punar** = again; **nīyate** = puts together, connects; **manasā** = mind; **kalpyate** = creates, imagines, forms, fashions; **bandhaḥ** = bondage; **mokṣa** = liberation.

dehādi-sarva-viṣaye parikalpya rāgaṁ
badhnāti tena puruṣaṁ paśuvad guṇena |
vairasyam-atra viṣavat suvidhāya paścāt
enaṁ vimocayati tan-mana eva bandhāt ||175||

The mind produces an attachment to the body, all the sense objects and so on. This rope of attachment binds a person as if they were an animal. Subsequently, the same mind creates an aversion for these sense objects and liberates one from that self-same bondage.

The mind is like a river which flows in the bed of the body ceaselessly. How can an unsteady mind make itself steady? It cannot. It is the nature of the mind to roam. One must go beyond the mind.

dehādi = body and so on; **sarva-viṣaye** = all sense objects; **parikalpya** = strongly creates or produces **rāgaṁ** = attachment; **badhnāti** = binds; **puruṣaṁ** = person; **paśu** = animal; **guṇena** = rope; **vairasyam** = tastelessness, aversion; **vimocayati** = liberates, frees.

tasmān manaḥ kāraṇam-asya jantoḥ
bandhasya mokṣasya ca vā vidhāne |
bandhasya hetuḥ malinaṁ rajo-guṇaiḥ
mokṣasya śuddham virajas-tamaskam ||176||

Therefore, the mind is the cause in producing both bondage and liberation. When tainted by active qualities, the mind is the cause of bondage. When it is free from active qualities and dullness it is the cause of liberation.

The mind covers up the Self like the moon which obscures the sun. The mind is like a thief. You must watch it constantly – not because you want anything from it, but because you don't want it to steal.

See MaitrīUp 6.34, 'Mind, in truth, is the cause of bondage and liberation'; see also AmṛtabinduUp 2.

tasmān = therefore; **manaḥ** = mind; **kāraṇam** = cause; **vidhāne** = to produce, perform, effect, cause, grant, bestow, distribute; **malina** = tainted; **rajo-guṇaiḥ** = active qualities; **śuddham** = free; **tamas** = dullness, laziness, darkness.

viveka-vairāgya-guṇātirekāt
śuddhatvamāsādya mano vimuktyai |
bhavatyato buddhimato mumukṣoḥ
tābhyāṁ dṛḍhābhyāṁ bhavitavyam agre ||177||

When the mind attains purity through discrimination and detachment, it turns towards liberation. An intelligent seeker of liberation must first be firmly established in them.

Discrimination and detachment are the first two limbs of the four-fold prerequisites prescribed in verse 17. When they are present, the mind naturally becomes introverted and ceases to thirst for sense objects in the external world.

See V. 11, 138, 150, 178, 183, 276–77, 315, 336, 361–63, 367, 370–71, 384, and 408 for purification of the mind.

viveka = discrimination; **vairāgya** = detachment; **śuddhatvam** = purity; **buddhimato** = an intelligent seeker; **dṛḍhābhyāṁ** = fixed, firm, steady.

mano nāma mahā-vyāghro viṣayāraṇya-bhūmiṣu |
caratyatra na gacchantu sādhavo ye mumukṣavaḥ ||178||

A great tiger called the mind wanders in the vast forest of sense objects. Let not good people who have a longing for liberation ever go there.

Sense objects are dangerous. They are like an infinitely vast and deep forest. If one wanders among them, one is sure to be lost. Thus, it behooves a person who is desirous of liberation, to shun them. The mind is like a fierce tiger who wanders this forest at will. It feels invulnerable even though a little discrimination will reveal that this is not the case. The KaUp says, 'A wise person, desiring immortality, turning their eyes inward, saw the inner Self.'

See V. 3, 19, 28, 29, 30, 31, 44, 84, 120, and 576 for references to *mumukṣutva*.
See V. 38, 41, and 43 on the forest.

mano = mind; **nāma** = called; **mahā-vyāghro** = great tiger; **viṣayāraṇya** = forest of sense obects; **caratyatra** = wanders; **sādhavo** = good people, spiritual aspirants; **mumukṣavaḥ** = burning desire for liberation.

manaḥ prasūte viṣayān aśeṣān
sthūlātmanā sūkṣmatayā ca bhoktuḥ |
śarīra-varṇāśrama-jāti-bhedān
guṇa-kriyā-hetu-phalāni nityam ||179||

The mind continually creates for the experiencer, experiences of all sense objects, gross and subtle; distinctions based upon body, caste, station in life, class, qualities, actions, causes, and effects.

The mind is involved in all experiences, both regarding the objects, subtle and gross, as well as the enjoyer of the experiences, the individual perceiver.

sthūla = gross; **sūkṣma** = subtle; **bhoktuḥ** = experiencer; **śarīra** = body; **varṇāśrama** = caste and stages of life; **jāti** = class, family; **bhedān** = differences, distinctions; **guṇa** = quality; **kriyā** = action; **hetu** = cause; **phalāni** = fruits, effects, results; **nityam** = continually, eternal.

asaṅga-cidrūpam amuṁ vimohya
dehendriya-prāṇa-guṇair-nibadhya |
ahaṁ mameti bhramayatyajasraṁ
manas-svakṛtyeṣu phalopa-bhuktiṣu ||180||

Deluding the individual, who is of the nature of unattached pure Consciousness, and binding it with the ties of the body, sense organs, and vital airs, the mind causes him to wander with a sense of 'I' and 'mine' experiencing the varied experiences of results done by itself.

Not only does the mind deceive the individual into becoming attached to sense objects, but it also deceives the individual, him or herself, into forgetting their real nature. The Self is never deluded, just as a person awake is not deluded by the dreams of the dreamer. It is the mind which perpetuates the delusion by superimposing the body upon the Self.

asaṅga = unattached; **cidrūpam** = Consciousness, intelligence; **vimohya** = deluding; **dehendriya-prāṇa** = body, sense organs, vital airs; **guṇair-nibadhya** = binding with a rope; **ahaṁ** = 'I'; **mameti** = mine; **bhrama** = delusion, error; **svakṛtyeṣu** = actions done by oneself; **phala** = fruits, results.

adhyāsa-doṣāt puruṣasya saṁsṛtiḥ
adhyāsa-bandhas tv amunaiva kalpitaḥ |
rajas-tamo-doṣavato'vivekino
janmādi-duḥkhasya nidānam-etat ||181||

An individual's involvement in worldly life is caused by superimposition and the bondage of superimposition is created by the mind alone. For a person of non-discrimination who is tainted by active qualities and darkness and dullness, it is the original cause for the sufferings of birth and so on.

Superimposition (*adhyāsa* – see verse 140) is defined by Śaṅkara in his BSBh Preamble (*Adhyāsa Bhāṣya*) as 'cognizing something as something else' (*atasmiṅ tad-buddhiḥ*). See V. 39, 269, 271, 279–86, 307, 393, 407, and 462 on superimposition.

adhyāsa = superimposition; **puruṣasya** = individual, person; **rajas**-active qualities; **tamo** = darkness, dullness, laziness; **doṣa** = defect, taint; **aviveka** = non-discrimination; **janmādi** = birth and so on; **duḥkhasya** = suffering; **nidānam** = primal cause, original cause.

ataḥ prāhur-mano'vidyāṁ paṇḍitās-tattva-darśinaḥ |
yenaiva bhrāmyate viśvaṁ vāyunevābhra-maṇḍalam ||182||

Hence the wise, who know the Truth, have declared that the mind itself is ignorance. It is solely by this that the universe is tossed about like the clouds by the wind.

Don't rely on the mind for liberation. It is the mind which brings one into bondage. Why think of changing the mind – it is already changing all the time.

ataḥ = hence, so, therefore; **prāhurmano'vidyām** = mind alone is ignorance; **paṇḍitāḥ** = the wise, great scholars; **tattva-darśinaḥ** = those who have seen or know the truth; **yenaiva** = solely; **bhrāmyate** = purposelessly changing, tossed; **viśvaṁ** = universe; **vāyunevābhra** = clouds by the wind; **maṇḍalam** = whirled around.

tan-manaḥśodhanaṁ kāryaṁ prayatnena mumukṣuṇā |
viśuddhe sati caitasmin muktiḥ kara-phalāyate ||183||

Therefore, the mind must be diligently purified by those who earnestly seek liberation. When the mind is purified, liberation is as easy of access as a fruit in the palm of one's hand.

See V. 11, 138, 150, 177–78, 276–77, 315, 336, 361–63, 367, 370–71, 384, and 408 for purification of the mind.

See KaUp 1.2.25; MuṇḍUp 3.1.5, 3.1.8; BṛhUp 4.4.23 on this verse.

tat = therefore (for the reason stated earlier); **manaḥśodhanaṁ** = purify the mind; **prayatnena** = diligently, by great effort; **viśuddhe** = purified; **caitasmin** = (*ca* = indicates the reason) *caiti-asmin* = in this mind; **kara** = palm; **phala** = fruit.

mokṣaika-saktyā viṣayeṣu rāgaṁ
nirmūlya saṁnyasya ca sarva-karma |
sacchraddhayā yaḥ śravaṇādi-niṣṭho
rajas-svabhāvaṁ sa dhunoti buddheḥ ||184||

That person who, by means of a one-pointed dedication to liberation, completely uproots attachment to the sense objects, renounces all actions, possesses an unswerving faith in Truth, and is firmly established in hearing and so on, completely destroys the flickering nature of the mind.

Hearing and so on = the discipline of hearing the truth (*śravana*), reflecting on its meaning (*manana*), and becoming firm in one's understanding (*nididhyāsana*).

mokṣaikasaktyā = by supreme or one-pointed dedication to liberation; **rāga** = attachment, desire; **nirmūlya** = completely uproots, removes; **saṁnyasya** = giving up, renouncing; **sarva-karma** = all actions; **sacchra-ddhayā** = earnest dedication to the truth; **śravaṇādi-niṣṭho** = established in hearing and so on; **rajas** = quivering, flickering; **svabhāvaṁ** = nature; **dhunoti** = completely destroys; **buddheḥ** = mind.

manomayo nāpi bhavet parātmā
hyādyantavattvāt pariṇāmi-bhāvāt |
duḥkhātmakatvāt viṣayatva-hetoḥ
draṣṭā hi dṛśyātmatayā na dṛṣṭaḥ ||185||

The mental sheath cannot be the supreme Self as it has a beginning and an end; as it is subject to modifications; as it is of the nature of suffering; as it is an object. The seeing subject cannot be the seen object.

See V. 169–70 on the mental sheath.

manomayo = mental sheath; **parātmā** = supreme Self; **ādyanta-vattvāt** = as it has a beginning and an end; **pariṇāmi-bhāvāt** = it is subject to modifications; **duḥkhātmakatvāt** = its nature is comprised of suffering, grief; **viṣayatva-hetoḥ** = because it is an object of cognition; **draṣṭā hi dṛśyātmatayā na dṛṣṭaḥ** = the seeing subject is nowhere seen to be the seen object.

buddhir-buddhīndriyaiḥ sārdhaṁ savṛttiḥ kartṛ-lakṣaṇaḥ |
vijñāna-maya-kośaḥ syāt puṁsaḥ saṁsāra-kāraṇam ||186||

The intellect, with its organs of knowledge along with its modifications, is known as the knowledge sheath. It has the characteristics of an agent which is the cause of worldly existence.

See V. 187, 189–90, and 208 on the intellectual sheath. Also see see V. 128, 151, 153, 156, and 167–70 on the five sheaths.

buddhi = intellect; **buddhīndriyaiḥ** = organs of knowledge; **sārdhaṁ** = along with; **savṛttiḥ** = modifications of the mind; **kartṛ-lakṣaṇaḥ** = the mark or quality of a doer; **vijñāna-maya-kośaḥ** = sheath of knowledge; **saṁsāra-kāraṇam** = cause of worldly existence.

anuvrajaccit-pratibimba-śaktiḥ
vijñānasaṁjñaḥ prakṛter vikāraḥ |
jñāna-kriyāvān aham-ityajasram
dehendriyādiṣvabhimanyate bhṛśam ||187||

The knowledge sheath has the power of reflection of the light of Consciousness which it accompanies. It is a modification of primordial matter. Its functions are knowledge and action and it is always completely identified with the body, the sense organs, and so on.

See V. 186, 189–90, and 208 on the intellectual sheath. Also see V. 128, 151, 153, 156, and 167–70 on the five sheaths.

anuvrajaccit = to go along with, or pervasion of Consciousness; **pratibiṁba** = reflection; **śaktiḥ** = power; **vijñānasaṁjñaḥ** = is known as the knowledge sheath; **prakṛter** = primordial nature; **vikāraḥ** = modification; **jñāna** = knowledge; **kriyā** = action; **dehendriyādiṣu** = in the body and the sense organs; **abhimanyate** = egoism, attachment, conceit; **bhṛśam** = strong, powerful.

anādi-kālo'yam ahaṁ-svabhāvaḥ
jīvaḥ-samasta-vyavahāra-voḍhā |
karoti karmāṇy-anupūrva-vāsanaḥ
puṇyānyapuṇyāni ca tat-phalāni ||188||

The nature of this 'I' is without beginning. It is called the 'individual' and undertakes all worldly activities. It performs auspicious and inauspicious actions according to previous latent impressions, and experiences their results.

How does any individual refer to him or herself – only as 'I', one single syllable. Everyone says 'I' but who knows what this 'I' is? It is not the body, the mind, etc. The body belongs to one. Who knows this? It is the 'I' which knows. The 'I' is the first thought upon waking after sleep and it is the last thought before dropping off into sleep. Enquire. Where does this 'I' arise from? Discover that.

anādikālo'yam = time that is beginningless, eternal, it cannot be said when it began; **vyavahāra** = worldly; **anupūrva-vāsanaḥ** = previous latent impressions; **puṇyānya puṇyāni** = auspicious and inauspicious; **phalāni** = the results or effects.

bhuṅkte vicitrāsvapi yoniṣu vrajan
āyāti nirātyadha ūrdhvam-eṣaḥ |
asyaiva vijñāna-mayasya jāgrat-
svapnādyavasthāḥ sukha-duḥkha-bhogaḥ ||189||

Born in various bodies, it comes and goes, above and below. The waking, dreaming and other states, and experiences of joy and sorrow, belong to the intellectual sheath.

See V. 186–87, 190, and 208 on the intellectual sheath. Also see V. 128, 151, 153, 156, and 167–170 on the five sheaths.

See V. 127, 172, 213, and 219 on the three states of existence.

yoniṣu = bodies, womb; **āyāti nirātyadha** = comes and goes; **ūrdhvam** = above; **eṣaḥ** = hastens near or towards; **asyaiva** = down, below; **vijñāna-mayasya** = intellectual sheath;

jāgrat-svapnādy-avasthāḥ = waking, dreaming and other states; **sukha-duḥkha-bhogaḥ** = experiences joys and sorrows.

dehādi-niṣṭhāśrama-dharma-karma-
guṇābhimānaḥ satataṁ mameti |
vijñāna-kośo'yam-atiprakāśaḥ
prakṛṣṭa-sānnidhya-vaśāt parātmanaḥ |
ato bhavatyeṣa upādhir-asya
yadātmadhīḥ saṁsarati bhrameṇa ||190||

The intellectual sheath always considers as its own the stages of life, duties, actions, attributes, and functions which belong to the body. It is extremely luminous owing to its close proximity to the supreme Self. It is a limiting adjunct on the Self, which, deluded by it, is therefore subject to worldly existence.

See V. 186–87, 189, and 208 on the intellectual sheath. Also see V. 128, 151, 153, 156, and 167–70 on the five sheaths.

dehādi = body and so on; **niṣṭhā** = always; **āśrama** = stages of life; **dharma** = qualities; **karma** = actions; **guṇa** = attributes; **vijñāna-kośo** = intellectual sheath; **atiprakāśaḥ** = very luminous; **sānnidhyavaśāt** = dwelling closeby, near; **parātmanaḥ** = supreme Self; **bhrameṇa** = deluded, error.

yo'yaṁ vijñāna-mayaḥ prāṇeṣu hṛdi sphurat svayaṁjyotiḥ |
kūṭasthaḥ san nātmā kartā bhoktā bhavaty-upādhisthaḥ ||191||

The self-effulgent[1] Self, which is all-pervasive knowledge, shines in the heart, extremely near the vital airs.[2] Though immutable, it becomes a doer and enjoyer because of limiting adjuncts.

Why are you looking for God in city after city, temple after temple? God dwells in the heart within. Why look in the East and in the West? Don't look for God, look for the Guru. God dwells within you; in truth, you are God. You don't need to find God, you need to find a Guru who will guide you to yourself.

See V. 219, and 257 on the heart.

vijñāna-mayaḥ = all-pervasive knowledge; **prāṇeṣu** = vital airs; **hṛdi sphurat** = shines in the heart; **svayaṁjyotiḥ** = self-effulgent; **kūṭasthaḥ** = immutable, changeless; **kartā** = doer; **bhoktā** = enjoyer; **upādhisthaḥ** = limiting adjuncts, adventitious conditions.

svayaṁ paricchedam upetya buddheḥ
tādātmya-doṣeṇa paraṁ mṛṣātmanaḥ |
sarvātmakaḥ sann api vīkṣate svayaṁ
svataḥ pṛthaktvena mṛdo ghaṭān iva ||192||

---

1 See BṛhUp 4.3.7, *yo'yaṁ vijñāna-mayaḥ prāṇeṣu hṛdy antarjyotiḥ puruṣaḥ* – the first part of this verse is a direct quotation. In this context, Yājñavalkya answers Janaka's question about, 'Which of these is the Self?' and says, '. . . the vital airs (*prāṇa*) stand for the sense organs (*indriya*).' It is a case of *sāmīpya saptamī like* 'the tree in the stone', i.e., tree near the stone (*pāṣāṇe vṛkṣaḥ*).

2 See US 1.11.11; MuṇḍUp 2.2.10–11. Also see V. 100, 153, 213, 221, 240, 508, and 536 on self-luminous.

Though the Self of all, by the defect of a false identification of the intellect which limits itself, it looks upon itself as something different, like pots from clay.

Clay may take different forms in a potter's hands and thus become known as pots, cups, plates, etc. Really, they are all clay through and through though they are individually called by various names. Each is a form in which the same clay appears. Even so, the Absolute appears in different forms and is called by various names. To concentrate on the form makes one forget the basis. A potter is indifferent to the various manifestations and knows that each item is only clay. The objects are so many forms in which the Reality appears. The appearances are invested with a name and form but what abides is the Reality. See V. 230–31, 253, and 392 on clay.

See ChānUp 6.1.4, 'Just as by means of one lump of clay all that is made of clay becomes known, the modification being only a name arising from speech while the truth is that it is just clay.'

paricchedam = limitation; **buddheḥ** = intellect; **doṣeṇa** = defect; **mṛṣātmanaḥ** = false identification; **sarvātmakaḥ** = Self of all; **mṛdo** = clay; **ghaṭān** = pot.

upadhi-saṁbandha-vaśāt parātmā-
hy upādhi-dharmān anubhāti tadguṇaḥ |
ayo-vikārān avikāri-vahnivat
sadaika-rūpo'pi paraḥ svabhāvāt ||193||

Even though the supreme Self is perfect and eternally unchanging, due to its association with the limiting adjuncts, it assumes the qualities of these limiting adjuncts and appears to act, even as the formless fire appears in the form of iron.

See fire/iron KaUp 2.2.9, 'As fire, which is one, entering this world becomes varied in shape according to the object, so also the one Self within all beings becomes varied according to whatever.' Also see ChānUp 6.1.4, 'Just as by means of one nail-cutter all that is made of iron becomes known, the modification being only a name arising from speech while the truth is that it is just iron'; see also MaitrīUp 3.3; V. 135, 350, and 507 on fire in iron.

upadhi = limiting adjunct; **saṁbandha** = association; **parātmā** = supreme Self; **vahni** = fire.

śiṣya uvāca
bhrameṇāpyanyathā vāstu jīvabhāvaḥ parātmanaḥ |
tad-upādher anāditvāt nānāder nāśa iṣyate ||194||

The student said:
Whether due to delusion or otherwise that the supreme Self assumes that it is an individual, that limiting adjunct is beginningless. Of what is beginningless, there can be no destruction.

The student makes an (invalid) inference stating that, 'if the individual is beginningless, then it must be immortal, for, whatever is beginningless is immortal.' In V. 188, the teacher said that the individual is beginningless and thus the student enquires, in V. 195, how to become liberated?

bhramenāpyanyathā = delusion or otherwise; **jīvabhāvaḥ** = individuality, state of being an individual; **parātmanaḥ** = supreme Self; **upādher** = limiting adjunct; **anādi** = beginningless, eternal; **nāśa** = destruction.

ato'sya'jīva-bhāvo'pi nityā bhavati saṁsṛtiḥ |
na nivarteta tan mokṣaḥ kathaṁ me śrīguro vada ||195||

Therefore, the individuality of the supreme Self will be eternal. How then can there be liberation from worldly existence? Please instruct me, revered Master.

The disciple, after hearing the Master elucidate the nature of the individual, asks, how is liberation from worldly existence possible if individuality is eternal? If *māyā* is beginningless and if that which is beginningless is also endless, then how can one become free? Ignorance seems to be indestructible. Again, if the supreme Self has entered into the individual self, and if the supreme Self is eternal then liberation is impossible.

nityā = eternal; **saṁsṛtiḥ** = worldly existence; **mokṣaḥ** = liberation; **kathaṁ** = how; **vada** = instruct me, speak.

śrīgurur-uvāca
samyak pṛṣṭaṁ tvayā vidvan sāvadhānena tac chṛṇu |
prāmāṇikī na bhavati bhrāntyā mohita-kalpanā ||196||

The revered Master said:
Learned one, you have asked a good question. Listen attentively. Things formed in the imagination cannot be valid for they, themselves, are due to delusion.

The Master responds to the disciple's question by elucidating the nature of delusion.

samyak = good, right; **pṛṣṭaṁ** = question; **vidvan** = learned one, intelligent one; **sāvadhānena** = determine well; **śṛṇu** = listen; **prāmāṇikī** = validity; **bhrāntyā** = false; **mohita** = delusion; **kalpanā** = forming, fashioning, making, creating in the mind.

bhrāntiṁ vinā tvasaṅgasya niṣkriyasya nirākṛteḥ |
na ghaṭetārtha saṁbandho nabhaso nīlatādivat ||197||

The Self is unattached,[1] actionless,[2] and formless;[3] thus without delusion there can be no connection with the objects of the world, even as blueness has no connection with the sky.

See BSBh, 'Young childen without discrimination superimpose black, yellow, blue, and so on on the invisible sky.'

bhrāntiṁ = delusion, false; **asaṅgasya** = unattached, devoid of association; **niṣkriyasya** = actionless; **nirākṛteḥ** = unchanging; **ghaṭetārtha** = objects of the world; **saṁbandho** = connection; **nabhaso** = sky; **nīla** = blue.

---

1 See BṛhUp 4.4.22 (*asangaḥ*) on the unattached Self.
2 See on actionless BṛhUp 4.4.22.
3 See ŚvetUp 6.19, 'without parts, without activity' (*niṣkalam niṣkriyam*); also 6.12.

svasya draṣṭur nirguṇasyākriyasya
pratyag-bodhānanda-rūpasya buddheḥ |
bhrāntyā prāpto jīva-bhāvo na satyo
mohāpāye nāstyavastu-svabhāvāt ||198||

The witness[1] is without qualities, immutable, and is realized within as knowledge and bliss absolute. Its individuality is a confusion of a deluded mind and is not real. As it is by nature not real, it vanishes with the destruction of delusion.

The *sakṣin* and the individual are distinguishable, though not separable. The *sakṣin* is not identical to the Self because the *sakṣin* is always associated with the *antaḥkaraṇa*. This association is both real and potential. It is real in the waking and dreaming states. It is potential in the deep sleep state (thus the individual loses its individuality in deep sleep).

See KaivUp 1.18 on witness.

draṣṭur = seer, witness; **nirguṇa** = without qualities; **ākriyasya** = immutable, changeless; **pratyag** = within, inner; **bodhānanda** = knowledge and bliss; **bhrāntyā** = confusion, error, mistake; **na satyo** = not real; **mohāpāye** = by the destruction of delusion.

yāvad bhrāntis tāvad evāsya sattā
mithyā-jñānojjṛmbhitasya pramādāt |
rajjvāṁ sarpo bhrānti-kālīna eva
bhrānter nāśe naiva sarpo'pi tadvat ||199||

Its (individuality) exists only so long as delusion persists, as it is born of false knowledge. The rope is mistaken for a snake only as long as the delusion lasts; there is no more a snake once the delusion is destroyed. So, too, in this case.

The rope is the cause of the snake in the sense that the snake pre-existed (so to speak) in the rope. It was sustained by the rope and finally disappeared back into the rope. All the time there was nothing else there than the rope. The rope never ceased being a rope, even while it appeared as the snake. This is the very essence of the idea – a thing appearing differently without ceasing to be itself even during the different appearance. See V. 12, 63, 112, 140, 248, 303, 388, 405, 407, and 550 for references to a snake.

bhrānti = delusion, error; **sattā** = exists; **mithyā-jñāna** = false knowledge, illusion; **rajjvāṁ** = rope; **sarpo** = snake; **bhrānti-kālīna** = delusion lasts or persists; **nāśe** = destroyed.

anāditvam avidyāyāḥ kāryasyāpi tatheṣyate |
utpannāyāṁ tu vidyāyāṁ āvidyakam-anādy-api ||200||
prabodhe svapnavat sarvaṁ saha-mūlaṁ vinaśyati |
anādyapīdaṁ no nityaṁ prāgabhāva iva sphuṭam ||201||

Ignorance and its effects are declared to be beginningless. But with the rise of knowledge, the entire effects of ignorance, even though beginningless, are destroyed along with its root, even as dreams vanish on waking. Though ignorance is beginningless, it is not eternal, like prior non-existence, yet evident.

---

[1] See ŚvetUp 6.19, 'without parts, without activity' (*niṣkalam niṣkriyam*); also 6.12.

In the Advaita tradition, ignorance (*avidyā*) is characterized by six marks: it is beginningless (*anādi*), it is removed by right knowledge (*jñāna nivartya*), it is a positive entity of the nature of an existent (*bhāvarūpa*), it is indescribable (*anirvacanīya*), it has the two powers of concealment and projection (*āvaraṇa and vikṣepa*), and its locus is either in the individual self (*jīva*) or in the Absolute (*Brahman*).

This verse is controversial since it refers to non-existence (*prāgabhāva*). See my Introduction (p. 000).

See V. 110–112 for a defintion of ignorance.

anāditvam = beginningless; **avidyā** = ignorance; **kāryasyāpi** = its effects; **utpannāyāṁ** = with the rise of; **vidyāyāṁ** = knowledge; **svapna** = dream state; **sarvaṁ** = all; **saha-mūlaṁ** = along with its root; **vinaśyati** = destroyed, completely removed; **no nityaṁ** = not eternal; **prāgabhāva** = prior-non-existence; **sphuṭam** = evident, clear, manifest, distinct.

anāder api vidhvaṁsaḥ prāgabhāvasya vīkṣitaḥ |
yad buddhyupādhi-saṁbandhāt parikalpitam ātmani ||202||
jīvatvaṁ na tato'nyas tu svarūpeṇa vilakṣaṇaḥ |
saṁbandhaḥ svātmano buddhyā mithyā-jñāna purassaraḥ ||203||

Prior non-existence, although beginningless, is observed to have an end. So too, individuality, which is imagined in the Self, due to its association with the limited adjuncts, is not real; for the other is really different from it in its essential nature. The relation of the Self and the intellect is due to false knowledge.

Non-existence (*abhāva*) has two main divisions: the absence of one entity in another (*saṁsarga abhāva*), which is of three kinds: prior non-existence, annihilative non-existence, and absolute non-existence; and one object not being another (*anyonya abhāva*) or reciprocal non-existence. The non-existence of an object before it comes into being is said to be beginningless, but this non-existence obviously comes to an end when the object in question is brought into being.

anāder-api = though beginningless; **vidhvaṁsaḥ** = destruction, end; **prāgabhāvasya** = prior non-existence; **vīkṣitaḥ** = is seen, is observed; **parikalpitam** = imaginary, not-real, illusory; **jīvatvaṁ** = individuality; **svarūpeṇa** = essential nature; **vilakṣàṇaḥ** = other than, different from; **saṁbandhaḥ** = relation; **svātmano** = one's Self; **mithyā-jñāna** = false knowledge; **purassaraḥ** = arises.

vinivṛttir bhavet tasya samyag-jñānena nānyathā |
brahmātmaikatva-vijñānaṁ samyag-jñānaṁ śruter matam ||204||

The disappearance of false knowledge takes place through correct knowledge; not otherwise. Correct knowledge, according to the scriptures, is the realization of the identity of the individual and the Absolute.

The great sayings (*mahāvākya*) of the *Upaniṣads* posit the essential identity between the individual and the Absolute. According to Advaita, the Self (*Ātman*) is one and non-dual. The pluralistic universe of an individual's day to day experience, which appears to one as real, is an illusory superimposition which is neither real nor unreal. This appearance is rooted in ignorance (*avidyā*) which conceals the real (*sat*) and projects the unreal (*asat*). One's entire experience of life seems to involve differentiations like, 'I am male, I am old, I am hungry, I am meditating, I am seeking liberation, I am having a vision' and so on. These differentiations are based on the superimposition of one thing on another or the attributes of one thing on another due to ignorance.

If the Self is one and non-dual, what is the status of the world, what is the status of all this multiplicity, including myself – what I think I am and what I think the world is? Even if it is true that appearances are illusory superimpositions, it still appears that there is a duality. The Self may exist, and I seem to exist, and this 'I' may even be the Self. But there seems to be something else, an 'other' or second, if you will. Even if what I think I am is illusory, still it is 'something' illusory. To put it another way, if the Self and the world are non-dual, one and the same, then there is no reason to seek the Self (for there is nothing that it is not). Yet, if that is the case, why am I miserable and happy, by turns? That seems to imply duality. On the other hand, if the world and the Self are different, then surely that is duality. To answer this question, Advaita relates a tale . . .

One day a washerman was taking his donkeys to the forest to graze them. He happened to chance upon a new-born lion cub. The lion cub did not know that it was a lion and so the cub grew up with the donkeys. As time passed, by living in their company, the lion began to speak like the donkeys, to eat with them, and to travel back and forth to the river carrying laundry on its back. The lion grew up thinking of himself as a donkey. One day, when he was grazing on the river bank with his donkey brothers, another lion came down to the river to drink. While he was drinking he caught sight of this young lion and was shocked and puzzled to see him standing in the midst of donkeys in such a pitiful condition. He came closer to the young lion and said, 'Brother, what are you up to?' The young lion replied, 'I am grazing with my brothers'. Shocked, the elder lion said, 'How can you call them brothers? They are asses and you are a lion. Come with me and look at your reflection in the water. Look at your reflection and then look at my reflection. Is there anything similar about us?' The young lion gazed down at his reflection and saw that he looked just like the old lion. The old lion demanded, 'Are they your brothers or am I your brother? Now stop braying like a donkey and roar like a lion.' The young lion began to roar. All the donkeys as well as the washerman ran away.

Was the young lion ever a donkey? No. He only thought he was a donkey. Was the young prince ever not a prince? No. He only thought he wasn't. The human being is not a limited, unhappy, imperfect being. Human beings only believe they are small, finite, mortal creatures. Once one discards this ignorant superimposition, one will manifest the strength, the glory, the majesty that one is, and always has been. It is only one's awareness that need be changed. We never were limited, and never will be limited, because we are the Self. Although a mirage appears in the desert, there never was, is not now, nor ever will be, water there. Although subjects and objects appear in one's nightly dreams, they are not real. Upon waking the next morning, one remarks, 'Oh, it was but a dream'. It is an improper question to ask, 'Where did they go?'

See AitUp 3.1.3, 'Consciousness is the Absolute' (*prajñānam brahma*); MāṇḍUp 2.7, 'This Self is the Absolute' (*ayam ātmā brahma*); BṛhUp 1.4.10, 'I am the Absolute' (*aham brahmāsmi*); ChānUp 6.8.7, 'That thou art' (*tat tvam asi*); also AitUp 1.3.13; ŚvetUp 3.10.4.

samyag-jñānena = correct knowledge; **nānyathā** = not otherwise; **brahmātmaikatva** = the identity or oneness of the Absolute and the individual; **śruter** = primary scripture.

tad ātmā-anātmanoḥ samyag vivekenaiva siddhyati |
tato vivekaḥ kartavyaḥ pratyag-ātmāsadātmanoḥ ||205||

That (correct knowledge) only is attained by right discrimination between the Self and not-self. Therefore, discrimination must be made between the inner Self and the non-real individual.

The *Vivekacūḍāmaṇi* is called such to emphasize the paramount importance of discrimination (*viveka*) in the quest for liberation. To be caught in the cycle of birth and death is the effect of one's actions, whether good or bad. Action is prompted by desire. Desire arises because one feels one is incomplete, due to ignorance. Why does one feel one is incomplete? Because one has identified oneself with their body. How to overcome this confusion? Discrimination. See V. 2 and 11 on discrimination.

ātmā-anātmanoḥ = the Self and not-self; **samyag vivekenaiva** = only by right discrimination; **siddhyati** = attainment; arises; **kartavyaḥ** = actions which must be performed; **pratyag-ātma** = inner Self; **asadātmanoḥ** = non-real individual.

jalaṁ paṅkavad-atyantam paṅkāpāye jalaṁ sphuṭam |
yathā bhāti tathātmāpi doṣābhāve sphuṭa-prabhaḥ ||206||

Water associated with mud is not clear, but becomes clear when the mud is removed. Similarly, the Self shines effulgently when whatever tainted it is removed.

When the Guru's initial instructions do not result in a permanent and complete manifestation of one's true nature, the Guru takes recourse in instructing the student to perform some prerequisite actions which will have the effect of purifying the intellect and removing the defects which hide one's inner Self. These are: (1) Discriminate (*viveka*) between what is permanent and what is impermanent, between the Self and the not-self; (2) practice detachment (*vairagya*) from all the sense objects of this or any other world; (3) cultivate the virtues such as sense control, equanimity, and faith; (4) cultivate an intense, burning desire for liberation (*mumukṣutva*). When these prerequisites are being cultivated, one becomes eligible to practice what Vedānta terms the primary means of liberation. This primary practice is known as *Śravana*, *manana*, and *nididhyāsana* or 'Hear the Truth; contemplate the Truth or practice the teachings; and finally, become firmly, completely, and eternally established in one's inner Self.' Thus, according to Vedānta, spiritual practices are not performed in order to gain the great inner Self – for one is already that, but to remove the impurities which cover it up and hide its presence from one. Get rid of what you haven't got (the impurities which hide the Self which you already are).

jalaṁ = water; **paṅka** = mud; **doṣābhāve** = defect, taint is non-existent; **sphuṭa-prabhaḥ** = shines clearly.

asan-nivṛttau tu sadātmanāḥ sphuṭam
pratītir etasya bhavet pratīcaḥ |
tato nirāsaḥ karaṇīya evā
sadātmanaḥ sādhvaham ādi vastunaḥ ||207||

Only when the unreal ceases to appear will there be the clear ascertainment of this real innermost Self. Therefore, one should completely remove everything beginning with egoism, and so on from the real Self (or, if read as *evāsadātmanaḥ* = therefore, one must strive to completely remove the unreal individuality comprised of the ego and so on).

Why does one need to do perform spiritual practices? *Sādhana* is engaged in in order for the guru's words to be fruitful. Mere listening isn't enough. The aspirant needs strength and purity of mind. Seeds sprout only in a well tilled field. Even though one reads countless books and hears countless discourses, why isn't one enlightened? Why does one still experience delusion? Because one's mind is not purified, and thus the senses lead one astray. In order for one to attain liberation, one must learn to vanquish one's enemies.

asat = unreal; **tu** = only; **nivṛttau** = ceases; **etasya** = of this; **sadāt-manaḥ** = real Self; **sphuṭa-pratītiḥ** = clearly apprehended or ascertained; **pratīcaḥ** = innermost; **tataḥ** = therefore; **nirāsaḥ** = completely remove; **aham-ādi-vastunaḥ** = from all things beginning with egoism.

ato nāyaṁ parātmā syāt vijñānamaya-śabdabhāk |
vikāritvāt jaḍatvāt ca paricchinnatva-hetutaḥ |
dṛśyatvād vyabhicāritvān nānityo nitya iṣyate ||208||

Hence, the intellectual sheath, which has been spoken of, cannot be the supreme Self because it is subject to change, it is insentient, it is limited, it is an object of perception, it changes. The non-eternal cannot be proclaimed to be the eternal.

See TaittUp 2.5.1 for a description of the intellectual sheath. See V. 186–87 and 189–90 on the intellectual sheath.

See KaUp 5.13, 'He is the eternal in the midst of the non-eternals' (*nityo'nityānaṁ*).

ataḥ = hence, from this (for reasons that will be stated); **parātmā** = supreme Self; **vijñānamaya** = intellectual sheath; **vikāritvāt** = subject to change, destructible; **jaḍatvāt** = insentient; **paricchinna** = limited, finite determination; **dṛśyatvād** = perceivable; **vyabhicāritvān** = changeability, to come apart; **nānityo** = non-eternal; **nitya** = eternal.

ānandapratibimba-cumbita-tanuḥ vṛttis tamo jṛmbhitā
syād ānandamayaḥ priyādi-guṇakaḥ sveṣṭārtha-lābhodayaḥ |
puṇyasyānubhave vibhāti kṛtināṁ ānanda-rūpaḥ svayaṁ
sarvo nandati yatra sādhu tanubhṛn-mātraḥ prayatnaṁ vinā ||209||

The sheath of bliss is a modification of ignorance and appears as a reflection of the Self which is bliss absolute. Its attributes are pleasures. It appears in view when some object agreeable to oneself presents itself. The fortunate spontaneously experience it shining by itself as joy when the fruits of their meritorious actions are manifest.

Finer than the intellectual sheath, this sheath of bliss should not be confused with the supreme Bliss of the Self. This is controversial for, without a doubt, Śaṅkara does not posit that the Self is the sheath of bliss. But it is a debatable point whether he accepts that the Self is of the nature of Bliss (see his TaittUpBh).

The sheath of bliss is not the Self, for it exists only at certain times. The bliss which is being spoken of here is an effect and thus is not the supreme Bliss which is the Self. The sheath of bliss occurs in a context in which the other sheaths are being described. Thus, like the other sheaths, the bliss sheath is a modification and merely the reflection of the Bliss which is the Self. See V. 128, 151, 153, 156, and 167–70 on the five sheaths.

ānandapratibimba = reflection of bliss; **cumbita** = closely or softly touched; **tanuḥ** = body; **vṛttis** = modification or fluctuation; **tamo** = darkness, ignorance; **jṛmbhitā** = produced by; **ānandamayaḥ** = sheath of bliss; **priyādi** = what is dear, pleasures; **lābha** = getting, obtaining; **udayaḥ** = production; **puṇyasyānubhave** = experiencing meritorious effects; **vibhāti** = shines; **kṛtinām** = the fortunate, those who have done meritorious deeds; **tanubhṛn-mātraḥ** = embodied persons; **prayatnaṁ vinā** = without effort.

ānanda-maya-kośasya suṣuptau sphūrtir-utkaṭā |
svapna-jāgarayor īṣad iṣṭa-sandarśan'ādinā ||210||

The sheath of bliss is fully manifest in the deep sleep state. In the waking and dream states it is only partially manifest, occasioned by the sight of desired objects.

The TaittUp describes the Self as hidden in the cavity of the five sheaths. Like deep sleep, since the bliss sheath is not permanent, it cannot be the Self. Even though this sheath is turned inwards and reflects bliss, it is a passive enjoyer, a mere reflection, and not the unconditioned Self. See TaittUp 2.5.1; 2.7.1., 2.8.1, 2.9.1 for a description of the sheath of bliss.

ānanda-maya-kośasya = sheath of bliss; **suṣuptau** = deep sleep state; **sphūrtir-utkaṭā** = fully, clearly manifest; **svapna** = dream state; **jāgarayor** = waking state; **īṣad iṣṭa sandarśanaādi** = sight of desired objects.

naivāyam ānandamayaḥ parātmā
sopādhikatvāt prakṛter vikārāt |
kāryatva-hetoḥ sukṛta-kriyāyā
vikāra-saṅghāta-samāhitatvāt ||211||

The sheath of bliss is not the supreme Self because it is connected with limiting adjuncts; it is a modification of primordial nature; it is an effect of good deeds; it is associated with groups of other modifications.

See TaittUp 2.5.1, 2.7.1., 2.8.1, and 2.9.1 for a description of the sheath of bliss. See V. 128, 151, 153, 156, and 167–70 on the five sheaths.

sopādhikatvāt = connected with limiting adjuncts; **prakṛter vikārāt** = modification of primordial nature; **sukṛta-kriyāyāḥ** = effect or modification of good deeds; **vikāra-saṅghāta-samāhitatvāt** = associated with groups of other modifications.

pañcānām api kośānāṁ niṣedhe yuktitaḥ kṛte |
tan niṣedhāvadhi sākṣī bodharūpo'vaśiṣyate ||212||

When all the five sheaths have been eliminated by analytical reasoning, what remains is the substratum of all, the witness, knowledge-absolute.

The witness self is consciousness marked by the internal organ (*antaḥkaraṇa upahita caitanya*). It is always in relation to consciousness and the witness thereof. It is self-luminous and ever-present. It never appears by itself but is always in association with the internal organ. See KaivUp 1.18 on witness. For references to witness (*sākṣī*) see V. 101, 127, 137, 159, 213, 217, 218, 223, 270, 295, 352, 370, 381, 384, 495, 506, 507, and 552.

See V. 128, 151, 153, 156, 167–70, 185–87, 189–90, 208–14, and 245 on the five sheaths.

pañcānām kośānāṁ = five sheaths; **api** = all (implies totality); **niṣedhe** = removed, elimanated; **yuktitaḥ** = analytical reasoning, logic; **āvadhi** = culmination, limit; **sākṣī** = witness; **bodharūpa** = knowledge absolute.

yo'yaṁ ātmā svayaṁ-jyotiḥ pañcakośa-vilakṣaṇaḥ I
avasthā-traya-sākṣī san nirvikāro nirañjanaḥ I
sadānandaḥ sa vijñeyaḥ svātmatvena vipaścitā II213II

This Self is self-effulgent,[1] distinct from the five sheaths, witness of the three states,[2] real, changeless, taintless, eternally blissful, this is to be realized by the wise as one's own true Self.

See V. 128, 151, 153, 156, 167–70, 185–87, 189–90, 208–14, and 245 on the five sheaths.

See V. 127–28, 172, 213, and 219 on the three states.

ātmā = Self; **svayaṁ-jyotiḥ** = self-effulgent; **pañcakośa** = five sheaths; **vilakṣaṇaḥ** = other than, distinct from; **avasthā-traya** = three states of existence; **sākṣī** = witness; **sat** = Real, True, Existence; **nirvikāro** = changeless; **nirañjanaḥ** = taintless, without blemish; **sadānandaḥ** = eternal bliss; **vipaścitā** = the wise, those who know.

śiṣya uvāca
mithyātvena niṣiddheṣu kośeṣveteṣu pañcasu I
sarvābhāvaṁ vinā kiñcinna paśyāmy atra he guro I
vijñeyaṁ kimu vastvasti svātmanātra vipaścitā II214II

The student said:
O Master! After these five sheaths have been eliminated as not real, I am nothing but an absolute void. By which entity, then, should the wise realize their identity with the Self?

The non-dual *Brahman* is suggested by a series of 'negations' or 'no's': 'Not course, not fine, not short, not long . . .' (BṛhUp 3.8.8). And again as, 'Not to be heard, not to be felt' (KaUp 1.3.15). As it is beyond all the relative categories of thought, it is easier spoken of by what it is not, than by what it is. Thus it is called indeterminate (*nirguṇa*) to distinguish it from all attributes. *Nirguṇa* means that it transcends the phenomenal realm. It is undefinable and unknowable, meaning that it is too great for words to describe and the finite mind to fathom (see TaittUpBhVār 2.721). Thus it is said, 'An absolutely pure, utterly differenceless Being is very difficult to conceive in

---

1 See KaivUp 1.18 on witness: 'In the three states of consciousness whatever appears as the object of enjoyment or the enjoyer or the enjoyment, I am different from them, the witness, pure consciousness, the eternal Śiva' (*sākṣī*). See V. 101, 127, 137, 159, 212, 217, 218, 223, 270, 295, 352, 370, 381, 384, 495, 506, 507, and 552 for references to witness (*sākṣī*).

2 See US 1.11.11, 'Just as it is seen that a sword shines when it is drawn from its sheath, so the Knower, separated in the dreaming state from cause and effect, is seen to be self-effulgent.' See V. 100, 153, 191, 219, 221, 240, 508, and 536 on self-luminous. 'In the golden space of the heart dwells the Absolute, without parts, without stain. Pure, the light of lights. This light is reflected in all. That shining, everything shines' (MuṇḍUp 2.2.10–11).

our imagination, that is, due to biological reasons, pictorial and practical.' This Reality appears to thought as a bare nothing or a contentless blank. Hegel said, 'To be completely free from any determination is just what we mean by nothing.' Bradley observed, 'I still insist that for thought what is not relative is nothing.' The Reality of the Advaitins is so similar to a seeming nothingness, a night in which all cows are black, that Śaṅkara was called a crypto-Buddhist is disguise. However, Śaṅkara foresaw this objection and possible misconception, for he said: '*Brahman*, free from space, attributes, motion, fruition, and difference, being in the highest sense and without second, seems to the slow of mind no more than non-being' (ChānUpBh 8.1.1, BSBh 3.2.22).

See V. 128, 151, 153, 156, 167–70, 185–87, 189–90, 208–14, and 245 on the five sheaths.

mithyātvena = not real, illusory; **niṣiddheṣu** = eliminated, negated; **kośeṣveteṣu pañcasu** = five sheaths; **sarvābhāvaṁ** = non-existent; **he guro** = O Master; **vijñeyaṁ** = realize; **kimu** = by which; **vipaścitā** = the wise, those who know.

śrī gurur-uvāca
satyam uktaṁ tvayā vidvan nipuṇo'si vicāraṇe |
ahamādi-vikārās te tad abhāvo'yamapyatha ||215||
sarve yenānubhūyante yaḥ svayaṁ nānubhūyate |
tam ātmānaṁ veditāraṁ viddhi buddhyā susūkṣmayā ||216||

The revered Master said:
Learned one! You have spoken truly. You are indeed clever in enquiry. He by whom the modifications of the ego and so on, as well as their subsequent absence, are perceived, but who is not himself perceived, knows that by your sharp intellect, knows the Self, the knower.

See KaUp 3.14, 'Arise! Awake! Pay attention, when you've attained your wishes! A razor's sharp edge is hard to cross, that, the poets say, is the difficultly of the path.'

See KaUp 3.12, 'The Self, though hidden in all beings, does not shine forth but can be seen by those subtle seers, through their sharp and subtle intelligence.'

satyam-uktaṁ tvayā = you have spoken truly; **vidvan** = wise; **nipuṇo'si** = clever, skillful, sharp; **vicāraṇe** = enquiry; **ahamādi** = 'I', ego and so on; **vikārā** = modifications; **abhāva** = non-existence; **sarve yenānu-bhūyante** = all the modifications that were experienced previously; **yaḥ svayaṁ nānubhūyate** = that which is itself not an object of experience; **buddhyā susūkṣmayā** = sharp, subtle intellect.

tat sākṣikaṁ bhavet tattadyad yad yen'ānubhūyate |
kasyāpy ananubhūt'ārthe sākṣitvaṁ n'opayujyate ||217||

That which is perceived by any one has that person as its witness. When an object is not perceived by any one, there is no meaning in speaking of a witness who perceives.

See KaivUp 1.18 on witness. See V. 101, 127, 137, 159, 212, 213, 218, 223, 270, 295, 352, 370, 381, 384, 495, 506, 507, and 552 for references to witness (*sākṣī*).

tat = that; **sākṣikaṁ** = witness.

asau sva-sākṣiko bhāvo yataḥ svenānubhūyate |
ataḥ paraṁ svayaṁ sākṣāt pratyag-ātmā na cetaraḥ ||218||

This non-existence is that of which the Self is the witness because it is perceived by the Self. Hence, the inner Self that witnesses is itself the supreme Self, and nothing else.

See KaivUp 1.18 on witness. See V. 101, 127, 137, 159, 212, 213, 217, 223, 270, 295, 352, 370, 381, 384, 495, 506, 507, and 552 for references to *sākṣī*.

svasākṣiko = self-witnessed; **svenānubhūyate** = self-experienced; **ataḥ** = hence; **paraṁ svayaṁ** = supreme Self; **sākṣāt** = witness; **pratyag-ātmā** = inner Self; **na ca itaraḥ** = not anything else.

jāgrat-svapna-suṣuptiṣu sphuṭataraṁ yo'sau samujjṛmbhate
pratyag-rūpatayā sadāham-aham ityantaḥ sphurannekadhā |
nānākāra-vikāra-bhāgina imān paśyann-ahaṁ-dhīmukhān
nityānanda-cidātmanā sphurati taṁ viddhi svam etaṁ hṛdi ||219||

That which clearly manifests itself in the waking, dreaming, and deep sleep states; which always inwardly shines in the same identical form giving an awareness of 'I'; which perceives the various modifications such as egoism, the intellect, and so on; which is self-effulgent;[1] know that in your heart as your Self, the eternal blissful conscious Self.

See KaivUp 1.17, 'The world which shines in the states of waking, dream, and dreamless sleep, knowing that it is the Absolute who I am.'

See KaUp 5.13, 'He is the eternal in the midst of the non-eternals, the principle of intelligence in all that are intelligent . . . the wise perceive him as existing within their own Self.'

jāgrat-svapna-suṣuptiṣu = waking, dreaming, deep sleep states; **sphuṭataraṁ** = very clearly; **samujjṛmbhate** = shines independently; **pratyag-rūpatayā** = the innermost; **sadā** = always; **aham** = 'I'; **sphuran** = self-effulgent; **ekadhā** = in the same form; **nānākāra-vikāra** = modifications of different kinds; **imān** = objects; **paśyan** = of perception; **nityānanda-cidātmanā sphurati hṛdi** = shines in the heart as the self-effulgent, eternally blissful, conscious Self; **viddhi** = know.

ghaṭodake biṁbitam arka-biṁbam
ālokya mūḍho ravim-eva manyate |
tathā cidābhāsam upādhi-saṁsthaṁ
bhrāntyāham-ity-eva jaḍobhimanyate ||220||

Looking at a reflection of the sun, mirrored in the water of a jar, a fool thinks it is the sun itself. Similarly, a stupid person, through delusion, imagines that the reflection of consciousness appearing in the limiting adjunct is the Self.

See BSBh. 3.2.20 for an illustration of the sun's reflection in water. The role of an illustration is to refer to some common feature(s). When two things are compared, they are compared only with reference to some particular point(s) they have in common. It is well-known that no comparison is ever totally equal, for, if that were the case, there would not be a comparison but identity. The special feature of the sun

---

[1] See US 1.11.11; Muṇḍ. Up 2.2.10–11. Also see V. 100, 153, 191, 213, 221, 240, 508, and 536 on self-luminous.

which warrents comparison in this case is known as 'participation in increase and decrease'. The reflected image of the sun increases when the water expands, and contracts when the water shrinks. Further, the reflected image trembles when the water is agitated and divides itself when the water is divided. Thus, the reflected image participates in all the conditions and attributes of the water even as the real sun remains unaffected all the while. Similarly, the Self, although changeless, participates, as it were, in the attributes and states of the body. One's image of who they are seemingly grows, shrinks, and so, as the body grows, shrinks, and so on.

See V. 119, 164, 221, 289, and 386 on *pratibimbavāda*.

See V. 4, 5, 77, 162, 163, and 549 for fools (*mūḍha*). Also see MuṇḍUp 1.2.8; KaUp 1.2.5; MaitrīUp 7.9; BG 17.5–6.

ghaṭa = jar; **biṁbitam** = reflection, mirrored; **arka** = sun; **biṁbam** = reflection; **mūḍho** = fool; **ravim-eva** = sun itself; **manyate** = thinks; **tathā** = similarly; **cidābhāsam** = reflection of consciousness; **upādhi** = limiting adjunct; **bhrāntyā** = delusion; **jaḍobhimanyate** = stupid person imagines.

ghaṭaṁ jalaṁ tadgatam-arka-bimbaṁ
vihāya sarvaṁ divi vikṣyate'rkaḥ |
taṭasthitaḥ tat-tritayāvabhāsakaḥ
svayaṁ-prakāśo viduṣā yathā tathā ||221||

A wise person rejects the pot, the water, and the sun's reflection in it and, indifferent and independent of them all, so sees the self-luminous[1] sun in the sky which illuminates these three.

When a person's attention is on the reflection it ignores the real sun in the sky. In order to perceive the original, one must turn one's attention from the reflection to the prototype. The sun does not include the pot, the water, and the reflection. If anything, they are there only to turn one's attention to the original. One should not mistake the reflection for the original.

See V. 119, 164, 220, 289, and 386 on *pratibimbavāda*.

ghaṭaṁ = pot; **jalaṁ** = water; **arka-bimbaṁ** = sun's reflection; **sarvaṁ** = all; **divi vikṣyate** = seen in the sky; **arkaḥ** = sun; **taṭasthitaḥ** = indifferent; **tat-tritayāvabhāsakaḥ** = illuminating those three; **svayaṁ-prakāśo** = self-luminous; **yathā** = as is.

dehaṁ dhiyaṁ cit-pratibimbam-evaṁ
visṛjya buddhau nihitaṁ guhāyām |
draṣṭāram-ātmānam akhaṇḍa-bodhaṁ
sarva-prakāśaṁ sad-asad-vilakṣaṇam ||222||
nityaṁ vibhuṁ sarva-gataṁ su-sūkṣmaṁ
antarbahiś-śūnyam ananyam ātmanaḥ |
vijñāya samyaṅ nija-rūpametat
pumān vipāpmā virajo vimṛtyuḥ ||223||

---

[1] See US 1.11.11, 'Just as it is seen that a sword shines when it is drawn from its sheath, so the Knower, separated in the dreaming state from cause and effect, is seen to be self-effulgent.' See V. 100, 153, 191, 213, 219, 240, 508, and 536 on self-luminous. 'In the golden space of the heart dwells the Absolute, without parts, without stain. Pure, the light of lights. This light is reflected in all. That shining, everything shines' (Muṇḍ. Up. 2.2.10–11).

Discarding the body, the intellect, and the reflection of consciousness in it, and realizing hidden in the intellect the innermost Self, the witness, which is knowledge absolute, all-luminous, other than the Real or the unreal, eternal, infinite, omnipresent, supremely subtle, devoid of anything interior or exterior, nothing other than the Self, and, realizing the real nature of the Self, becomes free from taint and immortal.

See BṛhUp 3.8.8; TaittUp 2.2; ŚvetUp 3.8 on this verse.

See KaivUp 1.18 per witness, 'In the three states of consciousness whatever appears as the object of enjoyment or the enjoyer or the enjoyment, I am different from them, the witness, pure consciousness, the eternal Śiva' (*sākṣī*). See V. 101, 127, 137, 159, 212, 213, 217, 218, 270, 295, 352, 370, 381, 384, 495, 506, 507, and 552 for references to witness (*sākṣī*).

See ChānUp 8.3.4, 'This is *Brahman*, immortal and fearless'.

dehaṁ = body; **dhiyaṁ** = intellect; **cit-pratibimbam** = reflection of consciousness; **visṛjya** = discarding, abandoning; **buddhau** = intellect; **nihitaṁ** = placed, bestowed; **guhāyām** = hidden, innermost; **draṣṭāram** = seer, witness; **akhaṇḍa-bodhaṁ** = unlimited knowledge; **sarva-prakāśaṁ** = all-luminous; **sad-asad-vilakṣaṇam** = other than the Real or unreal; **nityaṁ** = eternal; **vibhuṁ** = infinite; **sarva-gataṁ** = omnipresent; **su-sūkṣmaṁ** = supremely subtle; **antarbahiś-śūnyam** = devoid of anything internal or external; **ananyam** = nothing other than; **ātmanaḥ** = the Self; **vijñāya** = realizing; **pumān** = individual; **vipāpmā** = free from taint, defect; **vimṛtyuḥ** = deathless, immortal.

viśokaānanda-ghano vipaścit
svayaṁ kutaścin na bibheti kaścit |
nānyo'sti panthā bhava-bandha-mukteḥ
vinā sva-tattvāvagamaṁ mumukṣoḥ ||224||

The wise, free from sorrow, an embodiment of bliss, have no fear[1] of anything anywhere. For the ardent seeker of liberation there is no other path for freedom from the world's bondage than the realization of one's true nature.

Advaita posits that this Reality can be known only through knowledge of one's own Self. Those who want to know the Reality must make an enquiry. Without enquiry, the sacred teaching is incapable of generating the liberating knowledge.

viśoka = free from grief/sorrow; **ānanda** = bliss; **ghano** = compact, solid, material, firm, dense; **vipaścit** = knowledge of everything, wise, learned; **kutaścit** = realizes everything; **na bibheti** = no fear; **nānyo'sti panthā** = no other path; **bhava-bandha-mukteḥ** = freedom from the bondage of worldly existence; **vinā** = without, no other; **sva-tattvāvagamaṁ** = realization of one's own true nature; **mumukṣoḥ** = ardent seeker of liberation.

brahmābhinnatva-vijñānaṁ bhava-mokṣasya kāraṇam |
yenādvitīyam-ānandaṁ brahma sampadyate budhaiḥ ||225||

---

[1] See TaittUp 2.7.1, 'reached fearlessness' (*so'bhayaṁ gato bhavati*). Also see ChānUp 8.3.4, 'This is *Brahman*, immortal and fearless' (*amṛtam abhayam*). Also BṛhUp 1.4.2, 1.5.3, 3.9.26, 4.2.4, 4.3.20, 4.4.22, and 4.5.15; ChānUp 1.3.1, 8.9.1, 8.10.1, and 8.11.1; TaittUp 2.4; KaUp 3.2 and 6.2–3 on freedom from fear.

The realization of one's non-difference from the Absolute is the cause of liberation from worldly life. By that the wise attain the Absolute, the one without a second,[1] the supreme Bliss.

See MuṇḍUp 2.2.11, 'Brahman alone is all this.' ChānUp 6.2.1, 'It is One alone, without a second.' BṛhUp 4.4.19, 'In *Brahman* there is no diversity whatsoever.'

See MuṇḍUp 3.2.9, 'the knower of the Absolute becomes the Absolute' (*brahmaveda brahmaiva bhavati*). This does not mean a change of state or an attainment. The Sanskrit root '*bhū*' from which '*bhavati*' (becomes) is derived, means both 'being' and 'becoming'. In the present context it refers to 'being'. One is what one always is. To attain the unattained, action is necessary. But to attain the already attained, no action is required. Knowledge of the fact as-it-is will dispel the darkness of ignorance which covers it.

brahmābhinnatva-vijñānaṁ = realization of one's non-difference from the Absolute; **bhava** = worldly life; **mokṣasya** = freedom, liberation; **kāraṇam** = cause, instrument; **advitīyam** = non-dual, one without a second; **ānandaṁ** = bliss; **brahma** = the Absolute; **saṁpadyate** = to succeed, to become full, complete; **budhaiḥ** = the wise.

brahmabhūtastu saṁsṛtyai vidvān nāvartate punaḥ |
vijñātavyam ataḥ samyag brahmābhinnatvam-ātmanaḥ ||226||

The wise, having become the Absolute, never again return to worldly existence. Therefore, the individual's non-difference from the Absolute has to be fully realized.

Brahmabhūtam is an expression employed in the BG meaning, 'One who has become of the nature of the Absolute'. When a river flows into the ocean, it becomes one with the ocean. When an individual realizes his/her identity with the Absolute, (s)he becomes the Absolute.

See ChānUp 8.15, 'He does not return again.'

brahmabhūtastu = one who has become the Absolute; **saṁsṛtyai** = worldly existence; **vidvān** = the wise; **nāvartate** = do not return; **punaḥ** = again; **ataḥ** = therefore; **brahmābhinna-tvam** = non-difference from the Absolute.

satyaṁ jñānam anantaṁ brahma viśuddhaṁ paraṁ svatassiddham |
nityānandaika-rasaṁ pratyag-abhinnaṁ nirantaraṁ jayati ||227||

The Absolute is Existence, Knowledge, Infinitude,[2] pure, supreme, self-established, the essence of eternal bliss, non-different from the indweller, partless. It is ever victorious.

satyaṁ = Existence, Real; Truth; **jñānam** = Knowledge; **anantaṁ** = Infinitude; **brahma** = the Absolute; **viśuddhaṅ** = supremely pure; **paraṁ** = supreme, highest; **svatassiddham** = self-established, independent; **nityānandaika** = one with eternal bliss; **rasaṁ** = essence; **pratyag-abhinnaṁ** = non-different from the indweller; **nirantaraṁ** = partless, undivided; **jayati** = victorious.

sad-idaṁ paramādvaitaṁ svasmād-anyasya vastuno'bhāvāt |
na hy-anyad-asti kiñcit samyak-paramārtha-tattva-bodha-daśāyām ||228||

---

1 See ChanUp 6.2.1 (*ekam evādvitīyam*); BṛhUp 1.4.17 (*eka eva*); AitUp 1.1.1.

2 See TaittUp 2.1.1, 'know the Absolute as Existence, Knowledge, Infinitude'.

This Real is the supremely non-dual[1] reality since nothing else exists different from it. Truly, there is nothing which is other in realization of the absolute Truth.

Advaita is often spoken of as a type of monism. However, Advaita or non-dualism is not a monism as this term is generally understood in the West. Advaita emphasizes 'non'; it negates *all* duality and difference. Differences are said to be of three kinds: between members of the same class, between different species, or, last, internal differences (*sajātīya, vijātīya, svagatabheda*). A mere monism may not allow the first two types of difference, but is compatible with the last type. However, Advaita rejects all three types of difference. For this very same reason, Advaitins reject a view of the ultimate Reality as a Person (as is advocated by theism). Thus, to call Advaita 'monism', one should be aware that it is really an 'absolute monism', or a 'complete monism' (so as to distinguish it from all other types of monism).

ad-idaṁ = this Real; **paramādvaitaṁ** = supremely non-dual; **svasmād** = since, because; **anyasya** = nothing else different than; **vastuno'bhāvāt** = exists; **na hyanyad-asti** = there is nothing other that is; **kiñcit** = which; **para-mārtha** = absolute.

yad-idaṁ sakalaṁ viśvaṁ nānā-rupam pratītam-ajñānāt |
tat-sarvaṁ brahmaiva pratyastāśeṣa-bhāvanā-doṣam ||229||

This entire universe, which appears to be of diverse forms through ignorance; is only the Absolute freed from all defective understanding.

The universe, filled with attachments and aversions, appears to be real as long as one remains ignorant, but becomes unreal when one is enlightened. Dream appearances appear to be real as long as the dream lasts.

See BṛhUp 4.4.19, 'Only by the mind is it to be perceived. In it there is no diversity.'

idaṁ = this; **sakalaṁ** = determinate; **viśvaṁ** = universe; **nānā-rūpaṁ** = diverse forms; **pratītam** = appears to be; **ajñānāt** = ignorance; **tat-sarvaṁ brahmaiva** = all that is the Absolute; **doṣam** = defect.

mṛt-kārya-bhūto'pi mṛdo na bhinnaḥ
kumbho'sti sarvatra tu mṛt-svarūpāt |
na kumbha-rūpaṁ pṛthag asti kumbhaḥ
kuto mṛṣā kalpita-nāma-mātraḥ ||230||

A jar, though a modification of clay, is not different from it as it is essentially all clay. There is no separate entity of the form of the jar apart from the clay. Why, then, call it a jar? It is merely a false imagined name.

A thing is said to be real when it does not change the nature which is determined to be its own. In regards to clay, the nature which is determined to be its own, clay, does not change. But it is another thing in regards to the objects made of clay. What is known as a pot at one time may be seen later in the form of bits and pieces. The pot, as an effect, changes. The form does not remain the same. Thus the forms are declared to be unreal while the clay, which is changeless, is said to be real. See ChānUp 6.1.4,

[1] See Chan.Up 6.2.1 (*ekam evādvitīyam*); BṛhUp 1.4.17 (*eka eva*); AitUp 1.1.1.

'Just as by means of one lump of clay all that is made of clay becomes known, the modification being only a name arising from speech while the truth is that it is just clay.' See V. 192, 231, 253, and 392 on clay.

mṛt = clay; **kārya** = modification, change; **kumbha-rūpaṁ** = form of the jar; **mṛṣā** = false; **kalpita** = imagined; **nāma** = name.

kenāpi mṛd-bhinnatayā svarūpaṁ
ghaṭasya saṁdarśayituṁ na śakyate |
ato ghaṭaḥ kalpita eva mohāṭ
mṛdeva satyaṁ paramārtha-bhūtam ||231||

No one is capable of showing the essence of the pot to be other than the clay. Hence, the pot is imagined only due to delusion. Clay alone is the true abiding reality of the pot.

Take the instance of a clay pot. When the form of the pot is perceived without knowledge that the pot is made of clay, it is obvious that no one would deny the truth of its form or the validity of one's perception of the pot on the grounds that one had no knowledge of the substance (clay) from which it was made. The true character of the pot is clay and yet that true character may not be known even while one knows about the shape of the pot. Likewise, one need not deny the form of the pot when one knows the material it is made from. Both statements are true statements about the pot. Neither statement contradicts the other nor is incompatible with it. The predication that the pot is made of clay does not negate the shape of the pot nor does the shape of the pot negate the substantial truth that the pot is but clay in a particular shape. Therefore, each statement is from a particular viewpoint. One viewpoint is formal and pertains to the pot's shape while the other viewpoint points to the pot's essential nature. However, it should be noted that the form depends upon the substance, and not vice versa. See V. 192, 230, 253, and 392 on clay.

kenāpi = by any one; **mṛd** = clay; **bhinnatayā** = different than, other than; **svarūpaṁ** = essence, self-nature; **ghaṭasya** = pot; **saṁdarśayi-tuṁ** = showing; **na śakyate** = not capable, not able; **kalpita** = imagined; **eva** = only; **mohāṭ** = delusion; satyaṁ = true; paramārtha = absolute, supreme.

sadbrahmakāryam sakalaṁ sadaiva
san-mātram-etan na tato'nyad asti |
astīti yo vakti na tasya moho
vinirgato nidritavat-prajalpah ||232||

All that is, being the effect of the Existent Absolute, can be nothing but the Existent. It is pure Existence. Nothing exists other than it. If anyone says there is, their delusion has not vanished and they babble like one in sleep.

See 'All this is only the Absolute' (*sarvam khalvidam brahma*). See also MuṇḍUp 2.2.11, '*Brahman* alone is all this.' The Vedic verse, 'This universe is the Supreme Absolute' declares that nothing is which is not That. BG 2.16 says, 'The unreal has no existence; the real never ceases to be.'

sat = Existence, Real; **brahmakāryam** = effect of the Absolute; **moho** = delusion; **vinirgato** = vanished; **nidritavat-prajalpah** = babble like one in sleep.

brahmaivedaṁ viśvam ityeva vāṇī
śrautī brūte'tharva-niṣṭhā variṣṭhā |
tasmād-etad brahma-mātraṁ hi viśvaṁ
nādhiṣṭhānād bhinnatāropitasya ||233||

In truth, 'All this universe is the Absolute', is the supreme declaration of the *Atharva Veda*. Therefore, this universe is nothing but the Absolute for that which is superimposed is not different from its substratum.

ChānUp 3.14.1 declares, 'All this is the Absolute' (*sarvam khalvidam brahma*). See BṛhUp 4.4.6, 'There is no diversity whatsoever in It. He goes from death to death who seems to see diversity in It.'
See MuṇḍUp 2.2.11; ChānUp 6.2.1; BṛhUp 4.4.19 on *Brahman*.

brahmaivedaṁ viśvam variṣṭhā = this universe is the supreme Absolute; **eva** = only; **śrautī** = pertaining to the scriptures; **brūte** = declaration; **atharva** = Atharva Veda; **ādhiṣṭhānād** = substratum, foundation; **bhinnata** = difference; **āropitasya** = made, raised.

satyaṁ yadi syāj-jagadetad ātmano
'nantatva-hānir-nigam-āpramāṇatā |
asatya-vāditvam apīśituḥ syāt
naitat trayaṁ sādhu hitaṁ mahātmanām ||234||

If the universe is real, the infinitude of the Self will be affected; the scriptures will no longer be authoritative; the Lord will be proclaimed a speaker of untruth. Great Ones consider these three neither good nor beneficial.

If the universe were to be real this would have certain logical consequences. It would mean that the Self, being part of the universe, would be limited and finite. It would mean that the scriptures are no longer authoritative since they declare, in various places, that the Absolute is real and the world is unreal. It would mean that Lord Kṛṣṇa's declarations that the world is just a projection which has no reality would be false.

satyaṁ = real; **jagad** = universe; **ātmano'nantatva** = infinitude of the Self; **hānir** = affected; **nigama** = scriptures; **āpramāṇatā** = not authoritative; **asatya** = untruth; **vāditvam** = spoken, proclaimed; **trayaṁ** = hree; **sādhu** = good; **hitaṁ** = desirable, beneficial; **mahātmanām** = Great Ones.

īśvaro vastu-tattvajño 'na cāhaṁ teṣvavasthitaḥ |
na ca mat-sthāni bhūtānī' tyevameva vyacīkathat ||235||

The Lord, who knows the Truth about things, declared: I do not abide in them nor do beings abide in me.

Waves take their origin from the sea but the sea is not constrained in the waves.
See BG 9.4, 'All this universe is pervaded by Me in My unmanifested form; All beings abide in Me but I do not abide in them.'

īśvaro = the Lord; **vastu-tattvajño** = knows the truth about things; **na cāhaṁ** = I do not; **teṣvavasthitaḥ** = abide in things; **na** = not; **ca** = and; **mat-sthāni bhūtānī** = things abide in me.

yadi satyaṁ bhaved viśvaṁ suṣuptāvupalabhyatām |
yan-nopalabhyate kiñcid ato'sat svapnavan-mṛṣā ||236||

If the universe is real, let it be perceived in deep sleep also. Since it is not at all perceived in deep sleep, it is false and unreal like a dream.

There cannot be experience without an experiencer. On the other hand, the Self is the experiencing factor in every experience and thus, validates the multiplicity of experiences. The universe, and all experience which flows from it, come and go. Thus, they cannot be real.

See KaivUp 1.13, 'In the state of dreamless sleep in which all things disappear.'

yadi = if; **satyaṁ** = real; **viś vaṁ** = universe; **suṣupti** = deep sleep; **āvupa-labhyatām** = let it be perceived; **yannopalabhyate kiñcid** = since it is not perceived; **asat** = unreal; **svapnavan** = dream; **mṛṣā** = false.

ataḥ pṛthaṅ nāsti jagat parātmanaḥ
pṛthak-pratītis tu mṛṣā guṇāhivat |
āropitasyāsti kim arthavattā
adhiṣṭhnam-ābhāti tathā bhrameṇa ||237||

Therefore, the universe does not exist apart from the supreme Self; perception of its separateness is false like a snake appearing as a rope. Does the superimposed have the quality of producing its appropriate effect? It is the substratum which appears like that due to delusion.

See V. 12, 63, 112, 140, 199, 248, 303, 388, 405, 407, and 550 wherein Śaṅkara makes references to a snake.

ataḥ = therefore; **pṛthaṅ** = apart from, separate; **nāsti** = does not exist; **jagat** = world; **parātmanaḥ** = supreme Self; **pṛthak** = perception; **pratītis** = separateness; **mṛṣā** = false; **guṇāhivat** = snake rope; **āropita-syāsti** = superimposed, deposited on; **kim** = does; **arthavattā** = appropriate effect; **adhiṣṭhnam** = substratum; **bhrameṇa** = delusion; error.

bhrāntasya yad yad bhramataḥ pratītaṁ
brahmaiva tat tad rajataṁ hi śuktiḥ |
idaṁtayā brahma sadaiva rūpyate
tvāropitaṁ brahmaṇi nāma-mātram ||238||

Whatever appears to a deluded person, under the hold of delusion, is the Absolute alone. Silver is nothing but mother-of-pearl. The Absolute is the reality of whatever is referred to as 'this'. Whatever is superimposed on the Absolute is merely a name.

The fundamental cause of suffering is ignorance or superimposition. Ignorance by itself is not enough. In ignorance, one doesn't see what is there. Then one superimposes what is not upon that which is. A human being superimposes upon the Self ideas like, 'I am deficient, inadequate right now'. Why? The evidence for this is compulsiveness/desiring/pursuit of pleasure and security. Why is the gain of security and pleasure so important? It is going to be the means of fulfillment, the means to escape want, inadequacy, incompleteness, bondage. The urge to be complete is what drives all actions.

Compare Śaṅkara's concept of the Absolute which indicates not so much the absence of any character as the impossibility of attributing any conceptual category to Reality. Śaṅkara's Being is not a being among beings. The Being that is the substance cannot be categorized. '*Yato vaco nivartante aprapya manasa saha*' – 'whence words return along with the mind, not attaining it.' Śaṅkara's Being is merest Being or Pure Being.

See ChānUp 6.1.4, 'By means of just one lump of clay one would perceive everything made of clay – the transformation is a verbal handle, a name, while the reality is just clay.' Also see BṛhUp 1.4.7. See V. 357 and 399 on names.

bhrāntasya = deluded person; **bhramataḥ** = delusion; **brahmaiva** = the Absolute alone; **rajataṁ** = silver; **śuktiḥ** = pearl oyster, mother of pearl; **idaṁ** = this; **rūpyate** = reality, form; **tvāropitaṁ** = superimposed on; **brahmaṇi** = the Absolute; **nāma** = name.

ataḥ paraṁ brahma sad-advitīyaṁ
viśuddha-vijñāna-ghanaṁ nirañjanam ǀ
praśāntam-ādyanta-vihīnam akriyaṁ
nirantarānanda-rasa-svarūpam ǁ239ǁ
nirasta-māyā-kṛta-sarva-bhedaṁ
nityaṁ dhruvam niṣkalam-aprameyam ǀ
arūpaṁ-avyaktam-anākhyam avyayaṁ
jyotiḥ svayaṁ kiñcid idaṁ cakāsti ǁ240ǁ

Therefore, this supreme Absolute is Real, non-dual,[1] utterly pure, the essence of knowledge, taintless, supremely peaceful, without beginning or end, actionless, of the nature of never-ending bliss, free from all differences due to illusion, eternal, unchanging, without parts, ineffable, formless, unmanifest, nameless, immutable, self-luminous.[2] This something shines.

See MāṇḍUp 7, '. . . neither inside nor outside nor both; unseen (*adṛṣṭam*), can't be spoken of (*avyavaharyam*), ungraspable (*agrāhyam*), without distinguishable marks (*alakṣanam*), unthinkable (*acintyam*), unnameable (*avyapadeśyam*), peaceful (*śāntam*), non-dual (*advaitam*), auspicious (śivam).'

See ŚvetUp 6.19, 'without parts, without activity' (*niṣkalam niṣkriyam*); also 6.12.

See also KaivUp 1.20–23 on the Absolute.

ataḥ = therefore; **paraṁ brahma** = supreme Absolute; **sat** = Real, Existence; **advitīyaṁ** = nonn-dual, one without a second; **viśuddha** = utterly pure; **vijñāna-ghanaṁ** = essence or homogenous mass of knowledge, wisdom; **nirañjanam** = stainless, taintless; **praśāntam** = supremely peaceful, highest peace; **ādyanta-vihīnam** = without beginning or end; **akriyaṁ** = actionless; **nirantarānanda-rasa-svarūpam** = of the nature of never-ending bliss; **nirasta-māyā-kṛta-sarva-bhedaṁ** = that from which all differences due to illusion have been cast off; **nityaṁ**-eternal; **dhruvam** = unchanging; **niṣkalam** = without parts, complete; **aprameyam** = ineffable, beyond the faculty of reasoning, immeasurable; **arūpaṁ** = formless; **avyaktam** = unmanifest, subtle; **anākhyam** = nameless; **avyayaṁ** = immutable; **jyotiḥ svayaṁ** = self-effulgent, self-luminous; **kiñcit** = something; **idaṁ** = this; **cakāsti** = shines.

[1] See ChanUp 6.2.1 (*ekam evādvitīyaṁ*); Bṛh Up 1.4.17 (*eka eva*); AitUp 1.1.1.

[2] See US 1.11.11; MuṇḍUp 2.2.10–11. Also see V. 100, 153, 191, 213, 221, 508, and 536 on self-luminous.

jñātṛ-jñeya-jñāna-śūnyam anantaṁ nirvikalpakam |
kevalākhaṇḍa-cinmātraṁ paraṁ tattvaṁ vidur-budhāḥ ||241||

The wise realize the supreme Truth, which is void of the distinctions of knower, the object known, and act of knowledge; which is infinite, indeterminate, totally unbroken pure consciousness.

Truth is a tantalizer. It is the immense mystery which knowledge cannot contain. It is a pathless land. It is the song which calls to every person who seeks to find the basic, intrinsically intelligible bedrock of it all from which everything arises and into which experience culminates.

jñātr = knower; **jñeya** = known; **jñāna** = knowledge; **śūnyam** = devoid of; **anantaṁ** = infinite; **nirvikalpakam** = indeterminate, impartite; **keva-lākhandamātraṁ** = totally unbroken pure consciousness; **paraṁ tattvaṁ** = supreme truth; **vidur-budhāḥ** = the wise realize.

aheyam-anupādeyaṁ mano-vācām-agocaram |
aprameyam-anādyantaṁ brahma pūrṇaṁ mahan-mahaḥ ||242||

It can neither be thrown away nor taken up; it is beyond mind and speech, immeasurable, without beginning or end; it is the Absolute, full, the greatest of the great.

The Self cannot be thrown away, for it is one's essential nature and it cannot be taken up, for it is already present.

See BṛhUp 5.1.1, 'This is full, that is full' (*pūrṇam adaḥ pūrṇam idam*); see also MuṇḍUp 2.2.11, '*Brahman* alone is all this'. ChānUp 6.2.1, 'It is One alone, without a second'. BṛhUp 4.4.19, 'In *Brahman* there is no diversity whatsoever'.

aheya = thrown away; **anupādeyaṁ** = taken up; **mano** = mind; **vācām** = speech; **agocaram** = beyond, unattainable; **aprameyam** = immeasurable, beyond the faculty of reasoning; **anādyantaṁ** = without beginning or end; **brahma** = the Absolute; **pūrṇaṁ** = full, complete; **mahan-mahaḥ** = greatest of the great.

tat-tvaṁ-padābhyāṁ abhidhīya-mānayoḥ
brahmātmanoḥ śodhitayor yadīttham |
śrutyā tayos-tat-tvam-asīti samyak
ekatvam-eva pratipādyate muhuḥ ||243||

The scriptural statement, That thou art, repeatedly establishes the absolute oneness of the Absolute and the individual, thus indicated by the words That and thou, and whose meanings have been examined and determined.

The knowledge that one obtains through *śruti* texts like *tat tvam asi* is immediate and non-relational. Such texts signify the transcendental non-dual Reality. *Tat tvam asi* – That thou art. 'That' (*tat*) refers to the Absolute or *Brahman*. 'Thou' (*tvam*) refers to the individual. 'Art' (*asi*) points to the essential non-difference between the two. *Brahman*, by nature, is infinite, omnipotent, omnipresent, omniscient, immortal, and so on. The individual, seemingly is finite, mortal, limited, and so on. How can that which is Infinite and immortal be non-different from that which is finite and mortal?

Before we actually interpret the *mahāvākya 'tat tvam asi'*, it should be noted that an understanding of a *mahāvākya* involves a two-fold benefit. Even in an empirical statement which involves grammatical coordination, there is this two-fold benefit. For instance, in the phrase, 'blue lotus', both the color 'blue' benefits as well as the flower 'lotus'. The idea of 'blueness' removes all other possible colors from the lotus and 'that' which is blue is precisely a 'lotus'. Thus, each is enriched and benefits from their association.

In a similar manner, '*tat*', by its association with '*tvam*' removes the misconception that it is remote, unattainable, hidden, and reveals itself as that which is ever-manifest, immediate, direct, and the innermost Self. In a similar manner, '*tvam*', in its association with '*tat*' removes the misconception that it is mortal, finite, bound, and imperfect and reveals itself as that which is self-existent, ever-pure, ever-free, and immortal. Thus, what was conceived of as the farthest of the far is revealed as nearer than the nearest; what appeared to be unattainable is already attained; what is hidden is really self-manifest (see MundUp 3.1.7–8).

See ChānUp 6.8.7 on '*Tat tvam asi*'. See V. 251, 253–65, and 284 on *Tat tvam asi*.

tat = That; **tvaṁ** = thou; **padābhyām** = meaning; **abhidhīya-mānayoḥ** = examined and determined; **brahmātmanoḥ** = the Absolute and the individual; **śrutyā** = scripture; **tat-tvam-asīti** = That thou art; **ekatvam-eva** = absolute oneness, oneness alone; **pratipādyate** = attains, acknowledges, establishes, answered affirmatively; **muhuḥ** = constantly, repeatedly.

aikyaṁ tayor lakṣitayor na vācyayoḥ
nigadyate'nyonya-viruddha-dharmiṇoḥ |
khadyota-bhānvor-iva rāja-bhṛtyayoḥ
kūpāmbu-rāśyoḥ paramāṇu-mervoḥ ||244||

These two have qualities, mutually contradictory to each other, like a firefly and the sun, like a servant and the king, like a well and the ocean, like an atom or Mount Meru. Divesting these terms of their relative associations, identity is affirmed between them taking, not their literal meaning, but their implied meaning.

These two' are 'tat = That' and 'tvam = thou'. That has the qualities of omniscience, omnipotence, omnipresence, infinitude, immortality, and so on. Thou has the qualities of limitedness, finitude, mortality, stupidity, and so on. When the primary meaning of a term does not make sense, one should resort to its secondary meaning in order to do so. See V. 244 on *tat tvam asi*. Also see V. 251, 253–65, and 284.

aikya = identity; **laksitayor** = implied meaning; **na vācyayo** = not literal meaning; **nigadyate** = to speak; **anyonya-viruddha-dharmiṇoḥ** = mutually contradictory qualities; **khadyota** = firefly, glow-worm; **bhānvor** = sun; **rāja** = king; **bhṛtyayoḥ** = servant; **kūpāmbu** = well; **rāśyoḥ** = ocean; **paramāṇu** = atom; **mervoḥ** = Mount Meru.

tayor-virodho'yaṁ upādhi-kalpito
na vāstavaḥ kaścid-upādhireṣaḥ |
īśasya māyā mahad-ādi-kāraṇaṁ
jīvasya kāryaṁ śṛṇu pañcakośam ||245||

The opposition between them is imagined due to their limiting adjuncts. These adjuncts are not real. Listen! *Māyā* is the limiting adjunct of the Lord and the cause of 'the great' and so on; the five sheaths, which are the effects of *māyā*, are the limiting adjuncts of the individual.

The opposition between 'That' and 'thou' is in their literal meanings. This opposition is not real. By employing the secondary meaning of the terms in the *mahāvākya*, one removes the incompatible determinants of each term. By removing omniscience, omnipotence, etc., from 'That' and by removing limitedness, boundness, fallibility, etc., from 'thou', while retaining the common element between them, i.e., consciousness, *tat tvam asi* conveys a sense of non-relational identity. Some implications from this interpretation include: What we usually associate with 'thou' (such as suffering) is canceled by its association with 'That' and what we usually associate with 'That' (remoteness, etc.) is canceled by its association with 'thou'.

See V. 67, 110–112, 125, 406, 497, and 574 on *māyā*.

virodha = opposition; **jīvasya** = individual; **upādhi-kalpito** = imaginary limiting adjuncts; **na vāstavaḥ** = not real; **īśasya** = the Lord; **māyā** = illusion; **mahad-ādi** = the Great, the first evolution of primordial nature and so on; **pañcakośam** = five sheaths.

etāv-upādhī para-jīvayos-tayoḥ
samyaṅ nirāse na paro na jīvaḥ |
rājyaṁ narendrasya bhaṭasya kheṭakaḥ
tayor-apohe na bhaṭo na rājā ||246||

When the limiting adjuncts of the Lord and of the individual are completely rejected, there is no Lord and there is no individual. A kingdom is the symbol of a king, and a shield of a soldier. When they are removed, there is neither king nor soldier.

The limiting adjunct of the Lord is *māyā*, which is the cause of the entire world. The limiting adjunct of the individual is the five sheaths. However, they are not real.

upādhī = limiting adjuncts; **samyaṅ nirāse** = completely rejected; **na paro** = no Lord; **rājyaṁ** = king; **narendrasya** = kingdom; **bhaṭasya** = soldier; **kheṭakaḥ** = removed.

athāta ādeśa iti śruthi-svayaṁ
niṣedhati brahmaṇi kalpitaṁ dvayam |
śruti-pramāṇānugṛhīta-yuktyā
tayor-nirāsaḥ karaṇīya evam ||247||

The scripture itself, by the words, 'Now, this is the injunction', forbids imagined duality in the Absolute. The removal of the two is thus to be facilitated by reasoning supported by scriptural texts.

See BṛhUp 2.3.6, 'Here, then, is the rule of substitution: "not this, not this", for there is nothing beyond this "not".'

ādeśa = injunction; **iti** = his; **śruthi-svayaṁ**-scripture itself; **niṣedhati** = forbids; **brahmaṇi** = the Absolute; **kalpitaṁ dvayam** = imagined duality; **śruti-pramā** = scriptural truth; **aṇānugṛhīta** = promoting, facilitating.

nedaṁ nedaṁ kalpitatvān na satyaṁ
rajju dṛṣṭa-vyālavat svapnavat ca |
itthaṁ dṛśyaṁ sādhu-yuktyā vyapohya
jñeyaḥ paścād eka-bhāvas-tayor yaḥ ||248||

Neither this, nor this, because they are imagined like the snake and the rope, and like objects seen in a dream, are not real. Thus, by proper reasoning, completely eliminate the seen in this way, and realize their identity.

See BṛhUp 2.3.6, 'not this, not this' (*na iti, na iti – neti, neti*); see also BṛhUp 3.8.8.
See V. 12, 63, 112, 140, 199, 237, 303, 388, 405, 407, and 550 wherein Śaṅkara makes references to a snake.

nedaṁ = this is not, neither this; **kalpitatvān** = imagined; **na satyaṁ** = not real; **rajju** = rope; **dṛṣṭa** = seen; **svapnavat** = dream; **dṛśyaṁ** = objects seen; **sādhu-yuktyā** = proper reasoning; **vyapohya** = remove, destroy, elimianate; **eka-bhāvas** = oneness, identity, absence of difference.

tatas-tu tau lakṣaṇayā sulakṣyau
tayor-akhaṇḍaika-rasatva-siddhaye |
nālaṁ jahatyā na tathājahatyā
kintūbhayārthātmikayaiva bhāvyam ||249||

Hence, the two terms are to be correctly understood through their implied meanings in order to clearly establish the import of absolute identity between them. Neither the method of total rejection nor total non-rejection will suffice; but by a combination of both meanings.

Besides their primary meanings, words also have implied meanings. When in a given context the primary meaning of a word is found to be unintelligible, then the word must be understood in a secondary sense. For instance, the sentence, 'the hamlet on the Ganges', cannot be interpreted literally and remain meaningful. Villages are not literally 'on the water'. Thus the implied meaning, 'on the bank of the river', must be supplied to convey the import of the sentence. Secondary implication has been divided into three kinds: exclusive (*jahallakṣaṇā*), inclusive (*ajahallakṣaṇā*), and quasi-inclusive (*jahad-ajahallakṣaṇā*). Exclusive implication is when the implied meaning of a word or an expression excludes the primary meaning. In this type, the implied meaning is other than, but nonetheless related to, the primary meaning which is completely given up. In the sentence, 'the hamlet on the Ganges', the primary meaning of the word 'Ganges' is completely given up and the bank which is related to the river is implied. Inclusive implication includes the primary meaning in the implied sense. In this type, a meaning is implied which is other than the primary meaning of the word, yet which is related to it with the primary meaning not being given up. In the sentence, 'the school works today', the word 'school' indicates the members of the school. Thus the primary sense is maintained and included in the implied meaning. And, last, quasi-inclusive implication is when part of the primary sense of a word is given up and part of it is retained. For instance, in the sentence, 'this is that Devadatta', the meaning of the word 'this' refers to Devadatta as qualified by present time and place, and the meaning of the word 'that' refers to the same Devadatta as qualified by past time and place. The primary meanings of the two terms are incompatible. Thus, in quasi-inclusive implication, part of the meaning of the words 'this' and 'that' *viz.*, the individual Devadatta, is accepted and the other part of their meanings, *viz.*, 'as qualified by temporal and spatial qualifications, etc.' is rejected.

tataḥ = therefore; **lakṣaṇayā** = implied, secondary meanings; **sulakṣyau** = correctly understood; **akhaṇḍaika** = absolute identity, impartite oneness; **rasatva** = essesnce;

siddhaye = established; **nālaṁ jahatyā** = neither the method of total rejection, exclusive implication; **na tathājahatyā** = nor that of total non-rejection, non-exclusive implication; **kintūbhayārthāt-mikayaiva** = but by a combination of both meanings.

sa devadatto'yam-itīha caikatā
viruddha-dharmāṁśam apāsya kathyate |
yathā tathā tat-tvam-asīti vākye
viruddha-dharmān ubhayatra hitvā ||250||
saṁlakṣya cin-mātratayā sadātmanoḥ
akhaṇḍa-bhāvaḥ paricīyate budhaiḥ |
evaṁ mahā-vākya-śatena kathyate
brahmātmanor-aikyam akhaṇḍa-bhāvaḥ ||251||

Just as in the sentence, 'This is that Devadatta', the identity is expressed by eliminating the contradictory qualities, so in the sentence, 'That thou art', by rejecting the contradictory qualities in both words, the wise experience the true Self as being limitless consciousness.[1] Thus, the identity of the Absolute and the individual and their unlimited nature is conveyed by hundreds of great statements.

Each of these great sayings imparts a two-fold knowledge which gives a proper understanding of the scripture. First, they remove the deep-seated misconception of an individual that they are finite, bound, imperfect, and mortal beings. They reveal that the true Self of each individual is infinite, ever-free, ever-perfect, and immortal. And second, they remove the deep-rooted misconception that the supreme Reality is remote, unattainable, hidden, and they declare that the supreme Reality is the innermost self of all, the self manifest, immediate, and direct: 'That *Brahman* is vast, self-luminous, inconceivable, subtler than the subtle. That shines forth. That is far beyond what is far, and yet here very near at hand. That is seen here, dwelling in the cave of the heart of conscious beings' (MuṇḍUp 3.1.7). Thus, the unattainable becomes the already attained, and the farthest of the far becomes the nearest of the near.

See ChānUp 6.8.7, '*tat tvam asi*'. See, for *tat tvam asi*, V. 243, 253–65, and 284.

sa **devadatto'yam** = this is that Devadatta; **aikatā** = identity, oneness; **viruddha-dharmāṁśam** = contrary qualities; **apāsya** = throw away, elimanate; **tat-tvam-asi** = That thou art; **hitvā** = the wise; **cinmātratayā** = limitless consciousness; **sadātmanoḥ** = the true Self; **akhaṇḍa-bhāvaḥ** = unlimited, unbroken nature; **mahā-vākya-śatena** = hundreds of great sayings; **kathyate** = conveyed, spoken; **brahmātmanor-aikyam** = oneness of the Absolute and the individual (or Self).

asthūlam ityetad asan nirasya
siddhaṁ svato vyomavad-apratarkyam |
ato mṛṣā-mātram-idaṁ pratītam
jahīhi yat-svātmatayā gṛhītam |
brahmāham-ityeva viśuddha-buddhyā
viddhi svam-ātmānam akhaṇḍa-bodham ||252||

[1] See BṛhUp 2.4.12, 'limitless mass of consciousness only'.

After rejecting the false, in accordance with such statements as, 'Not gross, and so on',[1] one realizes the Self, which is self-established, which is beyond reasoning like the sky. Therefore, let go of this, which you think to be your own Self. With a purified understanding that 'I am the Absolute',[2] know your own Self to be indivisible intelligence.

Rejecting the false implies ceasing to dwell on sense objects. The root of bondage is the perception of difference between the Self and the not-self. The pursuit of sense objects increases the binding tendencies. Stop thinking of them. When the heart is peaceful, the Self becomes manifest.

asthūlam = not gross; **nirasya** = reject; **siddhaṁ svato** = self-established; **vyomavad-apratarkyam** = beyond reasoning like the sky; **mṛṣā** = false; **jahīhi** = discard; **gṛhītam** = caught hold of; **brahm-āham** = I am the Absolute; **viśuddha-buddhyā** = purified understanding; **viddhi** = know; **svam-ātmanam** = own Self; **akhaṇḍa-bodham** = indivisible intelligence, knowledge.

mṛt-kāryaṁ sakalaṁ ghaṭādi satataṁ mṛn-mātram-evābhitaḥ
tadvat saj-janitaṁ sadātmakam idaṁ san-mātram-evākhilam |
yasmān-nāsti sataḥ paraṁ kim-api tat satyaṁ sa ātmā svayam
tasmāt tat-tvam-asi praśāntam-amalaṁ brahmādvayaṁ yat-param ||253||

Whatever is made of clay, like a pot and so on, is only and always entirely nothing but clay. Similarly, all this that is the effect of the Real, is the Real itself, and entirely nothing but the Real. Because nothing exists, anywhere, anytime, other than the Real, That is the Truth, your own Self. Therefore, That thou art, supremely serene, pure, the Supreme, the non-dual[3] Absolute.

See ChānUp 6.1.4, 'Just as by means of one lump of clay all that is made of clay becomes known, the modification being only a name arising from speech while the truth is that it is just clay.' See V. 192, 230–31, and 392 on clay.

See ChānUp 6.8.7, 'That is the truth. That is the Self. That thou art' (*tat satyam, sa ātmā, tat tvam asi*). See V. 243, 251, 253–65, and 284 on *tat tvam asi*.

mṛt-kāryaṁ = made of clay; **ghaṭādi** = pot; **satataṁ mṛn-mātram-evābhitaḥ** = is only and always, entirely nothing but clay; **tadvat** = similarly; **nāsti** = it is not, nothing exists; **satyaṁ** = truth; **ātmā svayam** = own Self; **tasmāt** = therefore; **tat-tvam-asi** = That thou art; **praśāntam** = supreme peace; **amalaṁ** = pure, stainless, without defects; **brahmādvayaṁ**-the non-dual Absolute; **param** = supreme.

nidrā-kalpita-deśa-kāla-viṣaya-jñātrādi sarvaṁ yathā
mithyā tadvad-ihāpi jāgrat jagat svājñāna-kāryatvataḥ |
yasmād-evam idaṁ śarīra-karaṇa-prāṇāhamādyapyasat
tasmāt tat-tvam-asi praśāntam amalaṁ brahmādvayaṁ yat param ||254||

Just as place, time, objects, their knower and so on imagined during sleep are all unreal, so too, here in the waking state the world is a projection of one's own ignorance. Likewise, this body, the sense organs, the vital breath, the ego, and so on, are all unreal. Therefore, That thou art, supremely serene, pure, the Supreme, the non-dual[4] Absolute.

---

1 See BṛhUp 3.8.8, 'neither gross nor fine . . .' (*asthūlam anaṇu*); see also BṛhUp 2.3.6.
2 See BṛhUp 1.4.10, 'I am the Absolute' (*aham brahmāsmi*).
3 See ChānUp 6.2.1, BṛhUp 1.4.17, AitUp 1.1.1.
4 See ChānUp 6.2.1 (*ekam evādvitīyam*); BṛhUp 1.4.17; AitUp 1.1.1.

See ChānUp 6.8.7, 'That is the Self. That thou art' (*sa ātmā, tat tvam asi*). See, on *tat tvam asi*, V. 243, 251, 253–65, and 284.

nidrā = sleep; **kalpita** = imagined; **deśa** = place; **kāla** = time; **viṣaya** = objects; **jñātrādi** = knower and so on; **sarvaṁ** = all; **yathā** = just as; **mithyā** = unreal, illusory; **tadvadihāpi** = so too, here; **jāgrat** = waking state; **jagat** = world; **svājñāna-kāryatvataḥ** = projection of one's own ignorance; **idaṁ śarīra** = this body; **karaṇa** = sense organs; **prāṇāhamādi** = vital breath, egoism.

jāti-nīti-kula-gotra-dūragaṁ
nāma-rūpa-guṇa-doṣa-varjitam |
deśa-kāla-viṣayātivarti yat
brahma tat-tvam-asi bhāvayātmani ||255||

That Absolute, which is far from caste, creed, family, and lineage; which excludes the defects of name and form and qualities; which transcends place, time, and sense objects; meditate in your mind, That thou art.

The Great Saying gives a two-fold knowledge: by declaring oneness of the individual with the Absolute, it removes the deep-seated misconception about oneself that one is bound, mortal, finite, and impure, and reveals that one is ever free, immortal, etc. By declaring that the Absolute is the innermost Self of everyone, this removes one's misconceptions about the Divine that it is far away, inaccessible and reveals that it is immediate/direct/nearer than the nearest. The unattainable is already attained

See ChānUp 6.8.7, '*tat tvam asi*'. See, on *tat tvam asi*, V. 243, 251, 253–65, and 284.

jāti = caste; **nīti** = creed, rules for ethical living; **kula** = family; **gotra** = lineage; **dūragaṁ** = far from; **nāma** = name; **rūpa** = form; **guṇa** = qualities; **doṣa** = defects; **varjitam** = exclude, abandon; **deśa** = place; **kāla** = time; **viṣayātivarti** = transcends sense objects.

yatparaṁ sakalavāgagocaraṁ
gocaraṁ vimala-bodha-cakṣuṣaḥ |
śuddha-cidghanam anādivastu yad
brahma tat-tvam-asi bhāvayātmani ||256||

That Absolute, which is supreme; beyond words, yet attainable by an eye of wisdom which is totally free from defects; which is an embodiment of pure consciousness; which eternally exists; meditate in your mind, That thou art.

See ChānUp 6.8.7, '*tat tvam asi*'. See, on *tat tvam asi*, V. 243, 251, 253–65, and 284.

paraṁ = supreme; **sakalavāgagocaraṁ** = beyond words, beyond the reach of all speech; **gocaraṁ vimala-bodha-cakṣuṣaḥ** = attainable by the eye of wisdom which is extremely pure, taintless; **śuddha-cidghanam** = and embodiment of, compacted of pure consciousness; **anādivastu** = that which is the eternal being, which exists eternally.

ṣaḍbhir-ūrmibhir-ayogi yogi-hṛd-
bhāvitaṁ na karaṇair-vibhāvitam |
buddhyavedyam anavadyabhūti yad
brahma tat-tvam-asi bhāvayātmani ||257||

That Absolute, which is untouched by the six waves; which is meditated on in the hearts of yogis; which cannot be known by the sense organs; which cannot be known by the intellect; which is of an untainted excellence; meditate in your mind, That thou art.

The six waves are hunger, thirst, grief, delusion, old age, and death.

Compare KenaUp 3, 'It is other than all that is known, and It is also beyond the unknown.'

See ChānUp 6.8.7, '*tat tvam asi*'. See, on *tat tvam asi*, V. 243, 251, 253–65, and 284.

ṣaḍbhir = six: **ūrmibhir** = waves; **ayogi** = untouched, not affected by; **yogihṛd-bhāvitaṁ** = meditated on in the hearts of yogis; **na karaṇair-vibhāvitam** = not apprehended by the sense organs; **buddhyavedyam** = not knowable by the intellect; **anavadyabhūti** = of an untainted, flawless excellence.

bhrānti-kalpita-jagat-kalāśrayaṁ
svāśrayaṁ ca sad-asad-vilakṣaṇam |
niṣkalaṁ nirupamānaṁ ṛddhimat
brahma tat-tvam-asi bhāvayātmani ||258||

That Absolute, which is the substratum of the limited universe which is erroneously imagined upon it; which is self-established and other than the Real or the unreal; which is without parts; which is beyond compare and magnificent; meditate in your mind, That thou art.

The space within a pot is the same as the space outside the pot. A wave (limited by name/form) is but a small part of the ocean. As water the wave is identical with water. One is the water of the wave and not the individual drop of water.

See ŚvetUp 6.19, 'without parts' (*niṣkalamm*); also 6.12.

See ChānUp 6.8.7, '*tat tvam asi*'. See, on *tat tvam asi*, V. 243, 251, 253–65, and 284.

bhrānti-kalpita = erroneously imagined or superimposed; **jagat-kalāśrayaṁ** = limited universe, restricted basis; **svāśrayaṁ** = established in itself; **sad-asad-vilakṣaṇam** = other than the Real or the unreal; **niṣkalaṁ** = without parts; **nirupamānam** = incomparable; **ṛddhimat** = magnificient.

janma-vṛddhi-pariṇatyapakṣaya-
vyādhi-nāśana-vihīnam avyayam |
viśva sṛṣṭyavavighāta-kāraṇaṁ
brahma tat-tvam-asi bhāvayātmani ||259||

That Absolute, which is devoid of birth, growth, change, decay, disease, and death; which is indestructible; which is the cause of the creation, preservation, and dissolution of the universe; meditate in your mind, That thou art.

See ChānUp 6.8.7, '*tat tvam asi*'. See, on *tat tvam asi*, V. 243, 251, 253–65, and 284.

janma = birth; **vṛddhi** = growth; **pariṇatiḥ** = change; **apakṣaya** = decay; **vyādhi** = disease; **nāśana** = death; **vihīnam** = devoid of; **avyayam** = indestructible; **viśva** = universe; **sṛṣṭyava-vighāta-kāraṇaṁ** = cause of the creation, preservation, and dissolution.

asta-bhedam anapāsta-lakṣaṇaṁ
nistaraṅga-jalarāśi-niścalam |
nityamuktam-avibhakta-mūrti yad
brahma tat-tvam-asi bhāvayātmani ||260||

That Absolute, which is free from all differences; which is inseparably characterized by defining marks; which is calm like a waveless ocean; which is ever-free; which is of indivisible form; meditate in your mind, That thou art.

See ChānUp 6.8.7, '*tat tvam asi*'. See, on *tat tvam asi*, V. 243, 251, 253–65, and 284.

asta-bhedam = that which is free from all differences; **anapāsta-lakṣaṇaṁ** = inseparably characterized by defining marks; **nistaraṅga-jalarāśi-niścalam** = calm like a waveless ocean; **nityamuktam** = ever = free; **avibhakta-mūrti** = of indivisible form, undifferentiated nature.

ekam-eva sad-anekakāraṇaṁ
kāraṇāntara-nirāsya-kāraṇam |
kārya-kāraṇa-vilakṣaṇaṁ svayaṁ
brahma tat-tvam-asi bhāvayātmani ||261||

That Being, which is one only, is the cause of multiplicity; is itself without a cause; is other than both causes and effects being self-existent; meditate in your mind, That thou art.

Being constitutes the thread which gives certainty its allurement. Being (*sattā-mahāsamanya*) is the most universal concept, according to Śaṅkara, a universality which goes beyond that of any genus. At the same time, it is obscure and indefinite. 'Being-itself' cannot be comprehended by anything that is, and yet it is somehow a self-evident concept which can never be deduced from any higher concept nor represented by any lower one. All knowledge makes use of it, and yet it still remains incomprehensible.

See ChānUp 6.8.7, '*tat tvam asi*'. See, on *tat tvam asi*, V. 243, 251, 253–65, and 284.

ekam-eva = one only; **sat** = Being, Real, Existence; **anekakāraṇaṁ** = cause of multiplicity, manyness, duality; **kāraṇāntara-nirāsya-kāraṇam** = the causer itself has no cause; **kārya-kāraṇa-vilakṣaṇaṁ** = other than both causes and effects.

nirvikalpakam-analpam-akṣaraṁ
yat-kṣarākṣara-vilakṣaṇaṁ param |
nityam-avyaya-sukhaṁ nirāñjanaṁ
brahma tat-tvam-asi bhāvayātmani ||262||

That Absolute, which is without distinctions; infinite;[1] imperishable; other than the perishable and the imperishable; supreme; eternal; of undiminishing bliss; taintless; meditate in your mind, That thou art.

See ChānUp 6.8.7, '*tat tvam asi*'. See, on *tat tvam asi*, V. 243, 251, 253–65, and 284.

[1] See KaUp on infinite (*nityo nityānām*).

nirvikalpakam = impartite, without distinctions; **analpam** = huge, infinite; **akṣaraṁ** = imperishable, undecaying, all-enveloping; **yat-kṣarāk-ṣara-vilakṣaṇaṁ** = that which is other than the perishable or imperishable; **param** = supreme, superior; **nityam** = eternal; **avyaya-sukhaṁ** = of undiminishing bliss, eternal, imperishable bliss; **nirāñjanaṁ** = taintless, pure.

yad vibhāti sad-anekadhā bhramāt
nāma-rūpa-guṇa-vikriyātmanā |
hemavat svayam-avikriyaṁ sadā
brahma tat-tvam-asi bhāvayātmani ||263||

That Absolute, which, due to delusion, appears variously assuming names and forms, attributes and actions; which like gold, is itself always unchanging; meditate in your mind, That thou art.

Imagine a big building collapsing. Some rooms are in ruins, others intact. But can one speak of the space as ruined or intact? The structures suffer and change, not the space. A goldsmith melts down old ornaments to make new ones. Sometimes a good piece accidentally goes with the old. He is not worried. He knows that no gold has been lost.

See ChānUp 6.8.7, '*tat tvam asi*'. See, on *tat tvam asi*, V. 243, 251, 253–65, and 284.

vibhāti = appears; **bhramāt** = due to delusion, error, false; **nāma-rūpa** = names and forms; **guṇa-vikriyā** = attributes and actions; **hemavat** = like gold; **svayam-avikriyaṁ** = itself unchanging; **sadā** = always.

yac cakāstyanaparaṁ parāt-paraṁ
pratyag eka-rasam ātma-lakṣaṇam |
satya-cit-sukham anantam avyayaṁ
brahma tat-tvam-asi bhāvayātmani ||264||

That Absolute, shines, beyond which there is nothing before or after; which is beyond the supreme; the innermost Self; of a single essence; whose mark is the Self; which is of the nature of Existence, Consciousness, Bliss; infinite; eternal; meditate in your mind, That thou art.

See BṛhUp (*tadetad brahmāpūrvam anaparam*).

See MuṇḍUp (*akṣarāt parataḥ paraḥ*).

See PraśnaUp.

See ChānUp 6.8.7, '*tat tvam asi*'. See, on *tat tvam asi*, V. 243, 251, 253–65, and 284.

cakāstya = shines; **anaparaṁ** = beyond which there is nothing before or after; **parāt-paraṁ** = beyond the supreme; **pratyag** = innermost; **eka-rasam** = single essence; **ātma-lakṣaṇam** = whose mark is the Self; **satya-cit-sukham anantam avyayaṁ** = Truth, Existence, Consciousness, Bliss, infinite, eternal.

uktam-artham imam-ātmani svayaṁ
bhāvaya prathita-yuktibhir dhiyā |
saṁśayādi-rahitaṁ karāmbuvat
tena tattva-nigamo bhaviṣyati ||265||

You, yourself, meditate with a blemishless mind, employing authoritative reasoning, on this teaching which has been conveyed to you. By that means one will realize the Truth, free from doubt, like water in the palm of the hand.

Not only should one hear the Truth from another, but one must also meditate upon that Truth and reason about that Truth and, finally, experience it for oneself.

uktam-artham = this teaching; **svayaṁ bhāvaya** = yourself meditate; **prathita-yuktibhiḥ** = by famous or authoritative reasoning; **dhiyā** = blemishless mind; **saṁśayādi-rahitaṁ** = free from doubt; **karāmbuvat tena** = like water in the palm of the hand; **tattvanigam** = the truth arises.

svaṁ bodhamātraṁ pariśuddha-tattvaṁ
vijñāya saṅghe nṛpavac ca sainye |
tadātmanaivātmani sarvadā sthito
vilāpaya brahmaṇi viśva-jātam ||266||

Realizing yourself in this collection as pure knowledge, free from all false notions, like the king in an army, and being ever established in one's own Self, merge all that is brought into existence into the Absolute.

A king is identified by his army which consists of a multitude of men, their equipment and so on. Likewise, one should realize that their individuality is nothing but a combination of diverse elements. Merge all multiplicity into the Self: 'Merge the earth in water, the water in fire, fire in air, air in space, space in the unmanifest, the unmanifest in the Self. I am that Hari, the Pure.'

bodhamātraṁ = knowledge; **pariśuddha** = supremely pure; **tattvām** = real nature; **vijñāya** = realizing; **saṅghe** = collection, assembly; **nṛpa** = king; **sainye** = army **sarvadā sthito** = ever established; **viśva-jātam** = all that is brought into existence.

buddhau guhāyām sad-asad-vilakṣaṇaṁ
brahmāsti satyaṁ param-advitīyam |
tad-ātmanā yo'atra vased guhāyām
punar na tasyāṅga-guhā-praveśaḥ ||267||

In the cave of the intellect, there is the true, the supreme non-dual[1] Absolute which is other than the real or the unreal. For one who lives in this cave as that Self, there is no further return to the cave of the body.

See KaUp 2.1.12, 'The person of the size of a thumb resides in the middle of the body' (*aṅguṣṭha mātraḥ puruṣo madhya ātmani tiṣṭhati*); KaUp 1.3.13, 'Lodged in the secret place' (*loke guhām praviṣṭau*). See verse 134 for the cave and V. 191, 219, and 257 for the heart.

buddhau guhāyām = cave of the intellect; **sad-asad-vilakṣaṇaṁ** = other than the real or the unreal; **brahmāsti satyaṁ param-advitīyam** = there is the true, supreme non-dual Absolute; **punar na tasyāṅga-guhā-praveśaḥ** = there is no return again to the cave of the body.

---

[1] See ChanUp 6.2.1; BṛhUp 1.4.17 (*eka eva*); AitUp 1.1.1.

jñāte vastunyapi balavatī vāsanānādir-eṣā
kartā bhoktāpy-aham-iti dṛḍhā yāsya saṁsāra-hetuḥ |
pratyag-dṛṣṭātmani nivasatā sāpaneyā prayatnāt
muktiṁ prāhus-tad-iha munayo vāsanā-tānavaṁ yat ||268||

Even after the Self is known, there remain strong, beginningless, obstinate residual impressions such as doership and enjoyment, which are the cause of one's worldly existence. They have to be carefully removed with effort by living in a state of constant inward-viewing of the Self. Sages call this slaying of the residual impressions, liberation.

The seeker is who or what one is seeking. Looking (for it elsewhere) necessarily means it can't be found. Everything is within the Self. Know the Self and everything is known. That is why one is told to meditate on the Self, contemplate the Self, experience the Self, lose oneself in the Self.

balavatī = strong; **vāsanānādir** = beginningless residual impressions; **kartā bhoktāpi** = doership and enjoyment; **dṛḍhā** = strong, not easily broken, obstinate; **saṁsāra-hetuḥ** = cause of worldly existence; **pratyag-dṛṣṭāt-mani** = state of inward viewing; **nivasatā** = by living; **sāpaneyā prayatnāt** = it should be removed by effort; **muktiṁ** = liberation; **muni** = sages.

ahaṁ maneti yo bhāvo dehākṣādāv-anātmani |
adhyāso'yaṁ nirastavyo viduṣā svātma-niṣṭhayā ||269||

This idea of 'me' and 'mine' exists in the body, the sense organs, and so on, that are the not-self. The wise must destroy this superimposition by being firmly established in their own Self.

See V. 39, 181, 271, 279–86, 307, 393, 407, and 462 on superimposition.

ahaṁ = 'I'; **maneti** = mine; **anātmani** = are the not-self; **adhyāsa** = superimposition; **nirastavyo** = destroyed; **viduṣā** = the wise; **svātma-niṣṭhayā** = established in their own Self.

jñātvā svaṁ pratyag-ātmānaṁ buddhi-tad-vṛtti sākṣiṇaṁ |
so'ham-ityeva sad-vṛttyā' nātmanyātma-matiṁ jahi ||270||

Knowing one's own innermost Self, the witness of the intellect and its modifications, in this manner, conquer the Self in the not-self by the correct thought, 'I am That'.

So'ham means 'I am He' or 'I am That, the supreme Absolute'. Note the Great Saying, 'I am the Absolute' (*aham brahmāsmi*).

See KaivUp 1.18 on witness. See V. 101, 127, 137, 159, 212, 213, 217, 218, 223, 295, 352, 370, 381, 384, 495, 506, 507, and 552 for references to witness (*sākṣī*).

pratyag = innermost; **buddhi-tad-vṛtti sākṣiṇam** = witness of the intellect and its modifications; **so'ham** = I am That, I am he; **jahi** = conquer.

lokānuvartanaṁ tyaktvā tyaktvā dehānuvartanam |
śāstrānuvartanaṁ tyaktvā svādhyāsāpanayaṁ kuru ||271||

Give up the habit of pursuing the ways of the world; give up pursuing the body; give up pursuing the scriptures; accomplish the destruction of the superimposition which characterizes you.

See V. 39, 181, 269, 279–86, 307, 393, 407, and 462 on superimposition.

lokānuvartanaṁ tyaktvā = give up, renounce pursuing the ways of the world; **dehā** = body; **śāstrā** = scriptures; **ādhyāsāpanayaṁ kuru** = accomplish the destruction of superimposition.

loka-vāsanayā jantoḥ śāstra-vāsanayāpi ca |
deha-vāsanayā jñānaṁ yathāvan-naiva jāyate ||272||

True wisdom never arises in a living being who has worldly residual impressions or to those whose residual impressions thrive after scriptural learning or to those who are subject to bodily delusions.

Those who follow the temptations of the world will never experience true wisdom. Those who are subject to bodily delusions will never experience true wisdom. A person must accept certain teachings and put them into practice if they desire true wisdom.

loka-vāsanayā = worldly residual impressions; **śāstra-vāsana** = scriptural residual impressions; **deha-vāsanayā** = bodily residual impressions; **jñānaṁ** = wisdom; **naiva jāyate** = never arises.

saṁsāra-kārāgṛha-mokṣam-icchoḥ
ayomayaṁ pāda-nibandha-śṛṅkhalam |
vadanti tajjñāḥ paṭu-vāsanā-trayaṁ
yo'smād vimuktaḥ samupaiti muktim ||273||

The knowers of the Truth declare that, for those who desire to attain liberation from the prison of worldly life, these three residual impressions are strong iron fetters that bind one's feet. He who is free from them, attains liberation.

See AitUp 2.5, 'A hundred iron forts encaged me' (*śatam mā pura āyasīr arakṣann*).

saṁsāra = worldly life; **kārāgṛha** = prison; **mokṣamicchoḥ** = those who desire freedom, liberation; **ayomayaṁ pāda-nibandha-śṛṅkhalam** = iron fetters tied around one's feet.

jalādi-samparka-vaśāt prabhūta
durgandhadhūtāgaru-divya-vāsanā |
saṅgharṣaṇenaiva vibhāti samyak
vidhūyamāne sati bāhya-gandhe ||274||

The divine fragrance of sandalwood, which has become hidden by a bad odor due to its contact with water and so on, wafts fragrant only when the external odor is removed by rubbing.

Sandalwood, when left in water, emanates an obnoxious odor from the rotting wood. If the wood is taken out of the water and dried out and then rubbed, its essential fragrant nature will emerge once again.

jalādi = water and so on; **samparka** = to mix together, bring into contact, unite; **prabhūta** = come forth, appears, transforms into; **durgandha** = bad smell, stink; **dhūta** = agitated, destroyed; **dhūtāgaru** = sandalwood; **divya** = divine; **saṅgharṣaṇenaiva** = only by rubbing together; **vibhāti** = shines, becomes visible; **samyak** = well, good; **bāhya-gandhe** = external odor.

antaś-śritānanta-duranta-vāsanā
dhūlī-viliptā paramātma-vāsanā
prajñāti-saṅgharṣaṇato viśuddhā
pratīyate candana-gandhavat sphuṭam ||275||

The fragrance of the supreme Self is covered by the dust of endless inauspicious residual impressions. When it is purified by the constant friction of knowledge, it is clearly perceived, just like the fragrance of sandalwood.

Like the sandalwood, the essential nature of the Self will be clearly revealed once the dust of ignorance which has been covering it, is removed.

See BṛhUp 5.15.1 'The face of truth is covered with a golden disc. Unveil it'; also MaitrīUp 6.35.

antaś-śritānanta = imbedded inside; **duranta-vāsantạ** = inauspicious residual impressions; **dhūlī** = dust; **viliptā** = covered over; **paramātma** = supreme Self; **prajñāti-saṅghar-ṣaṇato** = constant association of rubbing with wisdom; **viśuddhā** = purified; **candana-gandhavat** = fragrance of sandalwood; **sphuṭam** = clearly perceived.

anātma-vāsanā-jālaiḥ tirobhūtātma-vāsanā
nityātma-niṣṭhayā teṣāṁ nāśe bhāti svayaṁ sphuṭā ||276||

Desire for the Self is obscured by innumerable desires for the not-self. When they have been destroyed by being constantly established in the Self, it shines clearly by itself.

The sun naturally appears after the destruction of the clouds which conceal it. Likewise, the Self naturally appears when the desires which cover it are destroyed. In a similar way, as light destroys darkness, knowledge destroys ignorance.

See BG 6.26, 'By whatever cause the wavering and unsteady mind wanders, let him curb it from that and subjugate it solely to the Self.'

See V. 11, 138, 150, 177–78, 183, 277, 315, 336, 361–63, 367, 370–71, 384, and 408 for purification of the mind.

anātma = not-self; **tirobhūtātma** = Self is obscured; **nāśe** = destroyed; **bhāti svayaṁ sphuṭā** = clearly shines by itself.

yathā yathā pratyag-avasthitaṁ manaḥ
tathā tathā muñcati bāhya-vāsanām |
niś śeṣa-mokṣe sati vāsanānāṁ
ātmānubhūtiḥ pratibandha-śūnyā ||277||

In that manner, as the mind is gradually established inward, it gives up the external residual impressions. When all the residual impressions have become extinct, there takes place the unobstructed realization of the Self.

The mind naturally begins to turn inwards when it ceases to dwell on external sense objects. The mind vibrates due to what strikes it (like a bell that is struck). If it is praise or pleasure, then it expands; if it is abuse or pain, then it contracts. The mind is the root of all bondage; every tendency comes from it. The mind is the root of all activities. It gives strength to desires. It awakens a sense of duality. It creates distinctions and differences and separates and divides and limits. The mind is the wall that stands between individual and the Absolute. It is the mind which brought the Self to the condition of a limited individual. It is the storehouse of all error/craving/passion/doubt/delusion/ignorance. It is a miraculous thought-producing machine. It creates in one moment and destroys in the next. It naturally runs towards objects. Its natural tendency of thought is outwards. Attachment is what drives thought outwards and attachment is the cause for all misery/pain/trouble. When the mind is attracted to something, there is bondage; when the mind is not attracted, there is freedom.

See V. 11, 138, 150, 177–78, 183, 276, 315, 336, 361–63, 367, 370–71, 384, and 408 for purification of the mind.

yathā yathā = in that manner, likewise; **pratyagavasthitaṁ** = established inwardly; **manaḥ** = mind; **muñcati** = gives up; **bāhya-vāsanām** = external residual impressions.

svātmanyeva sadā sthityā mano naśyati yoginaḥ |
vāsanānāṁ kṣayaścātaḥ svādhyāsāpanayaṁ kuru ||278||

Being solely and unceasingly established in one's own Self, the yogi's mind is no longer there. The residual impressions have been destroyed. Hence, destroy all your inauspicious superimpositions.

To be firmly established in the Self occurs as the result of a disciplined life. As the mind ceases to devitate into sense-indulgences, it becomes more and more fixed in the Self.

See BG 6.25, 'With his mind set in firmness, let him attain quietude little by little; with the mind fixed on the Self, let him not think of anything.'

svātmanyeva sadā sthityā = solely and always being established in oneself; **mano** = mind; **naśyati** = is not; **yoginaḥ** = yogi, spiritual practioner; **vāsanānāṁ kṣayaścātaḥ** = residual impressions have been destroyed; **svādhyāsa** = one's own superimpositions; **apanayaṁ** = taking away, leading away; bad or wicked conduct; **kuru** = therefore, hence.

tamo dvābhyāṁ rajaḥ sattvāt sattvaṁ śuddhena naśyati |
tasmāt sattvam avaṣṭabhya svādhyāsāpanayaṁ kuru ||279||

Darkness is destroyed by the two, active-energy and purity, light; active-energy is destroyed by purity; and purity by the Immaculate. Therefore, taking your stand in purity, destroy all your inauspicious superimpositions.

Darkness (*tamas*) is destroyed by the two (*sattva* and *rajas*); *rajas* is destroyed by *sattva*; *sattva* is destroyed by the Absolute: See V. 112–21 on the *guṇas*.

See V. 39, 181, 269, 271, 279–86, 307, 393, 407, and 462 on superimposition.

tamo = dullness, darkness, laziness; **dvābhyāṁ** = two, dual; **rajaḥ** = active-energy; sattvaṁ = purity, light; **śuddhena** = immaculate; **naśyati** = destroyed; **tasmāt** = therefore.

prārabdhaṁ puṣyati vapur iti niścitya niścalaḥ |
dhairyam ālambya yatnena svādhyāsāpanayaṁ kuru ||280||

Be courageous and fixed in the firm conviction that your previously performed actions will sustain this body, and with intelligent forethought destroy all your inauspicious superimpositions.

According to Advaita, destruction of ignorance alone is liberation (*avidyā-naśa*). White cloth is white. Dirt on it makes it look black. To make it white, wash it. It is not necessary to add whiteness to it.

See V. 39, 181, 269, 271, 279–86, 307, 393, 407, and 462 on superimposition.

See V. 280, 289, 417, 446–47, 452, 454–55, 459–64, and 552 on *prārabdha karma*.

dhairya = intelligence, forethought; **ālambya** = having supported, sustaining; **prārabdhaṁ** = karma-in-action, accumulated-past-actions; **puṣyati** = nourishment, sustain; **vapur** = having form, embodied; **niścitya** = one who has come to a conclusion, resolute upon; **niścalaḥ** = forethought, investigate, conviction, resolution; **dhairyam** = intelligent.

nāhaṁ jīvaḥ paraṁ brahmetyatad-vyāvṛtti-pūrvakam |
vāsanā-vegataḥ prāpta-svādhyāsāpanayaṁ kuru ||281||

Think, 'I am not the individual, but the supreme Absolute', proceeding by elimination, destroy all your inauspicious superimpositions formed by the agitation of residual impressions.

See *Nirvāṇaṣaṭkam* 1, 'I am neither the mind nor the intellect nor the ego nor the mind-stuff; neither the ears nor the tongue nor the senses of smell and sight; neither space nor air nor fire nor water nor earth. I am Consciousness and Bliss.'

See BṛhUp 1.4.10, 'I am the Absolute' (*ahaṁ brahmāsmi*).

See V. 39, 181, 269, 271, 279–86, 307, 393, 407, and 462 on superimposition.

nāhaṁ jīvaḥ = I am not an individual; **paraṁ brahmetyatad** = but the supreme Absolute; **vyāvṛtti** = proceed by elimination, get rid of; **pūrvakam vāsanā** = prior residual impressions; **vegataḥ** = violent, agitated.

śrutyā yuktyā svānubhūtyā jñātvā sārvātmyam ātmanaḥ |
kvacid ābhāsataḥ prāpta-svādhyāsapanayaṁ kuru ||282||

Knowing the Self as the Self of all through scriptures, through reasoning, and through your own realization, destroy all your inauspicious superimpositions which appear, here and there, as reflections.

Advaita is fond of delcaring that one knows through scripture (*śruti*), through reasoning (*yukti*) and through direct experience (*anubhava*). Of these three, direct exprience is always the final court of appeal. The first two are indirect and second hand while the latter is both immediate and direct.

Śaṅkara's Self is involved in each and every experience, both those of the experiencer as well as of the experienced. Thus, it is not open to the charge of being but a hypothetical postulate. It is a fact of direct experience. It cannot be doubted without a logical contradiction. Śaṅkara denied that it could ever be an object of knowledge. 'There is no knowing Reality but only being it.' Thought cannot hold the non-dual Reality in its grasp, for, unlike the world which is circumscribed by space–time conceptions, Reality is relationless. It is impossible to describe in words, that which is free from all distinctions.

See V. 39, 181, 269, 271, 279–86, 307, 393, 407, and 462 on superimposition.

śrutyā yuktyā = through scriptures and reasoning; **svānubhūtyā** = by one's own realization; **jñātvā sārvātmyam ātmanaḥ** = knowing the Self as the Self of all; **kvacid** = here, there, here and there, in various places; **ābhāsataḥ** = reflection.

annādāna-visargābhyām īṣan-nāsti kriyā muneḥ |
tad-ekaniṣṭhayā nityaṁ svādhyāsāpanayaṁ kuru ||283||

The sage has no connection whatsoever with action other than eating and evacuating. Being continually and solely established in That destroys all your inauspicious superimpositions.

In actual fact, the sage has nothing to do with any action, even the consumption of food or its expulsion. The sage knows that (s)he is not the body and thus whatever seemingly happens, in actual fact, nothing is happening. See BG 5.8–9, 'The sage centered in the Self should think, "I do nothing at all" – though seeing, hearing, touching, smelling, eating, going, sleeping, breathing, speaking, emptying, holding, opening and closing the eyes – firm in the thought that the senses move among sense objects.'

See V. 39, 181, 269, 271, 279–86, 307, 393, 407, and 462 on superimposition.

annādāna = taking of food, eating; **visargābhyām** = evacuating, expulsion; **īṣan** = to go, to fly away; **nāsti** = it is not; **kriyā** = action; **muneḥ** = the sage; **tat** = That; **ekaniṣṭhayā nityaṁ** = continually, eternally, and solely established.

tat-tvam-asyādi-vākyottha brahmātmaikatva-bodhataḥ |
brahmaṇyātmatva-dārḍhyāya svādhyāsāpanayaṁ kuru ||284||

For strengthening the sense of oneself in the Absolute, destroy all your inauspicious superimpositions by realizing the oneness of the Absolute and the Ṣelf declared in statements such as 'That thou art'.

See ChānUp 6.8.7, '*tat tvam asi*'. See, on *tat tvam asi*, V. 243, 251, 253–65.

See V. 39, 181, 269, 271, 279–86, 307, 393, 407, and 462 on superimposition.

tat-tvam-asyādi = That thou art and so on; **vākyottha** = declared, that has arisen or is produced in statements; **bodhataḥ** = realizing; **dārḍhyāya** = for strengthening.

ahaṁ-bhāvasya dehe'smin niśśeṣa-vilayāvadhi |
sāvadhānena yuktātmā svādhyāsāpanayaṁ kuru ||285||

With great vigilance and consideration, destroy the feeling 'I am this body', along with all your inauspicious superimpositions, and hence bring about the removal of your superimpositions.

How long should one do spiritual practices? So long as one's identification with them continues. One should do this with great vigilance and care.

See V. 39, 181, 269, 271, 279–86, 307, 393, 407, and 462 on superimposition.

ahaṁ-bhāvasya dehe'smin = the feeling, I am this body; **niśśeṣa-vilayāvadhi** = until the sense of 'I' is destroyed along with the residual impressions **sāvadhānena** = vigilance, to be careful; **yuktātmā** = consideration, reasoning.

pratītir-jīva-jagatoḥ svapnavad-bhāti yāvatā |
tāvan-nirantaraṁ vidvan svādhyāsāpanayaṁ kuru ||286||

Learned one, until the awareness of the individual and the world appears like a dream, ceaselessly remove all your inauspicious superimpositions.

These nine verses (V. 277–286) teach the removal of superimposition so that one will be established in the Self. See V. 39, 181, 269, 271, 279–86, 307, 393, and 407, and 462 on superimposition.

pratītir = appears, going towards, approaching; **jīva-jagatoḥ** svapnavad-**bhāti** = awareness of the individual and the world like a dream; **yāvatā** = as far as, to the end; **tāvan-niran-taraṁ** = ceaselessly, without a break, remove; **vidvan** = learned one.

nidrāyā loka-vārtāyāśśabdāder-api vismṛteḥ |
kvacin-nāvasaraṁ dattvā cintayātmānam-ātmani ||287||

Without giving even the slightest chance to forgetfulness arising from sleep, worldly talk, sounds, and so on, meditate on the Self in your mind.

This verse may also be translated to mean, 'do not give any room for sleep, worldly concerns, sense objects, and forgetfulness.'

See ChānUp 3.18.1, 'One should meditate on the mind as the Absolute' (*mano brahmety upāsītety adhyātman*); also BṛdUp 1.4.7 'the Self is to be meditated upon'.

nidrāyā = from sleep; **loka-vārtāyāśśabdāder** = worldly talk, gossip and objects of sound, music; **vismṛteḥ** = forgetfulness; **kvacin-nāvasaraṁ dattvā** = without, never, not even for a moment, giving the slightest chance; **cintayātmānam-ātmani** = meditate on the Self in your mind.

mātā-pitror-malodbhūtaṁ mala-māṁsa-mayaṁ vapuḥ |
tyaktvā cāṇḍālavad-dūraṁ brahmībhūya kṛtī bhava ||288||

Abandon far away, like an outcast, the body which is full of flesh and its impurities, born of the impurities of the mother and father, become the Absolute and be wise, attain your life's purpose.

The body is doubly impure. It is impure due to it production and it is impure due to its composition.

mātā-pitror = mother and father; **mala-māṁsa-mayaṁ vapuḥ** = the body full of flesh, defects, impurities; **tyaktvā** = abandon far away; **cāṇḍāla** = outcast; **brahmībhūya** = become, understand you are the Absolute; **kṛtī bhava** = attain, become what must be done, be wise.

ghaṭākāśaṁ mahākāśa ivātmānaṁ parātmani |
vilāpyākhaṇḍa-bhāvena tūṣṇīm bhava sadā mune ||289||

As the space in a pot merges into the universal space, merge the individual in the great Self and be ever silent, O sage.

Space is universal, located everywhere. Space enlcosed in a pot is known as *ghaṭākāśa*. This enclosed space is merely conventional. In actuality, space is space. Likewise, the Self appears enclosed by the body and its adjuncts but, in actual fact, this is only seemingly so.

See V. 136, 383, 386, 451, and 566 on space in a pot.
See V. 280, 417, 446–47, 452, 454–55, 459–64, and 552 on *prārabdha karma*.
See V. 119, 164, 220–21, and 386 on *pratibimbavāda*.

ghaṭākāśaṁ = pot-space; **mahākāśa** = universal space; **tūṣṇīm bhava sadā** = be ever silent; **mune** = sage.

sva-prakāśam adhiṣṭhānaṁ svayaṁbhūya sadātmanā |
brahmāṇḍam-api piṇḍāṇḍaṁ tyajyatāṁ mala-bhāṇḍavat ||290||

Being yourself the ever-existent Reality, which is the self-luminous foundation of everything, abandon the universe and your individual body like vessels filled with impurities.

Like separating rice from its husk, dross from gold, dirt from cloth, so too, separate the not-self from the Self.

See IśaUp 1 '. . . do not covet anyone's wealth'

sva-prakāśam = self-luminous; **adhiṣṭhānaṁ** = foundation, support· **svayaṁbhūya sadātmanā** = being yourself the ever-existent Reality; **brahmāṇḍam** = the cosmic egg, the universe; **piṇḍāṇḍaṁ** = individual body; **tyajyatāṁ** = give up, renounce, abandon, never think of; **mala** = defects, impurities, taints; **bhāṇḍavat** = pot, vessel, dish.

cid-ātmani sadānande dehārūḍhām ahaṁ dhiyam |
niveśya liṅgam utsṛjya kevalo bhava sarvadā ||291||

Transfer the 'I'-thought, which has sprung from the body, to the Self, which is consciousness and ever-blissful. Discard the subtle body and remain ever alone.

One's identification with the body is so deep-rooted that one takes it for granted and for certain that one is the body. Who doubts it? Yet, it is just this idea which must be enquired into and eventually discarded.

sadānande = ever-blissful; **dehārūḍhām** = risen, produced from, grown, sprung up from the body; **ahaṁ dhiyam** = 'I'-thought; **niveśya** = dwell, settle in; **liṅgam utsṛjya** = not identifying with the subtle body; **kevalo bhava sarvadā** = be always and ever unattached, alone.

yatraiṣa jagad-ābhāso darpaṇāntaḥ puraṁ yathā |
tad brahmāham iti jñātvā kṛtakṛtyo bhaviṣyasi ||292||

That, wherein this reflection of the world is like a city in a mirror, that Absolute I am. Knowing this, you will have attained fulfillment.

See BṛhUp 2.1.9, 'It is the person here in the mirror that I venerate as the Absolute'; also see ChānUp 8.7.4.

jagadābhāso = reflection of the world; **darpaṇāntaḥ** = mirror; **puraṁ** = city; **tad brahmāham** = that Absolute I am.

yat-satya-bhūtaṁ nija-rūpaṁ ādyaṁ
cid advayānandam arūpam akriyam |
tad-etya mithyā-vapur-utsṛjeta
śailūṣavad veṣam-upāttam-ātmanaḥ ||293||

Having attained that which is real, which is your essential nature, which is non-dual[1] bliss and consciousness, formless and actionless, reject this false body which has covered the Self, like an actor throwing off his mask.

See ŚvetUp 6.19, 'actionless' (*niṣkriyaṁ*).

yat-satya-bhūtaṁ nija-rūpam = your true nature, which is real; **ādyaṁ cid advayānandam** = non-dual bliss and consciousness; **arūpam** = formless; akriyam = actionless; **tad-etya** = having attained that; **mithyā-vapur** = false, unreal, illusory body; **utsṛjeta** = reject; **śailūṣavad veṣam-upāttam** = like an actor throwing off his mask.

sarvātmanā dṛśyam-idaṁ mṛṣaiva
naivāham-arthaḥ kṣaṇikatva-darśanāt |
jānāmyahaṁ sarvam-iti pratītiḥ
kuto'ham-ādeḥ kṣaṇikasya siddhyet ||294||

In all ways, this that is perceived is totally unreal. Neither is the ego real, for it is observed to be momentary. How can the belief, 'I know everything', be true of the ego, which is momentary?

Whatever is perceived is ultimately unreal. All perception begins with the idea of 'I' as the physical body. If the basis on which all perceptions is false, it follows that all perceptions will also be false.

sarvātmanā dṛśyam-idaṁ = in all ways this that is seen; **mṛṣaiva** = totally unreal, false; **kṣaṇikatva-darśanāt** = is observed to be momentary; **siddhyet** = be true, be established, be asserted.

ahaṁ-padārthastvahamādi-sākṣī
nityaṁ suṣuptāv-api bhāva-darśanāt |
brūte hyajo nitya iti śrutissvayaṁ
tat-pratyagātmā sad-asad-vilakṣaṇaḥ ||295||

That which is signified by the 'I' is the witness of the ego. It is eternal, even as seen in the state of deep sleep. The scripture itself says, 'It is unborn, eternal.' That innermost Self is other than the Real or the unreal.

See KaUp 1.1.18, 'It is unborn, eternal . . .'.

See BG 2.20, 'The Self is neither born nor does it die'.

The *sakṣin* and the individual are distinguishable, though not separable. The sakṣin is not identical to the Self because the *sakṣin* is always associated with the *antaḥkaraṇa*. This association is both real and potential. It is real in the waking and dreaming states. It is potential in the deep sleep state (thus the individual loses his individuality in deep sleep). See KaivUp 1.18 on witness. See V. 101, 127, 137, 159, 212, 213, 217, 218, 223, 270, 352, 370, 381, 384, 495, 506, 507, and 552 for references to witness (*sākṣī*).

---

[1] See ChanUp 6.2.1; BṛhUp 1.4.17; AitUp 1.1.1.

aham-padārtha-what is signified by the word 'I'; **sākṣī** = witness; **nityaṁ** = eternal; **suṣupti** = deep sleep; **bhāva-darśanāt** = as seen in; **brūte** = says; **ajo nitya** = unborn and eternal; **śrutissvayaṁ** = scripture itself; **tat-pratyagātmā** = that innermost Self; **sad-asad-vilakṣaṇaḥ** = other than the Real, or unreal.

vikāriṇāṁ sarva-vikāra-vettā
nityo'vikāro bhavituṁ samarhati |
manoratha-svapna-suṣuptiṣu sphuṭam
punaḥ punaḥ dṛṣṭam-asattvam-etayoḥ ||296||

The knower of all changes in things subject to change must doubtless be eternal and changeless. Again and again, the unreality of these two is clearly seen in imaginations, dreams, and deep sleep.

See V. 290 on 'these two' – the individual and the universe.

vikāriṇāṁ = things subject to change; **sarva-vikāra-vettā** = knower of all changes; **nityo'vikāro** = eternal and changeless; **manoratha** = imagination; **svapna-suṣuptiṣu** = dreams and deep sleep; **sphuṭam** = clearly; **punaḥ punaḥ** = again and again; **dṛṣṭam-asattvam** = unreality is seen.

ato'bhimānaṁ tyaja māṁsa-piṇḍe
piṇḍābhimāninyapi buddhi-kalpite |
kāla-trayābādhyaṁ akhaṇḍa-bodhaṁ
jñātvā svam-ātmānam upaihi śāntim ||297||

Therefore, give up your attachment to this lump of flesh, as well as to the ego which is attached to it, which are both imagined by the mind. Realizing your own Self, which is absolute knowledge and which cannot be sublated in any of the three periods of time, attain peace.

The three periods of time are the past, the present, and the future.

ataḥ = therefore; **abhimānaṁ** = attachment, vanity; **tyaja** = renounce, give up; **māṁsa-piṇḍe** = lump of flesh; **buddhi-kalpite** = imagined by the mind; **kāla-trayābādhyaṁ** = unsublatable three periods of time; **upaihi śāntim** = attain peace.

tyajābhimānaṁ kula-gotra-nāma-
rūpāśrameṣvārdra-śavāśriteṣu |
liṅgasya dharmān api kartṛtādīṁ-
styaktvā bhavākhaṇḍa-sukha-svarūpaḥ ||298||

Renounce attachment with family, lineage, name, form, and station in life, which dwell in this living corpse.[1] Similarly, renounce ideas of doership and so on, which are qualities of the subtle body, and remain an embodiment of unbroken bliss.

---

[1] See BṛhUp 1.2.7, 'Then he had this desire: I wish that this corpse of mine would become fit to be sacrificed so I could get myself a living body. Then that corpse became a horse. Because it bloated, it became fit to be sacrificed, that is what gave the name to and discloses the true nature of the horse sacrifice.'

tyajābhimānaṁ = renounce attachment; **kula-gotra-nāma-rūpāśrama** = family, lineage, name, form, and station in life; **ārdra** = soft, living, flowing through; **śavāśriteṣu** = attaching oneself to, dwelling in, inhabiting a dead body, belonging to a corpse; **liṅgasya dharmān** = qualities of the subtle body; **kartṛtādīṁ** = doership and so on; **bhavākhaṇḍa-sukha-svarūpaḥ** = an embodiment of unbroken bliss.

santyanye pratibandhāḥ puṁsaḥ saṁsāra-hetavo dṛṣṭāḥ |
teṣām-evaṁ mūlaṁ prathama-vikāro bhavatyahaṁkāraḥ ||299||

It is observed that there are other obstacles for human beings which cause worldly existence. Of these, egoism is the root, the first modification.

Obstacles to realization include superimposition, ignorance, and egoism. Egoism, or the 'I' thought, is the root cause of bondage.

anye = other than; **pratibandhāḥ** = obstacles; **puṁsaḥ** = human beings; **saṁsāra-hetavo** = cause of worldly existence; **mūlaṁ**-root; **prathama-vikāro** = first modification; **ahaṁkāraḥ** = egoism.

yāvat syāt svasya saṁbandho'haṁkāreṇa durātmanā |
tāvan na leśa-mātrāpi muktivārtā vilakṣaṇā ||300||

As long as one has any connection with the maleficent ego, there cannot be the least talk of liberation which is unique.

Liberation is so pristine and unique that it will not admit of even the slightest identification with the ego.

saṁbandho'haṁkāreṇa = connection with the ego; **durātmanā** = inauspicious nature, maleficent; **vilakṣaṇā** = unique, other than, opposed to.

ahaṁkāra-grahāt muktaḥ svarūpam upapadyate |
candravad vimalaḥ pūrṇaḥ sadānandaḥ svayaṁ-prabhaḥ ||301||

Freed from the grasp of egoism, like the moon freed from the eclipse, one attains one's real nature and is taintless, complete, ever-blissful, self-luminous.

See ChānUp 8.13.1, '. . . like the moon freeing itself from Rāhu's jaws'.
See MuṇḍUp 2.2.11, '*Brahman* alone is all this'. ChānUp 6.2.1, 'It is One alone, without a second'. BṛhUp 4.4.19, 'In *Brahman* there is no diversity whatsoever'.

ahaṁkāra-grahāt muktaḥ = freed from the grasp of egoism; **svarūpam upapadyate** = attains real nature; **candra** = moon; **vimalaḥ** = taintless; **pūrṇaḥ** = full, complete; **sadānandaḥ** = ever-blissful; **svayaṁ-prabhaḥ** = self-luminous.

yo vā puraiṣo'ham-iti pratītaḥ
buddhyā viklpas tamasātimūḍhayā |
tasyaiva niśśesatayā vināśe
brahmātma-bhāvaḥ partibandha-śūnyaḥ ||302||

It is well known that only when that which was perceived earlier to be the 'I' by a deluded intellect, clouded by the darkness of ignorance, is completely destroyed, is the sense of the identity between the Absolute and the individual devoid of obstruction.

See IsāUp 3, 'Into the worlds of the demons, enveloped in blinding darkness, verily do they repair after death who are slayers of the Self.'

va = (indicates what is well-known); **purā eṣaḥ aham iti pratītaḥ** = what was known earlier as 'I'; **tamasa** = ignorance, darkness; **atimūḍhayā** = deluded intellect which does not have the capacity to know; **tasyaiva niśśesatayā vināśe** = completely destroyed, removed without a trace; **partibandha-śūnyaḥ** = devoid of hindrance, obstruction.

brahmānanda-nidhir mahā-balavatā'haṁkāra ghorāhinā
saṁveṣṭyātmani rakṣyate guṇa-mayais-caṇḍais-tribhir mastakaiḥ |
vijñānākhya-mahāsinā dyutimatā vicchidya śīrṣa-trayaṁ
nirmūlyāhim-imaṁ nidhiṁ sukhakaraṁ dhīro'nubhoktuṁ kṣamaḥ ||303||

The treasure of the bliss of the Absolute is guarded by the extremely powerful and terrible snake of egoism who is coiled round it with its three fierce hoods, the *gunas*. The wise, who totally destroy it by severing the three heads with the great shining sword of wisdom, alone can enjoy this treasure which brings bliss.

Like the legendary dragon of old who guards treasure, the bliss of the Absolute is guarded by the serpent of egoism. In order to experience this inner Bliss, one must kill the serpent with the sword of wisdom.

See V. 12, 63, 112, 140, 199, 237, 248, 388, 405, 407, and 550 wherein Śaṅkara makes reference to a snake.

brahmānanda-nidhir = treasure of the bliss of the Absolute; **mahā-balavatā** = of great strength; **ahaṁkāra** = egoism; **ghorāhinā** = terrible snake; **saṁveṣṭyātmani** = having coiled around; **rakṣyate** = protecting, guarding; **guṇa-mayais-caṇḍais-tribhir mastakaiḥ** = by the three hoods forming the three qualities; **mahāsinā** = great sword; **dyutimatā** = which is shining (being sharp); **vicchidya** = completely destroying; **śīrṣa-trayaṁ** = three heads; **imaṁ nidhiṁ sukhakaraṁ** = this treasure which brings bliss; **dhīro** = the wise, one whose mind is controlled; **anubhoktuṁ kṣamaḥ** = has the capacity to enjoy.

yāvad-vā yat-kiñcid viṣa-doṣasphūrtir-asti ced-dehe |
katham-ārogyāya bhavet tadvad ahaṁtāpi yogino muktyai ||304||

As long as there is even a trace of poison in the body, how can one be healthy? Likewise is the effect of egoism in respect of a yogi's liberation.

To be one hundred percent healthy, there cannot be even a trace of poison in one's system. Egoism is analogous to poison.

yat-kiñcid = even a trace, even a small particle; **viṣa** = poison; **dehe** = in the body; **ārogyāya** = healthy.

ahamo'tyanta-nivṛttyā tat-kṛta-nānā-vikalpa-saṁhṛtyā |
pratyak-tattva-vivekād-ayam aham-asmīti vindate tattvam ||305||

By the complete cessation of egoism, by stopping the diverse imaginations created by it, and by discerning the inner reality, one realizes the Truth, 'I am This'.

See BṛhUp 1.4.10, 'I am the Absolute' (*aham brahmāsmi*).

ahamaḥ = egoism; **atyanta nivṛttyā** = completely destroying, total cessation; **tat-kṛta** = produced by it; **nānā-vikalpa** = different, various imaginations, ideas; **pratyak-tattva** = inner reality; **vivekād** = discrimination; **ayam aham-asmīti** = I am This.

ahaṁkartaryasmim ahamiti matiṁ muñca sahasā
vikārātmany-ātma-pratiphala-juṣi svasthitimuṣi |
yad-adhyāsāt prāptā jani-mṛti-jarā-duḥkha-bahulā
pratīcaścinmūrteḥ tava sukhatanoḥ saṁsṛtir-iyam ||306||

Renounce immediately your identification of this 'I' with the ego which, being a modification, is merely the reflected image of the Self and steals away its real nature. It is by such identification that you, who are essentially blissful consciousness, have come to be involved in empirical existence which is full of the miseries of birth, death, old age, and sorrow.

I am the doer, I am the experiencer, 'me and mine', (*ahaṁkāra*, *mamakāra*) are expressions of the ego. These feelings must be destroyed for they are the sources of misery and cover one's essentially blissful nature.

ahamiti matiṁ muñca = renounce immediately the sense of 'I'; **ātma-pratiphala-juṣi** = which captures the reflection of the Self; **svasthi-timuṣi** = that which steals, diverts one's own nature; **adhyāsāt** = superimposition; **prāptā** = appears as acquired; **jani-mṛti-jarā-duḥkha-bahulā** = full of the miseries of birth, death, old age, and sorrows; **pratīcaḥ** = which is inside; **cinmūrteḥ** = form of essential consciousness; **tava** = of you; **sukhatanoḥ** = compacted of bliss; **saṁsṛtiriyam** = this empirical existence.

sadaika-rūpasya cidātmano vibhor
ānanda-mūrter anavadya-kīrteḥ |
naivānyathā kvāpyavikāriṇas-te
vināham-adhyāsam-amuṣya saṁsṛtiḥ ||307||

But for your superimposition of the externally functioning ego, there cannot be worldly existence for you who are always of the same form, who are absolute knowledge, omnipresent, an embodiment of bliss, of untarnished glory, and immutable.

See BSBh, *Adhyāsa bhāṣya*; also ŚvetUp 6.19.
See V. 39, 181, 269, 271, 279–86, 307, 393, 407, and 462 on superimposition.

sadaika-rūpasya = always of the same form; **cidātmano vibhor ānanda-mūrter anavadya-kīrteḥ** = being infinite, made of consciousness, limitless, an embodiment of bliss, untarnished glory, immutable; **te vināham-adhyāsam** = without your superimposition.

tasmād-ahaṁkāram-imaṁ sva-śatruṁ
bhoktur-gale kaṇṭakavat pratītam |
vicchidya vijñāna-mahāsinā sphuṭam
bhuṅkṣvātma-sāmrājya-sukhaṁ yatheṣṭam ||308||

Therefore, uproot this egoism, which is your enemy and is like a thorn stuck in the throat of an eater, by the great sharp sword of knowledge, and then enjoy to your heart's content the bliss of the kingdom of the Self.

Once the ego is removed, one will continuously enjoy the bliss of the Self.

ahaṁkāram = egoism; **sva-śatruṁ** = one's enemy; **bhoktur** = enjoyer, eater; **gala** = throat; **kaṇṭa** = anything pointed, such as the point of a needle or pin; **vicchidya** = uproot; **vijñāna-mahāsinā** = by the great sharp sword of knowledge; **bhuṅkṣvā** = enjoy; **sāmrājya-sukhaṁ** = bliss of the kingdom; **yatheṣṭam** = to your heart's content, as much as you please.

tato'ham-āder vinivartya vṛttim
saṁtyakta-rāgaḥ paramārtha-lābhāt |
tūṣṇīṁ samāssvātma-sukhānubhūtyā
pūrṇātmanā brahmaṇi nirvikalpaḥ ||309||

Now, turning away from the ego, give up attachment to sense objects. Attain the supreme Reality. Dwell in silence. Experience the full bliss of the Self. Remain unchanging and realize your infinite nature in the Absolute.

Śaṅkara's slogan is: 'To experience itself'. The Self is involved in, and is the basis of, one's everyday experience. Immanently here and now, the quest begins and ends. Fundamental to Advaita is the message that ultimately there is no other shore, no bridge, and no path. The Reality is not to be attained, for it is already attained and present, here and now. To realize this is to be liberated. Thus silence is the best conceivable means to convey this wisdom. All else will only increase one's illusion and delusion. Silence – not because there is no answer, but because there is no question. Silence is eloquent because it exactly characterizes the Reality.

aham-ādeḥ = from egoism; **vinivartya** = turn away, desist from, extinguish; **saṁtyakta-rāgaḥ** = give up, renounce, turn away from attachment, desire, lust; **paramārtha-lābhāt** = attain the supreme; **tūṣṇīṁ** = silent; **samāssva** = remain; **ātma-sukhānu-bhūtyā pūrṇātmanā nirvikalpaḥ** = unchanging in the experience of total bliss of the Self.

samūla-kṛtto-pi mahān-ahaṁ punaḥ
vyullekhitaḥ-syād-yadi cetasā kṣaṇam |
sañjīvya vikṣepa-śataṁ karoti
nabhassvatā prāvṛṣi vārido yathā ||310||

Even though completely uprooted, if this mighty ego is allowed to sprout again in the mind, coming to life for even a moment, it will create hundreds of difficulties, like a cloud brought in by the wind during the rainy season.

samūla-kṛttopi = though completely cut asunder or uprooted; **mahān-ahaṁ** = mighty ego; **punaḥ** = again; **vyullekhitaḥ-syād-yadi cetasā kṣaṇam** = if allowed to sprout in the mind again, even for a moment; **vikṣepa-śataṁ** = hundreds of difficulties, perplexities, projections; **karoti** = causing, making, producing; **nabhassvatā** = clouds, rainy season; **prāvṛṣi** = rain; **vārido** = anything which covers or obstructs.

nigṛhya śatror-ahamóvakāśdḥ
kvacin na deyo viṣayānucintayā |
sa eva sañjīvana-hetur-asya
praksīna-jambīra-taror-ivāmbu ||311||

Conquer the enemy, egoism. Give no opportunity to it by thinking of sense objects. Like water sprinkled on a rose-apple tree which has dried up, it is the cause of rejuvenation.

See BG 2.62, 'When a person thinks of objects, attachment for them arises; from attachment comes desire; from desire; from desire comes anger; from anger comes delusion.'

nigṛhya = conquering, vanquishing; **śatror** = enemy; **na deyo** = don't give; **viṣayānu-cintayā** = thinking of sense objects; **sañjīvana-hetur** = cause of rejuvenation, returning to life; **praksīna** = diminished, decayed, vanished; **jambīra** = rose-apple tree; **ivāmbu** = like water.

dehātmanā saṁsthit eva kāmī
vilakṣaṇaḥ kāmayitā kathaṁ syāt |
ato'rtha-sandhāna-paratvam-eva
bheda-prasaktyā bhava-bandha-hetuḥ ||312||

That person alone, who has identified with their body, is greedy. How can one who is otherwise be afflicted with desire? Hence, the predisposition to think of sense objects is the cause of the bondage of worldly life, resulting from a sense of difference.

Who is the renunciant? A person who has given up the immortal Self for a handful of sense objects or one who has renounced a few trinkets and moments of pleasure for eternal Bliss? Belief in a body engenders greed and subsequently pain.

Sense enjoyment has a double sting: it takes off the edge of the sense organs by making them blunt and it sets the mind afire by making the mind desire for more of the same enjoyment. The mind wants enjoyment but the body can't take it. One burns the candle at both ends. One is roasted in one's own desires. Desires are the root of suffering.

dehātmanā saṁsthit eva = that person alone, who has identified with their body; **kāmī** = greedy.

kārya-pravardhanāt bīja-pravṛddhiḥ paridṛśyate |
kārya-nāśat bījanāśas tasmāt kāryaṁ nirodhayet ||313||

It is observable that, when an effect arises, its seed also arises. When the effect is destroyed, its source is destroyed. Therefore, one should subdue the effect.

A living tree produces myriad seeds which in turn will produce myriad trees. However, if the tree is destroyed, there will be no seeds and no future trees.

kārya-pravardhanāt = effect arises; **bīja-pravṛddhiḥ** = seed arises; **paridṛśyate** = observable, seen; **kārya-nāśat** = effect is destroyed.

vāsanā-vṛddhitaḥ kāryaṁ kārya-vṛddhyā ca vāsanā |
vardhate sarvathā puṁsaḥ saṁsāro na nivartate ||314||

Effects increase with the increase of residual impressions and residual impressions increase with the increase of effects. For such a person, worldly existence increases without end.

The previous verse explained how to prevent effects from producing future causes. Effects increase with the increase of latent impressions (*vāsana*). For a person who has residual impressions, worldly existence will be never ending. Thus, it behooves one to destroy one's residual impressions.

vāsanā = residual impressions; **vṛddhitaḥ kāryaṁ** = effects increase; **puṁsaḥ** = person, individual; **saṁsāro** = worldly existence.

saṁsāra-bandha-vicchittyai tad dvayaṁ pradahed yatiḥ |
vāsanā vṛddhir-etābhyām cintayā kriyayā bahiḥ ||315||

For breaking this bondage with worldly existence, a spiritual aspirant should completely burn to ashes these two. Inner thoughts and external actions stimulate residual impressions.

'These two' are effects and residual impressions.

See V. 11, 138, 150, 177–78, 183, 276–77, 336, 361–63, 367, 370–71, 384, and 408 for purification of the mind.

bandha = bondage; **vicchittyai** = complete breaking, destruction; **dvayaṁ** = two, double, duality; **pradahed** = set in motion, burn to ashes; **yatiḥ** = a person given to effort; **vṛddhir-etābhyām** = stimulate, impell; **cintayā** = inner thoughts; **kriyayā bahiḥ** = external actions.

tābhyāṁ pravardhamānā sā sūte saṁsṛtim-ātmanaḥ |
trayāṇāṁ ca kṣayopāyāḥ-sarvāvasthāsu sarvadā ||316||
sarvatra sarvataḥ sarvam brahma-mātrāvalokanaiḥ |
sad-bhava-vāsanādārḍhāt tat-trayaṁ layam-aśnute ||317||

An individual's involvement with worldly existence is nourished by these two. The way to destroy these three, however, is to look upon everything as the Absolute,[1] under all conditions, always, everywhere, and by all means. Through the strengthening of the residual impressions becoming the Absolute, those three are annihilated.

'These two' are effects and residual impressions. 'These three' are effects, residual impressions, and an involvement with worldly existence.

tābhyāṁ pravardhamānā sā = that which grows by these two; **sūte saṁsṛtim-ātmanaḥ** = produces an individual's involvement in worldly existence; **trayāṇāṁ** = three; **kṣayopāyāḥ** = cause of destruction; **sarvāvas-thāsu** = under all conditions, in all states; **sarvadā** = always; **sarvatra** = everywhere; **sarvataḥ** = by all means; **sarvam brahma-mātrāvalo-kanaiḥ** = see everything as the Absolute; **vāsanādārḍhāt** = strengthening of residual impressions.

kriyā-nāśe bhavec-cintānāśo'smād vāsanā-kṣayaḥ |
vāsanā-prakṣayo mokṣaḥ sa jīvan-muktir-iṣyate ||318||

With the destruction of action longing ceases, leading to the destruction of residual tendencies. The destruction of the residual tendencies is itself liberation. It is called liberated-while-living-in-a-body.

For liberated-while-living see BṛhUp 4.4.14, KaUp 2.3.14, MuṇḍUp 2.1.10, KenaUp 2.5, AitUp 2.1.5–6, BṛhUpBh 4.4.6, BG 5.23, BS 3.4.51, BS 4.1.

See V. 72, 419, 429–41, and 552 for liberated-while-living-in-a-body (*jīvanmukti*).

---

[1] See MāṇḍUp 1, 'All this is the Self' (*idam sarvam yadyamātmā*); MuṇḍUp 1, 'For this Absolute is everything'.

kriyā-nāśe = destruction of action; **bhavec-cintānāśo** = longing to become ceases; **vāsanā-kṣayaḥ** = destruction of residual impressions; **mokṣaḥ** = liberation; **jīvanmukti** = liberated-while-living-in-a-body.

sad-vāsanā-sphūrti-vijṛmbhaṇe sati
hy-asau vilīnā tvaham-ādi-vāsanā ।
ati-prakṛṣṭāpyaruṇa-prabhāyāṁ
vilīyate sādhu yathā tamisrā ॥319॥

Upon the manifestation of the residual impression of thinking oneself as the Real, the residual impressions of egoism and so on are completely dissolved even as the most intense darkness disappears in the radiant glow of the rising sun.

When light enters a room, darkness immediately and completely disappears, even if it has been there for millions of years. Likewise, when the sun rises, the darkness of night completely disappears.

hi = surely; **vilīnā** = completely lost, melted, dissolved; **aham-ādi-vāsanā** = residual impressions of egoism; **aruṇa-prabhāyāṁ** = radiant glow of the rising sun; **vilīyate** = disappears, destroyed; **tamisrā** = darkness, dark night.

tamas-tamaḥ-kāryam-anartha-jālaṁ
na dṛśyate satyudite dineśe ।
tathā'dvayānanda-rasānubhūtau
naivāsti bandho na ca duḥkha-gandhaḥ ॥320॥

Darkness and its inauspicious consequences are not seen when the sun has risen. So too, when the nectar of non-dual[1] bliss is experienced, there is no bondage nor even a trace of suffering.

tamas = darkness, laziness, dullness; **tamaḥ-kāryam** = things born of darkness, inauspicious consequences; **anartha** = suffering, harmful; **na dṛśyate** = not seen; **advayānanda-rasānubhūtau** = the exprience of the nectar of the non-dual bliss; **na bandha** = no bondage; **na duḥkha-gandhaḥ** = not even a trace of suffering.

dṛśyaṁ pratītaṁ pravilāpayan svayaṁ
san-mātram ānanda-ghanaṁ vibhāvayan ।
samāhitas-san bahir-antaram vā
kālaṁ nayethāḥ-sati karma-bandhe ॥321॥

Let perceived sense objects, both internal and external, vanish; meditate on the Reality which is an embodiment of bliss. Spend your time watchfully, for any binding residual karma-in-action.

Once one has destroyed their latent impressions, their thoughts, and their actions, meditating on the Reality becomes a real possibilitly.

dṛśyaṁ = seen, perceived; **pravilāpayan** = dissolve, disappear, vanish; **ānanda-ghanaṁ** = compacted of bliss; **vibhāvayan** = clearly perceived; **bahir-antaram** = internal and external; **kālaṁ**-time; **karma-bandhe** = binding actions.

---

[1] See ChanUp 6.2.1 (*ekam evādvitīyam*); BṛhUp 1.4.17; AitUp 1.1.1.

pramādo brahma-niṣṭhāyāṁ na kartavyaḥ kadācana |
pramādo mṛtyur-ityāha bhagavān brahmaṇaḥ sutaḥ ||322||

One should never be negligent in respect of being firmly established in the Absolute. Sanatsujāta, the divine son of the Creator, spoke of negligence as death.

In the *Mahābhārata*, *Udyoga Parvan*, Ch. 40–45, in what is known as the Sanatsujāta-Saṁvāda (the conversation between Sanatkumāra and King Dhṛtarāṣtra), there occur the following words, 'I say that negligence is death itself'.

pramāda = negligence; carelessness; **brahma-niṣṭhāyāṁ** = being firmly established in the Absolute; **na kartavyaḥ** = never be; **kadācana** = at any time; **mṛtyur** = death; **bhagavān brahmaṇaḥ sutaḥ** = the divine son of Brahmā, the Creator (i.e., Sanatsujāta).

na pramādād anartho'nyo jñāninaḥ sva-svarūpataḥ |
tato mohas-tato'haṁ-dhīḥ tato bandhaḥ-tato vyathā ||323||

There is no greater danger for a seeker of wisdom than negligence about one's own real nature. From this arises delusion; from delusion arises egoism; from egoism arises bondage; and from bondage arises misery.

Compare BG 2.62–63, 'When a person dwells in their mind on sense objects, attachment is produced. From attachment springs desire and from desire comes anger; from anger arises bewilderment, from bewilderment loss of memory, and from loss of memory, the destruction of intelligence and from the destruction of intelligence such a one perishes.'

pramādād = negligence, carelessness; **anartha** = harmful, dangerous; **jñāninaḥ** = seeker of wisdom; **sva-svarūpataḥ** = one's own real nature; **moha** = delusion, attachment; **ahaṁ** = egoism; **bandhaḥ** = bondage; **vyathā** = misery, agitation, disturbed mind.

viṣayābhimukhaṁ dṛṣṭvā vidvāṁsam api vismṛtiḥ |
vikṣepayati dhī-doṣaiḥ yoṣā jāram iva priyam ||324||

Finding one turned towards sense objects, forgetfulness, through a defective intellect, bewilders even a learned person, just as a young woman seducing her lover.

This is a reference to a spiritual aspirant who, though well-versed in book knowledge, is easily seduced by a lover.

Compare BG 2.62–63, 'Brooding on the sense objects, humans develop attachment to them; from attachment comes desire; from desire anger arises.'

viṣayābhimukhaṁ dṛṣṭvā = finding, seeing one facing, turned towards sense objects; **vidvāṁsam api** = even a learned person, a person with discrimination; **vismṛtiḥ** = forgetfulness; **vikṣepayati** = bewilders, confounds, drags far away; **dhī-doṣaiḥ** = defective intellect; **yoṣā jāram iva priyam** = like a young woman seducing her lover.

yathā-pakṛṣṭam śaivālaṁ kṣaṇa-mātraṁ na tiṣṭhati |
āvṛṇoti tathā māyā prājñaṁ vāpi parāṅmukham ||325||

Just as moss, even if removed, does not stay away for even a moment, but covers it again, so too, illusion covers the wise if their senses are outwards oriented.

This verse makes even clearer the idea expressed in the previous verse that attachment to sense objects will delude and destroy one. A neglected pond of still water easily becomes covered by moss. It floats on the surface and, from a distance, appears as something it is not, i.e., a large grassy field. Due to this moss the water will no longer reflect the sky, clouds, or the sun. When the moss is removed, the water regains its clarity. So it is likewise with the mind. See V. 151–152 on moss.

pakṛṣṭam = removed; **śaivālaṁ** = moss, algae; **kṣaṇa** = momentary; **āvṛṇoti** = seizes, grasps, covers; **māyā** = illusion; **parāṅmukham** = outward oriented, outward facing.

lakṣyacyutaṁ syād-yadi cittaṁ īṣad
bahir-mukhaṁ sannipatet tatas-tataḥ |
pramādataḥ pracyuta-keli-kandukaḥ
sopāna-paṅktau patito yathā tathā ||326||

If the mind, becoming outwardly inclined, strays ever so slightly from its ideal, it will continuously fall, like a ball inadvertently dropped at the top, falls down the stairs.

Compare the analogy of the bow and arrow in MuṇḍUp 2.2.3–4, 'Take, my friend, this bow, this great weapon of *upaniṣad*'.

lakṣyacyutaṁ = strays, slips from the ideal; **cittam** = mind; **bahir-mukhaṁ** = outwardly facing or inclined; **pracyuta** = to fall down, drop; **keli** = amusement, play; **kandukaḥ** = ball; **sopāna** = stairs, steps; **paṅktau patito** = falling down.

viṣayeṣvāviśac-cetaḥ saṁkalpayati tad-guṇān |
samyak saṁkalpanāt kāmaḥ kāmāt puṁsaḥ pravartanam ||327||

A mind attached to sense objects thinks of their qualities. From deeply thinking about them, desire for them arises. Desire for them leads to action.

See BG 2.62–63, 'When a person dwells in their mind on sense objects, attachment to them is produced. From attachment springs desire and from desire comes anger and so on.'

viṣayeṣvāviśaccetaḥ = a mind attached to sense objects; **saṁkalpayati** = thinks about; **tad-guṇān** = qualilties; **samyak saṁkalpanāt** = by deeply thinking about them; **kāmaḥ** = desire, attachment; **pravartanam** = action, effort to acquire, exhertion.

tataḥ svarūpavibhraṁśo vibhraṣṭastu patatyadhaḥ |
patitasya vinā nāśam punar nāroha īkṣyate ||
saṁkalpam varjayet tasmāt sarvānarthasya kāraṇam |
apathyāni hi vastūni vyādhigrasto yathotsṛjet ||328||

Hence, because of this, a person deviates from their real nature; deviating, they fall down. One who has fallen down comes to ruin and for such there is no rising again. Therefore, just as a sick person should avoid all prohibited edibles, one should totally give up thinking of sense objects, which is the cause of all undoing.

One is the Self, here and now. Forgetting this, when a person erroneously identifies with a body, with a separate 'me', the entire universe springs into existence. The instance one believes that one is distinct and separate from everything else, one falls, one deviates, one is deflected from the truth. Obviously there follows unhappiness, ruin, decay.

tataḥ svarūpavibhraṁśo = then, one wanders about, confused, deviates from one's true nature; **patatyadhaḥ** = one falls; **vinā nāśam** = apart from ruin; **punar** = again; **nāroha** = there is no rising; **sarvānarthasya** = all harmful; **kāraṇam** = causes; **apathyāni** = unsuitable, unwholesome food or drink; **vyādhigrasto** = seized or afflicted with disease.

ataḥ pramādānna paro'sti mṛtyuḥ
vivekino brahmavidaḥ samādhau |
samāhitaḥ siddhimupaiti samyak
samāhitātmā bhava sāvadhānaḥ ||329||

Therefore, for the discriminating one who is a knower of the Absolute, there is no greater death than negligence. But, the person who remains in deep concentration, attains perfection. Therefore, carefully remain in perfect concentration.

Negligence is death. Forgetfulness of one's Self is death.

ataḥ pramādānna = therefore, negligence, carelessness; **paro'sti mṛtyuḥ** = there is no greater death; **vivekino** = discriminating one; **brahmavidaḥ** = knower of the Absolute; **samādhau samāhitaḥ** = remains in one-pointed concentration; **siddhimupaiti** = attains perfection; **sāva-dhānaḥ** = attentive, heedful, careful.

jīvato yasya Kaivalyaṁ videhe sa ca kevalaḥ |
yat-kiñcit paśyato bhedaṁ bhayaṁ brūte yajuḥ śrutiḥ ||330||

One who is completely alone, even while living, is also alone after the body falls. The Yajurveda declares that there is fear for one who sees even the least difference.

See TaittUp 2.7, 'When, on the other hand, a person creates a hollow or fissure within it, then they experience fear' (*atha tasya bhayam bhavati*). Also BṛhUp 1.4.2, 'Since there is nothing else than myself, of what am I afraid? . . . Assuredly, it is from a second that fear arises.' Also BṛhUp 1.5.3, 3.9.26, 4.2.4, 4.3.20, 4.4.22, 4.5.15; ChānUp 1.3.1, 8.9.1, 8.10.1, 8.11.1; TaittUp 2.4; KaUp 3.2, 6.2–3 on freedom from fear.

jīvato = living, is alive; **Kaivalyaṁ** = one who is totally alone; **videhe sa ca** = even after the body falls; **bhedaṁ** = difference, duality; **bhayaṁ** = fear; **brūte** = declares; **yajuḥ** = Yajur; **śrutiḥ** = primary scripture, Veda.

yadā kadā vāpi vipaścid-eṣaḥ
brahmaṇyanante'pyaṇu-mātra-bhedam |
paśyatyathāmuṣya bhayaṁ tadeva
yadīkṣitaṁ bhinnatayā pramādāt ||331||

If, at any time, the wise perceive even the minutest difference in the infinite Absolute, at once, that which is inadvertently seen as different becomes a source of fear to them.

See BṛhUp 1.4.2, 'Since there is nothing else than myself, of what am I afraid? . . . assuredly, it is from a second that fear arises.'

yadā = if (used in this sense of yadi); **kadā vāpi** = at any time; **vipaścid-eṣaḥ** = the wise; **aṇu-mātra-bhedamapi** = even the slightest difference; **yadīkṣitaṁ bhinnatayā pramādāt** = whatever is inadvertently seen as different; **bhaya** = fear.

śruti-smṛti-nyāya-śatair niṣiddhe
dṛśye'tra yaḥ svātma-matiṁ karoti |
upaiti duḥkhopari duḥkha-jātaṁ
niṣiddha-kartā sa malimluco yathā ||332||

One who identifies their own self with perceived objects, which have been denied by hundreds of scriptural texts, scriptural traditions, and reasonings, experiences misery after misery like one with a guilty conscience for having committed a prohibited act.

Because one has forgotten their own Self, the reality they are, obviously their conscience bothers them. They are like a thief in that they lie every time they deny the truth of the ever-present reality and posit that which is not real as real.

śruti = primary scripture; **smṛti** = remembered secondary scriptures; **nyāya** = reason, logic; **śatair** = hundreds; **malimluco** = thief, one with a guilty conscience.

satyābhisandhāna-rato vimukto
mahattvam ātmīyam upaiti nityam |
mithyābhisandhāna-ratas-tu naśyet
dṛṣṭaṁ tad-etad yad acaura-caurayoḥ ||333||

One who is totally established in the Truth is liberated and attains the eternal glory of the Self. However, one who dwells on the unreal perishes. That this is so is illustrated in the case of a thief and of one who is not a thief.

In ChānUp 6.16, there is a story of a man who was accused of theft. 'Take, for example, a handcuffed man brought here by people shouting, "He's a thief! He has committed a theft. Heat an axe for him!" Now, if he is guilty of the crime, then he turns himself into a lie; uttering a falsehood and covering himself in falsehood, he takes hold of the axe and gets burnt, upon which he is executed. If, on the other hand, he is innocent of the crime, then he turns himself into the truth; uttering the truth and covering himself with the truth, he takes hold of the axe and is not burnt, upon which he is released.'

satyābhisandhāna-rato = one who is totally established in the truth; **nityam mahattvam ātmīyamthe** eternal glory of the Self; **upaiti** = attains; **mithyābhisandhāna** = one who dwells on the false, unreal; **caurayoḥ** = thief.

yatir-asad-anusandhiṁ bandha-hetuṁ vihāya
svayam-ayam-aham-asmītyātma-dṛṣṭyaiva tiṣṭhet |
sukhayati nanu niṣṭhā brahmaṇi svānubhūtyā
harati param-avidyā-kārya-duḥkhaṁ pratītam ||334||

A spiritual aspirant should give up all thoughts of the unreal, which cause bondage, and should remain steadfast in contemplation of the Self, in the form of, 'I am This'. Surely, steadfast contemplation and self-realization of the Absolute give rise to bliss and destroy the previously experienced intense sufferings caused by ignorance.

'I am This' is the great knowledge of Vedānta which boldly declares the identity of the individual and the Absolute (*mahāvākya*, the Great Sayings of the *Upaniṣads*). Traditionally, they are four in number: *prajñānam brahma* which occurs in the AitUp of the *Ṛg Veda; ayam ātma brahma* which occurs in the MāṇḍUp of the *Atharva Veda; tat tvam asi* which occurs in the ChānUp of the *Sāma Veda*; and *aham brahmāsmi* which occurs in the BṛhUp of the *Yajur Veda*).

yatir = spiritual aspirant; **asad** = unreal; **bandha-hetuṁ** = cause of bondage; **vihāya** = giving up; **ayam-aham** = I am This; **sukhayati** = causes happiness; **harati** = destroys; **param** = intense, extreme; **avidyā-kārya-duḥkhaṁ** = sufferings caused by ignorance.

bāhyānusandhiḥ parivardhayet phalaṁ
durvāsanām-eva tatas tato'dhikām |
jñātvā vivekaiḥ parihṛtya bāhyaṁ
svātmānusandhiṁ vidadhīta nityam ||335||

Attachment to external objects will only increase and intensify their fruits in the form of inauspicious tendencies. Therefore, knowing this by means of wise discrimination, abandon all that is external. Apply yourself in continuous uninterrupted contemplation of the Self.

bāhyānusandhiḥ = attachment to externals; **phalaṁ** = fruits, results; **durvāsanām** = inauspicious; **bāhyaṁ** = external; **svāt-mānu-sandhiṁ nityam** = continuous, eternal contemplation of the Self.

bāhye niruddhe manasaḥ prasannatā
manaḥ-prasāde paramātma-darśanam |
tasmin sudṛṣṭe bhava-bandha-nāśaḥ
bahir-nirodhaḥ padavī vimukteḥ ||336||

When the external abates, the mind becomes clear. When the mind is bright, there arises the vision of the great Self. When that is perfectly realized, bondage to the world is destroyed. Therefore, the cessation of the external is the initial step in attaining liberation.

See V. 11, 138, 150, 177–78, 183, 276–77, 315, 361–63, 367, 370–71, 384, and 408 for purification of the mind.

See BG 2.65, 'In tranquillity, all one's sorrow is destroyed. For the intellect of the tranquil-minded is soon established in equilibrium.'

bāhye = external; **niruddhe** = ceases, abates; **manasaḥ** = mind; **prasannatā** = bright, clear, pure; **prasāde** = bright; **paramātma-darśanam** = vision of the supreme Self; **sudṛṣṭe** = perfectly seen realized; **bhava-bandha-nāśaḥ** = destruction of worldly bondage; **bahir-nirodhaḥ padavī vimukteḥ** = cessation of the external is the initial step to liberation.

kaḥ paṇḍitaḥ-san sad-asad-vivekī
śruti-pramāṇaḥ paramārtha-darśī |
jānan hi kuryād asato'valambaṁ
svapāta-hetoḥ śiśuvan-mumukṣuḥ ||337||

Who, being learned, able to discriminate between the Real and the unreal, believing in the authority of the scriptures, qualified to realize the supreme Self, and a seeker of liberation, will, like a child, cling to what is unreal and which will surely be the cause of one's downfall?

See verse 4 in regard to this verse.

paṇḍitaḥ = learned, scholar; **sad-asad-vivekī** = discrimination between the Real and the unreal; **śruti-pramāṇaḥ** = scriptural authority; **paramārtha-darśī** = one qualified to see the supreme Self; **jānan hi** = knowing surely; **kuryād** = who will do; **avalambaṁ** = going in for support, cling to; **svapāta-hetoḥ** = which is the cause of one's downfall; **śiśuvan** = child.

dehādi-saṁsaktimato na muktiḥ
muktasya dehādyabhimatyabhāvaḥ |
suptasya no jāgaraṇaṁ na jāgrataḥ
svapnas tayor bhinna-guṇāśrayatvāt ||338||

There is no liberation for one who is attached to the body, and the liberated being has no attachment to the body. One who is asleep is not awake, and one who is awake does not dream, for these two refer to two different states.

If one wants to go North, one should not go South. One who is asleep is not awake and one is dreaming is not awake. This should be obvious.

dehādi = body and so on; **saṁsaktimato** = one who is attached to; **na muktiḥ** = no liberation; **dehādyabhimatyabhāvaḥ** = no attachment to the body; **suptasya** = one who is asleep; **no jāgaraṇaṁ** = not awake; **svapna** = dream.

antar-bahiḥ svaṁ sthira-jaṅgameṣu
jñānātmanādhāratayā vilokya |
tyaktākhilopādhir-akhaṇḍa-rūpaḥ
pūrṇātmanā yaḥ sthita eṣa muktaḥ ||339||

One is liberated who realizes the Self as knowledge, the substratum of all that moves and is unmoving, both internal and external; and who, abandoning all limitations, remains in an infinite and complete state.

See IśāUp 4, 'The Self is One, although not moving, It is swifter than the mind; the gods cannot catch it, as it speeds on in front. Standing, it outpaces others who run.'

antar-bahiḥ = internal and external; **sthira-jaṅgameṣu** = in objects which move and do not move; **jñānātmanādhāratayāvilokya** = who realizes the Self as knowledge; **tyaktākhilopādhir** = abandoning all residual limitations.

sarvātmanā bandha-vimukti-hetuḥ
sarvātma-bhāvān-na paro'sti kaścit |
dṛśyāgrahe satyupapadyate'sau
sarvātma-bhāvo'sya sadātma-niṣṭhayā ||340||

There is no other means for complete freedom from bondage than to identify oneself with the entire universe. This identification arises by rejecting the perceptible world by continuous meditation on the eternal Self.

See KaUp 5.13, 'He is the eternal in the midst of the non-eternals' (*nityo'nityānaṁ*).

bandha-vimukti-hetuḥ = the cause of freedom from bondage; **sarvātma-bhāvānna paro'sti** = identify oneself with the entire universe; **dṛśyāgrahe** = rejecting, not grasping the seen; **sadātma** = eternal Self; **niṣṭhayā** = continuous, established in.

dṛśyasyāgrahaṇaṁ kathaṁ nu ghaṭate dehātmanā tiṣṭhato
bāhyārthānubhava-prasakta-manasaḥ tat-tat-kriyāṁ kurvataḥ |
saṁnyastākhila-dharma-karma-viṣayaiḥ nityātma-niṣṭhā-paraiḥ
tattvajñaiḥ karaṇīyam ātmani sadānandecchubhir yatnataḥ ||341||

How will the non-perception of the visible universe be possible for one who lives identified with the physical body and whose mind is attached to enjoyment of external objects and acts accordingly? It can only be accomplished with great effort by spiritual aspirants, desirous of bliss, who have renounced all actions relating to sense objects and who are are established in the eternal Self.

dṛśyasyāgrahaṇaṁ = non-grasping; **kathaṁ nu ghaṭate** = how will it be possible?; **dehātmanā tiṣṭhato** = one who is established in a state of identifying the Self with the body; **bāhyārthānu-bhava-prasakta-manasaḥ** = one whose mind thinks of external objects; **kriyāṁ kurvataḥ** = doing specific actions; **saṁnyastākhila-dharma-karma-viṣayaiḥ** = those who have renounced all duties, actions, and sense objects; **nityātma-niṣṭhā** = those who are always established in the eternal Self.

sarvātma-siddhaye bhikṣoḥ kṛta-śravaṇa-karmaṇaḥ |
samādhiṁ vidadhātyeṣā śānto dānta iti śrutiḥ ||342||

For the renunciant, who has engaged in hearing[1] in order to accomplish universal identification, the scriptural passage beginning with, 'calmness, self-control, and so on',[2] prescribes one-pointed absorption of the intellect in That.

See V. 343, 354, 355, 358, 361, 363–67, 376, 408–411, and 474 on *samādhi*.

sarvātma = universal identification; **siddhaye** = accomplish, perfect; **bhikṣoḥ** = the renunciant; **kṛta-śravaṇa** = engaged in hearing; **samādhiṁ** = one = pointed absorption of the intellect in That, equal-mindedness; **vidadhāti** = prescribes, teaches; **śānto dānta** = calmness, self-control, etc.

ārūḍha-śakter-ahamo vināśaḥ
kartuṁ na śakyaḥ sahasāpi paṇḍitaiḥ |
ye nirvikalpākhya-samādhi-niścalāḥ
tān-antarā'nanta-bhavā hi vāsanāḥ ||343||

Even the learned cannot suddenly destroy egoism once its power has grown strong, except by those who are perfectly calm[3] and unmoving in an indeterminate one-pointed absorption of the intellect in That. For residual impressions are long-rooted and innumerable.

---

[1] See BṛhUp 2.4.5, 4.5.6, '. . . to be heard, to be reflected on, to be meditated upon'. See V. 67, 70, 72, and 365 on 'hearing'.

[2] See BṛhUp 4.4.23, '. . . having become calm, self-controlled, withdrawn, patient, and collected'.

[3] See BṛhUp 4.4.23, 'having become calm . . .' (*śānto*).

See V. 342, 354, 355, 358, 361, 363–67, 376, 408–411, and 474 on *samādhi*.

ārūḍha-śakter = power grown strong; **ahamo vināśaḥ** = destruction of the ego; **kartuṁ na śakyaḥ sahasā** = impossible to effect quickly; **paṇḍitaiḥ** = even by learned ones; **nirvikalpākhya-samādhi** = indeterminate one-pointed absorption of the intellect in That; **niścalāḥ** = unmoving; **tān-antarā** = except by them; **hi** = for; **vāsanāḥ** = residual tendencies; **anantabhavāḥ** = those which have numerous births or those produced by many objects.

ahaṁ-buddhyāiva mohinyā yojayitvāvṛter-balāt |
vikṣepa-śaktiḥ puruṣaṁ vikṣepayati tad-guṇaiḥ ||344||

The power of projection, aided by the power of concealment, causes a person to identify with egoism, thereby deluding him through the attributes of that.

See V. 115–17, 141, 146, 345, and 348 on veiling power.

mohinyā = deluding, perplexing, distracting; **ahaṁ-buddhyāiva-yojayitvā** = to connect or identity with a sense of egoism; **āvṛter-balāt** = produced by the power of projection; **vikṣepa-śaktiḥ** = power of concealment; **puruṣaṁ** = individual, person; **tad-guṇaiḥ** = the attributes of that.

vikṣepa-śakti-vijayo viṣamo vidhātuṁ
niśśeṣam-āvaraṇa-śakti-nivṛttyabhāve |
dṛg-dṛśyayoḥ sphuṭa-payojalavad-vibhāge
naśyet tad-āvaraṇam-ātmani ca svabhāvāt |
nissaṁśayena bhavati pratibandha-śūnyo
nikṣepaṇaṁ nahi tadā yadi cen mṛṣārthe ||345||

It is difficult to overcome the power of projection without the total removal of the power of concealment. The power of concealment will vanish naturally when a person can distinguish clearly the seer and the seen, like milk and water. This victory over the power of concealment is truly free from obstacles when there is no resting in false sense objects.

See V. 115–17, 141, 146, 344, and 348 on veiling power.

vikṣepa-śakti = power of projection; **vijayo** = overcome; **āvaraṇa-śakti** = power of concealment; **nivṛttyabhāve** = removal, negation, withdrawal; **dṛg-dṛśyayoḥ** = seer and the seen; **sphuṭa** = clearly; **payojalavad** = like water and milk; **śūnyo** = devoid of, free from; **mṛṣārthe** = false objects.

samyag-vivekaḥ sphuṭa-bodha-janyaḥ
vibhajya dṛg-dṛśya-padārtha-tattvam |
chinatti māyākṛta-moha-bandhaṁ
yasmād vimuktasya punar na saṁsṛtiḥ ||346||

Perfect discrimination is born from a clear knowledge separating the true nature of the seer and the seen. This breaks the bonds of delusion caused by illusion. From that arises liberation and there is no transmigration again.

See V. 2, and 11 on discrimination.

samyag-vivekaḥ = perfect discrimination; **sphuṭa-bodha-janyaḥ** = born of clear knowledge; **vibhajya** = separating; **dṛg-dṛśya** = seer and seen; **padārtha-tattvam** = the true nature; **chinatti** = breaks, destroys; **māyākṛta-moha-bandhaṁ** = the bonds of delusion caused by illusion; **punar na saṁsṛtiḥ** = no worldly existence or transmigration again.

parāvar'aikatva-viveka-vahniḥ
dahaty-avidyā-gahanaṁ hy-aśeṣam |
kiṁ syāt punaḥ saṁsaraṇasya bījam
advaita-bhāvaṁ samupeyuṣo'sya ||347||

For this reason, the discriminative knowledge of the oneness of the individual and the Absolute is a fire which entirely consumes the impenetrable forest of ignorance. For one who has attained this sense of oneness, what will remain of the seed of worldly existence?

para avara ekatva-viveka-vahniḥ = the discriminative knowledge which relates to the oneness of both is a fire; **dahat** = burns, consumes by fire; **avidyā** = ignorance; **gahanaṁ** = deep, dense, thick, impervious, impenetrable, hard to be understood, abyss, forest, cave, darkness; **hi** = for this reason; **aśeṣam** = along with all its products; **saṁsaraṇasya bījam** = seed of worldly existence; **advaita-bhāvaṁ** = sense of non-duality.

āvaraṇasya nivṛttir bhavati ca samyak padārtha-darśanataḥ |
mithyā-jñāna-vināśaḥ tad-vikṣepa janita-duḥkha-nivṛttiḥ ||348||

The power of concealment withdraws when a vision of reality is experienced. So too, the removal of illusory knowledge and suffering produced by false projections withdraws.

See V. 115–117, 141, 146, 344, and 345 on veiling power.

āvaraṇasya nivṛttir = power of concealment withdraws, is removed or negated; **samyak padārtha-darśanataḥ** = vision of reality; **mithyā-jñāna-vināśaḥ** = removal of illusory knowledge; **janita** = produced by; **duḥkha** = suffering.

etat tritayaṁ dṛṣṭaṁ samyag-rajju-svarūpa-vijñānāt |
tasmād vastu satattvaṁ jñātavyaṁ bandha-muktaye viduṣā ||349||

These three are seen in the rope when its true nature is correctly known. Therefore, the wise should know the true nature about things in order to be released from bondage.

'These three' are removal of the concealment of the rope; the destruction of the delusion of the snake; the removal of the grief ensuing in fear and trembling caused by the projection of the snake on the rope.

etat tritayaṁ = these three; **dṛṣṭaṁ** = are seen; **rajju** = rope; **svarūpa-vijñānāt** = true nature is known; **vastu satattvaṁ** = true nature of things; **viduṣā** = the wise.

ayo'gni-yogādiva sat-samanvayāt
mātrādi-rūpeṇa vijṛmbhate dhīḥ |
tat-kāryam-eva tritayam yato mṛṣā
dṛṣṭam bhrama-svapna-manorathesu ||350||

Like iron coming together with fire manifests as fire, the intellect takes various forms itself, as a knower and so on, through the inherence of the Absolute. As a result of it, these three are falsely seen in delusions, dreams, and imaginations.

See KaUp 2.2.9, 'As fire which is one, entering this world becomes varied in shape according to the object, so also the one Self within all beings becomes varied according to whatever it enters and also exists outside'; also Maitrī Up. 3.3. See V. 135, 193, and 507 on fire in iron.

The word *mātrādi* can be split two ways: as *mātrā* + *ādi* or as *mātṛ* + *ādi*. The former gives the meaning of 'sparks' while the latter means 'knower and known'.

'These three' are the seer, the seen, and the act of seeing. All acts of knowing involve these three (*tripuṭī*).

ayo = iron, metal; **agni** = fire; **yogādiva** = coming together like; **samanvayāt** = inherence; **mātrādi-rūpeṇa vijṛmbhate** = takes various forms; **dhīḥ** = intellect; **tritayam** = three; **mṛṣā dṛṣṭam** = falsely seen; **bhrama-svapna-manorathesu** = delusions, dreams, and imaginations.

tato vikārāḥ prakṛter ahaṁ-mukhāḥ
dehāvasānā viṣayāś ca sarve |
kṣaṇe'nyathā-bhāvina eṣa ātmā
nodeti nāpyeti kadāpi nānyathā ||351||

Therefore, all the modifications of primordial nature from egoism to the body to all sense objects are subject to continual change. But, the Self never changes, being never originated, never destroyed.

Advaita defines the real as that which never changes, the unreal as that which never appears, and the non-real as that which is sublated. BSBh 2.16 says, 'The division of real and non-real depends upon knowledge or experience: That is real whose knowledge does not miscarry; the non-real, on the other hand, is the object of a knowledge which fails or goes astray.' Also see BSBh 2.1.1 and 3.2.4. Thus, the real is that which lasts, which suffers no contradiction or sublation, which is eternal. Things of the world may be said to be (seemingly) real until they suffer sublation. Thus, they are known as non-real (*mithyā*).

vikārāḥ = changes, modifications; **prakṛter** = primordial nature; **ahaṁ-mukhāḥ** = egoism; **dehāvasānā** = bodily impressions; **viṣayāś** = sense objects.

nityādvayākhaṇḍa-cid-eka-rūpo
buddhyādi sākṣī sad-asad-vilakṣaṇaḥ |
ahaṁ-pada-pratyaya-lakṣitārthaḥ
pratyak sadānanda-ghanaḥ parātmā ||352||

The Supreme Self is eternal, non-dual,[1] indivisible consciousness, ever of the same form, the witness of the intelligence, and so on, other than the Real and the unreal, the implied meaning indicated of the word 'I', the innermost supreme Self, an embodiment of eternal bliss.

[1] See ChanUp 6.2.1 (*ekam evādvitīyam*); BṛhUp 1.4.17; AitUp 1.1.1.

See KaivUp 1.18 on witness. See V. 101, 127, 137, 159, 212, 213, 217, 218, 223, 270, 295, 370, 381, 384, 495, 506, 507, and 552 for references to witness.

nityādvayākhaṇḍa = eternal, non-dual, indivisible; **cid** = consciousness; **eka-rūpo** = single form; **buddhyādi sākṣī** = witness of the intellect; **sad-asad-vilakṣaṇaḥ** = other than the Real and the unreal; **ahaṁ-pada** = the word 'I'; **pratyaya** = innermost; **lakṣitārthaḥ** = implied meaning, sescondary meaning; **sadānanda-ghanaḥ** = compacted of eternal bliss; **parātmā** = supreme Self.

itthaṁ vipaścit sad-asad vibhajya
niścitya tattvaṁ nija-bodha-dṛṣṭā |
jñātvā svam-ātmānam akhaṇḍa-bodhaṁ
tebhyo vimuktaḥ svayam-eva śāmyati ||353||

Thus, the wise person, discriminating between the Real and the unreal, determining the Truth by one's own eye of wisdom, knowing one's own Self to be indivisible knowledge, freed from all that is the not-self, remains as the pure effulgent Self alone.

In V. 351–52, that which is unreal was explained. In verse 352, the Real was explained. A wise person will discriminate between the Real and the unreal.

See V. 20–21 for discrimination between the Real and the unreal.

itthaṁ = thus; **vipaścit** = wise person; **sad-asad vibhajya** = discriminating between the Real and the unreal; **niścitya tattvaṁ** = determining the truth; **nija-bodha-dṛṣṭājñātvā** = by one's own innate eye of wisdom; **akhaṇḍa-bodhaṁ** = indivisible knowledge; **tebhyo vimuktaḥ** = being completely freed from things; **svayam-eva śāmyati** = remaining alone as the pure effulgent Self.

ajñāna-hṛdaya-granther niśśesa-vilayas-tadā |
samādhinā'vikalpena yadādvaitātma-darśanam ||354||

When the non-dual[1] Self is directly experienced by means of impartite one-pointed absorption of the intellect in That, then the heart's knot of ignorance is completely destroyed.

Everyone says 'I', but who is making an effort to know what that 'I' exactly it is? One usually means this 'body.' On a deeper level we mean faculties of thinking/feeling/willing. One can easily understand that the body is not 'I' since it is insentient. This means that the body is always the known one, not the knower. If the body were you, why do you say, 'My body?' Does anyone ever say, 'I am the clothes, I am the gold?' It is mistaking this superimposition for a fact to think body is 'I'. Then, what is this 'I?' In the body arises a sense of awareness. As a collection this is usually called the mind. What is this mind – a collection of thoughts. And this collection is where the 'I' functions as their basis. Every thought relates to you, the 'I', either directly about you or connected with you as individuals, objects, things, events, opinions. In other words, every thought is rooted in your 'I'. So what is this 'I' – where is it rooted? Track it to its source. This is called *ātma vicāra* or an enquiry into the Self. This is the Self-enquiry which the *Vivekacūḍāmani* proclaims. One will realize that no amount of thought will enable one to realize that which is beyond thought. Thus, abide in the

[1] See ChanUp 6.2.1; BṛhUp 1.4.17; AitUp 1.1.1.

Self as it is. What is it that prevents us from doing this? The Self ever shines, ever present. Instead of abiding in Self, the ego arises, the thought that I am a separate individual who feels I am the body. This ego is the first root thought, the 'I' thought, all else needs this ego to exist. To remain as Self, all we need do is remove this initial obstruction, the first thought.

Between the ever-luminous Self (which neither rises nor sets) and the non-real not-self, the insentient body (which cannot of its own accord say, 'I'), arises a false 'I' which is limited to the body, the ego, called *cit-acit-granthi* – the knot between the sentient Self and the insentient body. Along with it arises ideas of bondage, desire, etc. How does this false 'I' arise – by grasping a form/a body. By grasping, it feeds upon forms and endures. Leaving one form, it grasps another, devouring, growing, enduring. So long as one does not enquire into who this false 'I' is, it will continue to live.

There is a story about this. Once, a man posed as a friend of both the bride and groom and attended their wedding. So long as everyone believed he was an invited guest, he got on very happily talking to both parties and feasting sumptuously. But as soon as an enquiry was started about him, as soon as people began to find out who he was, he disappeared. Such is the case with the ego – it poses as both Self and body. It seems to possess consciousness and shine with 'I' thought (which are properties of Self) and, at same time, it is limited to a form and it rises and sets.

Why does ego disappear when enquired into? It exists only when grasping forms. Without names and forms it cannot live. All thought, all objects, all knowledge of the second and third person (you/he/she/it) are only forms. It has no form of itself. To attend to itself is to lose strength, subside and finally disappear. There are not two 'I''s, the ego and the Self. There is not duality during spiritual practices and non-duality during liberation. There is only the ocean of the Self. In It all ideas/feelings/thoughts arise. Moreover, thoughts arise because we think them. They do not impose upon us. They have no power of their own. They gain power only by our attending to them. Pay them no attention; they will subside. Deny them, ignore them; you will be free. To accept them, and then to struggle with them, is to give them life. You will never win. Note that the mind functions only when the 'I' functions. Deep sleep shows this. All thoughts function only when the 'I'-thought is there. When the 'I'-thought is not there, the world, the mind and the body don't exist. Anyone can observe that the mind is quiet or disappears when one is deep asleeply, only to reppear when one wakes. This means that the 'I'-thought daily rises and sets. Follow the 'I'-thought back to its point of rising. See where it sets. This 'I'-thought is the only clue one has about oneself.

See MuṇḍUp 2.2.9, 'The knot of the heart is cut'; KaUp 2.3.15, 'When all the knots that fetter here the heart are cut asunder then a moral becomes immortal'; ChānUp 7.26.2, 'There is release from all the knots of the heart'.

See V. 342, 343, 355, 358, 361, 363–67, 376, 408–11, and 474 on *samādhi*.

ajñāna-hṛdaya-granther = heart's knot of ignorance; **niśśṣesa-vilayas** = completely destroyed; **tadā** = then, there arises; **samādhinā'vikalpena** = by means of impartite one-pointed absorption of the intellect in That; **yadād-vaitātma-darśanam** = when, sight of, direct experience of the non-dual Self.

tvam aham idam-itīyaṁ kalpanā buddhi-doṣāt
prabhavati paramātmanyadvaye nirviśeṣe |
pravilasati samādhāvasya sarvo vikalpo
vilayanam upagacchet vastu-tattvāvadhṛtyā ||355||

Imaginations of difference such as 'you', 'I', and 'this' arise in the qualityless, non-dual[1] supreme Self due to impurities of the mind. When this shines forth in one-pointed absorption of the intellect in That, all these imaginations will vanish because the Reality has been firmly apprehended.

See V. 342, 343, 354, 358, 361, 363–67, 376, 408–11, and 474 on *samādhi*.

tvam = you; aham = 'I'; idam = this; **buddhi-doṣāt** = impurities of the mind; **prabhavati** = arise; **paramātmanyadvaye nirviśeṣe** = qualityless non-dual supreme Self **sarvo vikalpo** = all doubts, imaginations; **upagacchet** = will attain; **vastu-tattvāvadhṛtyā** = firm apprehension of the reality, of the real nature of the Self.

śānto dāntaḥ param-uparataḥ kṣānti-yuktaḥ samādhiṁ
kurvan nityam kalayati yatiḥ svasya sarvātma-bhāvam |
tenāvidyā-timira-janitān sādhu dagdhvā vikalpān
brahmākṛtyā nivasati sukhaṁ niṣkriyo nirvikalpaḥ ||356||

Possessing tranquillity, self-control, perfectly with-drawn from all external activity, steadfast in forbearance, always being one-pointedly absorbed, a spiritual aspirant experiences oneness with everything. By these means, completely burning all wrong ideas caused by the darkness of ignorance, such a one remains in the blissful state of the Absolute, actionless and free from imaginations.

See BṛhUp 4.4.23, '. . . having become calm, self-controlled, withdrawn, patient, and collected sees the Self in one's own self, sees all in the Self.'
See ŚvetUp 6.19, 'actionless' (***niṣkriyaṁ***).

śānto = peace, tranquillity; **dāntaḥ** = self-control, restraint; **param-uparataḥ** = perfect power to ensure that the senses may not once again be tempted towards worldly objects; **kṣānti-yuktaḥ** = enduring the dualities with fortitude; **samādhiṁ** = one-pointed absorption of the intellect in That; **yatiḥ** = spiritual aspirant, renunciant; **svasya sarvātma-bhāvam** = experiencing oneness or aloneness with everything; **tenāvidyā** = by that ignorance; **timira** = darkness, obscuration; **vikalpān brahmākṛtyā nivasati sukhaṁ niṣkriyo nirvikalpaḥ** = actionless and free from imaginations, doubts, such a one remains, lives, in the blissful state of the Absolute.

samāhitā ye pravilāpya bāhyaṁ
śrotrādi cetaḥ svam-ahaṁ cid-ātmani |
ta eva muktā bhava-pāśa-bandhaiḥ
nānye tu pārokṣya-kathābhidhāyinaḥ ||357||

They alone are free from the binding noose of worldly life who merge the external things such as the ear and so on, the mind, and one's ego in the pure consciousness of the Self; never others who merely talk of a thing not experienced by them.

It is one thing to talk of the Self; it is quite another to be free from ignorance. See KaUp 6.12, 'Not by speech, not by the mind, not by sight can That be grasped'.

---

[1] See ChanUp 6.2.1 (*ekam evādvitīyam*); BṛhUp 1.4.17; AitUp 1.1.1.

samāhitā = held together, combined, one who has collected his thought together; **ye** = those persons; **pravilāpya** = apart from; **bāhyaṁ śrotrādi** = external things like the ear and so on; **cetaḥ** = the mind; **svam-ahaṁ** = one's ego; **ta eva** = they only; **muktā** = are freed; **bhava-pāśa-bandhaiḥ** = from the binding noose of worldly life; **nānye tu** = not others at all; **pārokṣya-kathābhidhāyinaḥ** = those who merely speak of a thing not experienced by them.

upādhi-yogāt svayam-eva bhidyate-
copādhyapohe svayam-eva kevalaḥ |
tasmād-upādheḥ vilayāya vidvān
vaset sadā'kalpa-samādhi-niṣṭhayā ||358||

By association with limiting adjuncts, one thinks oneself different. When the limiting adjuncts are removed, one remains alone. Therefore, the wise should remain forever established in one-pointed absorption of the intellect in That for the dissolution of the limiting adjuncts.

See KaUp 4.10, 'From death to death he goes, who sees here any kind of diversity'.
See V. 342, 343, 354, 355, 361, 363–67, 376, 408–11, and 474 on *samādhi*.

upādhi-yogāt = by association with limiting adjuncts; **upādhya-pohe** = removal of the limiting adjuncts; **kevalaḥ** = totally alone; **vilayāya** = dissolution, disappearance, death, destruction; **vidvān** = the wise; **vaset sadā'kalpa-samādhi-niṣṭhayā** = remain forever established in one-pointed absorption of the intellect in That.

sati sakto naro yāti sad-bhāvaṁ hyeka-niṣṭhayā |
kīṭako bhramaraṁ dhyāyan bhramaratvāya kalpate ||359||

A person one-pointedly fixed on the Real, becomes the Real. The worm, intently contemplating the bee, becomes that bee.

To illustrate this idea, the oft-quoted example of a pupa meditating upon a wasp is given. Thinking of the Self, one becomes the Self.

Compare KaUp 6.17, 'One should draw him out of the body with determination like a reed from the grass sheath.'

sati = Reality, the Real; **sakto** = fixed; **naro** = a person; **yāti sad-bhāvaṁ** = becomes the Real; **hi** = (indicates certainly); **eka-niṣṭhayā** = one-pointed fixing, establishing; **kīṭako** = a small worm, pupa; **bhramaraṁ** = bee; **dhyāyan** = contemplating, meditating.

kriyāntarāsaktim-apāsya kīṭako
dhyāyan alitvaṁ hyali-bhāvaṁ ṛcchati |
tathaiva yogī paramātma-tattvaṁ
dhyātvā samāyāti tad-eka-niṣṭhayā ||360||

Just as the worm, by giving up every other activity and thinking of nothing but the bee, becomes that bee, so too, the spiritual aspirant, one-pointedly contemplating the Reality that is the Supreme Self, becomes That.

Compare the oft-quoted phrases, 'As one thinks, so one becomes' (*yat bhāvo tat bhāvasi*) and 'As the mind, so the person' (*mana eva manuṣyanam*). Also see PraśnaUp 3.10.

kriyāntarāsaktim-apāsya = by giving up every other activity; **kīṭako** = worm; **dhyāyan** = meditating; **alitvam** = bee; **hi** = (indicates certainty); **ali-bhāvam** = becomes the bee; **yogī** = spiritual aspirant; **paramātma-tattvaṁ** = the reality that is the supreme Self.

atīva sūkṣmaṁ paramātma-tattvaṁ
na sthūla-dṛṣṭyā pratipattum-arhati |
samādhinā'tyanta-susūkṣma-vṛttyā
jñātavyam āryair ati-śuddha-buddhibhiḥ ||361||

The Truth that is the supreme Self is very subtle. It cannot be perceived by the gross, externally oriented mind. It is only accessible in one-pointed absorption of the intellect in That, to noble individuals of extremely pure intellect, through extraordinarily subtle mental states.[1]

See KaUp 1.3.12, 'The Self, though hidden in all beings, does not shine forth but can be seen by the seers of the subtle through their sharp intellect' (. . . *dṛśyate tvagryayā buddhyā sūkṣmadarśibhiḥ*). Also KaUp 6.9, 'His appearance is beyond the range of sight; no one can see him with his sight; within the heart, with insight, with thought, has he been contemplated; those who know this become immortal.'

See V. 11, 138, 150, 177–78, 183, 276–77, 315, 336, 362–63, 367, 370–71, 384, and 408 for purification of the mind.

See V. 342, 343, 354, 355, 358, 363–67, 376, 408–11, and 474 on *samādhi.*

atīva sūkṣmaṁ = very subtle; **paramātma-tattvaṁ** – the truth that is the supreme Self; **na sthūla-dṛṣṭyā** = not perceived by the gross; **samādhinā** = one-pointed absorption of the intellect in That; **atyanta-susūkṣma-vṛttyā** = very subtle mental modifications; **āryair** = great people, noble ones; **ati-śuddha-buddhibhiḥ** = by people of very pure intellects.

yathā suvarṇaṁ puṭa-pāka-śodhitaṁ
tyaktvā malaṁ svātma-guṇaṁ samṛcchati |
tathā manaḥ sattva-rajas-tamo-malaṁ
dhyānena saṁtyajya sameti tattvaṁ ||362||

Just as gold, when heated in a fire, gives up its impurities and is restored to its own lustre, so too does the mind, through meditation, shed the impurities, *sattva*, *rajas*, and *tamas*, and attain the Real.

Gold is already gold. Nothing need be added to gold to make it so. All that need be done is to melt it in a crucible and remove the dross which covers its purity. Likewise the Self is innately pure.

See BG 14.20, 'The embodied one having transcended these three *guṇas* out of which the body is evolved, is freed from birth, death, decay, pain, and attains immortality.'

---

[1] Extraordinarily subtle mental states (*atyanta-susūkṣma-vṛttyā*) point to the fact that there exists what may be termed 'a higher mind' or a 'pure mind' as well as the ordinary mental faculty or lower mind most people are familiar with. It is not this lower mind which can or will experience the Self. Thus, in order to experience the Self, there is the necessity of purifying the mind. Whether this higher mind is but the lower mind purified or whether it is a new instrument which functions when the obscuring tendencies of the lower mind are removed is not clear.

See V. 11, 138, 150, 177–78, 183, 276–77, 315, 336, 361, 363, 367, 370–71, 384, and 408 for purification of the mind.

suvarṇaṁ = gold; **puṭapāka** = a method of wrapping a thing, covering it with clay and then heating it in a fire; **śodhitaṁ** = purified, refined; **tyaktvā malaṁ svātma-guṇaṁ samṛcchati** = gold, giving up its impurities, attains its real nature of brightness; **manaḥ** = mind; **sattva-rajas-tamo-malaṁ** = taints or impurities of *sattva*, *rajas*, and *tamas*; **dhyānena** = through meditation

nirantarābhyāsa-vaśat tad-itthaṁ
pakvaṁ mano brahmaṇi līyate yadā |
tadā samādhiḥ sa vikalpa-varjitaḥ
svato'dvayānanda-rasānubhāvakaḥ ||363||

When the mind, thus purified by uninterrupted, continuous practice, merges in the Absolute, the state of one-pointed absorption of the intellect in That arises, free from imaginations and in which there is the experience of the nectar of non-dual[1] bliss.

The TaittUp declares that 'the Absolute is nectar'.

See V. 11, 138, 150, 177–78, 183, 276–77, 315, 336, 361–62, 367, 370–71, 384, and 408 for purification of the mind.

See V. 342, 343, 354, 355, 358, 361, 364–67, 376, 408–11, and 474 on *samādhi*.

nirantarābhyāsa = uninterrupted, continuous; **pakvaṁ** = purified; **mano** = mind; **brahmaṇi līyate** = merges in the Absolute; **samādhiḥ** = one-pointed absorption of the intellect in That; **vikalpa-varjitaḥ** = free from imaginations, fancies; **rasānu-bhāvakaḥ** = experience of nectar, elixir, essence; **advayānanda** = non-dual bliss.

samādhinānena samasta-vāsanā
granther vināśo'khila-karma-nāśaḥ |
antar-bahiḥ sarvata eva sarvadā
svarūpa-visphūrtir ayatnataḥ syāt ||364||

By this one-pointed absorption of the intellect in That, the knots of all residual impressions and the results of all actions are destroyed. One's own nature, within and without, everywhere and always, will, without effort, spontaneously arise.

See MuṇḍUp 2.2.9, 'The knot of the heart is cut' (*bhidyate hṛdaya granthis*); KaUp 2.3.15, 'When all the knots that here fetter the heart are cut asunder then a moral becomes immortal'; ChānUp 7.26.2, 'There is release from all the knots of the heart'. See V. 354, 424, and 559 on knots of the heart.

See V. 342, 343, 354, 355, 358, 361, 363–67, 376, 408–11, and 474 on *samādhi*.

samādhinānena = by this one-pointed absorption of the intellect in That; **samasta-vāsanā granther** = the knots of all residual impressions; **vināśa** = totally destroyed; **akhila-karma-nāśaḥ** = destruction of the results of all actions; **antar-bahiḥ** = within and without, inside and outside; **sarvata eva sarvadā** = everywhere and always; **svarūpa-visphūrtir ayatnataḥ syāt** = one's own nature will spontaneously arise without effort.

---

[1] See ChanUp 6.2.1; BṛhUp 1.4.17; AitUp 1.1.1.

śruteḥ śata-guṇaṁ vidyān mananaṁ mananād-api |
nidhidhyāsaṁ lakṣaguṇam anantaṁ nirvikalpakam ||365||

Reflection[1] is a hundred times superior to hearing; meditation is a hundred thousand times superior to reflection; impartite one-pointed absorption of the intellect in That is infinitely superior to all.

See V. 342, 343, 354, 355, 358, 361, 363–67, 376, 408–11. and 474 on *samādhi*.

śruteḥ = hearing; **śata** = one-hundred; **mananaṁ** = reflection, consideration; **nidhidhyāsaṁ** = meditation, contemplation, profound and repeated meditation; **nirvikalpakam** = impartite.

nirvikalpaka-samādhinā sphuṭaṁ
brahma-tattvam-avagamyate dhruvam |
nānyayathā calatayā manogateḥ
pratyayāntara-vimiśritaṁ bhavet ||366||

By impartite one-pointed absorption of the intellect in That, the Truth that is the Absolute is clearly and definitely realized, but not otherwise, for then, the mind, being unsteady, will become mixed with other modifications.

Nirvikalpa samādhi is a one-pointed impartite absorption in That, the Self.
See V. 342, 343, 354, 355, 358, 361, 363–67, 376, 408–11, and 474 on *samādhi*.

nirvikalpaka-samādhinā = impartite one-pointed absroption of the intellect in That; **sphuṭaṁ** = clearly; **dhruvam** = surely; **nānyayathā** = not-otherwise, it is not understood; **calatayā mano-gateḥ** = mind, being unsteady; **pratyayāntara-vimiśritaṁ bhavet** = will become mixed with other modifications.

ataḥ samādhatsva yatendriyas-san
nirantaraṁ śānta-manāḥ pratīci |
vidhvaṁsasya dhvāntam-anādyavidyayā
kṛtaṁ sad'ekatva-vilokanena ||367||

Therefore, remain in one-pointed absorption of the intellect in That, with the sense organs controlled, with a tranquil mind ever turned within, and, through the realization of your identity with the Absolute, destroy the darkness of beginningless ignorance.

See V. 11, 138, 150, 177–78, 183, 276–77, 315, 336, 361–63, 370–71, 384, and 408 for purification of the mind.
See V. 342, 343, 354, 355, 358, 361, 363–67, 376, 408–11, and 474 on witness.

samādhatsva = one-pointed absorption of the intellect in That; **indriya** = sense organs; **nirantaraṁ** = uninterrupted, perpetually; **śānta-manāḥ** = tranquil mind; **vidhvaṁsasya** = destroy; **dhvāntam** = darkness; **anādyavidyayā** = beginningless ignorance; **sad'ekatva** = oneness, identity with the Real; **vilokanena** = observe, contemplate.

---

[1] See BṛhUp 2.4.5; 4.5.6, 'Verily, *Maitreyī*, by the seeing of, by the hearing of, by the thinking of, by the understanding of the Self, all this is known'; also BṛhUp 4.5.6. See V. 67, 70, 72, and 342 on 'hearing, reflection, meditation'.

yogasya prathamaṁ dvāraṁ vāṅ-nirodho'parigrahaḥ I
nirāśā ca nirīhā ca nityam-ekānta-śīlatā II368II

The first doorways to union are silence, non-possession, freedom from desires, freedom from action, and always living by oneself.

The Self is within. Thus, silence is the door to the heart-cave. Keep quiet and realize that Self which is within. See verse 309 on silence.

yogasya = to union; **prathamaṁ dvāraṁ** = first, initial entrance, doorways; **vāṅ-nirodha** = cessation of speech, silence; **aparigrahaḥ** = non-possession; **nirāśā** = freedom from desires; **nirīhā** = cessation of actions; **nityam-ekānta-śīlatā** = always living alone.

ekānta-sthitir-indriyoparamaṇe hetur damaś cetasaḥ
saṁrodhe karaṇaṁ śamena vilayaṁ yāyād ahaṁ-vāsanā I
tenānanda-rasānubhūtir-acalā brāhmī sadā yoginaḥ
tasmāc-citta-nirodha eva satataṁ kāryaḥ prayatnāt muneḥ II369II

Living alone is the means to self-control, the stilling the activities of the sense organs. This leads to the control of the mind. By controlling the mind, the tendencies of the ego are destroyed. This gives the spiritual aspirant an eternal, immovable, unbroken realization of the bliss of the Absolute. Hence, the spiritual aspirant should always strive to control the mind with singlepointed effort.

See BG 2.60, 'The excited senses impetuously carry away the mind of even a wise man striving for perfection'.

ekānta-sthitir = living alone, living in an uninhabited place; **indriyo-paramaṇe** = stilling the activities of the sense organs; **hetur** = means, cause; **dama** = self-control, control of the sense organs, restraint; **cetasaḥ** = mind, consciousness; **saṁrodhe karaṇaṁ** = cause of tendencies, limitations, restrictions; **śamena** = ceases, extinguished; **vilayaṁ** = cause to disappear, be destroyed; **ahaṁ-vāsanā** = tendencies of the ego; **acalā** = immovable; **sadā** = always; **yoginaḥ** = spiritual aspirant; **citta-nirodha** = cessation of the mind; **muneḥ** = the wise.

vācaṁ niyacchātmani taṁ niyaccha
buddhau dhiyaṁ yaccha ca buddhi-sākṣiṇi I
taṁ cāpi pūrṇātmani nirvikalpe
vilāpya śāntiṁ paramāṁ bhajasva II370II

Restrain speech in the mind; restrain that in the intellect; restrain the intellect in the witness of the intellect; and merging that also in the infinite absolute Self, attain supreme peace.

See KaUp 1.3.13, 'The wise should restrain speech in the mind'.

See KaivUp 1.18 on witness: 'In the three states of consciousness whatever appears as the object of enjoyment or the enjoyer or the enjoyment, I am different from them, the witness, pure consciousness, the eternal Śiva' (*sākṣī*); See V. 101, 127, 137, 159, 212, 213, 217, 218, 223, 270, 295, 352, 381, 384, 495, 506, 507, and 552 for references to witness (*sākṣī*).

See V. 11, 138, 150, 177–78, 183, 276–77, 315, 336, 361–63, 367, 371, 384, and 408 for purification of the mind.

vācaṁ = speech; **ātmani** = in the mind; **niyaccha** = restrain, control; **buddhau** = intellect; **dhiyaṁ** = mind; **buddhi-sākṣiṇi** = witness of the intellect; **śāntiṁ paramāṁ bhajasva** = attaining supreme peace.

deha-prāṇendriya-mano-buddhyādibhir upādhibhiḥ |
yair yair vṛtteḥ samāyogaḥ tat-tad bhāvo'sya yoginaḥ ||371||

A spiritual aspirant's mind is modified and transformed into, as it were, according to its association with the various limiting adjuncts: the body, vital airs, sense organs, mind, intellect, and so on.

Whatever the mind associates with, it takes on those characteristics, just as a pure crystal takes on the color of its surrounding objects or as a pure cloth and so on.

See V. 11, 138, 150, 177–78, 183, 276–77, 315, 336, 361–63, 367, 370, 384, and 408 for purification of the mind.

deha = body; **prāṇendriya** = vital airs and sense organs; **mano-buddhyādibhir** = mind, intellect, and so on; **upādhibhiḥ** = limiting adjuncts; **samāyogaḥ** = connection with, association; **yoginaḥ** = spiritual aspirant.

tan-nivṛttyā muneḥ samyak sarvoparamaṇaṁ sukham |
sandṛśyate sadānanda-rasānubhava-viplavaḥ ||372||

When this is stopped, the wise easily detaches from everything and is seen immersed in a nectarine experience of everlasting bliss.

Here, 'this' means the association with thoughts, sense objects, and so on.

nivṛttyā = cessation, withdrawal; **muneḥ** = the wise; **samyak sarvopara-maṇaṁ** = easily detaches from everything; **sandṛśyate** = seen; **sadānanda-rasānubhava** = nectarine experience of eternal bliss; **viplavaḥ** = immersed in, full of.

antas-tyāgo bahis-tyāgo viraktasyaiva yujyate |
tyajatyantar bahiḥ-saṅgam viraktas-tu mumukṣayā ||373||

Only a detached person possesses both internal and external detachment. For the sake of liberation, only a detached person gives up both internal and external attachments.

Again and again there is the prerequisite of detachment prescribed for the earnest seeker of liberation. See V. 9, 17, and 21 for detachment.

antas-tyāgo = internal dispassion, detachment, renunciation; **bahis-tyāgo** = external detachment, renunciation; **viraktasyaiva** = only a detached person; **yujyate tyajatyantar bahiḥ-saṅgam** = gives up both internal and external attachments, associations; **mumukṣayā** = for the sake of liberation.

bahis-tu viṣayaiḥ saṅgam tathāntar-aham-ādibhiḥ |
virakta eva śaknoti tyaktuṁ brahmaṇi niṣṭhitaḥ ||374||

Being firmly established in the Absolute, a detached person alone is able to renounce external attachment to sense objects as well as internal attachment to egoism.

See V. 9, 17, 21 for detachment

bahis-tu viṣayaiḥ saṅgam = association with external sense objects; **āntara** = internal; **aham-ādibhiḥ** = egoism; **virakta** = renounce, give up; **brahmaṇi niṣṭhitaḥ** = established in the Absolute.

vairāgya-bodhau puruṣasya pakṣivat
pakṣau vijānīhi vicakaṣaṇa tvam |
vimukti-saudhāgratalādhirohaṇaṁ
tābhyāṁ vinā nānyatareṇa siddhyati ||375||

O learned one, know that detachment and wisdom are like the two wings of a bird. The ascent to the top story of the mansion of liberation cannot be gained by either of them individually.

It is declared that not by detachment alone nor by wisdom alone is liberation achieved. The analogy given is apt, for a bird cannot fly high into the sky without using both wings.

Compare the use of this analogy to make a different point in MuṇḍUp 3.1.1, 'Two birds, companions always united, cling to the self-same tree. Of these two, one eats the sweet fruit and the other looks on without eating.'

vairāgya-bodhau = detachment and wisdom; **pakṣivat** = as of a bird (the suffix *vat* is used for a simile meaning 'like'); **pakṣau vijānīhi** = know to be the two wings; **vicakaṣaṇa** = O learned one; **vimukti-saudhāgra-talādhirohaṇaṁ** = ascending to the top story of the mansion of liberation; **tābhyāṁ vinā** = without these two together; **nānyatareṇa** = not otherwise; **siddhyati** = gained, obtained, accomplished.

atyanta-vairāgyavataḥ samādhiḥ
samāhitasyaiva dṛḍha-prabodhaḥ |
prabuddha-tattvasya hi bandha-muktiḥ
muktātmano nitya-sukhānubhūtiḥ ||376||

Only a person of intense detachment can attain one-pointed absorption of the intellect in That. Only a person in one-pointed absorption has firm knowledge born of realization. Only a person who has realized the Truth is liberated from bondage. Only a person who is free experiences eternal bliss.

Samādhi is a one-pointed absorption in That. See V. 342, 343, 354, 355, 358, 361, 363–67, 408–11, and 474 on *samādhi*.

atyanta-vairāgyavataḥ = only a person of intense, very great, perpetual detachment; **samādhiḥ** = one-pointed absorption of the intellect in That; **samāhitasyaiva** = to that person alone whose mind is fixed on That; **dṛḍha-prabodhaḥ** = firm knowledge; **prabuddha-tattvasya** = he by whom the truth has been realized; **bandha-muktiḥ** = freedom from bondage; **nitya-sukhānubhūtiḥ** = experiences eternal bliss.

vairāgyān na paraṁ sukhasya janakaṁ paśyāmi vaśyātmanaḥ
tat cet śuddhatarātma-bodha-sahitaṁ svārājya-sāmrājya-dhuk |
etad dvāram ajasra-mukti-yuvateḥ yasmāt tvam-asmāt paraṁ
sarvatrāspṛhayā sadatmaṇi sadā prajñām kuru śreyase ||377||

For a person of self-control, I find no better producer of bliss than detachment and if that is combined with the realization of the supremely pure Self, there arises sovereignty, within and without. This is the door to the enjoyment of that everlasting state known as liberation. If, therefore, you seek the highest spiritual good, cultivate inner and outer detachment and always fix your mind on the eternal Self.

Detachment is the doorway to liberation and realization of the Self is its fruit.

vairāgyān = detachment; **na paraṁ sukhasya** = no greater bliss; **vaśyātmanaḥ** = a person of self-control; **śuddhatarātma-bodha** = realization of the supremely pure Self; **svārājya-sāmrājya** = sovereignty within and without; **dvāram** = door.

āśāṁ chindhi viṣopameṣu viṣayeṣveṣaiva mṛtyoḥ sṛtiḥ
tyaktvā jāti-kulāśrameṣvabhimatiṁ muñcāti-dūrāt kriyāḥ |
dehādāvasati tyajātma-dhiṣaṇāṁ prajñāṁ kuruṣvātmani
tvam draṣṭāsy'amalo'si nirdvaya-param-brahmāsi yad vastutaḥ ||378||

Sever your desire for sense objects, for they are like poison, the way to death. Renounce caste, family, and stages of life, abandoning from a great distance actions prompted by them. Renounce your identification of the idea of individuality, with the body, and so on, which are unreal and establish your mind on the Self. For, you are really the seer, pure, the non-dual Absolute.

See Swami Vivekananda's poem 'Song of the Sannyasin' (Strike off thy fetters, bonds that bind thee down, Of shining gold or darker baser ore. Love, hate, good, bad and all the dual throng. Know, slave is slave caressed or whipped not free for fetters, though of gold, are not less strong to bind. They know not truth who dream such vacant dreams as father, mother, children, wife and friend. The sexless Self, whose father He? whose child? whose friend? Whose foe is He who is but One? The Self is all in all, none else exists, and That thou art. Where seekest thou that Freedom friend, this world nor that can give. In books and temples vain thy search. Thine only in the hand that holds the rope that drags thee on. Then cease lament, let go thy hold. Truth never comes where lust and fame and greed of gain reside. No man who thinks of woman as his wife can ever perfect be. No woman who thinks of man as her husband can ever perfect be. Nor that person who owns the least of things, nor that one whom anger chains can ever pass through *māyā*'s gates).

chindhi = annihilate, destroy, cut off; **viṣopameṣu** = like poison; **viṣaya** = sense-objects; **mṛtyoḥ** = death; **sṛtiḥ** = path leading to; **tyaktvā** = give up, renounce; **jāti-kulāśrama** = caste, family, stages of life; **muñcāti-dūrāt** = abandon from a great distance; **dehādāvasati tyajātma-dhiṣaṇāṁ** = renounce your identification of the idea of individuality, with the body and so on; **prajñāṁ kuruṣvātmani** = establish the mind on your Self; **tvam draṣṭā** = you are the seer; **amalo'si** = you are pure.

lakṣye brahmaṇi mānasaṁ dṛḍhataraṁ saṁsthāpya bahyendriyaṁ
sva-sthāne viniveśya niścala-tanuścopekṣsya deha-sthitim |
brahmātmaikyam upetya tanmayatayā cākhaṇḍa-vṛttyāniśaṁ
brahmānanda-rasaṁ pibātmani mudā śunyaiḥ kim-anyair bhramaḥ ||379||

Establishing the mind firmly on the goal, the Absolute, resting the external sense organs in their respective centers; with your body unmoving, taking no thought for its maintenance; attaining identity of the individual and the Absolute, being one with it in the infinite expanse of your mind; in the plenitude of your bliss, drink the nectarine bliss of the Absolute. Of what joy are other things which are false and empty?

mānasaṁ = mind; **dṛḍha** = fixed, firm, established, certain, sure; **saṁsthāpya** = to stand together, abiding with, resting in; **bahyen-driyaṁ** = external sense organs; **svasthāne** = standing, abiding in oneself; **niścala** = unmoving; **tanuścopekṣsya** = making thin, taking no thought for its maintenance; **dehasthitim** = maintaining the body; **brahmātmai-kyam** = identifing the Absolute and the Self; **tanmayatayā cākhaṇḍa-vṛttyāniśaṁ** = being one with it in the infinite expanse of one's mind; **brahmānanda-rasaṁ pibātmani** = drink the nextarine bliss of the Absolute; **mudā** = pleasure, joy; **śunyaiḥ** = devoid, empty; **bhramaḥ** = false.

anātma-cintanaṁ tyaktvā kaśmalaṁ duḥkha-kāraṇam |
cintayātmānam ānanda-rūpaṁ yan-mukti-kāraṇam ||380||

Giving up all thought of the not-self, which is impure, and the cause of suffering, contemplate the Self, which is of the nature of bliss, and which leads to liberation.

anātma-cintanaṁ tyaktvā = give up, renounce all thought of the not-self; **kaśmalaṁ** = which is impure, defective; **duḥkha-kāraṇam** = cause of suffering, unhappiness; **cintayātmānam ānanda-rūpaṁ** = contemplate the Self which is of the nature of bliss; **yan-mukti-kāraṇam** = which leads to liberation.

eṣa svayaṁ-jyotir aśeṣa-sākṣī
vijñāna-kośo vilasatyajasram |
lakṣyaṁ vidhāyainam asad-vilakṣaṇam
akhaṇḍa-vṛttyātmatayānubhāvaya ||381||

This is self-luminous, the witness of everything, ever shining in the sheath of the intellect. Rest your mind on that which is other than the unreal; experience it yourself as impartite unlimited consciousness.

See KaivUp 1.18 on witness. See V. 101, 127, 137, 159, 212, 213, 217, 218, 223, 270, 295, 352, 370, 384, 495, 506, 507, and 552 for references to witness (*sākṣī*).

eṣa = this (Self); **svayaṁ-jyotir** = self-luminous; **aśeṣa-sākṣī** = witness of everything; **vijñāna-kośa** = sheath of the intellect; **vilasati** = ever-shining, fully shines; **vidhāyainam** = resting your mind; **asad-vilakṣaṇam** = other than the unreal; **akhaṇḍa-vṛttyātmata-yānubhāvaya** = experience, realize it yourself, nature, as unlimited consciousness.

etam-acchinnayā vṛttyā pratyayāntara-śūnyayā |
ullekhayan vijānīyāt sva-svarūpatayā sphuṭam ||382||

One should clearly realize this as one's own true nature, continuously contemplating it without any thoughts to the contrary.

acchinnayā = continuously, undivided; **ullekhayan** = causing to come forth, bringing forth; **vijānīyāt** = one should know, realize; **sva-svarūpatayā** = one's own true nature; **sphuṭam** = clearly.

atrātmatvaṁ dṛḍhī-kurvan aham-ādiṣu santyajan |
udāsīnatayā teṣu tiṣṭhed ghaṭapaṭādivat ||383||

Becoming convinced of one's identification with the Self and renouncing it in the ego and so on, one should remain indifferent to them as with the case of a pot, cloth, and so on.

A pot, cloth, and so on are one's possessions. They belong to one and never for a minute does one mistake them for oneself. Likewise with the body, one should realize that it belongs to one, is one's possession, and is not one's true Self.

From another angle, one often fails to distinguish a pot from the clay it is composed of, or a piece of cloth from the threads it is formed of. One should remain indifferent to the various names and forms an object takes and pay attention to its essence.

atrātmatvaṁ = the sense of one's true nature; **dṛḍhī-kurvan** = convinced of, firmly convinced; **aham-ādiṣu** = ego and so on; **santyajan** = rejecting, renouncing; **udāsīnatayā** = indifferent; **ghaṭa-paṭādivat** = pot, cloth, and so on.

viśuddham-antaḥkaraṇaṁ svarūpe
niveśya sākṣiṇyavabodha-mātre |
śanaiḥ śanair niścalatām-upānayan
pūrṇaṁ-svam-evānu-vilokayet tataḥ ||384||

Resting the purified inner organ in one's true Self, the witness consciousness, knowledge-absolute, gradually, little by little, attain a state of complete stillness. Then, one should continuously experience the state of fullness.

See V. 101, 127, 137, 159, 212, 213, 217, 218, 223, 270, 295, 352, 370, 381, 495, 506, 507, and 552 for references to witness (*sākṣī*). See KaivUp 1.18 on witness.

See V. 11, 138, 150, 177–78, 183, 276–77, 315, 336, 361–63, 367, 370–71, and 408 for purification of the mind.

viśuddham = purified; **antaḥkaraṇaṁ** = inner organ; **svarūpe** = one's own Self; **niveśya** = resting, dwelling, establishing; **sākṣiṇ** = witness; **śanaiḥ śanair niścalatām-upānayan** = gradually, little by little, attain a state of complete stillness; **pūrṇam** = fullness, completeness.

dehendriya-prāṇa-mano'ham-ādibhiḥ
svājñāna-kḷptair akhilair upādhibhiḥ |
vimuktam ātmānam akhaṇḍa-rūpaṁ
pūrṇaṁ mahākāśam ivāvalokayet ||385||

Realize the Self as full, like the all-pervading space, free from all limiting adjuncts such as the body, the sense organs, the vital airs, the mind, egoism and so on, which are projections due to one's ignorance.

'That is full and complete; this is full and complete. The full comes out of the full. Taking the full from the full, the full itself remains full and complete.' See also MuṇḍUp 2.2.11; ChānUp 6.2.1; BṛhUp 3.4.19.

dehendriya = body and sense organs; **prāṇa-mano'ham-ādibhiḥ** = vital airs, mind, egoism, and so on; **upādhibhiḥ vimuktam** = free from limiting adjuncts; **akhanda-rupam** = unlimited nature; **pūrṇaṁ** = full; **mahākāśam** = great space.

ghaṭa-kalaśa-kusūla-sūci-mukhyaiḥ
gaganam upādhi-śatair vimuktam ekam |
bhavati na vividhaṁ tathaiva śuddhaṁ
paraṁ ahamādi-vimuktaṁ ekam-eva ||386||

Space, divested of hundreds of limiting adjuncts such as a pot, a jar, a receptacle for grain, the eye of a needle, and so on, is one and not diverse. So, too, the supremely pure Self is one only, when divested of limiting adjuncts such as egoism, and so on.

See V. 136, 289, 383, 451, and 566 on space in a pot.
See V. 119, 164, 220–21, and 289 on *pratibimbavāda.*

ghaṭa = pot; **kalaśa** = jar; **kusūla** = storehouse of grains, grainery; **sūci-mukhyaiḥ** = eye of a needle; **gaganam** = space, sky; **upādhi-śatair vimuktam** = freed from, divested of hundreds of limiting adjuncts; **ekam** = one; **śuddhaṁ** = pure; **param** = supreme; **ahamādi-vimuktam** = free from egoism, etc; **ekam-eva** = one only.

brahmadi-stamba-paryantā mṛṣā-mātrā upādhayaḥ |
tataḥ pūrṇaṁ svam-ātmānaṁ paśyed ekātmanā sthitam ||387||

All limiting adjuncts, from the Creator down to a minute worm, are unreal. Therefore, one should realize one's essential nature as solely existent and complete.

Brahmā is the Lord of the fourteen worlds and creator of the universe, according to Indian thought; one of the purāṇic Indian trinity comprised of Brahmā, Viṣṇu, and Śiva.

brahmādi = Lord Brahmā, the Creator; **stamba** = tiny worm; **paryantā** = down to, ending with; **mṛṣā** = false, unreal, merely imagined; **upādhayaḥ** = limiting adjuncts; **pūrṇaṁ** = full, complete; **svamātmānam** = one's essential nature; **ekātmanā** = one, sole existence.

yatra bhrāntyā kalpitaṁ tad viveke
tat-tan-mātraṁ naiva tasmād vibhinnam |
bhrānter nāśe bhāti-dṛṣṭāhi-tattvaṁ
rajjus tasmad viśvamātma-svarūpam ||388||

That in which something is imagined to exist through error is, upon discrimination, not different from that something. When the delusion vanishes, the snake perceived through the error vanishes, and the rope appears as the Truth. Similarly, the entire universe is, in reality, the Self.

Whenever something is superimposed upon a substratum, the substratum is what is real, is what endures. A snake superimposed upon a rope is only a rope. The rope endures. In actuality, there never was a snake there, there is not now, and there will not be one there in the future. It is only a delusion which appears and a delusion which vanishes. However, one should note that, without the substratum, the delusion would not appear at all. Thus, the substratum is fundamental and persists whether the superimposed is there or not. It is said, 'Destruction of an imagined object leaves the substratum behind'.

When one's dream ceases upon awaking, one's dream universe, along with all of its manifold dream objects, vanishes.

See V. 12, 63, 112, 140, 199, 237, 248, 303, 405, 407, and 550 wherein Śaṅkara makes references to a snake.

bhrāntyā = wandering or roaming about; causing error or confusion; mistaking something for; erroneous perception; **kalpitaṁ** = imagined; **viveke** = discrimination; **bhrānter** = delusion; **nāśe** = vanishes, is destroyed; **dṛṣṭāhi** = perceived snake; **rajjus** = rope; **viśvam** = universe.

svayaṁ brahmā svayaṁ viṣṇuḥ svayaṁ-indraḥ svayaṁ śivaḥ |
svayaṁ viśvam-idaṁ sarvaṁ svasmād-anyan na kiñcana ||389||

The Self itself is Brahmā; the Self itself is Viṣṇu; the Self itself is Indra; the Self itself is Śiva; the Self itself is all this universe. Nothing exists other than the Self.

svayaṁ brahmā viṣṇuḥ indraḥ śivaḥ viśvam-idaṁ sarvaṁ = the Self is Brahmā, Viṣṇu, Indra, Siva, all this universe.

antaḥ svayaṁ cāpi bahiḥ svayaṁ ca
svayaṁ purastāt svayam-eva paścāt |
svayaṁ hy-avācyām svayam apyudīcyāṁ
tathopariṣṭāt svayam apyadhastāt ||390||

The Self itself is within and the Self itself is without; the Self itself is before and the Self itself is behind; the Self itself is in the south; the Self itself is in the north; likewise, the Self itself is above and below.

See MuṇḍUp 2.2.12, 'Verily, the Absolute is this immortal. The Absolute is is in front, the Absolute is behind, to the right and to the left. It spreads above and below' (*brahmaivedam amṛtam purastād brahma, paścād brahma, dakṣinataś cottareṇa*); also see ChānUp, 'I alone am below; the Self alone is below' (*ahamevādhastāt ātmaivādhastāt*).

antaḥ = within; **bahiḥ** = without; **purastāt** = before; **paścāt** = behind; **avācyām** = south; **udīcyāṁ** = north; **upariṣṭāt** = above; **adhastāt** = below.

taraṅga-phena-bhrama-budbudādi
sarvaṁ svarūpeṇa jalaṁ yathā tathā |
cid-eva dehādy'ham-antam-etat
sarvaṁ cid-evaika-rasaṁ viśuddham ||391||

Just as all things in the form of a wave, a whirlpool, a bubble, and so on, are in essence only water, similarly, consciousness alone is all this, from the body to the inner organ. All this is solely, pure consciousness.

The entire ocean is only water. Waves, whirlpools, bubbles, and drops of water are only water. They may be distinguished by names and forms but they are only water. See ChānUp 6.10, 'Now, take these rivers, son. The easterly ones flow towards the east, and the westerly ones flow towards the west. From the ocean, they merge into the very ocean; they become just the ocean.' Also see ChānUp Ch. 6.4, 'the transformation is a verbal handle, a name'. Likewise, gold is gold whether in the shape of an earring, a bangle, a ring, or a plate. Clay is clay whether in the shape of a pot, a mug, or a plate.

See MuṇḍUp 3.2.8, 'Just as rivers, as they flow, merge in the ocean giving up their separate names and forms, so the knowing one, freed from separateness arising from name and form, attains the luminous supreme Self.'

taraṅga = to move or wave about; **phena** = wave, foam; **bhrama** = whirlpool; **budbudādi** = bubble; **svarūpeṇa jalaṁ** = are in essence only water; **cid-eva** = consciousness alone; **cid-evaika-rasaṁ viśuddham** = all this is solely, pure consciousness.

sadevedaṁ sarvaṁ jagad-avagataṁ vāṅ-manasayoḥ
sato'nyan-nāstyeva prakṛti-para-sīmni sthitavataḥ |
pṛthak kiṁ mṛtsnāyāḥ kalaśa-ghaṭa-kumbhādyavagataṁ
vadatyeṣa bhrāntas tvam aham iti māyā-madirayā ||392||

This entire universe, known through speech and mind, is Existence alone. There is nothing other than this Existence for one established beyond the boundary of primordial nature. Are the jar, the pot, the vase, and so on, known to be other than clay? It is the deluded person, drunk with the wine of illusion, who speaks of 'I' and 'you'.

See ChānUp 6.1.4, 'Just as by means of one lump of clay all that is made of clay becomes known, the modification being only a name arising from speech while the truth is that it is just clay.' See V. 192, 230–31, and 253 on clay.

sarvaṁ = all, entire; **jagad** = universe; **avagataṁ** = known, conceived, under-stood; **vāṅ-manasayoḥ** = through speech and mind; **prakṛti-para** = beyond primordial nature; **kalaśa-ghaṭa-kumbhādi** = jar, pot, vase, etc.; **bhrānta** = error, delusion; **tvam** = you; **aham** = 'I'; **māyā-madirayā** = drunk with the wine of illusion.

kriyā-samabhihāreṇa yatra 'ānyad-iti śrutiḥ |
bravīti dvaita-rāhityaṁ mithyādhyāsa-nivṛttaye ||393||

The scripture, beginning with, 'Where one sees nothing else, and so on', speaks again and again of the absence of duality for the removal of the illusory superimpositions.

See ChānUp 7.24.1, 'Where one sees nothing else, hears nothing else, understands nothing else, that is the infinite.'

See V. 39, 181, 269, 271, 279–86, 307, 407, and 462 on superimposition.

kriyā-samabhihāreṇa = again and again; repetition; **dvaita-rāhityaṁ** = absence of duality; **mithyādhyāsa-nivṛttaye** = removal of illusory superimpositions.

ākāśavan-nirmala-nirvikalpam
nissīma-nisspandana-nirvikāram |
antar-bahiḥ śūnyam ananyam advayaṁ
svayaṁ paraṁ brahma kimasti bodhyam ||394||

The supreme Absolute is pure like the sky, impartite, infinite, motionless, changeless, devoid of interior or exterior, eternal, non-dual,[1] one's own Self. What else is there to know?

ākāśavan = sky; **nirmala** = stainless, pure; **nirvikalpam** = impartite, unchanging; **nissīma** = endless, infinite; **nisspandana** = actionless, motionless; **nirvikāram** = changeless; **antarbahiḥ śūnyam** = devoid of interior or exterior; **ananyam** = eternal; **advayaṁ** = non-dual; **svayaṁ** = one's own Self, self-established; **paraṁ** = supreme; **brahma** = Absolute; **kimasti bodhyam** = what else is there to know?

vaktavyaṁ kimu vidyate'tra bahudhā brahmaiva jīvaḥ svayam
brahmaitaj-jaga'ātatam nu sakalaṁ brahmādvitīyam śrutiḥ |
brahmaivāham-iti prabuddha-matayaḥ saṁtyakta-bāhyāḥ sphuṭaṁ
brahmī-bhūya vasanti santata-cidānandātmanaiva dhruvam ||395||

---

[1] See ChānUp 6.2.1 (*ekam evādvitīyam*); BṛhUp 1.4.17; AitUp 1.1.1.

What more needs to be said? The individual is none other than the Absolute only. This entire world, to the minutest atom, is the Absolute. The scripture declares that the Absolute is one without a second.[1] It is indubitable that those who have understood 'I am the Absolute only',[2] giving up all external attachments, certainly dwell unified in the Absolute as eternal Existence, Knowledge, and Bliss.[3]

vaktavyaṁ kimu = what more needs to be said; **bahudhā** = in many ways, repeatedly; **brahmaiva jīvaḥ** = the individual is the Absolute; **brahmādvitīyam** = the Absolute, one without a second; **brahmaivāham** = I am the Absolute only, alone; **prabuddha-matayaḥ** = those who have awakened, understood; **saṁtyakta-bāhyāḥ** = giving up externals; **santata-cidānanda** = eternal existence, consciousness, bliss.

jahi mala-maya-kośe'haṁ-dhiyotthāpitāśāṁ
prasabham-anila-kalpe liṅgadehe'pi paścāt |
nigama-gadita-kīrtiṁ nityamānanda-mūrtiṁ
svayam-iti paricīya brahma-rūpeṇa tiṣṭha ||396||

Destroy all desires generated by a sense of 'I' in the gross body, which is permeated by filth. Then, with great persistence, do the same with the air-like subtle body. Thus, realizing yourself, the embodiment of eternal bliss, whose glories the scriptures proclaim, remain as the Absolute.

The statement, '*Brahmaveda brahmaiva bhavati*, MuṇḍUp 3.2.9 (the knower of *Brahman* becomes *Brahman*), does not mean a change of state or an attainment. The Sanskrit root '*bhū*' from which '*bhavati*' (becomes) is derived means both 'being' and 'becoming'. In the present context it refers to 'being'. One is what one always has been. To attain the unattained, action is necessary. But to attain the already attained, no action is required. Knowledge of the fact as-it-is will dispel the darkness of ignorance which covers it.

jahi = destroy; **mala-maya** = permeated, compacted of defects; filth; **kośe'haṁ** = a sense of 'I' in the body; **utthāpita** = generated; **aśāṁ** = attachment; **prasabham** = with great force; **anilakalpe liṅgadehe** = air-like subtle body; **nigama** = scriptures; **nitya-mānanda-mūrtiṁ** = embodiment of eternal bliss; **brahma-rūpeṇa tiṣṭha** = remain as the Absolute.

śavākāraṁ yāvad bhajati manujas-tāvad-aśuciḥ
parebhyaḥ syāt kleśo janana-maraṇa-vyādhi-nilayaḥ |
yadātmānaṁ śuddhaṁ kalayati śivākāram-acalaṁ
tadā tebhyo mukto bhavati hi tadāha śrutir-api ||397||

So long as an individual thinks they are of the form of a corpse,[4] they are impure, and suffering will arise from enemies in the form of birth, death, and disease. When they think of themselves as pure, as the essence of auspiciousness, as immovable, then, assuredly, they become free of them. This is also attested to by the scriptures.

---

[1] See ChānUp 6.2.1 (*ekam evādvītīyam*); BṛhUp 1.4.17; AitUp 1.1.1.
[2] ChānUp 3.14.1 declares, 'All this is the Absolute'.
[3] See TaittUp 2.1.1, 'know the Absolute as Existence, Knowledge, Infinitude' (*brahmavid . . . satyaṁ jñānam anantam brahma*).
[4] See scriptural reference, ChānUp 8.12.1, 'O Indra, verily this body is mortal'.

See BṛhUp 2.4.6, 'May the priests/warriors/worlds/gods/beings/everyone forsake anyone who knows themself as different from the Self. All these, priests/warriors/ worlds/gods/beings/everyone are all this Self.' Also BṛhUp 1.4.2, 'So long as there is a second, there is fear.'

śavākāram bhajati = thinks of oneself as the form of a corpse; **aśuciḥ** = impure; **parebhyaḥ syāt kleśo** = there will be grief, defilements, from enemies; **janana-maraṇa-vyādhi** = birth, death, disease; **kalayati** = knows, realizes; **śuddha** = pure; **śavākāram** = essence of auspiciousness; **acalaṁ** = immovable.

svātmanyāropitāśeṣābhāsa-vastu-nirāsataḥ |
svayameva paraṁ brahma pūrṇam advayam akriyam ||398||

By the elimination of all impure qualities superimposed on oneself, oneself alone remains, as the supreme Absolute, complete, non-dual,[1] and actionless.

See ŚvetUp 6.19, 'actionless' (*niṣkriyaṁ*).

svātmani āropita = imagined, superimposed on oneself; **aśeṣābhāsa-vastu** = all things with impure qualities; **nirāsataḥ** = elimanated, destroyed; **paraṁ brahma** = supreme Absolute; **pūrṇam** = full; **advayam** = non-dual; **akriyam** = actionless.

samāhitāyāṁ sati citta-vṛttau
parātmani brahmaṇi nirvikalpe |
na dṛśyate kaścid-ayaṁ vikalpaḥ
prajalpa-mātraḥ pariśiṣyate yataḥ ||399||

When the mental fluctuations are established in the impartite supreme Self, in the Absolute, awareness of this phenomenal world is not experienced. What remains thereafter is merely a matter of meaningless words.

The definition of Yoga in the YS 2 is, 'Yoga is the cessation of the modifications of the mind' (*yogaś citta vṛtti nirodhaḥ*).
See ChānUp 7.1.3, 'But, venerable sir, I am only like one knowing the words and not a knower of the Self.' See V. 62, 64–65, and 474 on mere words.

citta-vṛttau = mental fluctuations; **parātmani brahmaṇi nirvikalpe** = impartite supreme Self, the Absolute; **na dṛśyate kaścid-ayaṁ vikalpaḥ** = awareness of this is not experienced; **prajalpa** = gossip, prattle.

asatkalpo vikalpo'yaṁ viśvam-ityekavastuni |
nirvikāre nirākāre nirviśeṣe bhidā kutaḥ ||400||

This universe, imagined in the one Reality, is an unreal appearance. How can there be any difference in that which is changeless, formless, qualityless?

asatkalpo = unreal appearance; **vikalpo** = imagined; **ayaṁ viśvam** = this universe; **nirvikāre** = changeless; **nirākāre** = formless; **nirviśeṣe** = qualityless.

---

[1] See ChanUp 6.2.1; BṛhUp 1.4.17; AitUp 1.1.1.

draṣṭṛ-darśana-dṛśyādi-bhāva-śūnyaika-vastuni |
nirvikāre nirākāre nirviśeṣe bhidā kutaḥ ||401||

The one Reality is devoid of the distinctions of seer, seeing, and seen. How can there be any difference in that which is changeless, formless, qualityless?

See V. 346 on seer/seeing/seen.

draṣṭṛ-darśana-dṛśyādi = seer, seeing, and seen, knower, knowing, known; **bhāva-śūnyaikā** = devoid of.

kalpārṇava ivātyanta-paripūrṇaika-vastuni |
nirvikāre nirākāre nirviśeṣe bhidā kutaḥ ||402||

The one Reality is supremely full like the ocean at the time of the cosmic dissolution. How can there be any difference in that which is changeless, formless, qualityless?

See MuṇḍUp 2.2.11, *Brahman* alone is all this. ChānUp 6.2.1, 'It is One alone, without a second.' BṛhUp 4.4.19, 'In *Brahman* there is no diversity whatsoever.'

kalpārṇava = cosmic dissolution; **atyanta** = excessive, very great, exceedingly full; **paripūrṇaika vastu** = belonging to the supremely full ocean.

tejasīva tamo yatra vilīnaṁ bhrānti-kāraṇam |
advitīye pare tattve nirviśeṣe bhidā kutaḥ ||403||

How can there be any difference in the supreme Reality, which is without a second[1] and qualityless, when the cause of delusion is dissolved, like darkness in light?

When light appears, darkness disappears. When knowledge of the Self arises, ignorance is completely and totally destroyed.

tejasīva tamo = like ignorance, darknesss in light; **bhrānti-kāraṇam** = cause of delusion, falsehood, error; **advitīye** = without a second, non-dual; **pare tattve** = supreme reality; **nirviśeṣe** = qualityless.

ekātmake pare tattve bheda-vārtā kathaṁ vaset |
suṣuptau sukha-mātrāyāṁ bhedaḥ kenāvalokitaḥ ||404||

How can there be any talk of difference when the supreme Reality is one only? Who has ever experienced difference in the bliss-filled state of deep sleep?

By definition, the state of deep sleep is devoid of all thoughts, all distinctions, all difference.
See BṛhUp.

ekātmake = one only; **pare tattve** = supreme reality; **bheda-vārtā** = talk of difference, duality; **kathaṁ** = how; **suṣuptau sukha-mātrāyāṁ** = bliss-filled state of deep sleep.

[1] See ChanUp 6.2.1; BṛhUp 1.4.17; AitUp 1.1.1.

na-hyasti viśvaṁ para-tattva-bodhāt
sadātmani brahmaṇi nirvikalpe |
kālatraye nāpyahirīkṣito guṇe
na-hyambu-bindur mṛga-tṛṣṇikāyām ||405||

Even before realization of the supreme reality, the universe does not ever exist in the impartite, ever-existent Absolute. In none of the three periods of time is the seen snake ever existent in the rope, nor do drops of water exist in a mirage.

The snake does not exist, ever. It didn't exist in the past; it doesn't exist in the present; it won't exist in the future. Likewise, there has never been any water in a mirage. As the BG says, 'Negation does not pertain to what is real' (*nābhāvo vidyate sataḥ*).

See V. 12, 63, 112, 140, 199, 237, 248, 303, 388, 407, and 550 wherein Śaṅkara makes reference to a snake.

na-hyasti = ever exists; **viśvaṁ** = universe; **para-tattva** = supreme reality; **bodhāt** = realization; **sadātmani brahmaṇi** = ever-existent Absolute; **nirvikalpe** = impartite; **kālatraye** = three periods of time; **nāpya-hirīkṣito** = seen snake is non-existent; **guṇe** = rope; **na-hyambu-bindur mṛga-tṛṣṇikāyām** = nor do drops of water exist in a mirage.

māyā-mātram idaṁ dvaitam advaitaṁ paramārthataḥ |
iti brūte śrutis-sākṣāt suṣuptāvanubhūyate ||406||

The scripture itself declares, this duality is only an appearance brought about by *māyā*. The absolute Truth is non-duality. This is directly experienced in deep sleep.

ŚvetUp 3.10 describes the world being created by the wonder-working power of God, *māyā*. See also RV 6.47.18.

See KaivUp, 'When everything has merged in the state of dreamless sleep'.

See ChānUp 8.3.1–3; BṛhUp 2.4.14; MuṇḍUp 2.2.1; KaUp 2.4.2; Īśa 2, 15.

See V. 67, 110–12, 125, 245, 497, and 574 on *māyā*.

māyā = illusion, that-which-does-not-exist; **dvaitam** = duality; **advaitaṁ** = non-duality; **paramārthataḥ** = absolute truth; **brūte śrutis** = the scripture declares; **sākṣāt** = directly; **suṣuptāvanu-bhūyate** = experienced in deep sleep.

ananyatvam adhiṣṭhānād āropyasya nirīkṣitam |
paṇḍitai rajju-sarpādau vikalpo bhrānti-jīvanaḥ ||407||

The wise observe that that which is superimposed is not other than the substratum. The imagined difference between the rope and the snake, and so on, persists due to delusion.

The projection upon a substratum, the snake upon the rope, has no existence apart from the substratum (rope). Never is the snake other than the rope; never is the superimposed other than the substratum. Silver is not apart from the shell; the post is not apart from the post; the mirage is not apart from the desert. Likewise, the world of phenomena cannot exist apart from the Self. One is never apart from the Self and must invoke the Self to even ask, 'Where is the Self?' How wonderful!

See V. 39, 181, 269, 271, 279–86, 307, 393, and 462 on superimposition.

See V. 12, 63, 112, 140, 199, 237, 248, 303, 388, 405, and 550 wherein Śaṅkara makes reference to a snake.

ananyatvam = not other than; **adhiṣṭhānād** = substratum; **āropyasya** = superimposed; **paṇḍitai** = the wise; **rajju-sarpādau** = rope-snake; **vikalpo** = imagined difference; **bhrānti-jīvanaḥ** = subsists, exists, persists by delusion, error, falsehood.

citta-mūlo vikalpo'yaṁ cittābhāve na kaścana |
atas cittaṁ samādhehi pratyag-rūpe parātmani ||408||

The mind is the source of this appearance of difference. When the mind does not exist, there is none. Therefore, stabilize the mind in one-pointed absorption on the innermost supreme Self.

The mind functions only by division. It selects and excludes in order to produce distinctions and thus knowledge. When this division does not take place, there is no diversity. Deep sleep is an obvious instantiation of this.

See V. 11, 138, 150, 177–78, 183, 276–77, 315, 336, 361–63, 367, 370–71, and 384, for purification of the mind.

See V. 342, 343, 354, 355, 358, 361, 363–67, 376, 409–411, and 474 on *samādhi*.

citta-mūlo = mind is the root or source; **vikalpa** = imagined difference, mental construct, hallucination; **cittābhāve** = when the mind does not exist; **na kaścana** = there is none, nothing; **ataḥ** = therefore; **cittaṁ** = mind; **samādhehi** = one-pointed absorption; **pratyag-rūpe parātmani** = innermost supreme Self.

kim-api satata-bodhaṁ kevalānanda-rūpaṁ
nirupamam ativelaṁ nitya-muktaṁ nirīhaṁ |
niravadhi gaganābhaṁ niṣkalaṁ nirvikalpaṁ
hṛdi kalayati vidvān brahma pūrṇaṁ samādhau ||409||

The wise realize in their heart through one-pointed absorption of the intellect in That the all-inclusive Absolute, of the nature of infinite knowledge, pure bliss, incomparable, beyond all limitations, ever-free, without desire, limitless like the sky, indivisible, and impartite.

Samādhi or meditative enstasis is a state wherein one experiences the non-dual Bliss of the Self.

For a discussion on 'no one can ever conceive that they are not', see BSBh 1.1.2.

MaṇḍUp 7 says, 'The Self is unseen (*adṛṣṭam*), incapable of being spoken of (*avyavahāryam*), ungraspable (*agrāhyam*), without any distinctive marks (*alakṣaṇam*), unthinkable (*acintyam*), unnameable (*avyapadeśyam*), the essence of the knowledge of the one Self (*ekātma-pratyaya-sāram*), that into which the world is resolved (*prapañcopaśamam*), peaceful (*śāntam*), auspicious (*śivam*), non-dual (*advaitam*).'

See BṛhUp 2.4.12, 'limitless mass of consciousness only'.

See ŚvetUp 6.19, 'without parts' (*niṣkalam*); also 6.12.

See V. 342, 343, 354, 355, 358, 361, 363–67, 376, 408–11, and 474 on *samādhi*.

kim-api = indescribable; **satata-bodhaṁ** = eternal and infinite knowledge; **kevalānanda-rūpaṁ** = of the nature of pure bliss; **nirupamam** = incom-parable; **ativelaṁ** = beyond all limitations; **nitya-muktaṁ** = ever-free; **nirīham** = without desires; **niravadhi gaganābhaṁ** = limitless, without end like the sky; **niṣkalaṁ** = without parts, indivisible; **nirvikalpaṁ** = impartite, changeless; **hṛdi** = heart; **vidvān** = the wise; **brahma pūrṇaṁ** = all-inclusive Absolute; **samādhau** = one-pointed absorption of the intellect in That.

prakṛti-vikṛti-śūnyaṁ bhāvanātītabhāvaṁ
samarasam asamānaṁ māna-saṁbandha-dūram |
nigama-vacana-siddhaṁ nityam asmat-prasiddhaṁ
hṛdi kalayati vidvān brahma pūrṇaṁ samādhau ||410||

The wise realize in their heart through one-pointed absorption of the intellect in That the all-inclusive Absolute, devoid of the ideas of cause and effect, whose nature is beyond comprehension, homogeneous, incomparable, beyond all canons of knowledge, established by the words of the scriptures, and eternally self-established.

See V. 342, 343, 354, 355, 358, 361, 363–67, 376, 408–11, and 474 on *samādhi.*

prakṛti-vikṛti-śūnyaṁ = devoid of any ideas of cause and effect; **bhāvanātīta-bhāvaṁ** = whose nature is beyond comprehension; **samarasam** = homogeneous, of identical nature, whose essence is the same; **asamānaṁ** = beyond compare; **māna-saṁbandha-dūram** = beyond all canons of knowledge, beyond connection with any means of knowledge; **nigama-vacana-siddhaṁ** = established by the words of the scriptures; **nityam asmat-prasiddhaṁ** = eternally self-established.

ajaram amaram astābhavā-vastu-svarūpaṁ
stimita-salila-rāśi-prakhyamākhyā-vihīnam |
śamita-guṇa-vikāram sasvatam śāntam-ekaṁ
hṛdi kalayati vidvān brahma pūrṇaṁ samādhau ||411||

The wise realize in their heart through one-pointed absorption of the intellect in That the all-inclusive Absolute, which is ever-young, immortal, that whose nature is free from all differences, unmoving like a vast expanse of water without waves, nameless, qualityless, changeless, eternal, peaceful, one.

See ChānUp 8.3.4, 'This is *Brahman*, immortal and fearless'.

See MāṇḍUp 7, '. . . neither inside nor outside nor both; unseen (*adṛṣṭam*), can't be spoken of (*avyavaharyam*), ungraspable (*agrāhyam*), without distinguishable marks (*alakṣaṇam*), unthinkable (*acintyam*), unnameable (*avyapadeśyam*), peaceful (*śāntam*), non-dual (*advaitam*), auspicious (*śivam*).'

See V. 342, 343, 354, 355, 358, 361, 363–67, 376, 408–11, and 474 on *samādhi.*

ajaram = undecaying, ever-young; **amaram** = immortal, devoid of destruction; **astābhavā-vastu-svarūpaṁ** = that whose nature is free from all differences; **stimita-salila-rāśi-prakhyam** = unmoving like a vast expanse of water without waves; **ākhyā-vihīnam** = without name, nameless; **śamita-guṇa-vikāram** = qualityless and changeless; **sasvatam** = eternal, beginningless; **śāntam** = peaceful; **ekaṁ** = one.

samāhitāntaḥkaraṇaḥ svarūpe
vilokayātmānam akhaṇḍa-vaibhavam |
vicchinddhi bandhaṁ bhava-gandha-gandhitaṁ
yatnena puṁstvaṁ saphalī-kuruṣva ||412||

With the internal organ firmly collected, clearly realize your own self in the Self of infinite glory. Cut off the bondage formed by the residual impressions of worldly existence and, with effort, make your birth as a human being worthwhile.

The purpose of birth is to destroy one's ignorance and realize the Self.

Compare BG 15.20, 'Knowing this, a person becomes enlightened and all his duties are accomplished'.

samāhitāntaḥkaraṇaḥ = with the internal organ collected, held together; **svarūpe vilokayātmānam** = realize your own self in the Self; **akhaṇḍa-vaibhavam** = of infinite glory; **vicchinddhi** = cut off, remove, destroy; **bandhaṁ** = bonds, ignorance; **bhava-gandha-gandhitaṁ** = compacted of, formed by the residual impressions of worldly existence; **yatnena** = with effort; **puṁstvaṁ** = human being, individual; **saphalī** = worthwhile, fruitful.

sarvopādhi-vinir-muktaṁ sac-cid-ānandam advayam |
bhāvayātmānam ātmasthaṁ na bhūyaḥ kalpase'dhvane ||413||

Meditate on the Self, existing in you, free of all limiting adjuncts, Existence, Knowledge, Bliss,[1] without a second, and you will never be ensnared in worldly existence again.

See ChānUp (*na sa punar āvartate*); BG 8.15, 'Having come to Me, great souls are no more subject to rebirth, which is transitory and the abode of pain; for they have reached the highest perfection.'

sarvopādhi-vinir-muktaṁ = completely free of all limiting adjuncts; **sac-cid-ānandam** = Existence, Knowledge, Bliss; **advayam** = non-dual, without a second; **bhāvayātmānam** = meditate on the Self; **ātmasthaṁ** = existing in you; **na bhūyaḥ kalpase'dhvane** = never be ensnared in worldly existence again.

chāyeva puṁsaḥ pari-dṛśyamānam
ābhāsa-rūpeṇa phalānubhūtyā |
śarīram-ārāt śavavan-nirastaṁ
punar na sandhatta idaṁ mahātmā ||414||

Great Ones, by reason of their fruitful realization, never again attach themselves to this body, though it is visible as an appearance, like a shadow, when once it has been cast off to a distance like a corpse.

Even as a person is neither attached to their shadow, nor does the shadow suffer wetness when exposed to water nor pain and so on, thus does the Great One know that their body is other than the Self.

See V. 165, 431, and 505 on shadow.

chāyeva = like a shadow; **paridṛśyamānam ābhāsa-rūpeṇa** = though it is visible like an appearance; **phalānubhūtyā** = experience of fruits, results, fruitful realization; **śarīram** = body; **śavavan** = corpse; **punar na** = never again; **mahātmā** = great ones; great souls.

satata-vimala-bodhānanda-rūpaṁ svametya
tyaja jaḍa-mala-rūpopādhim-etaṁ sudūre |
atha punar-api naiva smaryatāṁ vānta-vastu
smaraṇa-viṣaya-bhūtaṁ kalpate kutsanāya ||415||

[1] See TaittUp 2.1.1, '. . . know the Absolute as Existence, Knowledge, Infinitude'.

Realizing your own true nature, eternal, taintless, enlightened, bliss, fling far away this insentient, impure, limiting adjunct that is the body. Then, do not think of it again, for that which has been vomited brings only disgust when it is remembered.

MaṇḍUp 7 says, 'The Self is peaceful (*śāntam*), auspicious (*śivam*), non-dual (*advaitam*).'

satata = eternal; **vimala** = taintless, pure; **bodhānanda-rūpaṁ** = nature of enlightened bliss; **svametya** = attaining your own; **sudūre tyaja** = fling far off, renounce; **jaḍa-mala-rūpopādhim-etaṁ** = this body which is inert, insentient, impure, tainted limiting adjunct; **punarapi naiva** = never again; **vānta** = vomited; **smaraṇa** = remembered; **kutsanāya** = causing disgust.

samūlam-etam paridāhya vahnau
sadātmani brahmaṇi nirvikalpe |
tataḥ svayaṁ nitya-viśuddha-bodha-
ānandātmanā tiṣṭhati vid-variṣṭhaḥ ||416||

Burning this body, from its root, in the fire of the unchanging Absolute, the ever-existent Self, the greatest of knowers remains firmly established as the eternal, pure, enlightened, and blissful Self.

The fire of knowledge burns all duality to its very root.
See KaUp 5.13, 'He is the eternal'.

samūlam-etam paridāhya vahnau = burning this body from its root in the fire; **nitya-viśuddha-bodha-ānandātmanā** = eternal, pure, enlightened blissful Self; **tiṣṭhati** = firmly established; **vid-variṣṭhaḥ** = highest of knowers.

prārabdhasūtra-grathitaṁ śarīraṁ
prayātu vā tiṣṭhatu goriva srak |
na tat punaḥ paśyati tattva-vettā
ānandātmani brahmaṇi līna-vṛttiḥ ||417||

Let this body, formed by the thread of accumulated past actions, go or remain, like a garland tied around the neck of a cow. The knower of Truth does not care for it ever again, for their mental modifications are merged in the Absolute, the embodiment of bliss.

Even as a cow has no attachment to a garland around its neck, so too, there should be no attachment to one's body.
See V. 280, 289, 446–47, 452, 454–55, 459–64, and 552 on *prārabdha karma*.

prārabdha = accumulated past actions, *karma*-in-action; **sūtra** = thread, rope; **śarīraṁ** = body; **grathitam** = strung, tied; **prayātu tiṣṭhatu vā** = let it go or remain; **goriva** = like a cow; **srak** = garland; **na tat punaḥ paśyati** = does not care for it again; **tattva-vettā** = knower of truth; **līna-vṛttiḥ** = mental modifications merged into, absorbed, destroyed.

akhaṇḍānandam ātmānaṁ vijñāya sva-svarūpataḥ |
kim-icchan kasya vā hetor dehaṁ puṣṇāti tattva-vit ||418||

After realizing the ever-blissful Self as one's very own nature, desiring what, and for whose sake, will the knower of Truth nourish the body?

This passage, 'desiring what and for whose sake', echoes the words of BṛhUp 2.4.5, Yājñavalkya's teaching to his wife, Maitreyī: 'Not for the sake of all things, but for the sake of the Self are things dear' (*na vā are sarvasya kāmāya sarvaṁ priyam bhavati, ātmanas tu kāmāya sarvam priyam bhavati*). Also see BṛhUp 4.5.7.

akhaṇḍānandam ātmānaṁ = ever-blissful Self; **vijñāya** = realizing; **sva-svarūpataḥ** = one's very own nature; **kim-icchan** = desiring which or what; **tattva-vit** = knower of the truth.

saṁ-siddhasya phalaṁ tvetat jīvan-muktasya yoginaḥ ǀ
bahir-antaḥ sadānanda-rasāsvādanam ātmani ǀǀ419ǀǀ

The spiritual practitioner who has attained perfection and is liberated-while-living-in-a-body tastes the fruit of immortality, bliss eternal, the Self, both internal and external.

On liberated-while-living see BṛhUp 4.4.14; KaUp 2.3.14; MuṇḍUp 2.1.10; KenaUp 2.5; AitUp 2.1.5–6; BṛhUpBh. 4.4.6; BG 5.23; BS 3.4.51; BS 4.1–3.

See V. 72, 318, 429–41, and 552 on liberated-while-living-in-a-body (*jīvanmukti*).

saṁ-siddhasya = attained perfection; **phalaṁ** = fruit, result; **jīvan-muktasya** = one liberated-while-living; **yoginaḥ** = spiritual practitioner; **bahir-antaḥ** = internal and external.

vairāgyasya phalaṁ bodhaḥ bodhasyo-paratiḥ phalam ǀ
svānandānubhavāt śāntir eṣaivoparateḥ phalam ǀǀ420ǀǀ

The fruit of detachment is wisdom; the fruit of wisdom is withdrawal. That leads to the experience of the bliss of the Self, which in turn leads to peace.

See V. 377.

See V. 9, 17, 21, and 373–74 on detachment.

vairāgyasya phalaṁ = the fruit of detachment; **bodhaḥ** = knowledge, wisdom; **uparatiḥ** = once the sense organs have been restricted, the power to ensure that the senses may not once again be tempted towards sense objects; **svānandānubhavāt** = experience of the bliss of the Self; **śāntir** = peace, silence.

yad uttarottarābābhāvaḥ pūrva-pūrvam tu niṣphalam ǀ
nivṛttiḥ paramā tṛptiḥ ānando'nupamaḥ svataḥ ǀǀ421ǀǀ

If there is an absence of the latter stages, the prior ones are fruitless. Withdrawal, absolute satisfaction, incomparable bliss follow naturally.

Indian thought accepts the law of cause and effect (*karma*). If there is an absence of causes, then the preceding effects will also be absent.

uttarottarābābhāvaḥ = absence of the subsequent stages; **pūrva** = prior, earlier; **niṣphalam** = fruitless, useless; **nivṛttiḥ** = withdrawal, involution, the path of turning away from activity; **paramā tṛptiḥ** = absolute, supreme satisfaction; **ānando'nupamaḥ** = incomparable bliss; **svataḥ** = naturally.

dṛṣṭa-duḥkheṣvanudvegaḥ vidyāyāḥ prastutaṁ phalam |
yat-kṛtaṁ bhrānti-velāyāṁ nānā-karma jugupsitam |
paścān-naro vivekena tat kathaṁ kartum arhati ||422||

The result of knowledge, after the dawn of discrimination, will be the turning away from what is unreal. Absence of regret over perceived sorrows is the result of delusion. How can a person who did various despicable deeds during a state of delusion, do them later?

A person who does not both regret and cease from despicable deeds is not behaving in a noble fashion. A person who is deluded into thinking that there is water in a mirage, will strive to obtain it. However, when one knows that it is a mirage, no one will continue to possess it. The result of knowledge will destroy one's delusory notions and behavior.

dṛṣṭa-duḥkheṣvanudvegaḥ = absence of regret over perceived sorrows; **vidyāyāḥ prastutaṁ phalam** = pre-eminent fruit of knowledge; **bhrānti** = delusion, error; **nānā-karma** = various deeds; **jugupsitam** = disgusting; **paścān** = sunk **naro** = person; **viveka** = discrimination; **arhati** = to be able.

vidyā-phalaṁ syād-asato nivṛttiḥ
pravṛttir-ajñāna-phalaṁ tad-īkṣitam |
tajñājñayor yan-mṛga-tṛṣṇikādau
no-ced vidāṁ dṛṣṭa-phalaṁ kim-asmāt ||423||

The fruit of knowledge will be a turning away from what is unreal. Turning towards something is the fruit of ignorance. This distinction between one who knows and one who does not know is observed in the case of a mirage, and so on. Otherwise, how will the tangible fruit of one who knows be able to be withdrawn from the neal?

vidyā-phalaṁ = fruit of knowledge; **syād-asato nivṛttiḥ** = turning away from what is unreal; **pravṛttir-ajñāna-phalaṁ** = turning towards something is the fruit of ignorance; **mṛgatṛṣṇikādau** = in the mirage, and so on; **dṛṣṭa-phalaṁ** = tangible or seen fruit.

ajñāna-hṛdaya-granther vināśo yady-aśeṣataḥ |
anicchor viṣayaḥ kiṁ nu pravṛtteḥ kāraṇaṁ svataḥ ||424||

When the knot of ignorance in the heart has been completely destroyed, what cause can there be for inducing the wise, who have no desire of their own to satisfy, to turn outwards?

See MuṇḍUp 2.2.9, 'The knot of the heart is cut' (*bhidyate hṛdaya granthi*); KaUp 2.3.15, 'When all the knots that fetter here the heart are cut asunder then a moral becomes immortal'; ChānUp 7.26.2, 'There is release from all the knots of the heart.'

ajñāna-hṛdaya granther = knot of ignorance in the heart.

vāsanānudayo bhogye vairāgyasya tadāvadhiḥ |
ahaṁ-bhāvodayābhāvo bodhasya paramāvadhiḥ |
līnavṛttair anupattiḥ maryādoparates-tu sā ||425||

The culmination of detachment is when residual impressions no longer become excited in regards to objects of enjoyment. The supreme limit of knowledge is the non-arisal of the sense of 'I'. The limit of the withdrawal of the sense organs is when the mental modifications, which have ceased to arise, emerge no more.

The culmination of detachment is when there is no excitement in the mind even in the presence of (enticing) sense objects. The culmination of knowledge is when the 'I' no longer arises.

See BG, 'Even the mental tendencies of such a person withdraw when the Supreme is realized'.

See V. 9, 17, 21, and 373–74 on detachment.

vāsanānudayo = non-springing or non-arisal of residual impressions; **bhogye** = excitement, enjoyment; **vairāgyasya tadāvadhiḥ** = culmination or limit of detachment; **ahaṁbhāvodayābhāvo** = non-arisal of the sense of 'I'; **bodhasya paramāvadhiḥ** = supreme limit of knowledge; **uparati** = withdrawal, once the sense organs have been restricted, the power to ensure that the senses may not once again be tempted towards sense objects.

brahmākāratayā sadā sthitatayā nirmukta-bāhyārtha-dhīḥ
anyāvedita-bhogya-bhoga-kalano nidrāluvad bālavat |
svapna-ālokita-lokavat jagad-idaṁ paśyan kvacil-labdha-dhīḥ
āste kaścid ananta-puṇya-phala-bhug dhanyaḥ sa mānyo bhuvi ||426||

Completely freed from all awareness of external sense objects on account of always remaining established in the Absolute; only consuming what is necessary for bodily sustenance, as provided by others, like one asleep or like a child; perceiving this world as one seen in a dream, this rare person enjoys infinite merit. Such is to be honored on earth.

This verse, and the following ones, set forth the characteristics of a person of Self-realization.

sadā sthitatayā = always established in or remaining; **nirmukta** = completely freed; **bāhyārtha-dhīḥ** = external awareness of sense objects; **anyāvedita-bhogya-bhoga-kalano** = he whose means of subsistence is provided by others; **nidrāluvad** = like one asleep; **bālavat**-like a child; **svapna** = dream; **jagad-idaṁ** = this world; **kaścid** = this rare person; **ananta-puṇya** = infinite merit; **āste sa dhanyaḥ sa mānyo bhuvi** = such a blessed one exists on earth praised by all.

sthitaprajño yatir-ayaṁ yaḥ sadānandam aśnute |
brahmaṇyeva vilīnātmā nirvikāro viniṣkriyaḥ ||427||

This spiritual aspirant, whose mind has merged in the Absolute, enjoys eternal bliss, is changeless, and free from all activity, is a person established in wisdom.

See BG 2.55–68 describing a person of wisdom.

sthitaprajño = one whose mind is established in wisdom, steadfast wisdom; **yatir** = the spiritual aspirant; **sadānandam** = eternal bliss; **nirvikāro** = changeless; **viniṣkriyaḥ** = devoid of all changes, free from activity.

brahmātmanoḥ śodhitayor eka-bhāvāvagāhinī I
nirvikalpā ca cinmātrā vṛttiḥ prajñeti kathyate I
sā sarvadā bhaved-yasya sa jīvanmukta iṣyate II428II

That impartite mental modification, which comprehends only the identity of the Absolute and the Self after analyzing them, impartite and pure knowledge, is called wise. That person who possesses steadfast wisdom is always said to be liberated-while-living-in-a-body.

In Advaita parlance, 'an impartite modal cogition' (*akhaṇḍākāra-vṛtti-jñāna*) is the liberating knowledge the object of which is the Absolute. This modification is called the ultimate modification as it destroys every other type of modification, giving rise to the direct perception of the Self and then it also perishes, leaving only the Self. Since liberation occurs with the destruction of ignorance, the continuation of the physical body is in no way incompatible with it. Since the physical body is not real, its continued appearance is of no consequence. The liberated-while-living-in-a-body is one who lives in the world but is not of it. Whether such a one has a body or not is of no consequence.

See V. 72, 318, 419, 429–41, and 452 on liberated-while-living-in-a-body (*jīvanmukti*).

śodhitayor = after analyzing, justifying; **nirvikalpā** = impartite; **ca cinmātrā** = and pure knowledge; **vṛttiḥ** = mental modifications; **kathyate** = is called; **sthitaprajñaḥ** = steadfast wisdom; **ucyate** = is said to be; **jīvanmukta** = liberated-while-living.

yasya sthitā bhavet prajñā yasyānando nirantaraḥ I
prapañco vismṛta-prāyaḥ sa jīvanmukta iṣyate II429II

One is said to be liberated-while-living-in-a-body whose wisdom is firmly established, whose bliss is constant, and to whom the world is as a thing forgotten.

The concept of liberation-while-living (*jīvanmukti*) is certainly one of the most original and inspirational ideas that India has contributed to the world. Of all the Indian philosophical systems which propound this concept of *jīvanmukti*, Advaita Vedānta is unique in that it is the only school which must *necessarily* embrace the concept. It is a debatable question as to exactly when and how the term '*jīvanmukti*' originated. The most commonly accepted designation has post-Śaṅkara Advaita Vedānta propounding the concept with Sāṅkhya-Yoga, Śaiva Siddhānta, and Kāśmīrī Śaivism following thereafter. However, the concept itself, if not the term, has ancient roots. That is, doctrinally, Advaita's metaphysics has a built-in necessity which *demands* the concept. If one grants Advaita's presuppositions, *jīvanmukti* is not only a logical consequent, but necessarily so. The word '*jīvanmukti*' does not occur in the canonical texts of Vedānta. It is not found in the *Vedas*, nor in the earlier *Upaniṣads*, the *Bhagavadgītā*, or the *Brahmasūtras*. However, the concept of liberated-while-living can be found scattered throughout the literature. To mention but a few references: 'Verily, while we are here we may know this' (BṛhUp 4.4.14); 'A mortal becomes immortal, attains *Brahman*, even here, when the knots of the heart are destroyed' (KaUp 2.3.14); 'He who knows that which is set in the cave of the heart, he, here on earth, cuts the knot of ignorance' (MuṇḍUp 2.1.10); 'Whosoever, O *Gārgi*, in this world, without knowing this Imperishable . . . departs from this world is pitiable' (BṛhUp 3.8.10); 'There is truth if a person knows it here and if not there is a great loss' (KenaUp 2.5); 'When, to one who knows, all beings have, verily, become one with his own Self, then what delusion and what sorrow can be to him who has seen the oneness?' (ĪśaUp 1.7); 'While I (Vāmadeva) was in the womb I realized (the Self) and subsequently lived a long and productive life'; (AitUp 2.1.5–6); Śaṅkara's commentary on BṛhUp 4.4.6, 'The man free from desires realizes Brahman even here'; 'Before he is released from the body, if a *yogi* has perfect control over his mind and attains identity with *Brahman*, he is eternally liberated' (BG 5.23.28); '*Brahman*-knowledge takes place even in this life' (BS 3.4.51).

See V. 72, 318, 429–41, and 452 on liberated-while-living-in-a-body (*jīvanmukti*).

sthitā bhavet prajñā = wisdom is firmly established; **ānando nirantaraḥ** = bliss is constant; **prapañco vismṛta-prāyaḥ** = the world is as a thing forgotten.

līnadhīr-api jāgarti yo jāgrad-dharma-vivarjitaḥ |
bodho nirvāsano yasya sa jīvanmukta iṣyate ||430||

One is said to be liberated-while-living-in-a-body who, while having one's mind merged in the Absolute, is nevertheless awake, yet at the same time free from the characteristics of the waking state, and whose awareness is free from residual tendencies.

See V. 72, 318, 429–41, and 452 on liberated-while-living-in-a-body (*jīvanmukti*).

līnadhīr = mind is merged; **jāgrat** = awake; **bodho nirvāsano** = awareness is free from residual tendencies.

śānta-saṁsāra-kalanaḥ kalāvān-api niṣkalaḥ
yaḥ sacitto'pi niścintaḥ sa jīvanmukta iṣyate ||431||

One is said to be liberated-while-living-in-a-body whose limitations of worldly life are pacified, who, though learned, yet is, as it were, without learning, and who, though possessed of a mind, is yet free from the mind.

See V. 72, 318, 429–41, and 452 on liberated-while-living-in-a-body (*jīvanmukti*).

śānta = peaceful, pacified; **saṁsāra-kalanaḥ** = limitations of worldly life; **kalāvān-api** = though adept in all the various types of knowledge; **niṣkalaḥ** = without learning; **yaḥ sacitto'pi niścintaḥ** = though possessed of a mind, is yet free from the mind.

vartamāne'pi dehe'smiṁs-chāyāvad-anuvartini |
ahaṁtā-mamatā-abhāvo jīvanmuktasya lakṣaṇam ||432||

The mark of one liberated-while-living-in-a-body is an absence of any sense of 'I' and 'mine' in this body, though it follows like a shadow.

See V. 72, 318, 429–41, and 452 on liberated-while-living-in-a-body (*jīvanmukti*).
See V. 165, 414, and 505 on shadow.

dehe = body; **chāyāvad-anuvartini** = follows like a shadow; **ahamtā-mamatā-abhāvo** = absence, without any sense of 'I' and mine; **lakṣaṇam** = the mark.

atītānanusandhānaṁ bhaviṣyad-avicāraṇam |
audāsīnyam-api prāpte jīvanmuktasya lakṣaṇam ||433||

The mark of one liberated-while-living-in-a-body is not to dwell on the past, not to think about the future, to be indifferent about the present.

See V. 72, 318, 429–41, and 452 on liberated-while-living-in-a-body (*jīvanmukti*).

atītānanusandhānaṁ = not remembering, not dwelling on the past; **bhaviṣyad-avicāraṇam** = not thinking about the future; **audāsīnyam** = indifferent; **prāpte** = the present; **jīvanmuktasya lakṣaṇam** = the mark of one liberated-while-living.

guṇa-doṣa-viśiṣṭe'smin svabhāvena vilakṣaṇe |
sarvatra sama-darśitvaṁ jīvanmuktasya lakṣaṇam ||434||

The mark of one liberated-while-living-in-a-body is seeing everything with an eye of equality, though its nature is otherwise, being qualified by auspicious and inauspicious characteristics.

See BG 5.19, 'Even here the created is overcome by those who minds are established in equality'.

See V. 72, 318, 429–41, and 452 on liberated-while-living-in-a-body (*jīvanmukti*).

guṇa-doṣa-viśiṣṭe'smin = qualified by auspicious and inauspicious characteristics; **svabhāvena** = its own nature; **vilakṣaṇe** = otherwise; **sarvatra sama-darśitvaṁ** = seeing everything with an eye of equality.

iṣṭāniṣṭārtha-saṁprāptau sama-darśitayā'tmani |
ubhayatrāvikāritvaṁ jīvanmuktasya lakṣaṇam ||435||

The mark of one liberated-while-living-in-a-body is being changeless in respect of both the favorable and the unfavorable, due to seeing everything with an eye of equality.

See V. 72, 318, 429–41, and 452 on liberated-while-living-in-a-body (*jīvanmukti*).

iṣṭāniṣṭārtha = favorable and unfavorable; **ubhayatrāvikāri-tvaṁ** = changeless in respect of both.

brahmānanda-rasāsvādāsakta-cittatayā yateḥ |
antar-bahir-avijñānaṁ jīvanmuktasya lakṣaṇam ||436||

The mark of one liberated-while-living-in-a-body is an absence of all ideas of interior and exterior because their mind is completely engrossed in experiencing the ambrosial bliss of the Absolute.

See V. 72, 318, 429–41, and 452 on liberated-while-living-in-a-body (*jīvanmukti*).

brahmānanda = bliss of the Absolute; **rasāsvādāsakta** = experiencing the essence or ambrosia; **cittatayā** = mind; **antar-bahir-avijñānaṁ** = absence of knowledge of interior and exterior.

dehendriyādau kartavye mamāhaṁ-bhāva-varjitaḥ |
audāsīnyena yas-tiṣṭhet sa jīvanmukta iṣyate ||437||

One is said to be liberated-while-living-in-a-body who is free from all sense of 'I' and 'mine' with regard to the actions of the body and its sense organs, and so on, and remains indifferent to them.

See V. 72, 318, 429–41, and 452 on liberated-while-living-in-a-body (*jīvanmukti*).

dehendriyādau = body, sense organs, and so on; **kartavye** = prescribed actions; **mamāhaṁ-bhāva-varjitaḥ** = free from all sense of 'I' and mine; **audāsīnyena yas-tiṣṭhet** = remains indifferent to them.

vijñāta ātmano yasya brahma-bhāvaḥ śruter-balāt |
bhava-bandha-vinirmuktaḥ sa jīvanmukta iṣyate ||438||

One is said to be liberated-while-living-in-a-body who has realized, by the force of scriptural declarations, that their individuality is inherently the Absolute, and is free from the bonds of worldly life.

See V. 72, 318, 429–41, and 452 on liberated-while-living-in-a-body (*jīvanmukti*).

vijñāta ātmano = has realized their individuality is; **śruter-balāt** = by the force of scriptural declarations; **bhava-bandha-vinirmuktaḥ** = free from the bonds of worldly life.

dehendriyeṣvahaṁ-bhāva idaṁ-bhāvas-tadanyake |
yasya no bhavataḥ kvāpi sa jīvanmukta iṣyate ||439||

One is said to be liberated-while-living-in-a-body who never again has a sense of 'I' with regard to the body, the sense organs, nor the sense of 'this' in other things.

See V. 72, 318, 429–41, and 452 on liberated-while-living-in-a-body (*jīvanmukti*).

dehendriyeṣvahaṁ = body, sense organs, a sense of 'I'-am; **idaṁ** = this; **tadanyake** = in any other things; **no bhavataḥ** = never has a sense of, does not exist; **kvāpi** = at any time.

na pratyag-brahmaṇor bhedaṁ kadāpi brahma-sargayoḥ |
prajñayā yo vijānāti sa jīvanmukta iṣyate ||440||

One is said to be liberated-while-living-in-a-body who is never aware of a difference between the inner and the Absolute, nor the Absolute and the world.

See V. 72, 318, 429–41, and 452 on liberated-while-living-in-a-body (*jīvanmukti*).

na pratyag-brahmaṇor bhedaṁ = no difference between the inner and the Absolute; **sargayoḥ** = world.

sādhubhiḥ pūjyamāne'smin pīḍyamāne'pi durjanaiḥ
sama-bhāvo bhaved yasya sa jīvanmukta iṣyate ||441||

One is said to be liberated-while-living-in-a-body who has perfect equality whether adored by the good or tormented by the wicked.

See V. 72, 318, 429–41, and 452 on liberated-while-living-in-a-body (*jīvanmukti*).

sādhubhiḥ pūjyamāne = adored by the good; **pīḍyamāne'pi durjanaiḥ** = tormented or afflicted by the wicked; **samabhāvo** = equanimity; tranquillity, perfect equality.

yatra praviṣṭā viṣayāḥ pareritā
nadī-pravāhā iva vāri-rāśau |
linanti san-mātratayā na vikriyāṁ
utpādayantyeṣa yatir vimuktaḥ ||442||

That renunciant is indeed liberated in whom the sense objects directed by others are merged, producing no change, like rivers flowing into the ocean, because of his being established in the Truth.

See MuṇḍUp 3.2.8, 'Just as rivers, as they flow, merge in the ocean giving up their separate names and forms, so the knowing one, freed from separateness arising from name and form, attains the luminous supreme Self.'

viṣayāḥ = sense objects; **pareritā** = by others indeed; **nadī** = channel; **pravāhā** = stream, river; **linanti** = merge, engulf, disappear; **na vikriyāṁ utpādayant-yeṣa** = do not produce any change; **yatir** = the renunciant; **vimuktaḥ** = liberated, freed.

vijñāta-brahma-tattvasya yathā-pūrvaṁ na saṁsṛtiḥ |
asti cen-na sa vijñāta-brahma-bhāvo bahir-mukhaḥ ||443||

For one who has realized the Truth of the Absolute, there is no more worldly life as before. If such worldly life still persists, it means that such a one has not realized the Absolute but is still externally faced.

So it is said (*asti cet*), 'If worldly life persists, then one has not realized the Self'. This means that one still shuns what is painful and desires what is pleasurable, becomes excited and anxious, and is subject to all the myriad pulls of the universe of multiplicity.

vijñāta-brahma-tattvasya = one who has realized the truth of the Absolute; **pūrvaṁ** = former, as before; **na saṁsṛtiḥ** = no worldly life; **asti** = it is, persists; **bahir-mukhaḥ** = externally faced, facing outwards.

prācīna-vāsanā-vegād asau saṁsaratīti cet |
na sad-ekatva-vijñānāt mandī-bhavati vāsanā ||444||

If it is said that this person is again bound to worldly life by the momentum of past residual impressions, it is not so, for residual impressions become ineffectual on realization of the one Reality.

prācīna-vāsanā = prior residual impressions; **vegād** = force, momentum; **sad-ekatva-vijñānāt** = realization of the one reality; **mandī-bhavati vāsanā** = residual impressions become ineffectual.

atyanta-kāmukasyāpi śaktiḥ kuṇṭhati mātari |
tathaiva brahmaṇi jñāte pūrṇānande manīṣiṇaḥ ||445||

Even the mind of one given to extreme lust is restrained before his mother. Likewise is the case for those immersed in the all-encompassing bliss of the Absolute.

kāma = lust; **kuṇṭhati** = weak-minded, stupid, dull; **mātari** = before his mother; **brahmaṇi jñāte pūrṇānande** = realization of the all-encompassing bliss of the Absolute; **manīṣiṇaḥ** = the wise.

nididhyāsana-śīlasya bāhya-pratyaya īkṣyate |
bravīti śrutir-etasya prārabdhaṁ phala-darśanāt ||446||

One who practices constant meditation is still said to have external awareness. The scripture[1] speaks of accumulated past actions and it can be confirmed from results actually seen.

Nididhyāsana śīlasya means 'one still given to the practice of contemplation for the removal of incorrect impressions.' So long as one still has an external awareness, one will continue to exert to establish one's mind in the Self.

Prārabdha or accumulated past actions, the fruits of which are experienced now and cannot be erased, is that part of the accumulated effect of past deeds which has begun to take effect with the creation of the present physical body, and which is responsible for the continuance of the body even after release is attained. It is destroyed only when its force is spent. It cannot be averted, avoided, or changed, though either by knowledge or by grace, its impact can be minimized or rendered nil to the perceiver as the case may be.

See V. 280, 289, 417, 447, 452, 454–55, 459–64, and 552 on *prārabdha karma*.

nididhyāsana = constant meditation, one-pointed absorption; **śīlasya** = one who is given to, practices; **bāhya-pratyaya īkṣyate** = is said to have external awareness; **bravīti śrutir-etasya** = the scriptures speak of; **prārabdhaṁ** = accumulated past actions; **phala-darśanāt** = results seen.

sukhādyanubhavo yāvat tāvat prārabdham-iṣyate |
phalodayaḥ kriyā-pūrvo niṣkriyo na-hi kutracit ||447||

Accumulated past actions are said to persist as long as one experiences pleasure and so on. Every effect is preceded by a prior action, and nowhere is there an effect that happens without such.

See V. 280, 289, 417, 446, 452, 454–55, 459–64, and 552 on *prārabdha karma*.

sukhādi = pleasure and so on; **anubhavo** = experiences; **phalodayaḥ** = every effect; **kriyā-pūrvo** = prior action; **kutracit** = nowhere.

ahaṁ brahmeti vijñānāt kalpa-koṭi-śatārjitam |
sañcitaṁ vilayaṁ yāti prabodhāt svapna-karmavat ||448||

Through the realization, 'I am the Absolute', actions accumulated through hundreds of millions of cycles of eons are destroyed, even as actions performed in a dream disappear upon waking.

Upon realization of the Self, all *karmas*, past, present, and yet to fructify, are destroyed, like last night's dreams to one now awake, like seeds that are burnt will never sprout again.

The ChānUp 3.14.1 declares, 'All this is the Absolute' (*sarvam khalvidam brahma*). This is the great knowledge of Vedānta which boldly declares the identity of the individual and the Absolute; also *ayam ātma brahma* which occurs in the *Māṇḍūkya Upaniṣad* of the *Atharva Veda*; and *aham brahmāsmi* which occurs in the *Bṛhadāraṇyaka Upaniṣad* of the *Yajur Veda*.

---

1 See ChānUp 6.14.2, 'I shall remain here only so long as I shall not be released' (*tasya tāvad eva ciram yāvan na vimokṣye*).

See BṛhUp 1.4.1, 'This is I' (*aham ayam ity*) and BṛhUp 1.4.5, 'I indeed am this creation, for I produced all this' (*ahaṁ vāva sṛṣṭir asmi, ahaṁ hīdaṁ sarvam asṛkṣīti*).

ahaṁ brahmeti = I am the Absolute; **kalpa-koṭi-śatārjitam sañcitaṁ** = actions accumulated through hundreds of millions of cycles of eons; **vilayaṁ** = are destroyed; **yāti** = attains; **prabodhāt** = on waking; **svapna** = dream.

yat-kṛtaṁ svapna-velāyāṁ puṇyaṁ vā pāpam-ulbaṇam ǀ
suptotthitasya kiṁ tat syāt svargāya naraḳāya vā ǁ449ǁ

Will even the greatest beneficial or harmful actions performed during a dream lead to heaven or hell for one who has awakened from the dream?

Some may contend that there is activity even for the liberated, that is, a *jīvanmukta* may seem to be engaged in various activities. However, this contention is based on a mistaken view. Since ignorance, which is the cause of bondage, has been destroyed, the embodied state of the liberated one and the so-called activities in which he is supposed to be engaged *from the standpoint of others*, do not bind him anymore. Since the root cause of activity has been destroyed, the residual karmas which account for the continuance of his body have already been rendered ineffective. What one sees is not action but a semblance of activity.

svapna = dream; **puṇyaṁ** = meritorious; **pāpam** = demeritorious, harmful, wicked; **ulbaṇam** = anything laid over in addition, superfluous, abundant; **suptotthitasya** = awakened from a dream; **svargāya** = heaven; **narakāya** = hell.

svam-asaṅgam udāsīnaṁ parijñāya nabho yathā ǀ
na śliṣyate yatiḥ kiñcit kadācid bhāvi-karmanabhiḥ ǁ450ǁ

Realizing oneself as unattached and indifferent as the sky, a renunciant is not in the least affected by actions yet to be performed.

Even as clouds pass through the sky never leaving a trace so, too, the awakened one is unattached and indifferent to all types of action.

asaṅgam = single, one, alone, unattached; **udāsīnaṁ** = indifferent; **parijñāya** = perfectly experiencing; **nabho** = sky; **na śliṣyate** = not affected, clinging, adhering to; **yatiḥ** = renunciant.

na nabho ghaṭa-yogena surā-gandhena lipyate ǀ
tathātmopādhi-yogena tad-dharmair naiva lipyate ǁ451ǁ

Though connected with a jar, space is not tainted by the odor of the liquor in it. Similarly, the Self is not tainted by the qualities of the limited adjuncts with which it is connected.

See V. 136, 289, 383, 386, and 566 on space.

na nabho = space is not; **ghaṭa-yogena** = connected with a jar; **surā-gandhena** = odor of liquor; **lipyate** = tainted, defiled, poluted; **dharmair** = qualities, attributes.

jñānodayāt purārabdhaṁ karma jñānān-na naśyati ǀ
adattvā svaphalaṁ lakṣyam uddiśyotsṛṣṭa-bāṇavat ǁ452ǁ

Like an arrow shot towards its target, accumulated past actions begun before the dawn of knowledge and which have now begun to fructify, are not destroyed by that knowledge without yielding its fruits.

Compare the arrow analogy in MuṇḍUp 2.2.4, 'The bow is *om*, the arrow's the self, the target is the Absolute.'

See V. 72, 318, and 429–41 on liberated-while-living-in-a-body (*jīvanmukti*).

See V. 280, 289, 417, 446–47, 454–55, 459–64, and 552 on *prārabdha karma*.

purārabdhaṁ = goes before, shot towards; **naśyati** = not destroyed; **lakṣyam uddiśyotsṛṣṭa** = aimed at its target; **bāṇavat** = arrow.

vyāghra-buddhyā vinirmukto bāṇaḥ paścāt-tu gomatau |
na tiṣṭhati chinatty-eva lakṣyam vegena nirbharam ||453||

The arrow which is released from the bow under an impression that the target is a tiger, does not halt upon the realization that it is a cow, but surely pierces its target with great speed.

Any action which has already started to produce its results before the rise of Self-realization will not become destroyed upon it, just as an arrow, released at a target in ignorance, will not cease in mid-flight. Similarly, a fan which has been switched off will continue to rotate until its centrifugal force comes to a halt.

vyāghra = tiger; **vinirmukto** = freed towrds; **bāṇaḥ** = arrow; **paścāt** = from behind; **gomatau** = a cow; **na tiṣṭhati** = not established, does not halt; **lakṣyam** = target, mark; **vegena** = great speed, force; **nirbharam** = deeply, soundly.

prārabdhaṁ balavattaraṁ khalu vidāṁ bhogena tasya kṣayaḥ
samyag-jñāna-hutāśanena vilayaḥ prāk sañcitāgāminām |
brahmātmaikyam-avekṣya tan-mayatayā ye sarvadā saṁsthitāḥ
teṣāṁ tat tritayaṁ nahi kvacidapi brahmaiva te nirguṇam ||454||

Accumulated past actions which have now begun to fructify are very strong indeed. For the wise, they are destroyed only by enjoying them. Of the accumulated-past-actions-which-have-not-begun-to-fructify and of actions-yet-to-come, their destruction takes place in the fire of perfect knowledge. But none of these three affects those who realize their identity with the Absolute, and who are always established in it. They are verily the attributeless Absolute.

Karma or actions, rites, deeds, is the accumulated effect of deeds in lives, past and present. *Karma* is divided into *Sañcita-karma* or the residue produced by acts performed either in this life or in a previous one, but which remain latent during this present life; *Āgāmi-karma* or the result of acts performed during this present life which will mature in the normal course of events; and *Prārabdha-karma* or the residue of acts that are working themselves out during the present life.

See V. 280, 289, 417, 446–47, 452, 454–55, 459–64, and 552 on *prārabdha karma*.

prārabdhaṁ = accumulated-past-actions which have now begun to fructify; **balavattaraṁ** = very strong; **khalu** = certainly, truly; **vidāṁ** = the wise; **bhogena** = experiencing, enjoying; **kṣayaḥ** = destroyed; **samyag-jñāna** = perfect knowledge; **hutāśanena** = fire; **sañcitāgāminām** = accumulated-past-actions-which-have-not-begun-to-fructify and actions-yet-to-come; **brahmātmaikyam-avekṣya** = seeing, realizing the identify of the Self and the Absolute; **tan-mayatayā** = being compacted, of the form of; **sarvadā saṁsthitāḥ** = always established in; **tritayaṁ nahi** = none of the three; **nirguṇam** = attributeless.

upādhi-tādātmya-vihīna-kevala-
brahmātmanaivātmani tiṣṭhato muneḥ ।
prārabdha-sadbhāva-kathā na yuktā
svapnārtha-saṁbandha-katheva jāgrataḥ ॥455॥

For the sage who is established solely in himself as the Absolute, devoid of identification with limiting adjuncts, it is inappropriate to speak of the existence of accumulated-past-actions-which-have-begun-to-fructify even as a person who has awakened from a dream has no connection with objects seen in it.

It is meaningless to speak to a sage of the accumulated past actions which have begun to fructify. A sage has no connection or identification with either the body or the mind. Thus, even if it appears to another that the sage does things and things happen to a sage, from the point of view of the sage, 'nothing happens'.

See V. 280, 289, 417, 446–47, 452, 454–55, 459–64, and 552 on *prārabdha karma*.

upādhi = limiting adjuncts; **vihīna** = entirely abandoned, absent from; **kevala** = only, solely, along, perfectly; **tiṣṭhato** = established; **muneḥ** = sage; **svapnārtha** = objects in a dream; **na saṁbandhano** connection; **jāgrataḥ** = awakened.

na hi prabuddhaḥ pratibhāsa-dehe
dehopayoginyapi ca prapañce ।
karotyahamtām mamatām-idaṁtāṁ
kiṁtu svayaṁ tiṣṭhati jāgareṇa ॥456॥

The spiritual aspirant who has awakened from a dream does not have any sense of 'I', 'mine', and 'this' with regard to his dream body and objects seen in it, but remains quite awake as his own Self.

na = not; **hi** = certainly; **prabuddhaḥ** = he who has awakened; **pratibhāsa-dehe** = in the dream body; **yogin** = spiritual aspirant; **ahamtām mamatām-idaṁtāṁ** = any sense of 'I', mine, this; **svayaṁ** = own self; **tiṣṭhati** = established in; **jāgareṇa** = waking state.

na tasya mithyārtha-samarthanecchā
na saṅgrahaḥ taj-jagato'pi dṛṣṭaḥ ।
tatrānuvṛttir-yadi tan-mṛṣārthe
na nidrayā mukta itīṣyate dhruvam ॥457॥

Such a one has no desire to affirm the false objects seen in the dream world nor do they act in regard to them. If such a one still clings to those false objects, it surely should be declared that they have not yet awakened from the dream.

mithyārtha = false objects; **na samarthanecchā** = not acting in regard to them; **saṅgrahaḥ** = accepting, affirming; **taj-jagat** = dream world; **dṛṣṭaḥ** = seen; **tatrānuvṛttir** = clings to; **mṛṣārthe** = false objects; **na nidrayā mukta** = not awakened from the dream.

tadvat pare brahmaṇi vartamānaḥ
sadātmanā tiṣṭhati nānyad-īkṣate |
smṛtir-yathā svapna-vilokitārthe
tathā-vidaḥ prāśana-mocanādau ||458||

Similarly, one absorbed in the Absolute remains forever established in that Self and does not see anything else. Like a remembrance of objects seen in a dream, so are the reactions of the wise regarding eating, expulsion, and so on.

pare brahmaṇi vartamānaḥ = being forever absorbed in, abiding in the Absolute; **sadātmanā tiṣṭhati** = abiding in, remaining in the form of the Self; **smṛtir-yathā** = like something remembered; **svapna** = dream; **vidaḥ** = the wise; **prāśana** = eating; **mocanādau** = explusion, rejecting, and so on.

karmaṇā nirmito dehaḥ prārabdhaṁ tasya kalpyatām |
nānāder ātmano yuktaṁ naivātmā karma-nirmitaḥ ||459||

The body is created out of an accumulation-of-past-actions which may be imagined with reference to it. But such is not appropriate with reference to the beginningless Self, for the Self is never the outcome of an accumulation-of-past-actions.

KaUp 1.2.18 declares, 'The Self is unborn, permanent, eternal, ancient'. Gauḍapāda advanced the doctrine which he is best known for, 'nothing is ever born' or the theory of non-origination (*ajātivāda*). BG 2.20 says, 'The Self is neither born nor does it die'.

See V. 280, 289, 417, 446–47, 452, 454–55, 459–64, and 552 on *prārabdha karma*.

nirmito = created, fashioned; **dehaḥ** = body; **prārabdhaṁ** = accumulated-past-actions; **kalpyatām** = may be imagined; **nānāder** = never.

ajo nitya iti brūte śrutir-eṣa tvamoghavāk |
tadātmanā tiṣṭhato'sya kutaḥ prārabdha-kalpanā ||460||

The scriptures,[1] whose words are infallible, declare that This is unborn and eternal. How then, can there be an imagination of accumulated-past-actions-which-have-begun-to-fructify to one who remains as That, the Self?

See V. 280, 289, 417, 446–47, 452, 454–55, 459–64, and 552 on *prārabdha karma*.

ajo nitya = unborn and eternal; **tvamoghavāk** = words are infallible; **tadātmanā tiṣṭhato'sya** = of one who remains as the Self; **kalpanā** = imagination.

prārabdhaṁ sidhyati tadā yadā dehātmanā sthitiḥ |
dehātma-bhāvo naiveṣṭaḥ prārabdhaṁ tyajyatām-ataḥ |
śarīrasyāpi prārabdha-kalpanā bhrāntir-eva hi ||461||

---

[1] See KaUp 1.2.18, 'The knowing Self is never born, eternal . . .' (*na jāyate mriyate vā vipaścin*). BG 2.20, 'The Self is neither born nor does it die'.

Accumulated-past-actions-which-have-begun-to-fructify are meaningful only so long as there is an identification with the body. But the sense of the body being the Self is not valid, hence the accumulated-past-actions-which-have-begun-to-fructify have to be rejected. Attributing accumulated past actions which have begun to fructify to the body is also a delusion.

See V. 280, 289, 417, 446–47, 452, 454–55, 459–64, and 552 on *prārabdha karma.*

prārabdhaṁ = accumulated-past-actions-which-have-begun-to-fructify; **siddhyati** = meaningful, relevant; **dehātmanā sthitiḥ** = identification with the body; **tyajyatām-ataḥ** = hence, therefore rejected, renounced, given up; **śarīra** = to the body; **kalpanā** = imagining; **bhrāntir** = delusion, false; **hi** = certainly.

adhyastasya kutaḥ sattvam asattvasya kuto janiḥ |
ajātasya kuto nāśaḥ prārabdham asataḥ kutaḥ ||462||

How can something that is superimposed be said to be real, and how can that which is not real be said to have a birth? Where, then, is the destruction of the unborn? Where are the unreal accumulated-past-actions-which-have-begun-to-fructify?

The famous BG verse 2.16, 'Of the real there is no non-being and of the non-real there is no being' (*nā'sato vidyate bhāvo, nā'bhāvo vidyate sataḥ*) declares that that which exists, exists forever and that that which does not exist, never is.

See V. 39, 181, 269, 271, 279–86, 307, 393, and 407 on superimposition.

See V. 280, 289, 417, 446–47, 452, 454–55, 459–64, and 552 on *prārabdha karma.*

adhyastasya = that is superimposed; **kutaḥ** = how; **sattvam** = real; **asattvasya** = not real; **janiḥ** = have a birth; **ajātasya kuto nāśaḥ** = where in the destruction of the unborn; **asataḥ** = unreal.

jñānenājñāna-kāryasya samūlasya layo yadi |
tiṣṭhatiyayaṁ kathaṁ deha iti śaṅkāvato jaḍān |
samādhātuṁ bāhya-dṛṣṭyā prārabdhaṁ vadati śrutiḥ ||463||
na-tu dehādi-satyatva-bodhanāya vipaścitām |
yataḥ śruter abhiprāyaḥ paramārthaikagocaraḥ ||464||

In reply to the fools who asked how the body continues to live if the effects of ignorance, along with their root, are destroyed by knowledge, the scripture speaks of accumulated-past-actions-which-have-begun-to-fructify from an empirical point of view. But not to teach the learned the reality of the body, and so on. The purport of the scripture relates only to the Absolute.

The most famous example of this is the analogy of a fan blade which continues to spin until its centrifugal force is spent.

See V. 280, 289, 417, 446–47, 452, 454–55, 459–64, and 552 on *prārabdha karma.*

jñānena = by knowledge, by realization; **ajñāna-kāryasya** = whatever is the result of ignorance; **samūlasya** = associated with its root, with ignorance; **layo yadi** = if there is cancelation; **tiṣṭhatiyayaṁ kathaṁ deha** = how does the body continue to live; **jaḍān** = fools; **samādhātuṁ** = to reply; **bāhya-dṛṣṭyā** = empirical viewpoint, external sight; **śrutiḥ** = scripture; **dehādi** = body and so on; **satyatva** = reality, truthfulness; **bodhanāya na tu vipaścitām** = not to teach the learned; **abhiprāyaḥ paramārthaika** = relates to, approaches the Absolute; **gocaraḥ** = purport, come within range.

paripūrṇam anādyantam aprameyam avikriyam |
ekam evādvayaṁ brahma neha nānāsti kiñcana ||465||

There is only the Absolute, one without a second,[1] complete, infinite, without beginning or end, inscrutable, changeless. There is not even an iota of duality here.

See MāṇḍUp 7, '... without distinguishable marks (*alakṣanam*), unthinkable (*acintyam*), non-dual (*advaitam*).

paripūrṇam = devoid of spatial limitation, complete, full; **anādyantam** = infinite, without beginning or end; **aprameyam** = inscrutable, ineffable; **avikriyam** = changeless; **ekam evādvayaṁ** = one without a second; **brahma** = the Absolute; **neha** = not in the Absolute; **nānāsti** = does not exist; **kiñcana** = even a little.

sad-ghanaṁ cid-ghanaṁ nityam ānanda-ghanam akriyam |
ekam-evādvayam brahma neha nānāsti kiñcana ||466||

There is only the Absolute, one without a second,[2] eternal, an embodiment of Existence, Consciousness, and Bliss, actionless. There is not even an iota of duality here.

See ŚvetUp 6.19, 'actionless' (*niṣkriyaṁ*).

sad-ghanaṁ = of the form of Existence, compacted of Existence; **cid-ghanaṁ** = of the form of Consciousness, compacted of Consciousness; **nityam** = eternal; **ānanda-ghanam** = of the form of Bliss, compacted of Bliss; **akriyam** = actionless.

pratyag-eka-rasaṁ pūrṇam anantaṁ sarvato-mukham |
ekam-evādvayaṁ brahma neha nānāsti kiñcana ||467||

There is only the Absolute, one without a second, internal, homogeneous, complete, infinite, all-pervading.[3] There is not even an iota of duality here.

pratyag = internal; **eka-rasaṁ** = homogeneous; one essence; **pūrṇam** = full, complete; **anantaṁ** = infinite; **sarvato-mukham** = all-pervading, facing everywhere.

aheyam anupādeyam anādeyam anāśrayam |
ekam-evādvayaṁ brahma neha nānāsti kiñcana ||468||

There is only the Absolute, one without a second, which can neither be discarded nor accepted, which does not rest upon another nor has any support. There is not even an iota of duality here.

aheyam = cannot be discarded; **anupādeyam** = cannot be taken up; **anādeyam** = does not rest upon another; **anāśrayam** = has no support.

nirguṇaṁ niṣkalaṁ sūkṣmaṁ nirvikalpaṁ nirañjanam |
ekam-evādvayaṁ brahma neha nānāsti kiñcana ||469||

---

1 See ChanUp 6.2.1 (*ekam evādvitīyam*); BṛhUp 1.4.17; AitUp 1.1.1.
2 See ChanUp 6.2.1 (*ekam evādvitīyam*); BṛhUp 1.4.17; AitUp 1.1.1.
3 See KaUp 1.2.22 '... all-pervading (*vibhum*).

There is only the Absolute, one without a second, attributeless, partless, subtle, changeless, taintless. There is not even an iota of duality here.

The non-dual *Brahman* is suggested by a series of 'negations' or 'no's': 'Not coarse, not fine, not short, not long . . .' (BṛhUp 3.8.8), and again as, 'Not to be heard, not to be felt' (KaUp 1.3.15). As it is beyond all the relative categories of thought, it is easier spoken of by what it is not, than by what it is. Thus it is called indeterminate (*nirguṇa*) only to distinguish it from all attributes. *Nirguṇa* means that it transcends the phenomenal realm. It is undefinable and unknowable, meaning that it is too great for words to describe and the finite mind to fathom.

Thus an absolutely pure, utterly differenceless Being is very difficult to conceive in one's imagination, that is, due to biological reasons, pictorial and practical. This Reality appears to thought as a bare nothing or a content-less blank. The Reality of the Advaitins is so similar to a seeming nothingness, a night in which all cows are black, that Śaṅkara was called a crypto-Buddhist is disguise. However, Śaṅkara foresaw this objection and possible misconception, for he said: '*Brahman*, free from space, attributes, motion, fruition, and difference, being in the highest sense and without second, seems to the slow of mind no more than non-being' (ChānUpBh 8.1.1 and BSB 3.2.22).

nirguṇaṁ = attributeless; formless; **niṣkalaṁ** = partless; **sūkṣmaṁ** = subtle; **nirvikalpaṁ** = changeless; **nirañjanam** = without blemish, taintless, pure.

anirūpya-svarūpaṁ yan mano-vācām-agocaram |
ekam-evādvayaṁ brahma neha nānāsti kiñcana ||470||

There is only the Absolute, one without a second, formless, whose nature is inscrutable, beyond thought and word. There is not even an iota of duality here.

Śaṅkara's concept of the attributeless Absolute (*nirguṇa Brahman*) indicates not so much the absence of any character as the impossibility of attributing any conceptual category to Reality. Śaṅkara's Being is not a being among beings. The Being that is the substance cannot be categorized: '*Yato vaco nivartante aprapya manasa saha*' -- 'whence words return along with the mind, not attaining it'. Śaṅkara's Being is merest Being or Pure Being.

anirūpya = formless; **svarūpaṁ yan manovācām-agocaram** = whose nature is inscrutable, beyond thought and word.

sat-samṛddhaṁ svatas-siddhaṁ śuddhaṁ buddham anīdṛśam |
ekam-evādvayaṁ brahma neha nānāsti kiñcana ||471||

There is only the Absolute, one without a second, the Reality, of the nature of infinite bliss, self-established, pure, knowledge, incomparable. There is not even an iota of duality here.

sat = Existent, Real; **samṛddhaṁ** = of the nature of infinite bliss; **svatassiddhaṁ** = self-established; **śuddhaṁ** = pure, taintless; **buddham** = of the nature of knowledge; **anīdṛśam**-not seen like this, incomparable.

nirasta-rāgā nirapāsta-bhogāḥ
śāntāḥ sudāntā yatayo mahāntaḥ |
vijñāya tattvaṁ param-etad-ante
prāptāḥ parāṁ nirvṛtim-ātma-yogāt ||472||

The great spiritual aspirants who have abandoned all attachments and discarded all pleasures, perfectly restraining themselves and at peace, realize the supreme Truth, and, at the end, gain supreme bliss through their realization of the Self.

nirasta-rāgā nirapāsta-bhogāḥ = those who have abandoned all desires and pleasures; **śāntāḥ** = peaceful; **sudāntā** = those whose external organs are restrained; **yatayo** = those given to effort; **mahāntaḥ** = great spiritual aspirants; **vijñāya tattvaṁ param** = realize the supreme truth; **prāptāḥ** = attained.

bhavān-apīdaṁ para-tattvam-ātmanaḥ
svarūpamyānanda-ghanaṁ nicāyya |
vidhūya mohaṁ sva-manaḥ-prakalpitaṁ
muktaḥ kṛtārtho bhavatu prabuddhaḥ ||473||

You too, realize this supreme Truth of the nature of the Self, which is an embodiment of bliss, and destroy delusion which is a product of your mind's imagination, awaken, be freed, and fulfill the goal of your life.

The supreme goal of life is declared to be the realization of the Self, e.g., see 'The knower of the Absolute attains the highest' (*brahmaividāpnoti param*).

bhavān-apīdaṁ = you too; **para-tattvam-ātmanaḥ** = supreme truth of the Self; **svarūpamyānanda-ghanaṁ** = whose nature is of compacted bliss; **nicāyya** = realizing; **vidhūya** = destroy; **mohaṁ** = delusion; **sva-manaḥ-prakalpitaṁ** = imaginations of one's own mind; **muktaḥ** = freed, liberated; **kṛtārtho bhavatu** = fulfill the goal of life, attain life's purpose; **prabuddhaḥ** = awakened.

samādhinā sādhu viniścalātmanā
paśyātma-tattvaṁ sphuṭa-bodha-cakṣuṣā |
nissaṁśayaṁ samyag-avekṣitaś cet
śrutaḥ padārtho na punar-vikalpyate ||474||

Through one-pointed absorption in which the mind has been perfectly stilled, realize the Truth of the Self with the clear eye of knowledge. If it is directly experienced, the meaning of the words of the scripture will never cause any doubt again.

See V. 342, 343, 354, 355, 358, 361, 363–67, 376, and 408–411 on *samādhi*.

See ChānUp 7.1.3, 'But, venerable sir, I am only like one knowing the words and not a knower of the Self'. See V. 62, 64–65, and 399 on mere words.

samādhinā sādhu viniścalātmanā = by one-pointed absorption in That by which the individual is perfectly still; **paśyātma-tattvaṁ** = realize the truth of the Self; **sphuṭa-bodha-cakṣuṣā** = by clear perception, by the clear eye of wisdom; **nissaṁśayaṁ** = free from all doubt; **śrutaḥ padārtho** = meaning of the words of the scriptures; **na punar-vikalpyate** = does not doubt again.

svasyāvidyā-bandha-saṁbandha-mokṣāt
satya-jñānānanda-rūpātma-labdhau |
śāstraṁ yuktir deśikoktiḥ pramāṇaṁ
cāntas-siddhā svānubhūtiḥ pramāṇam ||475||

Regarding realization of the Self, which is of the form of Existence, Knowledge, Bliss,[1] attaining freedom from one's connection with the bondage of ignorance, the proofs are the scriptures, reasoning, and the words of the Master. Another proof is one's own experience accomplished by internal realization.

This is very subtle. According to Advaita, as long as the seeker regards himself as a separate individual and the Master as also separate, no matter what one does, it will not help liberation and in fact, will only tighten one's bonds. The 'seeker' will only go round and round like a dog chasing his own tail. One is not a 'seeker' and the 'Master' is not someone separate who 'knows'. And yet, the Master does help. His help is negative in that he negates his own individual presence and lives as 'no one'. The Master always supplies what is necessary, he does the needful without doing it himself.

svasya = of oneself; **āvidyā-bandha-saṁbandha-mokṣāt** = freedom from any connection with the bonds of ignorance; **satya-jñānānanda-rūpātma** = the Self in the form of Existence, Knowledge, Bliss; **śāstraṁ** = scriptures; **yuktir** = reasoning, logic; **deśikoktiḥ** = words of the Master; **pramāṇaṁ** = proofs, means of valid knowledge; **cāntas-siddhā** = accomplished by internal realization; **svānubhūtiḥ** = one's own experience; **pramāṇam** = proof.

bandho mokṣaś ca tṛptiś ca cintārogya-kṣudādayaḥ |
svenaiva vedyā yaj-jñānaṁ pareṣām-ānumānikam ||476||

Bondage, liberation, contentment, anxiety, health, hunger, and so on, are to be known only by oneself. Knowledge of these by others is indirect, inferential.

There is nothing, absolutely nothing, that the Master or anyone else can do for you as an individual in regard to the liberation you are seeking. Just as a person must eat to appease their own hunger, so too, one must realize the Self oneself.

bandho = bondage; **mokṣaś** = liberation; **ca** = and; **tṛptiś** = contentment; **cintā** = anxiety; **ārogya** = health; **kṣut** = hunger; **ādayaḥ** = and so on; **svenaiva vedyā** = to be known only by oneself; **yaj-jñānaṁ** = because knowledge; **pareṣām** = by others; **ānumānikam** = is indirect, inferential.

taṭa-sthitā bodhayanti guravaḥ śrutayo yathā |
prajñayaiva tared vidvān īśvarānugṛhītayā ||477||

Masters, like the scriptures, teach while remaining on the shore. The learned must cross by their own wisdom backed by the grace of God.

The Master will never be seen in his true nature as long as the seeker observes and treats him as just another individual. The Master seemingly has a body but does not identify with it. The Master is without name and form and yet appears to have such. The sun has never seen darkness and yet is called the enemy of darkness. Note the scriptural saying, 'Words return along with the mind, not attaining It' (*yato vāco nivartante, aprāpya manasā saha* – TaittUp 2.4.1).

See V. 3, 29, 42, 50, 138, 149, 489, 518, and 519 for references to grace.

---

[1] See TaittUp 2.1.1, '. . . know the Absolute as Existence, Knowledge, Infinitude' (*brahmavid . . . satyaṁ jñānam anantam brahma*).

taṭasthitā bodhayanti = teach while remaining on the shore; **guravaḥ** = Masters; **śrutayo** = scriptures; **prajñayaiva tared** = must cross by their own wisdom; **vidvān** = the learned; **īśvarānugṛhītayā** = supported by God's grace.

svānubhūtyā svayaṁ jñātvā svamātmānam-akhaṇḍitam |
saṁsiddhaḥ susukhaṁ tiṣṭhen-nirvikalpātmanātmani ||478||

Realizing oneself to be the indivisible Self by one's own experience, let one be established blissfully in the Self, beyond all conceptualization.

svānubhūtyā = by one's own experience; **jñātvā** = realizing; **sva-mātmānam** = oneself; **akhaṇḍitam** = unlimited; **saṁsiddhaḥ** = perfectly accomplished; **susukhaṁ** = blissfully; **tiṣṭhen-nirvikalpātmanātmani** = established in the Self beyond all conceptualization.

vedānta-siddhānta-niruktir-eṣā
brahmaiva jīvaḥ sakalaṁ jagat ca |
akhaṇḍa-rūpa-sthitir-eva mokṣaḥ
brahmādvitīyam śrutayaḥ pramāṇam ||479||

The final established view of Vedānta is that the individual and the entire universe are nothing but the Absolute. Liberation abides solely in the form of the indivisible. Scripture is the valid means of knowledge that the Absolute is one without a second.

The established conclusion (*siddhānta*) of Vedānta is 'You are That' here and now. The first verse of the *Vivekacūḍāmaṇi* stated, 'The Divine Master is the goal of all Vedāntic truths' and the individual is not different therefrom.

Not only does Śaṅkara say that an individual must be qualified (*adhikāri*) to pursue the path of knowledge, but also that the Absolute can be known *only* through religious statements (*śabda pramāṇa*). The distinctive cause of a valid cognition is a *pramāṇa* (valid means of knowledge). A valid cognition is defined as one whose content remains unsublated. Perception and all the other *pramāṇas*, except words-as-knowledge, produce cognitions which ultimately suffer sublation. (Provisionally, at the empirical level they are accepted as valid but ultimately, at the Absolute level, they do suffer sublation.) *Brahman*, which is the content of the cognition produced by religious discourse, always remains unsublated. Because *Brahman* is eternal, there is no possibility of its sublation at some later time. Thus, the cognition which religious discourse gives rise to is valid.

vedānta-siddhānta = the final, established view of Vedānta; **niruktir** = definitive, conclusive assertion; **brahmaiva jīvaḥ** = the individual and the Absolute are one only; **sakalaṁ jagat** = the entire world, universe; **akhaṇḍa-rūpa** = form of the indivisible; **sthitir-eva** = abides only, solely; **mokṣaḥ** = liberation; **brahmād-vitīyam** = the Absolute is one without a second; **śrutayaḥ pramāṇam** = scripture is the valid means of knowledge, the authority.

iti guru-vacanāt śruti-pramāṇāt
param-avagamya sa-tattvam-ātma-yuktyā |
praśamita-karaṇaḥ samāhitātmā
kvacid-acalākṛtir ātma-niṣṭhito'bhūt ||480||

Thus, having understood the supreme Truth on the authority of the scriptures, the instructions of the Master, and by one's own reasoning, with the sense organs perfectly controlled and the mind concentrated, the disciple became immovable in a lonely place, established in the Self.

iti = thus; **guru-vacanāt** = instructions of the Master; **śruti-pramāṇāt** = authority of the scriptures; **param-satattvam** = supreme truth; **avagamya** = on understanding, having understood; **ātma-yuktyā** = one's reasoning; **praśamita-karaṇaḥ** = one whose sense organs are perfectly controlled; **samāhitātmā** = a concentrated mind; **kvacit** = in a lonely place; **acalākṛtir** = immovable; **ātma-niṣṭhito** = established in the Self; **abhūt** = became.

kiṁcit-kālaṁ samādhāya pare brahmaṇi mānasam |
vyutthāya paramānandād idaṁ vacanam abravīt ||481||

Establishing his mind for some time in the supreme Absolute, he rose and out of an abundance of bliss, spoke as follows.

kiṁcit-kālaṁ = for some time; **samādhāya** = establishing, composing; **pare brahmaṇi** = supreme Absolute; **mānasam** = mind; **vyutthāya** = rising upwards; **paramānandād** = out of an abundance of bliss; **vacanam** = spoke.

buddhir vinaṣṭā galitā pravṛttiḥ
brahmātmanor ekatayādhigatyā |
idaṁ na jāne'pyanidaṁ na jāne
kiṁ vā kiyad-vā sukham-asya pāram ||482||

My mind has utterly vanished and all of its modifications have perished by a realization of the oneness of the Absolute and the Self. I know neither this nor not-this. I do not know what the nature or the extent of the boundless bliss is.

When the mind has vanished and one rests in That, That remains as the great mystery. It will always remain a mystery. It is so very secret that no one has ever been able to tell what it is. It is so secret that two cannot walk abreast there. Not even one. Not the body, the mind, the senses, the intellect.

buddhir = mind, intellect; **vinaṣṭā** = destroyed, utterly lost; **galitā** = perished; **pravṛttiḥ** = modifications; **brahmāt-manor ekatayādhi-gatyā** = by direct realization of the identity of the Absolute and the Self; **idaṁ na jāne'pyanidaṁ na jāne** = I know neither this nor not-this; **kiṁ vā kiyadvā** = I know not the nature of the extent; **sukham-pāram** = boundless bliss.

vācā vaktum aśakyam-eva manasā mantuṁ na vā śakyate
svānandāmṛta-pūra-pūrita-parabrahmāmbudher vaibhavam |
ambho-rāśi-viśīrṇa-vārṣika-śilā-bhāvaṁ bhajan me manaḥ
yasyāṁśāṁśa-lave vilīnam-adhunā'nandātmanā nirvṛtam ||483||

The majesty of the ocean of the supreme Absolute, full of the ambrosia of the bliss of the Self, cannot be adequately expressed in words nor conceived by the mind. My mind has melted like a hailstone becoming merged in an infinitesimal fraction of the ocean, is now satisfied by the enjoyment of that bliss.

MaṇḍUp 7 says, 'The Self is unseen (*adṛṣṭam*), incapable of being spoken of (*avyavahāryam*), ungraspable (*agrāhyam*), without any distinctive marks (*alakṣaṇam*), unthinkable (*acintyam*), unnameable (*avyapadeśyam*).'

vācā vaktum aśakyam-eva manasā mantuṁ na vā śakyate = cannot be adequately expressed in words or conceived by the mind; **svānandāmṛta** = ambrosia of the bliss of the Self; **pūra** = flooding, filling; **pūrita** = filled completely, full; **parabrahmāmbudher** = ocean of the supreme Absolute; **vaibhavam** = majesty, glory; **ambho** = water, ocean; **rāśi** = mass, heap, greatly; **viśīrṇa** = to be distinguished; **vārṣika-śilā** = hailstone; **bhajan** = sharing, participating in; **me** = my; **manaḥ** = mind; **āṁśāṁśa** = part of a part, fragment; **lave** = infinitesimal, a moment; **vilīnam** = merged in, absorbed in; **adhunā** = now, at this time; **ānandātmanā** = bliss of the Self; **nirvṛtam** = withdrawn.

kva gataṁ kena vā nītaṁ kutra līnam-idaṁ jagat |
adhunaiva mayā dṛṣṭaṁ nāsti kiṁ mahad-adbhutam ||484||

Where has this universe gone? By whom has it been removed? Where has it merged? It was seen by me just now. Has it ceased to be? What a great wonder!

Compare KenaUp 1, 'By whom willed and directed does the mind light on its objects?' (*keneṣitam patati preṣitam manaḥ*).

kva = where; **gataṁ** = gone; **kena** = by whom; **nītaṁ** = carried off, removed; **līnam** = merged; **idaṁ jagat** = this universe; **adhunaiva** = just now; **dṛṣṭaṁ** = seen; **nāsti** = it is not; **kiṁ mahadadbhutam** = what a great wonder.

kiṁ heyaṁ kim-upādeyaṁ kim-anyat kiṁ vilakṣaṇam |
akhaṇḍānanda-pīyūṣa-pūrṇe brahma-mahārnave ||485||

In the great ocean of the Absolute filled with the nectar of unbroken bliss, what is to be rejected and what accepted; what is different and what is other?

When one is the boundless Self, there is nothing to accept, nothing to reject; nothing to hold on to, nothing to let go of; nothing to grasp, nothing to renounce; nothing to embrace, nothing to relinquish.

heyaṁ = rejected, thrown down; **upādeyaṁ** = taken up, accepted; **anyat** = other, another; **vilakṣaṇam** = other than, different from; **akhaṇḍānanda-pīyūṣa-pūrṇe** = filled with the nectar of unbroken bliss; **brahma-mahārnave** = in the great ocean of the Absolute.

na kiñcid atra paśyāmi na śṛṇomi na vedmyahaṁ |
svātmanaiva sadānanda-rūpeṇāsmi vilakṣaṇaḥ ||486||

I neither see nor hear nor know anything here. I simply abide, distinct, in the form of my own Self, eternally blissful.

See KaivUp 21, 'I am without hands and feet, I see without eyes, I hear without ears'.

na paśyāmi = I neither see; **na śṛṇomi** = nor hear; **na vedmyahaṁ** = nor know anything.

namo namaste gurave mahātmane
vimukta-saṅgāya sad-uttamāya ǀ
nityādvayānanda-rasa-svarūpiṇe
bhūmne sadāparā-dayāmbu-dhāmne ǁ487ǁ

Salutations again and again, O Master, Great One, who is free from all attachment, the best of the best among the knowers of the Truth, an embodiment of the essence of eternal, non-dual bliss, infinite, and an eternal boundless ocean of compassion.

See 'Śrī Guru Pāduka Pañcakam' – Salutations again and again to the auspicious Guru's sandals (*namo namaḥ śrīgurupādukābhyaḥ*) There is an oft-quoted verse, 'In thought one should cultivate non-duality; not in action anywhere. Advaita is (permitted) in the three worlds, but not in respect of the Guru.' Even after Self-realization, the Guru has a special place in the respect and behavior of the disciple.

namo namaste = salutations again and again; **gurave** = O Master; **mahātmane** = Great One; **vimukta-saṅgāya** = free from attachment; **sad-uttamāya** = the best of the best among knowers of the truth; **nityādvayānanda** = eternal, non-dual bliss; **rasa-svarūpiṇe** = embodiment of the essence of; **bhūmne** = infinite; **sadāparā-dayāmbu-dhāmne** = eternal boundless ocean of compassion.

yat-kaṭākṣa-śaśi-saāndra-candrikā-
pāta-dhūta-bhava-tāpaja-śramaḥ ǀ
prāptavān-aham akhaṇḍa-vaibhava
ānandam ātma-padam akṣayaṁ kṣaṇāt ǁ488ǁ

By whose gracious glance, like a shower of the cool moon's concentrated moonbeams, the afflictions of the heat of worldly life have been removed, and, in a moment I have acquired the unbroken state of the Self which is of eternal bliss.

See verse 40 on the cool moon's rays.

kaṭākṣa = glance; **śaśi** = moon; **saāndra** = solid, full, concentrated; **candrikā** = moonbeams; **pāta** = unobsructed flow; **dhūta** = banished, removed; **bhava-tāpaja-śramaḥ** = afflictions of the heat of worldly life; **prāptavān-aham** = I have acquired; **akhaṇḍa-vaibhava ātma-padam** = the unbroken state of the Self; **akṣayaṁ** = eternal, undecaying; **kṣaṇāt** = instantly, in a moment.

dhanyo'haṁ kṛtakṛtyo-ahaṁ vimukto'haṁ bhava-grahāt ǀ
nityānanda-svarūpo'haṁ pūrṇo'haṁ tvad-anugrahāt ǁ489ǁ

Blessed am I. I have attained the consummation of life. I have been liberated from the clutches of worldly life. I am the essence of eternal bliss. I am complete, all through your grace.

Remember the lineage (*guruparampara*) *śloka*? It should be recited in remembrance every day. These individuals are the transmittors of the *brahma-vidyā* tradition. One after another they pass down the liberating knowledge. Thereby the lineage should be remembered with respect, reverence, and gratitude.

Even when one intellectually understands that one is the Self, the senses lead one astray. One needs some instrument, some device whereby one can overcome the pull, the tyranny of the senses. That instrument is the Guru. TaittUp says, 'The teacher is the first letter; the student is the last letter; knowledge is the meeting place; instruction is the link.'

See V. 3, 29, 42, 50, 138, 149, 477, 518, and 519 for references to grace.

dhanyo'haṁ = I am blessed; **kṛtakṛtyo-ahaṁ** = I have attained what needed to be attained; **vimukto'haṁ** = I am liberated; **bhavagrahāt** = from the grasp of worldly life; **pūrṇo'haṁ** = I am complete, full; **anugraha** = grace.

asaṅgo'ham anaṅgo'ham aliṅgo'ham abhaṅguraḥ |
praśānto'ham ananto'ham amalo'ham cirantanaḥ ||490||

I am unattached. I am not the body. I am not the subtle body. I am unchangeable. I am peaceful. I am infinite. I am taintless and eternal and free from weariness.

See MāṇḍUp 7, '. . . neither inside nor outside nor both; unseen (*adṛṣṭam*), ungraspable (*agrāhyam*), without distinguishable marks (*alakṣanam*), unthinkable (*acintyam*), unnameable (*avyapadeśyam*), peaceful (*śāntam*), non-dual (*advaitam*).'

asaṅgo'ham = I am unattached; **anaṅgo'ham** = I am not the body; **aliṅgo'ham** = I am not the subtle body; **abhaṅguraḥ** = unchangeable, invariable, not fragile; **praśānto'ham** = I am peaceful, silence; **ananto'ham** = I am infinite; **amalo'ham cirantanaḥ** = I am taintless, eternal, and free from weariness.

akartāham abhotkāham avikāro'ham akriyaḥ |
śuddha-bodha-svarūpo'haṁ kevalo'haṁ sadā-śivaḥ ||491||

I am not the doer. I am not the enjoyer. I am changeless and actionless. I am the essence of pure knowledge. I am perfect and ever-auspicious.[1]

See ŚvetUp 6.19, 'actionless' (*niṣkriyaṁ*).

akartāham = I am not the doer; **abhotkāham** = I am not the enjoyer; **avikāro'ham akriyaḥ** = I am changeless and actionless; **śuddha-bodha-svarūpo'haṁ** = I am the essence of pure knowledge; **kevalo'haṁ sadāśivaḥ** = I am perfect and ever-auspicious.

draṣṭuḥ śrotur vaktuḥ kartur bhoktur vibhinna evāham |
nitya-nirantara-niṣkriya-nissīmāsaṅga-pūrṇa-bodhātmā ||492||

I am indeed other than the seer, the hearer, the speaker, the doer, and the enjoyer. I am of the nature of what is permanent, without any break; actionless, boundless, complete, knowledge.

draṣṭuḥ = seer; **śrotur** = hearer; **vaktuḥ** = speaker; **kartur** = doer; **bhoktur** = enjoyer; **vibhinna** = other than; **evāham** = I am indeed; **nitya** = eternal, permanent; **nirantara** = without break; **niṣkriya** = actionless; **nissīmāsaṅga** = boundless; **pūrṇa-bodha** = complete knowledge.

nāham-idaṁ nāham-ado'py-ubhayor avabhāsakaṁ paraṁ śuddham |
bāhyābhyantaraśūnyaṁ pūrṇaṁ brahmādvitīyam-evāham ||493||

---

[1] See MāṇḍUp 7, '. . . auspicious' (*śivam*).

I am not this, I am not that, but the first, the illuminer of both, the supreme, the pure. I am indeed the Absolute, one without a second, devoid of anything external or internal, complete.

BṛhUp 2.3.6 says, 'Now therefore the description (of *Brahman*): "Not this, not this". Because there is no other and more appropriate description than this "not this".' Śaṅkara, commenting on this passage, says that the Absolute can never be properly denoted by any words – including the word 'Absolute' (*Ātman*). Thus the only appropriate way to indicate *Brahman* is to say, 'not this, not this'. Though no positive description of the Absolute is possible, Śaṅkara claims that a negative characterization may be comprehensible. Its import is not so much to say that there are no characteristics applicable to the Absolute, as to indicate the impossibility of attributing any conceptualization to it. Thus it becomes a linguistic device to avoid categorical mistakes. It is a methodological language symbol which draws attention to the ineffability of the Absolute. Thus 'not this, not this' has been called a way of expounding the Truth. Religious discourse is a conceptualization of the Reality which is destroyed as soon as it is conceptualized in thought. Yet conceptualization is necessary and cannot be avoided if self-knowledge is to arise. Thus one must use the concept in such a way as to recognize this paradoxical situation.

nāham-idaṁ = I am not this; **nāham adi** = I am not that; **ubhayor avabhāsakaṁ** = the illuminer of both; **paraṁ** = the supreme; **śuddham** = the pure; **bāhyābhyantara-śūnyaṁ** = devoid of anything external or internal; **pūrṇaṁ** = complete, full; **brahmādvitīyam-evāham** = I am indeed the Absolute, one without a second.

nirupamam anādi-tattvaṁ tvam aham idam ada iti kalpanā-dūram |
nityānandaika-rasaṁ satyaṁ brahmādvitīyam-evāham ||494||

I am indeed the Absolute, one without a second, incomparable, beginningless Truth, beyond all imagined distinctions such as 'you', 'I', 'this', 'that', of the essence of eternal bliss, the real.

See MāṇḍUp 2.7, 'This Self is the Absolute' (*ayam ātmā brahma*); BṛhUp 1.4.10, 'I am the Absolute' (*aham brahmāsmi*).

nirupamam = incomparable; **anādi-tattvaṁ** = beginningless truth; **tvam** = you; aham = 'I'; idam = this; **ada** = that; **kalpanā-dūram** = beyond imagined distinctions, imaginations.

nārāyaṇo'haṁ narakāntako'haṁ
purāntako'haṁ puruṣo'ham-īśaḥ |
akhaṇḍa-bodho'hamaśeṣa-sākṣī
nirīśvaro'haṁ nirahaṁ ca nirmamaḥ ||495||

I am Nārāyaṇa. I am the slayer of Naraka. I am the slayer of Tripurāsura. I am the supreme Person, the Lord. I am knowledge absolute, witness of all. I am not subject to another ruler. I am without a sense of 'I' or 'mine'.

Nārāyaṇa is one name for Viṣṇu, the all-pervading One. He slayed the demon Naraka. As Lord Śiva, he slayed the demon Tripurāsura.

See KaivUp 1.18 on the witness.

See V. 101, 127, 137, 159, 212, 213, 217, 218, 223, 270, 295, 352, 370, 381, 384, 506, 507, and 552 for references to witness (*sākṣī*).

nārāyaṇo'haṁ = I am Nārāyaṇa; **narakāntako'haṁ** = I am the slayer of Naraka; **purāntako'haṁ** = I am the slayer of Tripurāsura; **puruṣo'ham-īśaḥ** = I am the supreme person, the Lord; **akhaṇḍa-bodha** = knowledge absolute; **ahamaśeṣa-sākṣī** = I am the witness of all; **nirīśvaro'haṁ** = I am not subject to another ruler; **nirahaṁ ca nirmamaḥ** = I am without a sense of 'I' or mine.

sarveṣu bhūteṣvaham-eva saṁsthitaḥ
jñātrātmanāntar-bahir-āśrayaḥ san |
bhoktā ca bhogyaṁ svayam-eva sarvaṁ
tadyat-pṛthag-dṛṣṭam idaṁtayā purā ||496||

I alone abide in all beings, in the form of the knower, as their internal and external support. I, myself, am the enjoyer and I, myself, am all that is enjoyed; whatever I looked upon as distinctly 'this' previously is nothing but me.

See BG 2.30, 'This, the indweller in all bodies, is indestructible'.

sarveṣu bhūteṣvaham-eva saṁsthitaḥ = I alone abide in all beings; **jñātrātman** = in the form of the knower; **antarbahir-āśrayaḥ** = internal and external support; **bhoktā ca bhogyaṁ** = enjoyer and enjoyed; **tadyat-pṛthagdṛṣṭam idaṁtayā purā** = of whatever is seen in front distinctly as 'this' earlier.

mayy-akhaṇḍa-sukhāmbhodhau bahudhā viśva-vīcayaḥ |
utpadyante vilīyante māyā-māruta-vibhramāt ||497||

By the flurry of the winds of *māyā*, the various waves of the universe arise and are merged in me, the infinite ocean of bliss.

See V. 67, 110–12, 125, 245, 406, and 574 on *māyā*.

See V. 442 and 483 on waves merging in the ocean.

mayyakhaṇḍa-sukhāmbhodhau = in me, the infinite ocean of bliss; **bahudhā** = great multitude; **viśva-vīcayaḥ** = waves of the universe; **utpadyante** = arise; **vilīyante** = merge; **māyā-māruta** = winds of illusion; **vibhramāt** = whirling about, agitated, flurry.

sthūlādi-bhāvā mayi kalpitā bhramāt
āropitānusphuraṇena lokaiḥ |
kāle yathā kalpaka-vatsarāyaṇa
ṛtvādayo niṣkala-nirvikalpe ||498||

Such ideas as gross, and so on, are erroneously imagined in me by people through the manifestation of things superimposed (or of what is superimposed on me by delusion), just as in time, which is indivisible and partless, distinctions are made of eons, years, half-years, seasons, and so on.

See V. 39, 181, 269, 271, 279–86, 307, 393, 407, and 462 on superimposition.

sthūlādi = gross and so on; **kalpitā bhramāt** = erroneously imagined; **āropitānusphuraṇena** = manifestation superimposed; **kāle** = time; **kalpaka** = eons; **vatsarāyaṇa** = years and half years; **ṛtvādi** = seasons and so on.

āropitaṁ nāśraya-dūṣakaṁ bhavet
kad-āpi mūḍhair mati-doṣa-dūṣitaiḥ |
nārdrīkarotyūṣara-bhūmi-bhāgaṁ
marīcikā-vāri-mahā-pravāhaḥ ||499||

That which is superimposed by fools affected by defects of the mind cannot affect the substratum. A great flood of water seen in a mirage does not wet the desert sand.

āropitaṁ = that which is superimposed; **nāśraya-dūṣakaṁ bhavet** = cannot affect the substratum; **mūḍhair** = by fools; **mati-doṣa-dūṣitaiḥ** = affected by defects of the mind; **nārdrīkarot-yūṣara-bhūmi** = does not wet the desert sand; **bhāgaṁ** = part; **marīcikā** = mirage; **mahā-pravāhaḥ** = great flood of water.

ākāśavat kalpa-vidūrago'ham
ādityavad bhāsya-vilakṣaṇo'ham |
ahāryavat nitya-viniścalo'ham
ambhodhivat pāra-vivarjito'ham ||500||

Like space, I am beyond all temporal limitations. Like the sun, I am different from things illuminated. Like the mountain, I am permanent and unmoving. Like the ocean, I am without a shore.

ākāśavat = like space; **kalpa-vidūraga** = beyond, unlimited by time; **ādityavad** = like the sun; **bhāsya-vilakṣaṇo'ham** = I am other than the illumined; **ahāryavat** = like the mountain; **nitya-viniścalo'ham** = I am permanent, eternal, and unmoving; **ambhodhivat** = like the ocean; **pāra-vivarjito'ham** = I am free from, without a shore, limitless, boundary, the end or limit of anything, the utmost reach.

na me dehena sambandho megheneva vihāyasaḥ |
ataḥ kuto me tad-dharmā jāgrat-svapna-suṣuptayaḥ ||501||

I am not connected with the body, as the sky with clouds. How then will its qualities like waking, dreaming, and deep sleep affect me?

na me dehena sambandho = I am not connected with the body; **megheneva vihāyasaḥ** = as the sky with clouds; **dharmā** = qualities; **jāgrat-svapna-suṣupti** = waking, dreaming, deep sleep.

upādhir-āyāti sa eva gacchati
sa eva karmāṇi karoti bhuṅkte |
sa eva jīvan mriyate sadāhaṁ
kulādrivan niścala eva saṁsthitaḥ ||502||

It is the limiting adjuncts alone which come, and they alone go; that performs actions and enjoys; that alone lives and dies. Like the Kulādri Mountains, I stand ever unmoving.[1]

upādhir = limiting adjuncts; **āyāti** = coming; **gacchati** = going; **eva** = only; **karmāṇi karoti** = performing actions; **bhuṅkte** = enjoying; **jīvan mriya** = lives and dies; **kulādrivan** = like the Kulādri Mountains; **sadāhaṁ niścala eva saṁsthitaḥ** = I stand ever unmoving.

---

[1] See IśāUp 4, 'The Self is One, although not moving. It is swifter than the mind; the gods cannot catch it, as it speeds on in front. Standing, it outpaces others who run.'

na me pravṛttir na ca me nivṛttiḥ
sadaika-rūpasya niramśakasya |
ekātmako yo nibiḍo nirantaro
vyomeva pūrṇaḥ sa kathaṁ nu ceṣṭate ||503||

For me, ever of the same form, without parts, there is neither activity nor withdrawal. How can that which is one, complete, compacted, and without parts, ever act?

See ŚvetUp 6.19, 'without parts, without activity' (*niṣkalam niṣkriyam*); also 6.12.

na pravṛttir = neither activity; **na nivṛttiḥ** = nor withdrawal; **sadaika-rūpasya** = ever of the same form; **niramśakasya** = partless; **ekātmako** = that which is one; **nibiḍo** = compacted; **nirantaro** = without parts; **vyomeva** = ever act, move; **pūrṇaḥ** = complete, full; **ceṣṭate** = move, struggle, act, strive.

puṇyāni pāpāni nirindriyasya
niścetaso nirvikṛter nirākṛteḥ |
kuto mamākhaṇḍa-sukhānubhūteḥ
brūte hy-ananvāgatam ityapi śrutiḥ ||504||

How can there be merits and demerits[1] for me who am without sense organs, without mind, without change, and without form; who experiences infinite bliss? The scripture also declares this in the passage, 'not touched'.

puṇyāni = merits, auspiciousness; **pāpāni** = demerits, inauspiciousness, wickedness; **nirindriyasya** = without sense organs; **niścetaso** = without mind; **nirvikṛter** = without change; **nirākṛteḥ** = without form; **mamākhaṇḍa-sukhānubhūteḥ** = for me who experiences infinite bliss; **brūte hy-ananvāgatamthe ityapi śrutiḥ** = the scripture declares this in the 'untouched, unconnected' passage.

chāyayā spṛṣṭam uṣṇaṁ vā śītam vā suṣṭhu duṣṭhu vā |
na spṛśatyeva yat-kiñcit puruṣaṁ tad-vilakṣaṇam ||505||

If heat or cold, good or bad touches the shadow of a person, it does not affect in the least the person who is distinct from the shadow.

The original is least affected by its reflection. The body is least affected by its shadow.
See V. 165, 414, 431, and 505 on shadow.
See BG 2.23, 'Weapons do not hurt the Self, fire does not burn it, water does not wet it, wind does not dry it.'

chāyayā = shadow; **spṛṣṭam** = touches; **uṣṇaṁ vā śītam** = heat or cold; **suṣṭhu vā duṣṭhu** = good or bad; **puruṣaṁ** = person; **tadvilakṣaṇam** = distinct from, other than that.

na sākṣiṇaṁ sākṣya-dharmāḥ samspṛśanti vilakṣaṇam |
avikāram udāsīnam gṛha-dharmāḥ pradīpavat |
dehendriya-manodharmāḥ naivātmanam spṛśantyaho ||506||

---

[1] See BṛhUp 4.3.22, 'Untouched by merits and demerits, for he is then beyond all the afflictions of the heart.'

The qualities of things observed do not affect the witness who is other than them; the qualities of the body, the sense organs, and the mind do not affect the Self even as the qualities of the objects in a house do not affect the lamp which illuminates them.

See BG 2.23, 'This Self cannot be cut, cannot be burnt, cannot be wet, cannot be dried. It is eternal, all-pervading, stable, immovable, and everlasting.'

See KaivUp 1.18 on the witness.

See V. 101, 127, 137, 159, 212, 213, 217, 218, 223, 270, 295, 352, 370, 381, 384, 495, 507, and 552 for references to witness (*sākṣī*).

na = not; **sākṣiṇaṁ** = witness; **dharmāḥ** = qualities; **samspṛśanti** = touch, affect; **vilakṣaṇam** = other than, distinct from; **avikāram** = does not change; **udāsīnam** = indifferent, free from; **gṛha** = house; **dehendriya** = body and sense organs; **mano** = mind.

raver yathā karmaṇi sākṣi-bhāvo
vahner yathā vā'yasi-dāhakatvam |
rajjor yathā'ropita-vastu-saṅgaḥ
tathaiva kūṭastha-cid-ātmano me ||507||

As the sun is merely a witness of action, as the fire makes for the burning quality of iron, as the rope is associated with the object superimposed upon it, so too is what pertains to me who am the immutable consciousness.

See KaivUp 1.18 on witness.

See V. 101, 127, 137, 159, 212, 213, 217, 218, 223, 270, 295, 352, 370, 381, 384, 495, 506, and 552 for references to witness (*sākṣī*).

See V. 135, 193, and 350 on fire in iron.

raver = sun; **sākṣi** = witness; **vahner** = fire; **ayasi** = iron; **dāhakatvam** = burning quality; **rajjor** = rope; **aropita** = superimposed; **saṅgaḥ** = associated with; **tathaiva** = likewise, so too; **kūṭastha-cid** = immutable consciousness.

kartāpi vā kārayitāpi nāhaṁ
bhoktāpi vā bhojayitāpi nāham |
draṣṭāpi vā darśayitāpi nāhaṁ
so'haṁ svayaṁ-jyotir-anīdṛg-ātmā ||508||

I am neither the doer nor one who makes others act. I am neither the enjoyer nor one who makes others enjoy. I am neither the seer nor one who makes others see. I am the self-effulgent, indescribable Self.

See BG 4.13, 'Know me to be actionless and changeless (*akartāram avyayam*)'. Also see ŚvetUp. 6.19, 'actionless' (*niṣkriyaṁ*).

See US 1.11.11, 'Just as it is seen that a sword (shines) when it is drawn from its sheath, so the Knower, separated in the dreaming state from cause and effect, is seen to be self-effulgent'; MuṇḍUp. 2.2.10–11. Also see V. 100, 153, 191, 213, 221, 240, and 536 on self-luminous.

kartāpi = doer; **vā kārayitāpi** = nor one who makes others act; **nāhaṁ bhoktāpi** = I am not the enjoyer; **vā bhojayitāpi** = nor one who makes others enjoy; **nāham draṣṭāpi**

= I am neither the seer; **vā darśayitāpi** = nor one who makes others see; **so'haṁ svayaṁ-jyotir-anīdṛg-ātmā** = I am the self-effulgent, indescribable Self.

calatyupādhau pratibimba-laulyam
aupādhikaṁ mūdha-dhiyo nayanti |
sva-bimba-bhūtaṁ ravivad viniṣ-kriyam
kartāsmi bhoktāsmi hato'smi heti ||509||

When the limiting adjunct moves, the movement of its reflection is ascribed by fools to the original, like the sun which is unmoving. Likewise, one thinks 'I am the doer', 'I am the enjoyer', 'I am lost', alas!

calatyupādhau = limiting adjunct moves; **pratibimba** = reflection; **laulyam** = restlessness, fickleness; **aupādhikaṁ** = imposter; **mūdha-dhiyo** = foolish-minded ones; **sva-bimba-bhūta** = one's own original being; **ravivad** = sun; **viniṣ-kriyam** = not moving; **kartāsmi** = I am the doer; **bhoktāsmi** = I am the enjoyer; **hato'smi** = I am lost; **heti** = alas.

jale vāpi sthale vāpi luṭhatveṣa jaḍātmakaḥ |
nāhaṁ vilipye tad-dharmaiḥ ghaṭa-dharmair nabho yathā ||510||

Whether on water or on land, let this insentient body wallow. I am not affected by their qualities, even as the space is not affected by the qualities of the pot.

jale = water; **vāpi** = be strewn, be cast; **sthale** = dry land; **luṭhatveṣa** = to wallow, roll; **jaḍātmakaḥ** = insentient, inert body; **nāhaṁ** = space; **vilipye** = affected, concealed; **dharmaiḥ** = qualities; **ghaṭa** = pot.

kartṛtva-bhoktṛtva-khalatva-mattatā-
jaḍatva-baddhatva-vimuktatādayaḥ |
buddher vikalpā na tu santi vastutaḥ
svasmin pare brahmaṇi kevale'dvaye ||511||

The imaginations of the intellect like agency, enjoyment, cunning, drunkenness, dullness, bondage, and liberation do not exist, in reality, in one's own Self, or in the supreme Absolute, which is one, without a second.

kartṛtva = agency; **bhoktṛtva** = enjoyment; **khalatva** = cunning; **mattatā** = drunkenness; **jaḍatva** = dullness; **baddhatva** = bondage; **vimuktatādayaḥ** = liberation; **buddher vikalpā** = imaginations of the intellect.

santu vikārāḥ prakṛter daśadhā śatadhā sahasradhā vāpi |
taiḥ kiṁ me'saṅga-citaḥ na hyambudaḍambaro'mbaraṁ spṛśati ||512||

Let there be changes in primordial nature in tens, hundreds, or thousands. What is my connection with them? I am the unconnected consciousness. For the thunder of the clouds does not touch the sky.

vikārāḥ = changes; **prakṛter** = primordial nature; **daśadhā** = tens; **śatadhā** = hundreds; **sahasradhā** = thousands; **vāpi** = changes; **taikihkim me'sanga-citah** = (connection with them); **na hyambudaḍambaro'mbaraṁ spṛśati** = the thunder of the clouds does not touch the sky.

avyaktādi sthūla-paryantam-etad
viśvaṁ yatrābhāsa-mātraṁ pratītam |
vyoma-prakhyaṁ sūkṣmam-ādyanta-hīnaṁ
brahmādvaitaṁ yat-tad-evāham-asmi ||513||

I am verily that Absolute, the one without a second, which is like the sky, subtle, without beginning or end, in which the entire universe from the unmanifested to the gross, appears as an appearance.

According to Śaṅkara, nothing is more certain than the fact of one's own existence. It is self-evident, immediate, and direct. No one is able to disbelieve in one's own existence. 'A man may doubt of many things, of anything else; but he can never doubt his own being' (BSBh 2.3.7). This is because the very act of doubting would be but an affirmation of one's very existence. In the act of saying, 'I don't exist', who is the 'I' who is doing the doubting?

avyaktādi = unmanifest; **sthūla** = gross; **paryantam** = entirely, all together; **viśvaṁ** = universe; **yatrābhāsa-mātraṁ** = appears as an appearnce; **vyoma** = sky; **sūkṣmam** = subtle.

sarvādhāraṁ sarva-vastu-prakāśaṁ
sarvākāraṁ sarvagaṁ sarva-śūnyam |
nityaṁ śuddhaṁ niścalam nirvikalpaṁ
brahmādvaitaṁ yat-tad-evāham-asmi ||514||

I am verily that Absolute, the one without a second, which is the support of all, which illuminates all things, which has all forms, which is omnipresent, which is the great void, eternal, pure, changeless, and impartite.

sarvādhāraṁ = support of all; **sarva-vastu-prakāśaṁ** = illumines all things; **sarvākāraṁ** = all forms; **sarvagaṁ** = omnipresent; **sarva-śūnyam** = devoid of all forms; **nityaṁ** = eternal; **śuddhaṁ** = pure; **niścalam** = changeless; **nirvikalpaṁ** = impartite.

yasminnastā śeṣa-māyā-viśeṣaṁ
pratyag-rūpaṁ pratyayāgamyamānam |
satya-jñānāntam ānanda-rūpaṁ
brahmādvaitaṁ yat-tad-evāham-asmi ||515||

I am verily that Absolute, the one without a second, which transcends the endless differentiations of *māyā*, which is the innermost essence, which cannot be comprehended by the mere intellect, and which is the essence of Existence, Knowledge, Infinitude, Bliss.

See TaittUp 2.1.1, '. . . know the Absolute as Existence, Knowledge, Infinitude'.

yasminnastā śeṣa-māyā-viśeṣaṁ = transcends the endless differentiations of illusion; **pratyag-rūpaṁ** = innermost essence; **pratyayāgam-yamānam** = cannot be comprehended by the intellect; **satya-jñānāntam ānanda-rūpaṁ** = the essence of Existence, Knowledge, Bliss.

niṣkriyo'smy-avikāro'smi
niṣkalo'smi nirākṛtiḥ |
nirvikalpo'smi nityo'smi
nirālambo'smi nirdvayaḥ ||516||

I am actionless, changeless, partless, formless. I am without differences. I am eternal. I have no other support, being without a second.

niṣkriyo'smy = I am actionless; **avikāro'smi** = I am changeless; **niṣkalo'smi** = I am partless; **nirākṛtiḥ** = I am formless; **nirvikalpo'smi** = I am without modifications; **nityo'smi** = I am eternal; **nirālambo'smi** = I am supportless; **nirdvayaḥ** = without a second.

sarvātmako'ham sarvo'haṁ sarvātīto'ham advayaḥ |
kevalākhaṇḍa-bodho'ham ānando'ham nirantaram ||517||

I am the Self of all. I am everything. I am beyond everything. I am non-dual. I am the single, infinite wisdom. I am bliss and indivisible.

sarvātmako'ham = I am the Self of all; **sarvo'haṁ** = I am everything; **sarvātīto'ham** = I am beyond everything; **advayaḥ kevalākhaṇḍa-bodho'ham** = I am non-dual, infinite, wisdom; **ānando'ham** = I am bliss; **nirantaram** = indivisible.

svārājya-sāmrājya-vibhūtir-eṣā
bhavat-kṛpā-śrī-mahita-prasādāt |
prāptā mayā śrī-gurave mahātmane
namo namaste'stu punar namo'stu ||518||

My salutations to you, again and again, salutations to you, O supreme, auspicious Master. It is by your grace and by your auspicious, supreme blessings that I have attained the splendor of this self-sovereignty and lordship over all.

See V. 3, 29, 42, 50, 138, 149, 477, 489, and 519 for references to grace.

svārājya = self-sovereignty; **sāmrājya** = lordship, sovereignty; **vibhūtir** = splendor; **kṛpā** = grace; **śrī-mahita-prasādāt** = auspicious, supreme blessings; **śrī-gurave** = auspicious Master; **mahātmane** = great one; **namo namaste'stu punar namo'stu** = salutations to you, again and again.

mahā-svapne māyā-kṛta-jani-jarā-mṛtyu-gahane
bhramantaṁ kliśyantaṁ bahula-tara-tāpair anukalam |
ahaṁkāra-vyāghra-vyathitam imam atyanta-kṛpayā
prabodhya prasvāpāt param avitavān māmasi guro ||519||

O Master, by your infinite grace, you have awakened me from sleep and saved me, who was wandering in a great dream in the forest of birth, old age, and death created by *māyā*. I was exhausted by countless illusory afflictions which tormented me every moment. I was tormented by the tiger of egoism.

The very concept of bondage is itself bondage because, whichever way it is considered, there is no 'one' to be bound and no 'one' to be liberated. The concept of bondage is tied to the illusion that there is a 'me', independent; an imagined entity. The Master points out to the seeker that he himself already is, has always been, what he thinks he is seeking. The eye is seeking that which it is already seeing.

See V. 3, 29, 42, 50, 138, 149, 477, 489, and 518 for references to grace.

mahā-svapne = great dream; **māyā-kṛta** = created by illusion; **jani** = birth; **jarā** = old age; **mṛtyu** = death; **gahane bhramantaṁ kliśyantaṁ** = countless illusory, false afflictions; **bahula** = thick, dense; **tara** = carrying across; **tāpair** = sorrow, afflictions; **anukalam** = every moment; **ahaṁkāra** = egoism; **vyāghra** = tiger; **vyathitam** = to be agitated, restless, tormented; **atyanta-kṛpayā** = infinite grace; **prabodhya** = awakened; **guro** = O Master.

namas tasmai sad-ekasmai namaś cinmahase muhuḥ |
yad-etad-viśva-rūpeṇa rājate gurū-rāja te ||520||

Salutations to you, O king among Masters, who is always the same. Salutations to you again, whose glorious consciousness manifests as the entire universe.

The Master is a living example of the fact that there is no entity with a separate existence. There is no 'he', no 'me', no 'you'.

namas = salultations; **sad-ekasmai** = who are always one; **cinmahase** = glorious consciousness; **muhuḥ** = constantly, incessantly; **viśva-rūpeṇa** = entire universe; **rājate gurū-rāja** = king among Masters.

iti natam-avalokya śiṣya-varyaṁ
samadhigatātma-sukhaṁ prabuddha-tattvam |
pramudita-hṛdayam sa deśikendraḥ
punar-idam-āha vacaḥ paraṁ mahātmā ||521||

Perceiving this best among students, who, bowing down, has perfectly realized the bliss of the Self and who has awakened to the Truth, with a joyful heart, that supreme Great One again spoke these wise words.

iti = this; **natam-avalokya** = bowing down; **śiṣya-varyaṁ** = best among students; **samadhigatātma-sukhaṁ** = who has perfectly realized the bliss of the Self; **prabuddha-tattvam** = awakened to the truth; **pramudita-hṛdayam** = joyful heart; **sa deśikendraḥ** = these wise instructions; **punar** = again; **idam-āha** = this command; **vacaḥ** = spoke; **paraṁ mahātmā** = supreme Great One.

brahma-pratyaya-santatir jagad-ato brahmaiva sat sarvataḥ
paśyādhyātma-dṛśā praśānta-manasā sarvāsvavasthāsvapi |
rūpād-anyad-avekṣitaṁ kim-abhitaś cakṣuṣmatām vidyate
tad-vad brahma-vidaḥ sataḥ kim-apraṁ buddher-vihārāspadam ||522||

The universe is an unbroken stream of perceptions of the Absolute. Hence, it is in all respects solely the Absolute. See this in all one's states by the inner vision of the Self with a serene mind. For those with eyes, is there anything to sense other than forms? Similarly, for those who have known the Absolute, is there anything other than it to engage their intellect?

ChānUp 3.14.1 declares, 'All this is the Absolute' (*sarvam khalvidam brahma*). To a person of realization, nothing exists which is not That.

brahma-pratyaya-santatir = unbroken stream of perceptions of the Absolute; **jagad** = universe; **paśyādhyātma-dṛśā** = see this in all one's states by inner vision; **praśānta-manasā** = serene mind; **rūpād-anyad** = other than forms; **cakṣuṣmatām** = for those with eyes; **kim-apraṁ** = what is there other.

kastāṁ parānanda-rasānubhūtim
utsṛjya śūnyeṣu rameta vidvān |
candre mahālādini dīpamane
citrendum ālokayituṁ ka icchet ||523||

What wise one will indulge in the void, abandoning the nectarine experience of supreme bliss? When the moon is shining giving infinite delight, who will desire to look at a painted moon?

parānanda-rasānubhūtim = nectarine experience of supreme bliss; **utsṛjya** = abandoning; **śūnyeṣu** = the void; **rameta** = pleasing; **vidvān** = wise one; **candre** = moon; **mahālādini** = infinitely delightful; **dīpa** = luminous, shining; **ka· icchet** = who will desire.

asat-padārthānubhavena kiñcit
na-hyasti tṛptir na ca duḥkha-hāniḥ |
tad-advayānanda-rasānubhūtyā
tṛptaḥ sukhaṁ tiṣṭha sadātma-niṣṭhayā ||524||

In the enjoyment of unreal things, there is neither satisfaction nor a cessation of misery. Therefore, remain satisfied and happy in the realization of the existent Self, enjoying the nectarine experience of that non-dual[1] bliss.

asat-padārthānubhavena = experience of unreal things; **na-hyasti tṛptir** = there is neither satisfaction; **na duḥkha-hāniḥ** = nor cessation of misery; **advayānanda** = non-dual bliss; **rasānubhūtyā** = nectarine experience.

svam-eva sarvathā paśyan manya-mānaḥ svam-advayam |
svānandam anubhuñjānaḥ kālam naya mahāmate ||525||

Great One! Spend your time beholding yourself alone, everywhere, thinking of yourself as non-dual, experiencing yourself as bliss.

eva = alone, one; **sarvathā** = everywhere; **paśyan** = seeing, observing; **advayam** = non-dual; **ānandam** = blissful; **mahāmate** = Great One.

akhaṇḍa-bodhātmani nirvikalpe
vikalpanaṁ vyomni puraḥ-prakalpanam |
tad-advayānanda-mayātmanā sadā
śāntiṁ parām-etya bhajasva maunam ||526||

Attributing distinctions in the Self, the impartite infinite knowledge, is like imagining castles in the sky. Therefore, remain silent, always identifying yourself with That, the Self, non-dual bliss, to attain supreme peace.

akhaṇḍa-bodhātmani = infinite knowledge; **nirvikalpe** = impartite; **vikalpanaṁ** = imagining distinctions, mental constructs; **vyomni** = sky; **puraḥ-prakalpanam** = imagining cities, castles; **advayānanda** = non-dual bliss; **sadā** = always; **śāntiṁ** = calm, peace; **maunam** = silence.

---

[1] Compare the famous verse from the *Śrīmad Bhāgavatam* 9.19.14, 'Never is desire appeased by the enjoyment of sense pleasures'.

tūṣṇīm-avasthā paramopaśāntiḥ
buddher asatkalpa-vikalpa-hetoḥ |
brahmātmanā brahma-vido mahātmano
yatrādvayānanda-sukhaṁ nirantaram ||527||

To a Great One, who is a knower of the Absolute, the mind, which is the cause of imagined unrealities, becomes supremely silent by reason of one's being the Absolute in the enjoyment of eternal non-dual bliss.

tūṣṇīm-avasthā = becomes. silent; **paramopaśāntiḥ** = supremely silent, peaceful; **buddher** = mind, intellect; **asatkalpa-vikalpa** = imagined unrealities; **hetoḥ** = cause of; **mahātmano** = Great One.

nāsti nirvāsanāt maunāt paraṁ sukhakṛd-uttamam |
vijñātātma-svarūpasya svānanda-rasa-pāyinaḥ ||528||

To one who has known their Self, their own nature, and drinks the nectar of the bliss of the Self, there is no greater source of joy than the silence free from every desire.

maunāt = silence; **paraṁ** = supreme; **sukhakṛd-uttamam** = giver, maker of the highest happiness.

gacchaṁ-stiṣṭhan-upaviśan śayāno vānyathāpi vā |
yathecchayā vased vidvān ātmārāmaḥ sadā muniḥ ||529||

The sage, delighting in the Self, ever lives at ease, whether going, remaining, sitting, reclining, or in any other condition.

gacchaṁ = going; **stiṣṭhan** = remaining; **upaviśan** = sitting; **śayāno** = reclining; **vānyathāpi** = any other condition; **ātmārāmaḥ** = delighting in the Self; **sadā** = always; **muniḥ** = sage.

na deśa-kālāsana-dig-yamādi-
lakṣyādyapekṣāpratibaddha-vṛtteḥ |
saṁsiddha-tattvasya mahātmano'sti
svavedane kā niyamādyavasthā ||530||

The Great One, who has perfectly realized the Truth, whose mental modifications have been rendered ineffective, does not depend upon place, time, posture, direction, abstentions, and so on. What disciplines can there be in knowing one's own Self?

na deśa-kālāsana-dig-yamādi = neither place, time, posture, direction, abstentions, and so on; **lakṣyādyapekṣāpratibaddha-vṛtteḥ** = mental modifications have been rendered ineffective; **saṁsiddha-tattvasya** = perfectly realized the truth; **mahātmano** = Great One; **svavedane** = knowing one's own Self; **kā niyamādya-vasthā** = what abstention practices.

ghaṭo'yam-iti vijñātuṁ niyamaḥ ko'nvapekṣyate |
vinā pramāṇa-suṣṭhutvaṁ yasmin sati padārtha-dhīḥ ||531||

Truly, what discipline is needed to know, 'this is a jar', save that the means of knowledge be without any defects, which alone ensures perception of the object?

ghaṭo'yam-iti = this is a jar; **vijñātuṁ** = to know; **niyamaḥ** = disciplines; **apekṣyate** = with regard to, considering; **vinā** = without; **pramāṇa** = source of knowledge; **susṭhutvaṁ** = to establish, settle well; **padārtha-dhīḥ** = perception of an object.

ayam-ātmā nitya-siddhaḥ pramāṇe sati bhāsate ।
na deśaṁ nāpi vā kālaṁ na śuddhiṁ vāpyapekṣate ॥532॥

This Self is eternally perfect and shines when apprehended by proper canons of knowledge. It does not depend upon place, time, or purity.

ayam-ātmā = this Self; **nitya-siddhaḥ** = eternally perfect; **pramāṇe** = valid means of knowledge; **bhāsate** = shines; **deśaṁ** = place; **kālaṁ** = time; **śuddhiṁ** = purity.

devadatto'ham-ity-etad-vijñānaṁ nirapekṣakam ।
tadvad brahmavido'pyasya brahmāham-iti vedanam ॥533॥

The knowledge, 'I am Devadatta', does not depend on anything else. Likewise is the Self-realization in the declaration, 'I am That', for one who has realized the Absolute.

devadatto'ham = I am Devadatta; **nirapekṣakam** = does not depend upon; **brahmāham** = I am the Absolute.

bhānuneva jagat sarvaṁ bhāsate yasya tejasā ।
anātmakam asat tucchaṁ kiṁ nu tasyāvabhāsaskam ॥534॥

What, indeed, can illuminate That, whose effulgence, like the sun, causes the entire false, unreal and without substance universe to appear at all?

bhānu = the sun; **jagat** = universe, world; **sarvaṁ** = all, entire; **bhāsate** = illuminate; **tejasā** = splendor, effulgence; **anātmakam** = not-self; **asat** = unreal; **tucchaṁ** = false.

veda-śāstra-purāṇāni bhūtāni sakalānyapi ।
yenārthavanti taṁ kiṁ nu vijñātāraṁ prakāśayet ॥535॥

What can illuminate that supreme knower by whom the Vedas, the *śāstras*, the *Purāṇas*, and all things are endowed with meaning?

veda = Vedas, primary scripture; **śāstra** = *śāstras*, scriptures in general; **purāṇāni** = *Purāṇas*, sacred, legendary historical books containing stories, legends, and hymns about the creation of the universe and the incarnations of the divine.

eṣa svayaṁjyotir ananta-śaktir
ātmā'prameyaḥ sakalānubhūtiḥ ।
yam-eva vijñāya vimukta-bandhaḥ
jayatyayaṁ brahmavid uttamottamaḥ ॥536॥

This is the self-effulgent Self, of infinite power, beyond all valid means of conditioned knowledge, yet the direct experience of all. Freed from bondage, realizing this alone, the incomparable knower of the Absolute lives victoriously.

See US 1.11.11; MuṇḍUp 2.2.10–11. Also see V. 100, 153, 191, 213, 221, 240, 508, and 536 on self-luminous.

svayaṁjyotir = self-effulgent; **ananta-śaktir** = infinite power; **ātmā'prameyaḥ** = the Self is indefinable; **sakala** = conditioned; **anubhūtiḥ** = directly experienced; **vimukta-bandhaḥ** = freed from bondage; **jayatyayaṁ** = lives victoriously; **brahmavid uttamottamaḥ** = incomparable, highest knower of the Absolute.

na khidyate no viṣayaiḥ pramodate
na sajjate nāpi virajyate ca |
svasmin sadā krīḍati nandati svayaṁ
nirantarānanda-rasena tṛptaḥ ||537||

He is neither grieved nor pleased by sense objects, and he is neither attached nor averse to them. He sports and delights in his own Self, ever content in the elixir of unending bliss.

See BG 14.24, 'He who regards pain and pleasure alike, who dwells in his own Self' (*samaduḥkhasukhaḥ svasthaḥ*).

na khidyate = neither grieved; **no viṣayaiḥ pramodate** = nor pleased by sense objects; **na sajjate** = neither attached; **nāpi virajyate** = nor averse; **sadā** = always; **krīḍati** = sports; **nandati** = delights; **nirantarānanda-rasena** = in the elixir of unending bliss; **tṛptaḥ** = content.

kṣudhāṁ deha-vyathāṁ tyaktvā bālaḥ krīḍati vastuni |
tathaiva vidvān ramate nirmamo nirahaṁ sukhī ||538||

A child plays unmindful of bodily afflictions and hunger. Likewise, the realized person delights without any sense of 'my' and 'I' and is happy.

kṣudhāṁ = hunger; **deha-vyathāṁ** = bodily afflictions; **tyaktvā** = unmindful, free from; **bālaḥ** = child; **krīḍati** = plays; **vidvān** = realized person, knower; **ramate** = delights; **nirmamo** = without mine; **nirahaṁ** = without 'I'; **sukhī** = happy.

cintā-śūnyam adainya-bhaikṣam-aśanaṁ pānaṁ sarid-vāriṣu
svātantryeṇa niraṅkuśā-sthitir abhīr nidrā śmaśāne vane |
vastraṁ kṣālana-śoṣaṇādi-rahitaṁ dig-vāstu śayyā mahī
sañcāro nigamānta-vīthiṣu vidāṁ krīḍā pare brahmaṇi ||539||

The realized individual sports in the supreme Absolute, eating carefree, on alms obtained without humiliation, drinking water from rivers, living freely without restraint, sleeping without fear in the cremation ground or in the forest, covered in clothes, unwashed and undried, or even naked, clothed in space, sleeping on the earth, the wise roam the highways of the scriptures and sport in the supreme Absolute.

Compare Swami Vivekananda's poem, 'Song of the Sannyasin' to this verse.

cintā-śūnyam = without worry, devoid of thoughts, carefree; **adainya** = without humiliation; **bhaikṣam-aśanaṁ** = food obtained by begging; **pānaṁ sarid-vāriṣu** = drinking river water; **abhīr** = without any fear; **nidrā śmaśāne vane** = sleeping in a cremation ground or forest; **vastraṁ** = cloth; **kṣālana-śoṣaṇādi-rahitaṁ** = unwashed, undried and so on; **dig-vāstu** = clothed in space, naked; **śayyā** = sleeping; **mahī** = earth; **sañcāro** = moving about, roaming; **nigamānta** = passages of the scriptures; **vīthiṣu** = roads, streets, highways; **krīḍā** = sport.

vimānam-ālambya śarīram-etat
bhunaktyaśeṣān viṣayān-upasthitān |
parecchayā bālavadātmavettā
yo'vyakta-liṅgo'nanuṣakta-bāhyaḥ ||540||

Without any manifest marks or external attachments, the knower of the Absolute, like a child, experiences all sense objects through the body as they come to him by the wishes of others, but without any identification with them.

vimānam = measuring out; **ālambya** = depending on, sustaining; **śarīram** = body; **viṣayān** = sense objects; **bālavad** = like a child; **yo'vyakta-liṅgo'nanuṣakta-bāhyaḥ** = without any manifest marks or external attachments.

dig-ambaro vāpi ca sāmbaro vā
tvag-ambaro vāpi cid-ambara-sthaḥ |
unmattavad vāpi ca bālavad-vā
piśācavad vāpi caratyavanyām ||541||

Established in the ethereal space of consciousness, he wanders on the earth naked or clothed or clad in skins, like one drunk, or like a child or a ghost.

dig-ambaro = naked, clothed in space; **vāpi** = clothed; **cidambarasthaḥ** = established in the space of consciousness; **unmattavad** = drunk, intoxicated, mad; **bālavad-vā** = or like a child; **piśācavad** = like a ghost; **caratyavanyām** = wanders on the earth.

kāmān-ni kāmarūpī saṁś-caratyekacaro muniḥ |
svātmanaiva sadā tuṣṭaḥ svayam sarvātmanā sthitah ||542||

Being of the nature of desireless desires, the sage roams by himself seemingly enjoying everything while ever remaining satisfied as the Self of all.

kāmān-ni kāmarūpī = nature of desireless desires; **cara** = roams, wanders; **muniḥ** = sage; **sadā** = always; **tuṣṭaḥ** = enjoying, content, happy with everything; **sarvātmanā sthitah** = remaining as the Self of all.

kvacin-mūḍho vidvān kvacid-api mahārāja-vibhavaḥ
kvacid bhrāntaḥ saumyaḥ kvacid ajagarācāra-kalitaḥ |
kvacid pātrī-bhūtaḥ kvacid-avamataḥ kvapyaviditaḥ
caratyevaṁ prājñaḥ satata-paramānanda-sukhitaḥ ||543||

The realized person, ever enjoying supreme bliss, is sometimes like a fool, sometimes like a sage, sometimes like a king with royal splendor, sometimes like one mad, sometimes like one calm and silent, sometimes unmoving like a python, sometimes respected, sometimes insulted, and sometimes unknown to anyone.

kvacin-mūḍho = sometimes like a fool; **vidvān kvacid** = sometimes like a sage; **mahārāja-vibhavaḥ kvacid** = sometimes like a king with royal splendor; **bhrāntaḥ** = mad; **saumyaḥ kvacid** = sometimes like one calm and silent; **ajagarācāra-kalitaḥ kvacid** = sometimes unmoving like a python; **pātrī-bhūtaḥ avamataḥ kvapya-viditaḥ** = sometimes respected, insulted, unknown.

nirdhano'pi sadā tuṣṭo'py-asahāyo mahābalaḥ |
nitya-tṛpto'py-abhuñjāno'py-asamaḥ samadarśanaḥ ||544||

Though without wealth, yet ever content; though helpless, yet extremely strong; though not enjoying sense objects, yet eternally satisfied; though without an equal, yet seeing all with an equal eye.

No one is superior, no one is inferior, for the same Self is within all and this Truth has been realized.

nirdhano = without wealth; **sadā tuṣṭo** = always contented, satisfied, happy; asahāyo = helpless; **mahābalaḥ** = very strong; **nitya-tṛpto** = eternally satisfied; samadarśanaḥ = seeing all with an equal eye, equal sighted.

api kurvan-na-kurvāṇaś cābhoktā phala-bhogyapi |
śarīryapyaśarīryeṣa paricchinno'pi sarvagaḥ ||545||

Though acting, yet inactive; though experiencing the fruits of actions, yet not enjoying them; though embodied, yet not identified with it; though limited, yet omnipresent.

api kurvan-na-kurvāṇaś = though acting, inactive; **cābhoktā phala-bhogyapi** = experiencing the fruits of action yet not enjoying them; śarīryapyaśarīryeṣa = though embodied, not identified with it; **paricchinno'pi sarvagaḥ** = though limited, yet omnipresent.

aśarīraṁ sadā santam-imam brahma-vidaṁ kvacit |
priyāpriye na spṛśatas tathaiva ca śubhāśubhe ||546||

Neither pleasure nor pain nor good nor bad ever affects this knower of the Absolute who ever remains without a body.

See ChānUp 8.12.1, 'Free from pleasure and pain'.

aśarīraṁ sadā = ever without a body; **brahma-vidaṁ** = knower of the Absolute; **priyāpriye na** = neither pleasure nor pain; **spṛśatas** = touch; **śubhāśubhe** = good or bad.

sthūlādi-saṁbandhavato'bhimāninaḥ
sukhaṁ ca duḥkhaṁ ca śubhāśubhe ca |
vidhvasta-bandhasya sadātmano muneḥ
kutaḥ śubhaṁ vāpyaśubhaṁ phalaṁ vā ||547||

Joy and sorrow, good and bad, pertain to one who is connected with the gross body and is attached to it. For the sage, who has broken his bonds and has realized the Self, how will there arise the fruits of good or bad?

sthūlādi-saṁbandha = connected to the body and so on; **sukhaṁ ca duḥkhaṁ** = joy and sorrow; **śubhāśubhe** = good and bad; **vidhvasta-bandhasya** = broken his bonds; **muneḥ** = the sage; **śubhaṁ aśubhaṁ phalaṁ vā** = the fruits of good or bad.

tamasā grastavad-bhānād agrasto'pi ravir janaiḥ |
grasta ityucyate bhrāntyā hyajñātvā vastu-lakṣaṇam ||548||

On account of delusion, without knowing the Truth, people say that the sun is swallowed, its brightness being hidden by darkness.

See IsāUp 3, 'Into the worlds of the demons, enveloped in blinding darkness, verily do they repair after death who are slayers of the Self.'

tamasā = darkness, dullness; **bhānād** = brightness; **ravir** = sun; **grasta** = swallowed, eaten; **ityucyate** = it is said; **bhrāntyā** = delusion.

tadvad dehādi-bandhebhyo vimuktaṁ brahma-vittamam |
paśyanti dehivan mūḍhāḥ śarīrābhāsa-darśanāt ||549||

Similarly, fools, seeing a supreme knower of the Absolute who is free from the bonds of the body and so on, perceive merely the appearance of a body.

See V. 4, 5, 77, 162, 163, 220, and 549 for fools (*mūḍha*). Also see MuṇḍUp 1.2.8; KaUp 1.2.5; MaitrīUp 7.9; BG 17.5–6.

dehādi-bandhebhyo vimuktaṁ = free from the bonds of the body; **brahma-vittamam** = supreme knower of the Absolute; **paśyanti** = perceive; **dehi** = body; **mūḍhāḥ** = fools; **śarīrābhāsa-darsanāt** = see the appearance of a body.

ahir-nirlvayanīm-vāyaṁ muktvā-deham-tu tiṣṭhati |
itas-tataś cālyamāno yat-kiñcit prāṇavāyunā ||550||

The body of one who is liberated moves here and there, by the vital airs, just as the slough of a snake.[1]

See V. 12, 63, 112, 140, 199, 237, 248, 303, 388, 405, and 407 wherein Śaṅkara makes reference to a snake.

ahir = snake; **nirlvayanīm-vāyaṁ** = to scrape off, slough; **muktvā-deham-tu** = the body of one who is liberated; **tiṣṭhati** = remains; **itas-tataś** = here and there; **cālyamāno** = moving; **prāṇavāyunā** = by the vital airs.

srotasā nīyate dāru yathā nimnonnata-sthalam |
daivena nīyate deho yathā-kālopabhuktiṣu ||551||

Just as a piece of wood is tossed by the current to high or low ground, so too a body is carried here and there by destiny as determined by the momentum of its past actions.

srotasā = current of a river; **nīyate** = carried, tossed; **dāru** = piece of wood; **nimnonnata** = high and low; **sthalam** = ground, earth; **daivena** = destiny; **deho** = body.

prārabdha-karma-parikalpita-vāsanābhiḥ
saṁsārivat carati bhuktiṣu mukta-dehaḥ |
siddhaḥ svayaṁ vasati sākṣivad-atra tūṣṇīṁ
cakrasya mūlam-iva kalpa-vikalpa-śūnyaḥ ||552||

---

[1] See BṛhUp 4.4.7, 'Just as the slough of a snake lies on an anthill, dead, cast off, even so lies this body.'

Free from the body, a person of perfection moves amidst objects of enjoyment like a worldly person due to the imaginary residual impressions forged by the fruition of accumulated-past-actions-the-fruits-of-which-are-now-being-experienced. However, such a one lives like a witness, free from mental imaginations, unmoving like the nave of a wheel.

See BṛhUp 4.4.14, 'Verily, while we are here we may know this'; KaUp 2.3.14, 'A mortal becomes immortal, attains the Absolute even here, when the knots of the heart are destroyed'; MuṇḍUp 2.1.10, 'He who knows that which is set in the cave of the heart, he, here on earth, cuts the knot of ignorance'; KenaUp 2.5, 'There is truth if a person knows it here and if not there is a great loss'; AitUp 2.1.5–6, 'While I (Vāmadeva) was in the womb I realized (the Self and subsequently lived a long and productive life'; Śaṅkara's commentary on BṛhUp 4.4.6, 'The man free from desires realizes the Absolute even here'; BG 5.23, 'Before he is released from the body, if a yogi has perfect control over his mind and attains identity with the Absolute, he is eternally liberated'. BS 3.4.51, 'Knowledge of the Absolute takes place even in this life'; BS 4.1.13, 'On the realization of the Absolute, non-attachment and the destruction of both prior and subsequent actions occurs'; BS 4.1–3, 'Having reached the Self, the soul attains liberation.'

See KaivUp 1.18 on witness, 'In the three states of consciousness whatever appears as the object of enjoyment or the enjoyer or the enjoyment, I am different from them, the witness, pure consciousness, the eternal Śiva' (*sākṣī*).

See V. 101, 127, 137, 159, 212, 213, 217, 218, 223, 270, 295, 352, 370, 381, 384, 495, 506, and 507 for references to witness (*sākṣī*).

See V. 280, 289, 417, 446–47, 452, 454–55, and 459–64 on *prārabdha karma.*

prārabdha-karma = accumulated-past-actions-the-fruits-of-which-are-now-being-experienced; **parikalpita** = illusory, imagined; **vāsanābhiḥ** = residual impressions; **saṁsārivat** = worldly person; **carati** = moves; **bhuktiṣu** = enjoyment; **mukta-dehaḥ** = one free of the body; **siddhaḥ svayaṁ** = person of perfection; **vasati** = lives; **sākṣivad** = like a witness; **tūṣṇīṁ** = unmoving; **cakrasya mūlam-iva** = like the nave of a wheel; **kalpa-vikalpa-śūnyaḥ** = devoid of mental imaginations.

naivendriyāṇi viṣayeṣu niyuṅkta eṣa
naivāpayuṅkta upadarśana-lakṣaṇasthaḥ |
naiva kriyā-phalam-apīṣad-avekṣate sa
svānanda-sāndra-rasa-pāna-sumatta-cittaḥ ||553||

With his mind full of ecstasy from drinking the elixir of the bliss of the Self, he does not direct his sense organs towards sense objects, nor does he use them. He is merely an unconcerned spectator and does not care, even in the least, for the fruits of actions.

naivendriyāṇi viṣayeṣu niyuṅkta = does not direct sense organs towards sense objects; eṣa = to attain, hasten towards; **upadarśana-lakṣaṇasthaḥ** = unconcerned spectator; **kriyā-phalam** = fruits of actions; **ānanda** = bliss; **sāndra** = dense, solid; rasa = elixir; **pāna** = drinking; **sumatta-cittaḥ** = mind full of.

lakṣyālakṣya-gatiṁ tyaktvā yas-tiṣṭhet kevalātmanā |
śiva eva svayaṁ sākṣād-ayaṁ brahma-vid-uttamaḥ ||554||

He who, giving up all consideration of reaching the goal and of not reaching the goal, remains as the one and only Self, is verily auspiciousness itself. Such a one is indeed the best among knowers of the Absolute.

lakṣyālakṣya-gatiṁ tyaktvā = he who has renounced all anxiety concerning reaching the goal or not reaching the goal; **kevalātmanā** = remains alone; **śiva** = Siva, auspicious; **eva** = only, one; **vid-uttamaḥ** = best among knowers.

jīvanneva sadā muktaḥ kṛtārtho brahma-vittamaḥ |
upādhi-nāśād brahmaiva sad-brahmāpyeti nirdvayam ||555||

Even while living, he is ever free. He is a supreme knower of the Absolute. He is the Absolute alone, through the destruction of the limiting adjuncts. He attains the non-dual reality which is the Absolute.

jīvanneva = even while living; **sadā muktaḥ** = ever free, liberated; **vittamaḥ** = supreme knower; **upādhi-nāśād** = destruction of limiting adjuncts.

śailūṣo veṣa-sadbhāvābhāvayoś ca yathā pumān |
tathaiva brahmavit-śreṣṭhaḥ sadā brahmaiva nāparaḥ ||556||

As an actor is always the same person whether he puts on the dress of his part or does not, so, too, the supreme knower of the Absolute is always the Absolute and nothing else.

śailūṣo = actor; **veṣa** = dress, attire; **pumān** = person; **brahmavit-śreṣṭhaḥ** = supreme knower of the Absolute; **sadā brahmaiva** = always the Absolute; **nāparaḥ** = nothing else.

yatra kvāpi viśīrṇaṁ parṇam-iva taror vapuḥ-patanāt |
brahmī-bhūtasya yateḥ prāg-eva hi tad cidagninā dagdhaṁ ||557||

Let the body of the spiritual aspirant, who has realized the Absolute, fall anywhere like the leaf of a tree, for it has already been burnt by his fire of knowledge.

parṇam-iva = like a leaf; **taror** = tree; **vapuḥ** = fall, be scattered; **patanāt** = falls; **cidagninā** = fire of knowledge; **dagdham** = burnt.

sadātmani brahmaṇi tiṣṭhato muneḥ
pūrṇādvayānanda-mayātmanā sadā |
na deśa-kālādyucita-pratīkṣā
tvaṅ-māṁsa-viṭpiṇḍa-visarjanāya ||558||

To the sage, who always remains in the reality, the Absolute, the ever-full, non-dual, and infinite bliss of the Self, there is no consideration of place, time, or appropriateness in discarding the body consisting of skin, flesh, or excrement.

brahmaṇi tiṣṭhato = firmly established in the Absolute; **muneḥ** = the sage; **pūrṇādvayānanda** = ever-full, non-dual bliss; **deśa** = place, space; **kālādyucita** = time or appropriateness; **tvaṅ-māṁsa-viṭpiṇḍa** = skin, flesh, filth; **visarjanāya** = discarding, abandoning, giving up.

dehasya mokṣo no mokṣo na daṇḍasya kamaṇḍaloḥ |
avidyā-hṛdaya-granthi-mokṣo mokṣo yatastataḥ ||559||

The abandoning of the body is not liberation, nor that of the staff, nor the water pot. Real liberation is the freedom from the knot of ignorance in the heart.

See MuṇḍUp 2.2.9, 'The knot of the heart is cut' (*bhidyate hṛdaya granthis*); KaUp 2.3.15, 'When all the knots that fetter here the heart are cut asunder then a moral becomes immortal'; ChānUp 7.26.2, 'There is release from all the knots of the heart.'

daṇḍasya = staff; **kamaṇḍaloḥ** = water pot; **avidyā-hṛdaya granthi** = knot of ignorance in the heart.

kulyāyām-atha nadyāṁ vā śiva-kṣetre'pi catvare |
parṇaṁ patati cet tena taroḥ kiṁ nu śubhāśubham ||560||

Whether a leaf falls in a small stream or in a river or in auspicious places of pilgrimage or where the four roads meet, what does it matter, good or bad, to the tree?

kulyāyām vā nadyāṁ = small stream or a river; **śiva-kṣetre** = auspicious places of pilgrimage; **catvare** = place where four roads meet; **parṇaṁ** = leaf; **patati** = falls; **taroḥ** = tree; **śubhāśubham** = good or bad.

patrasya puṣpasya phalasya nāśavat
dehendriya-prāṇa-dhiyāṁ vināśaḥ |
naivātmanaḥ svasya sadātmakasya
ānandākṛter vṛkṣavadāsta eṣaḥ ||561||

The destruction of the body, the sense organs, the vital breath, and the mind are like the destruction of the leaf, the flower, and the fruit. It does not mean the destruction of the reality, one's true nature as the blissful Self, which survives like the tree.

patrasya = leaf; **puṣpasya** = flower; **phalasya** = fruit; **nāśavat** = destruction; **dehendriya-prāṇa-dhiyāṁ** = body, sense organs, vital breath, intellect; **vṛkṣa** = tree.

prajñāna-ghana ityātma-lakṣaṇaṁ satya-sūcakam |
anūdddyaupādhikasyaiva kathayanti vināśranam ||562||

The nature of the Self is verily indicated by saying that it is an embodiment of wisdom. Having indicated its reality, the limiting adjunct alone is spoken of as subject to destruction.

See BṛhUp 4.5.13, 'As a lump of salt is without interior or exterior, whole, homogeneous salt mass, verily so is this Self'.

prajñāna-ghana = compacted of wisdom; **ityātma-lakṣaṇaṁ** = mark or nature of the Self; **satya** = truly, certainly indicated.

avināśī vā are'yam-ātmeti śrutirātmanaḥ |
prabravītyavināśitvaṁ vinaśyatsu vikāri ṣu ||563||

The scriptural passage, 'Verily, the Self is indestructible', declares its indestructibility amidst the changing things liable to destruction.

See BṛhUp 4.5.14, 'Verily this Self is imperishable, indestructible by its very nature.'

pāṣāṇa-vṛkṣa-tṛṇa-dhānya-kaḍaṅkarādyāḥ
dagdhā bhavanti hi mṛdeva yathā tathaiva |
dehendriyāsu-mana-ādi samasta-dṛśyaṁ
jñānāgni-dagdham upayāti parātma-bhāvam ||564||

Just as when a burnt stone, a tree, a blade of grass, wealth, grain, cloth and so on are reduced to clay, so too, all things seen like the body, the sense organs, the vital breaths, the mind, burnt by the fire of knowledge, become the supreme Self.

pāṣāṇa = stone; **vṛkṣa** = tree; **tṛṇa** = a blade of grass; **dhānya** = wealth; **kaḍa** = grain; **ādi** = and so on; **dagdhā** = burnt; **mṛdeva** = like clay, are reduced to earth; **dehendriyāsu-mana-ādi** = body, sense organs, vital breaths, mind; **samasta-dṛśyaṁ** = all things seen; **jñānāgni** = fire of knowledge; **dagdham** = burnt.

vilakṣaṇam yathā dhvāntaṁ līyate bhānu-tejasi |
tathaiva sakalaṁ dṛśyaṁ brahmaṇi pravilīyate ||565||

As darkness, which is distinct, vanishes in the radiance of the sun, similarly, all perceptible things merge in the Absolute.

vilakṣaṇam = distinct, other than; **dhvāntaṁ** = darkness, covered; **līyate** = vanishes, disappears; **bhānu-tejasi** = radiance of the sun; **sakalaṁ dṛśyaṁ** = all perceptible things; **pravilīyate** = melt into, dissolve.

ghaṭe naṣṭe yathā vyoma vyomaiva bhavati sphuṭam |
tathāivopādhi-vilaye brahmaiva brahmavit svayam ||566||

As when the pot is broken, the space (within) becomes one with the space (without), so too, the supreme knower of the Absolute becomes the Absolute itself when the limiting adjuncts vanish.

ghaṭe = pot; **naṣṭe** = broken, is not; **vyoma** = space.

kṣīram kṣīre yathā kṣiptam tailam taile jalam jale |
samyuktam ekatām yāti tathātmanyātmavin muniḥ ||567||

As milk poured into milk, oil into oil, water into water, becomes united and one with it, so the sage, who is a knower of the Self, attains oneness with the Self.

See KaUp 2.1.15, 'As pure water poured forth into pure becomes the very same'; MuṇḍUp 3.2.8, 'Just as the flowing rivers disappear in the ocean casting off name and shape'.

See MuṇḍUp 3.2.8, 'Just as rivers, as they flow, merge in the ocean, giving up their separate names and forms, so the knowing one, freed from separateness arising from name and form, attains the luminous supreme Self.'

kṣīram = milk; **kṣiptam** = poured into; **ṭailam** = oil; **jalam** = water; **samyuktam** = united with; **eka** = one.

evam videha-kaivalyam san-mātratvam-akhaṇḍitam |
brahma-bhāvam prapadyaiṣa yatir nāvartate punaḥ ||568||

Attaining the Absolute, marked by freedom from embodiment, eternally identified with the reality, the sage does not come back again.

videha-kaivalyam = freedom from embodiment; **yatir** = the sage; **nāvartate punaḥ** = does not return again.

sadātmaikatva-vijñāna-dagdhāvidyādi-varṣmaṇaḥ |
amuṣya brahma-bhūtatvād brahmaṇaḥ kuta udbhavaḥ ||569||

By realizing the oneness of the individual with the Absolute, his bodies, consisting of ignorance and so on, are burnt and he becomes the Absolute itself. How can there be birth?

sadātmaikatva-vijñāna = realizing the oneness of the individual and the Absolute; **dagdhāvidyādi** = ignorance and so on burnt; **varṣmaṇaḥ** = having bodies; **kuta udbhavaḥ** = how can there be birth?

māyā-klptau bandha-mokṣau na staḥ svātmani vastutaḥ |
yathā rajjau niṣkriyāyām sarpābhāsa-vinirgamau ||570||

Bondage and liberation are imaginations due to *māyā*; they do not pertain to the Self, one's reality. It is like the appearance and disappearance of the snake in the rope which does not change.

māyā-klptau = imaginations due to illusion, ignorance; **bandha-mokṣau** = bondage and liberation; **rajja** = rope; **niṣkriyāyām** = does not change; **sarpābhāsa** = disappearance of the snake.

āvṛteḥ sad-asattvābhyāṁ vaktavye bandha-mokṣaṇe |
nāvṛtir brahmaṇaḥ kācid anyābhāvād anāvṛtam |
yadyastyadvaitahāniḥ syād dvaitaṁ no sahate śrutiḥ ||571||

Bondage and liberation may be spoken of when there is the presence or absence of concealment. But there can be no concealment of the Absolute, for there is no second thing to conceal it. If there is such a thing, non-duality will be contradicted, and duality is not suffered by the scriptures.

See ChānUp 6.2.1, 'One only, without a second' (*ekam evādvitīyam*); KaUp 2.1.11, 'There is no diversity here. From death to death he goes who sees here any kind of diversity here'; TaittUp 2.7; ChānUp 3.19.1; MaitrīUp 6.17; *Pañcadaśī* 1.19.

āvṛteḥ sad-asattvābhyāṁ = presence or absence of concealment; **vaktavye** = may be spoken of; **bandha-mokṣaṇe** = bondage and liberation; **anyābhāvād anāvṛtam** = there is nothing to conceal it; **yadyastyadvaitahāniḥ** = if there is, non-duality will be contradicted; **dvaitaṁ** = duality; **no sahate śrutih** = not supported, not endured, suffered by the scriptures.

bandhaś ca mokṣaś ca mṛṣaiva mūḍhāḥ
buddher guṇaṁ vastuni kalpayanti |
dṛgāvṛtiṁ megha-kṛtāṁ yathā ravau
yato'dvayāsaṅga-cidekam-akṣaram ||572||

Bondage and liberation are both false. Fools imagine the qualities of the intellect on the Self, as the covering of sight caused by a cloud is attributed to the sun, but it is consciousness, one alone, non-dual, unattached, and indestructible.

bandhaś ca mokṣaś ca mṛṣaiva = bondage and liberation are both false; **mūḍhāḥ** = fools; **guṇaṁ** = qualities; **kalpayanti** = imagining; **dṛgāvṛtiṁ** = sight-covering; **megha** = cloud; **ravau** = sun; **advayā-saṅga** = non-dual and unattached; **cidekam** = consciousness alone; **akṣaram** = indestructible.

astīti pratyayo yaś ca yaś ca nāstīti vastuni |
buddher-eva guṇāvetau na tu nityasya vastunaḥ ||573||

The expressions 'is' and 'is not' are only qualities of the intellect. They do not pertain to the eternal Reality.

I am this; I am not this. Give up such distinctions. Know that everything is the Self. When this is understood, all things are understood. Desires fall away and peace is found.

astīti = it is; **nāstīti** = it is not.

atas-tau māyayā kḷptau bandha-mokṣau na cātmani |
niṣkale niṣkriye śānte niravadye nirañjane |
advitīye pare tattve vyomavat kalpanā kutaḥ ||574||

Hence, these two, bondage and liberation, are imaginations of *māyā*. They do not pertain to the Self. How can there be any imaginations of the partless, actionless, peaceful, defectless, taintless, non-dual supreme reality which is like the sky?

The *Aṣṭāvakragītā* ends, 'What need is there for striving or stillness? What is freedom or bondage? What are holy books or teachings? What is the purpose of life? Who is the disciple, and who is the master? Nothing arises in me in whom nothing is single, nothing is double. Nothing is, nothing is not. What more is there to say?'

See V. 67, 110–12, 125, 245, 406, and 497 on *māyā*.

māyayā = illusion; **kḷptau** = imaginations, conjurations; **bandha-mokṣau** = bondage and liberation; **niṣkale** = partless; **niṣkriye** = actionless; **śānte** = peaceful; **niravadye** = defectless; **nirañjane** = taintless; **advitīye** = non-dual; **pare tattve** = supreme reality, truth; **vyomavat** = sky; **kalpanā** = imaginations.

na nirodho na cotpattir na baddho na ca sādhakaḥ |
na mumukṣur na-vai muktaḥ ityeṣā paramārthatā ||575||

The ultimate Truth is that there is no death, no birth, no bondage and no spiritual aspirant, no seeker with a burning desire for liberation, none liberated.

See AmṛtUp 10 (this is a verbatim quote).

See V. 3, 19, 28, 29, 30, 31, 44, 84, 120, 178, and 576 for references to *mumukṣutva*.

na nirodho = no death; **na cotpattir** = no birth; **na baddho** = no bondage; **na sādhakaḥ** = no spiritual aspirant; **na mumukṣur** = no aspirant with a burning desire for liberation; **na-vai muktaḥ** = none liberated; **paramārthatā** = the ultimate truth.

sakala-nigama-cūḍāsvānta-siddhānta-guhyaṁ
param-idam-ati-guhyaṁ darśitaṁ te mayādya |
apagata-kali-doṣam kāma-nirmukta-buddhiḥ
tadatulamasakṛt tvāṁ bhāvayedam mumukṣuḥ ||576||

O you with a burning desire for liberation! I have now revealed to you the secret conclusion which is the crown of all scriptures. With a mind rendered free from the defects of the dark age and free from desires, realize this incomparable secret Truth.

The dark age is the Kali Yuga, the modern age when righteousness is in decline. See V. 3, 28, 29, 30, 31, 44, 84, and 120 for references to *mumukṣutva.*

sakala-nigama = all scriptures; **cūdāsvānta** = crown, crest; **siddhānta-guhyaṁ** = secret conclusion, final and ultimate doctrine; **param-idam-ati-guhyaṁ** = this supreme secret; **darśitaṁ te** = I have revealed, I have shown to you; **kali-doṣam** = defects of the dark age; **kāma** = desires; **nirmukta-buddhiḥ** = mind free from; **mumukṣuḥ** = a seeker with a burning desire for liberation.

iti śrutvā guror vākyaṁ praśrayeṇa kṛtānâtiḥ |
sa tena samanujñāto yayau nirmukta-bandhanaḥ ||577||

Having listened with reverence to these words of the Master, and having prostrated before him with reverence, obtaining his permission he went his way freed from bondage.

śrutvā = hearing; **guror** = Master; **vākyaṁ** = words; **praśrayeṇa** = to go forth; **kṛtānatiḥ** = one who bends in reverence; **tena** = in that direction, in that manner; **nirmukta-bandhanaḥ** = freed from bondage.

gurur-eṣa sadānanda-sindhau nirmagna-mānasaḥ |
pāvayan vasudhāṁ sarvāṁ vicacāra nirantaraḥ ||578||

The Master, with his mind ever immersed in the ocean of bliss, forever roamed, completely sanctifying the entire world.

gurur = Master; **sadā** = ever, always; **ānanda-sindhau** = ocean of bliss; **nirmagna-mānasaḥ** = mind immersed; **pāvayan** = purified, sanctified; **vasudhāṁ** = doing good; **sarvām** = entire; **vicacāra** = roaming; **nirantaraḥ** = perpetually.

ityācāryasya śiṣyasya saṁvādenātma-lakṣaṇam |
nirūpitaṁ mumukṣūṇāṁ sukha-bodhopapattaye ||579||

Thus, this dialog between the Master and the disciple on the nature of the Self has been expounded for the easy comprehension of ardent seekers of liberation.

ityācāryasya śiṣyasya = thus the Master and the disciple; **saṁvādenātma-lakṣaṇam** = on the nature of the Self; **nirūpitaṁ** = has been expounded, given forth, indicated; **mumukṣūṇāṁ** = ardent seeker of liberation; **sukha-bodhopapattaye** = easy understanding, evidence, in the light of reasoning.

hitam-idam upadeśamādriyantām
vihita-nirasta-samasta-citta-doṣāḥ |
bhava-sukha-viratāḥ praśānta-cittāḥ
śruti-rasikā yatayo mumukṣavo ye ||580||

May spiritual aspirants who ardently seek liberation, who have been purged of all defects of the mind by the prescribed disciplines, who are averse to worldly pleasures, who have a supremely serene mind, who take delight in the scriptures, appreciate this valuable spiritual teaching.

hitam-idam = this good advice, valuable; **upadeśam** = spiritual teaching; **doṣāḥ** = defects; **bhavasukha-viratāḥ** = averse to worldly pleasures; **praśānta-cittāḥ** = supremely supreme, silent mind; **śruti-rasikā** = delight in the scriptures.

saṁsārādhvani tāpa-bhānu-kiraṇa-prodbhūta-dāhavyathā-
khinnānāṁ jala-kāṅkṣayā marubhuvi bhrāntyā paribhrāmyatām |
atyāsanna-sudhāmbudhiṁ sukhakaraṁ brahmādvayaṁ darśayat
yeṣā śaṁkara-bhāratī vijayate nirvāṇa-sandāyinī ||581||

For those who are afflicted by the scorching sun's rays of worldly life, who wander forth in quest of water in the mirages of desert sands, may this victorious voice of Śaṅkara pointing out the blissful ocean of the non-dual Absolute which is within easy reach, bestow liberation.

saṁsārādhvani = those who are afflicted by worldly life; **tāpa** = heat, austerity; **bhānu kiraṇa** = ray of light of the sun; **prodbhūta** = come forth, sprung up; **dāha** = burning; **vyathā** = tremble, waver; **khinnānāṁ** = suffer pain, exhausted; **jala** = water; **marubhuvi** = desert sand; **bhrāntyā** = mirages, illusion, false; **pari-bhrāmyatām** = wander about; **su-dhāmbu-dhiṁ sukhakaraṁ brah-mādvayaṁ** = blissful ocean of the non-dual Absolute; **śaṁkara-bhāratī** = voice of Śaṅkara; **vijayate** = victorious.

iti śrīmatparamahamsa-parivrājakācāryasya
śrīgovindabhagavatpūjyapādaśiṣyasya
śrīmacchaṁkarabhagavataḥ kṛtau vivekācūḍāmaṇiḥ

Thus ends the *Crown Jewel of Discrimination* written by Śrī Śaṅkara Bhagavatpāda, the disciple of Śrīmat Paramahamsa Parivrajakācārya Śrī Govinda Bhagavatpujyapāda.

Om Tat Sat

Variant Readings

My translation of the *Vivekacūḍāmaṇi* is based on the 1983 edition published by Samata Books in Madras. The 1983 edition, though based upon, is not a mere reproduction of its successor, the 20-volume edition which was first published in the original Sanskrit by Sri T.K. Balasubramania Iyer, Vani Vilas Press, Srirangam, 1910. This edition has been revised and rearranged to take modern scholarship into account. Though it is not a critical edition, it has taken into consideration manuscript information different from that used by the editors of that edition.

I have principally consulted five manuscripts that contained the original devanagari script and looked at five others (without the original text).

1. *Complete Works of Sri Sankaracharya*, vol III *Upadeśaracanāvalī* pp. 3–111. Madras: Samata Books. 1983. I have designated this as A. (This consists solely of the Sanskrit text.)
2. *Vivekacūḍāmaṇi of Śrī Śaṅkarācārya* . . . Swami Madhavananda, tr. Advaita Ashrama: Calcutta, 1966. I have designated this as B. (This is a more literal translation given by Swami Madhavananda, a monk of the Sri Ramakrishna Order.)
3. *Vivekacūḍāmaṇi of Śrī Śaṅkarācārya*. Swami Turiyananda, tr. Sri Ramakrishna Math: Madras, 1987. I have designated this as C. (This is Swami Turiyananda's freestyle translation given orally and recorded in shorthand by Ida Ansell, along with changes made in punctuation, spelling, syntax, and word choice to accord with contemporary modern English usage.)
4. *Vivekacūḍāmaṇi*. tr. and comm. by the Śaṅkarācārya of Sṛṅgeri. Bombay: Bharatiya Vidya Bhavan, 1988. I have designated this as D.
5. *Talks on Sankara's Vivekachoodamani* by Swami Chinmayananda. Bombay, 1970.

I also consulted:

6. *Saṅkara's Crest Jewel of Discrimination*. tr. by Swami Prabhavananda and Christopher Isherwood. Vedanta Press: Hollywood, 1947.
7. *The Crest-Jewel of Wisdom*. tr. by Charles Johnston. New York, 1925.
8. *Vivekacūḍāmaṇi or Crest-Jewel of Wisdom of Śrī Śaṅkarācārya*. tr. by Mohini Chatterji. Theosophical Society: Adyar, 1932.
9. *Vivekacūḍāmaṇi*, tr. C. Bohra. *Brahmavādin* 17, 1912: 394, 445, 480.
10. *Vivekacūḍāmaṇi*. Ed. and tr. by R. Balasubramanian, *The Voice of Samkara*, vol. 7, 1982, vol. 10, 1985.

A=Samata edition; B=Madhavananda; C=Turiyananda; D=Sṛṅgeri

Verse 2 *muktir no śata-koṭ i-janma sukṛ taiḥ* – A; B; D
(2) *muktiḥ no śata-janma-koṭ i sukṛ taiḥ* – C

Verse 4 *muktyau . . . sa ā tmahā* – A; D
(4) *muktau . . . sa hyā tmahā* – B; C

Verse 6 *vinā vimuktiḥ* – A; D
(6) *vin'ā pi muktiḥ* – B; C

Verse 21 *jugupsā* – A; D
(21) *jihā sā* – B; C

Verse 100 *yatra svayaṁ-jyotirayaṁ parātmā* – A; D
(99) *yatra svayaṁ-bhā ti hy'ayaṁ parātmā* – B; C

Verse 114 *etat tad* – A; D
(112) *esā tad* – B; C

Verse 156 *hyannena jī vati* – A; D
(154) *c'ā nnena jī vati* – B; C

Verse 168 *naivā tmā yam* – A; D
(166) *n'aiv'ā tm'ā pi* – B; C

Verse 169 *anupū rya* – A; D
(167) *abhipū rya* – B; C

Verse 176 *mokṣ asya śuddham* – A
(176) *mokṣ asya hetuḥ* – D

Verse 181 *yogāt* – D
(179) *doṣā t* – A; B; C

Verse 188 *anupū rva* – A; D
(186) *api pū rva* – B; C

Verse 191 *sphurat svayaṁ jyotiḥ* – A
(189) *sphuraty'ayaṁ jyotiḥ* – B; C

Verse 212 *yuktitaḥ kṛ te* – A; D
(210) *yuktitaḥ śruteḥ* – B; C

Verse 214 *vinā kiñcinna . . . svā tmanā tra ā tmanavipaścitā* – A
(214) *vinā na . . . svā tmanā tra ā tmanavipaścitā* – D
(212) *vinā kiñcinna . . . svā tmanā ā tmanavipaścitā* – B; C

Verse 215 *abhā vo'yamapyatha* – A
(215) *abhā vo'yamamopyatha* – D
(213) *abhā vo'ayam apy'anu* – B; C

Verse 221 *divi vikṣ yate* – A; D
(219) *vinirī kṣ yate* – B; C

Verse 235 *vyacī kathat* – A; D
(233) *vyacī kḷ pat* – B; C; D

Verse 237 guṇ ahivat – A; D
(235) guṇ adivat – B; C

Verse 240 *nityaṁ dhruvam* – A; D
(238) *nityaṁ sukham* – B; C

Verse 242 *pū rṇ aṁ mahan* – A; B; D
(241) *pū rṇ aṁ aham* – C

Verse 247 *pramā nāṇ ugṛ hī ta-yuktyā . . . evam* – A
(247) *pramā nāṇ ugṛ hī ta-yuktyā . . . ittham* – D
(245) *pramā nāṇ ugṛ hī ta-bodhā* – B; C

Verse 253 *evā bhitaḥ* – A; D
(251) *ev'ā hitam* – B; C

Verse (253) *yatra bhrā ntyā kalpitaṁ tad viveke*
tat tan-mā traṁ n'aiva tasmā d vibhinnam;
svapne naṣṭ aṁ svapna-viś vaṁ vicitraṁ
svasmā d-bhinnaṁ kinnu dṛṣṭ aṁ prabhodhe – B; C
(this verse not in A; D)

Verse 258 *nirupamā nam ṛ ddhimat* – A; D
(257) *nir-upamā navad-hi-yat* – C
(257) *nir-upamā navaddhi-yat* – B

Verse 265 *bhā vaya* – A; D
(264) *bhā vayet* – B; C

Verse 266 *svaṁ bodhamā traṁ . . . tadā tmanaivā t* – A; D
(265) *saṁ bodhamā traṁ . . . tadāś rayaḥ svā t* – B; C

Verse 274 *jalā di-saṁ parka* – A; D
(273) *jalā di-saṁ sarga* – B; C

Verse 278 *sthityā* – A; D
(277) *sthitvā* – B; C

Verse 302 *buddhyā vikḷ pas* – A
(302) *buddhyā aviviktas* – D
(301) *buddhyā prakḷ ptaḥ* – B; C

Verse 303 *dyutimatā* – A; D
(302) *śrutimatā* – B; C

Verse 305 *ayam aham* – A; D
(304) *idam aham* – B; C

Verse 306 *ahaṁ kartaryasmim* – A; D
(305) *ahaṁ-kā re kartary aham iti* – B; C

Verse 321 *pravilā payan svayam* – A; D
(320) *pravilā payan san* – B; C

Verse 325 *syā d yadi* – A; D
(324) *ced yadi* – B; C

Verse 328 *tataḥ svarū pavibhraṁ ṣo . . .* (the first three lines of this verse are nos 328 and part of 329 in B; C)
apathyā ni hi vastū ni byā dhigrasto yathotsṛ jet
(this line only occurs in A; D it does not in B; C)

Verse 329 *ataḥ pramā dā nna . . . sā vadhā naḥ* occurs in A; D and is verse no. 327 of B; C)

Verse 350 *tritayam* – A; D
(349) *dvitayam* – B; C

Verse 351 *kṣ aṇ e'nyathā-bhā vina eṣ a ā tmā*
nodeti nā pyeti kadā pi nā nyathā – A; D

(350)	*kṣ aṇ e'anyathā-bhā vitayā hi amīṣā m*
	asattvam ā tmā tu kadā pi n'ā nyathā – B; C
Verse 358	*upā dhi-yogā t* – A; D
(357)	*upā dhi bhedā t* – B; C
Verse 377	*na sukham devarā jasya na sukham cakravartinaḥ*
	yā dṛśam vī tarā gasya muner ekā ntaśī linaḥ
	yacca kā masukham loke yacca divyam mahat sukham
	tṛṣṇā kṣ ayasukhasyaite nā rhataḥ ṣ oḍ aśī m kalā m
	(this verse is not in A; B; C)
Verse 379	*kim-anyair bhramaḥ* – A
(379)	*kim-anyair bhramaiḥ* – D
(378)	*kim-anyair bhṛśam* – B; C
Verse 403	*vilī nam* – A; D
(402)	*pralī nam* – B; C
Verse 415	*svametya* – A; D
(414)	*sametya* – B; C
Verse 428	*sā sarvadā bhaved-yasya sa jī vanmukta iṣ yate* – A; D
(427)	*susthitā 'asau bhaved yasya sthitaprañaḥ sa ucyate* – B; C
Verse 433	*prā pte* – A; D
(432)	*prā ptam* – B; C
Verse 437, 438, 440, 441	*jī vanmukta iṣ yate* – A; D
(436, 437, 439, 440)	*jī vanmukta lakṣ aṇ aḥ* – B; C
Verse 460	*ajo nitya iti brū te śrutir-eṣ a tvamoghavā k* – A; D
(459)	*ajo nityaḥ śā śvata iti brūteś rutir amoghavā k* – B; C
Verse 464	*yataḥ śruter abhiprā yaḥ paramā rthaikagocaraḥ* – A; D
	(this verse does not appear in B; C)
Verse 472	*nirasta-rā gā nirapā sta-bhogāḥ* – A; D
(471)	*nirasta-rā gā vinirasta-bhogāḥ* – B; C
Verse 473	*nicā yya* – A; D
(472)	*vicā rya* – B; C
Verse 478	*susukham* – A; D
(477)	*sammukham* – B; C
Verse 482	*asya pā ram* – A; D
(481)	*asty'apā ram* – B; C
Verse 500	*ā kā śavat kalpa-vidū rago'ham* – A; D
(499)	*ā kā śaval lepa-vidū rago'aham* – B; C
Verse 506	*dehendriya-manodharmāḥ naivā tmanam spṛ śantyaho*
	(this verse is in A; D and not in B; C)
Verse 507	*vahner yathā vā 'yasi-dā hakatvam* – A; D
(506)	*vahner yathā dā ha-niyā makatvam* – B; C
Verse 512	*taiḥ kiṁ me'saṅ ga-citaḥ na hyambudaḍ ambaro'mbaraṁ spṛ śati* – A; D
(511)	*kiṁ me'asaṅ ga-citaḥ taiḥ na ghanah kvacit ambaraṁ spṛ śati* – B; C

Verse 515 *yasminnastā śeṣ a-mā yā-viśeṣ aṁ* – A; D
(514) *yat pratyast'ā śeṣ a-mā yā-viśeṣ aṁ*

Verse 520 *muhuh* – A; D
(519) *naṁah* – B; C

Verse 557 *parṇ am* – A; D
(556) *satparṇ am* – B; C

Select Bibliography

Editions of the *Vivekacūḍāmaṇi*

Vivekacūḍāmaṇi, tr. Chunilal C. Bohra, *Brahmavādin* 17, 1912: 394, 445, 480.

The Crest-Jewel of Wisdom, tr. Charles Johnston, New York, 1925.

Viveka-cūḍāmaṇi or Crest-Jewel of Wisdom of Śrī Śaṁkarācārya, tr. Mohini Chatterji, Theosophical Society, Adyar, 1932.

Saṅkara's Crest Jewel of Discrimination, tr. Swami Prabhavananda and Christopher Isherwood, Vedanta Press: Hollywood, 1947.

Vivekacūḍāmaṇi of Śrī Śaṅkarācārya, tr. Swami Turiyananda, Sri Ramakrishna Math, Madras.

Vivekacūḍāmaṇi Śrī Śaṅkarācārya, Swami Madhavananda, tr. Advaita Ashrama, Calcutta, 1966.

The Pinnacle of Indian Thought, Ernest Wood, Wheaton, IL, Theosophical Publishing House, 1967.

Talks on Sankara's Vivekachoodamani, Swami Chinmayananda, Bombay, 1970.

Complete Works of Sri Sankaracharya, Vol. III *Upadeśaracanāvalī*, pp. 3–111, Madras, Samata Books, 1983.

Vivekacūḍāmaṇi, ed. and tr. R. Balasubramanian, *The Voice of Sāmkara* 7, 1982, p. 10.

Vivekacūḍāmaṇi, tr. and comm. the Śaṅkarācārya of Sṛṅgeri, Bombay, Bharatiya Vidya Bhavan, 1988.

Vivekacūḍāmaṇi in *The Collected Works of Ramana Maharshi*, pp. 222–290, Tiruvannamalai, Sri Ramanasramam, 1996.

Secondary Works

Antarkar, W.R. (1961) 'Śaṅkara Vijayas: A Comparative and Critical Study', PhD dissertation from the University of Poona.

Bader, J. (1990) *Meditation in Śaṅkara's Vedanta*, New Delhi, Aditya Prakashan.

——— (1991) *Conquest of the Four Quarters: Traditional Accounts of the Life of Sankara*, PhD dissertation, Australian National University.

Balasubramanian, R. (1976) *Advaita Vedānta*, Madras, University of Madras.

——— (1978) in *Perspectives of Theism and Absolutism in Indian Philosophy*. 'Advaita Vedanta'. University of Madras.

Belvalkar, S.K. (1929) *Vedanta Philosophy*, Poona, Bilrakunja Publishing House.

——— (1929) *Sri Gopal Basu Mallik Lectures on Vedanta Philosophy*, Part 1, Poona.

Clooney, F.X. (2000) 'To Be Heard and Done, But Never Quite Seen: The Human Condition According to the *Vivekacūḍāmaṇi*' in *The Human Condition*, ed. Robert Cummings Neville, Albany, State University of New York Press.

Coburn, T. (1991) *Encountering the Goddess*, Albany, State University of New York Press.

Collins, A.Y. (ed.) (1985) *Feminist Perspectives on Biblical Scholarship*, Chico, Scholars Press.

Datta, D.M. (1972) *The Six Ways of Knowing*, Calcutta, University of Calcutta.

Grimes, J. (1989) *Quest for Certainty: A Comparative Study of Heidegger and Sankara*, New York, Lang Press.

——— (1990) *The Seven Great Untenables: Sapta Vidha Anupapatti*, Motilal Banarsidass.

——— (1991) *An Advaita Vedanta Perspective on Language*, Studies in Indian Traditions Series No. 3, Delhi, Indian Books Centre.

——— (1992) *The Naiskarmyasiddhi of Sureśvara: A Monogram*, Delhi, Sri Garib Dass Oriental Series, Sri Satguru Publications.

——— (1994) *Problems and Perspectives in Religious Discourse: Advaita Vedanta Implications*, Albany, State University of New York Press.

——— (1996) *A Concise Dictionary of Indian Philosophy*, Albany, State University of New York Press.

——— (forthcoming). 'Revisiting Śaṅkara's Authorship of the Vivekacūḍāmaṇi', *International Journal of Hindu Studies*.

Gussner, R.E. (1976) 'A Stylometric Study of the Authorship of Seventeen Sanskrit Hymns Attributed to Śaṅkara', *Journal of the American Oriental Society*, 96, pp. 259–267.

——— (1977) 'Śaṅkara's Crest Jewel of Discrimination: A Stylometric Approach to the Question of Authorship', *Journal of Indian Philosophy* 4, pp. 265–278.

Hacker, P. (1995) *Philology and Confrontation*, ed. Wilhelm Halbfass, Albany, State University of New York Press.

Halbfass, W. (1983) *Studies in Kumarila and Sankara*, Studien zur Indologie und Iranistik, Monographie 9, Reinbeck.

Ingalls, D.H.H. (1952) 'The Study of Saṁkarācārya', *Annals of the Bhandarkar Oriental Research Institute*, Vol. XXXII.

Kulkarni, S.D. (1987) *Adi Sankara: The Saviour of Mankind*, Bombay, Shri Bhagavan Vedavyasa Itihasa Samshodhana Mandira.

Kuppuswami, A. (1972) *Sri Bhagavatpada Sankaracarya*, Varanasi, Chowkhamba Publication.

Larson, G. (1981) 'The Song Celestial: Two Centuries of the Bhagavad Gītā in English', *Philosophy East and West* 31, no. 4, October, pp. 518–519.

Lorenzen, D. (1987) 'Śaṅkara', in Mircea Eliade (ed.) *The Encyclopedia of Religion*, XIII, New York, Macmillan, pp. 64–65.

Mahadevan, T.M.P. (1976) *The Philosophy of Advaita*, India, Arnold-Heinemann.

Marcaurelle, R. (1999) *Freedom Through Inner Renunciation: Śaṅkara's Philosophy in a New Light*, Albany, State University of New York Press.

Mayeda, S. (1992) *A Thousand Teachings: Upadeśasāhasrī*, Albany, State University of New York Press.

Nakamura, H. (1983) *A History of Early Vedanta Philosophy*, Delhi.

Neusner, J. (1981) *Method and Meaning in Ancient Judaism III*, Chico, Scholars Press.

Pande, G.C. (1994) *Life and Thought of Śaṅkarācārya*, Delhi, Motilal Banarsidass.

Pathak, K.B. (1892) 'The Date of Sankaracarya', *Indian Antiquary*, Vol. 2, London.

Potter, K. (1981) *Encyclopedia of Indian Philosophies, Advaita Vedanta up to Sankara and His Pupils*, Princeton, Princeton University Press.

Radhakrishnan, S. (1923) *Indian Philosophy*, 2 volumes, London, George Allen & Unwin.

Raja, K.K. (1960) 'On the Date of Samkaracarya and Allied Problems', *Adyar Library Bulletin*, Vol. 24, pts 3–4.

Vidyasankar, S. (forthcoming) 'Conflicting Hagiographies and History: The Place of Sankaravijaya texts in Advaita Tradition', *International Journal of Hindu Studies*.

General Index

Index to Verses